D1606472

# FROM WARM CENTER TO RAGGED EDGE

IOWA AND THE MIDWEST EXPERIENCE

Series editor, William B. Friedricks,
Iowa History Center at Simpson College

# JON K. LAUCK

# FROM WARM CENTER TO RAGGED EDGE

## THE EROSION OF MIDWESTERN LITERARY AND HISTORICAL REGIONALISM, 1920–1965

UNIVERSITY OF IOWA PRESS, IOWA CITY

University of Iowa Press, Iowa City 52242

Copyright © 2017 by the University of Iowa Press

www.uipress.uiowa.edu

Printed in the United States of America

TEXT DESIGN BY ALLIGATOR TREE GRAPHICS

The University of Iowa Press is a member of Green Press Initiative and is committed to preserving natural resources.

Printed on acid-free paper

LIBRARY OF CONGRESS CATALOGING-IN-PUBLICATION DATA

Names: Lauck, Jon, 1971– author.

Title: From warm center to ragged edge : the erosion of midwestern literary and historical regionalism, 1920–1965 / Jon K. Lauck.

Description: Iowa City : University of Iowa Press, 2017. | Series: Iowa and the midwest experience | Includes index.

Identifiers: LCCN 2016040307 | ISBN 978-1-60938-496-8 (pbk) | ISBN 978-1-60938-497-5 (ebk)

Subjects: LCSH: American literature—Middle West—History and criticism. | Literature and history—Middle West. | Middle West—In literature. | Middle West—Intellectual life. | BISAC: HISTORY / United States / State & Local / Midwest (IA, IL, IN, KS, MI, MN, MO, ND, NE, OH, SD, WI).

Classification: LCC PS273 .L38 2017 | DDC 810.9/977—dc23

LC record available at https://lccn.loc.gov/2016040307

For Jason Duncan,
Dave McMahon,
and Mark Milosch

# CONTENTS

Man is surprised to find that things
near are not less beautiful and
wondrous than things remote.

—Emerson

# ACKNOWLEDGMENTS

Books may often seem like solitary late-night projects pursued in dimly lit basements, but they take a lot of help and, in the end, require the extension of much gratitude and appreciation and many acknowledgments. For crucial assistance with this project I want to thank, in particular, the many members of the Society for the Study of Midwestern Literature who have helped me with my research on midwestern writers. Special thanks are due to SSML leaders such as Phil Greasley, Sara Kosiba, Marcia Noe, Andy Oler, and Tricia Oman. Additional thanks are extended to Marcia Noe for permission to use large parts of my essay "The Myth of the 'Revolt from the Village,'" which she first published in SSML's journal *MidAmerica* in volume 40 (2013). I also want to thank my friends and colleagues who made possible the launch of the new Midwestern History Association (MHA), especially Kathy Borkowski, Dana Brown, Jon Butler, Ted Frantz, Maria Howe, John Hudson, Zachary Michael Jack, Richard Jensen, James Madison, Paula Nelson, Joe Otto, David Pichaske, Pamela Riney-Kehrberg, Greg Schneider, Jim Seaton, Michael Skaggs, Kelly Wenig, and Robert Wuthnow. On a related note, I want to thank the leaders of the Western History Association, the Organization of American Historians, and the American Historical Association, who did so much to welcome and form partnerships with and generally assist the MHA, especially Stephen Aron, Jon Butler, Johnny Faragher, and Jim Grossman. Reviving midwestern studies would not be possible without strong journals, so special thanks are due to my *Middle West Review* colleagues Bill Barillas, Margaret Garb, David Good, Jason Heppler, Wally Hettle, Doug Kiel, Brian Craig Miller, Paul Mokrzycki,

Shannon Murray, Adam Ochonicky, Andrew Seal, Sharon Wood, and Eric Zimmer and my *Studies in Midwestern History* colleagues Michael Skaggs and Paul Putz. More generally, I want to thank the friends who have joined me for at least parts of the journey toward the completion of this book such as Mike Allen, Joe Anderson, Al Bogue, Jim Davis, Robert Dorman, Jason Duncan, Nicole Etcheson, Susan Gray, Kurt Hackemer, Ellis Hawley, Patrick Hicks, Jeff Helgeson, Joe Hogan, Ben Jones, David Kennedy, Mitch Kinsinger, James Leary, Deirdre McCloskey, John McGreevy, Dave McMahon, Hank Meijer, John Miller, Matt Moen, Mike Mullin, Paul Murphy, Paula Nelson, Dennis Papini, Ron Parsons, Matt Pehl, Will Prigge, Elizabeth Raymond, Bill Richardson, Molly Rozum, Michael Steiner, Harry Thompson, Mark Vinz, Emily Wanless, Will Weaver, and Gleaves Whitney. One of the greatest boosters of this project in its early stages and a peer reviewer for this manuscript was Drew Cayton, midwestern historian extraordinaire, who left us far too early in 2015, but not before giving great assistance to our efforts to rejuvenate midwestern history.

Once again, I want to thank my dad and mom, Dale and Pat Lauck, who grew up, along with their parents and grandparents, on little farms in eastern South Dakota and became farmers themselves. They have been long-time pillars of the old agrarian midwestern order that now seems to be fading rapidly. A son could not ask for more wonderful parents. Most importantly, I want to thank my wife, Amy, who has patiently endured many discussions and digressions about the Midwest and to whom I owe everything and for whom I have the greatest love. And, finally, I want to extend my love and affection to my children, Brendtly, Abigail, and Henry, all budding midwesterners, who, if this book hits the mark, will have a slightly better appreciation of their roots and their region's heritage

# FROM WARM CENTER
## TO RAGGED EDGE

INTRODUCTION

# THE PROMISE OF MIDWESTERN REGIONALISM

At the midpoint of his second annual address to Congress, written in the midst of national calamity and in the immediate shadow of Antietam—the bloodiest single day in American history—Abraham Lincoln dedicated precious space to the swift maturation of the nation's "great interior region," the third of the country that formed the "great body of the republic," a land of "provisions, grains, grasses, and all which proceed from them" that made the region "one of the most important in the world." Lincoln's Midwest—the "vast interior region" from which he sprang—and its civic republican foundations and agro-industrial brawn made it possible for him to win the Civil War and save the American republic.[1] In ensuing years, the midwestern economy boomed and the region's leaders dominated the presidency, winning the office six of seven times after 1860. During the fifty years after the Civil War, Bernard DeVoto explained, it was widely presumed that the "Mississippi Valley must eventually be the dominant culture of the United States."[2] Walt Whitman sang of the Midwest as the "crown and teeming paradise, so far, of time's accumulations."[3] In 1900, a historian declared that the "Mississippi Valley yields to no region in the world in interest, in romance, and in promise for the future. Here, if anywhere, is the real America—the field, the theater, and the basis of the civilization of the Western World."[4] In 1914, Sherwood Anderson thought that the "great basin of the Mississippi River . . . is one day to be the seat of the culture of the universe."[5] Before the end of the nineteenth century, the region found its historical muse in the form of Wisconsinite Frederick Jackson Turner, who confessed to a fellow midwestern historian, "I love my Middle

West," the rolling green expanse between the rivers Ohio and Missouri, as the "heart of the Republic."[6] After the turn of the century, Turner and his disciples diligently chronicled the development of this middling space of the American republic and gave life to an impressive corpus of regional history that articulated the Midwest's story to the nation and loosened the Northeast's grip on the American historical imagination.[7]

But by mid-century the old regional enthusiasms had passed, national crises followed on earlier traumas, new fashions crowded out old traditions, rosy regional expectations dimmed, foreign catastrophes intruded, and soon the Midwest was fast retreating to the edges of the history profession and the popular mind. For the past half century, the prevailing forces and trends in high and popular culture and in the American academy have not been conducive to the study of midwestern history and have cut against a focus on the Midwest as a particular region. After an uptick of regionalist thinking and writing during the interwar decades, World War II had the effect of focusing the nation's attention outward, and the decades-long commitment of the Cold War intensified this focus. The growth of radio and television and their natural inclination to produce a "mass culture" for a popular audience further eroded the capacity to retain regional identities. The hostility of intellectuals to the Midwest, which first took form in the 1920s, deterred some writers from telling the region's stories while those who tried were not taken seriously and lost in the national din. Recent academic trends—coupled with an earlier tradition of skepticism and criticism toward the purportedly monochromatic rural and small-town Midwest—and the emphasis on globalization and its "varieties of uprootedness" also drew attention and resources away from what many academicians and other commentators considered a staid and colorless rural interior, leaving the region trapped outside "historians' field of vision" and "unseen" and its history "etiolated."[8]

Underlying all of these trends is a stark geographic fact: the nation's dominant cultural institutions have historically tended to concentrate on the coasts and thereby heighten a persistent anxiety among intellectuals—an "ancient bogey," as the Minnesota writer Herbert Krause called it—about seeming provincial and being too far removed from the coastal culture complex and trapped, in James McManus's diagnosis of the condition, in a zone of "unedgy squareness."[9] As Willa Cather once observed, "Nebraska is distinctly déclassé as a literary background; its very name throws the delicately attuned critic into a clammy shiver of embarrassment."[10] Sherwood Anderson noted that too many New Yorkers "think the United States ends at Pittsburgh and believe there's nothing but desert and a few Indians and Hollywood on the other side."[11] In more recent years, in the era of "bicoastalism," the interior of the country has been dubbed "the fly-over."[12] Realizing the effects of these forces and attitudes is meant to serve as a partial explanation for how the Midwest was lost from our general modes of thought, both academic and popular, and how it is possible—and considered amusing to many—for the *Saturday Review* to publish a cartoon in the 1970s of a highway billboard with the caption: "Welcome to the Midwest, Butt of 1000 Cruel and Tasteless Jokes."[13] My primary purpose here is to analyze the forces that wilted midwestern identity by mid-century and, more generally, to bolster the new and concerted search for the history and culture of the lost region at the heart of our nation by studying what went wrong, or examining how the Midwest as a region faded from our collective imagination, fell off the map, and became an object of derision.

Such an effort has related precedents, however dimmed by the mists of time they may be. The Wisconsinite Frederick Jackson Turner, although mostly remembered—and often reviled—for his frontier thesis, also sought to promote midwestern studies and hoped his home region could maintain a regional "resistance to national homogeneity."[14] American regions should never cease "seeing nationally," he thought, because an expansive vision was vital to civic cooperation and making the country function, but he also thought regions such as the Midwest should maintain their identity and study their history.[15] Westerner and later Harvard philosopher Josiah Royce also articulated his fears about the coming flood of mass culture and the resulting homogenization of American life.[16] In a once well-known speech in Iowa City, Royce set forth his case for retaining regions' distinctiveness lest Americans lose their grounding in place and local traditions and succumb to a "dead level of harassed mediocrity."[17] He called for the preservation of the "independence" and "organic life" of the "provinces."[18] Midwesterners such as Hamlin Garland similarly sought to "combat literary centralization," especially in New York, and "to build up local centres" by recognizing the literature from the "great interior spaces."[19] Garland helped to form the Society of Midland Authors, for example, the culmination of several late nineteenth-century efforts to build a midwestern intelligentsia and strengthen the region's literary voices.[20] In the post–Civil War era, as the Great West became less of a transitory borderland zone filled with migrants and more of a settled space and as the idea of the Midwest as a region took root, writers and other intellectuals increasingly embraced a midwestern identity.[21] Buoyed by such gestures, the Midwestern Moment in the annals of American regionalism had arrived.

Despite these noble efforts and the sentiments underlying them, it was difficult to sustain the midwestern regionalist project and to combat what Walter Lippmann called the "acids of modernity" that dissolved local cultures and communities.[22] Many observers justifiably worried that the "last remnants" of an older American society would fade and that the "mass culture manufactured and promoted by Madison Avenue and Hollywood" would overwhelm local, regional, and folk cultures and undermine American pluralism.[23] One Nebraska regionalist, Lowry Charles Wimberly, who edited the recently formed literary journal *Prairie Schooner* in the 1930s, had his fears about the eclipse of regionalism confirmed by a speaker who denied any worthwhile literary production from the middle of the country and who, to make the point about where good literature was produced and where it was not, relied on a map displaying a dead cow over Wimberly's Nebraska.[24] The dead cow chart symbolized the belief that interior voices were growing faint and that regional influences were in decline. A few decades later, some critics argued that "we have no regions anymore," at least "not the regions of regionalism," or the regions of ante–World War II America.[25]

The realities of mass society and the diminishment of regional cultures are not to be dismissed, but I mean to suggest, at this critical early stage of the effort to revive the field of midwestern studies, that the death-of-regionalism findings are too stark. With greater focus and more resources and a cognizance of history or, as Kent Ryden counsels, if we simply "pay attention," we can see that regions persist.[26] "For even through an ivory tower the wind of the country blows," as George Stewart once observed, "bringing the smell of pine woods or perhaps of new-plowed land or perhaps of an oil refinery; but still it blows."[27] Geography and history and place and regional attachments still matter in the world.[28] Fargo is not San Diego.[29] The revolts of the Quebecois and Catalonian secession and Grexits and Brexits continue to lead the news and Scottish rebels still fight the 1707 Act of Union.[30] Regionalist impulses have much less drastic consequences in the Midwest, of course, where the debates are over where the Midwest ends and the plains begin or how far north one can go before ceasing to be midwestern or how much of Missouri is midwestern, but the impulses still exist.[31] Some midwesterners can still recall Bill Holm's wry call for the secession of Minnesota and the adaption of the Atlantic and Pacific oceans in the American "from sea to shining sea" anthem to the Minnesota-based substitutes of Lake Superior and Big Stone Lake.[32]

Wallace Stegner, a forgotten midwesterner now solely remembered for his western writings, was adept at describing the persisting power of place and the "physical and spiritual bonds that develop within a place and a society."[33] He could also detect the uneven power of place and regional nuances, including the distinctions between the scattered and complex subregions of the West and the "unity" of the "corn Midwest."[34] Stegner could see these distinctions better because, in addition to his time on the high plains and in the far West, he had midwestern roots. He was born in Lake Mills, Iowa, next to the Minnesota border, and he earned his PhD at the University of Iowa when it was a "citadel of Iowa regionalism."[35] Stegner's inner Iowan could help him see the distinctions between the older, agrarian Midwest and the fractious West and its cult of the "horseman," who would always be "more romantic than the plowman or the townsman" and would become a mass media franchise.[36] It was the farm and village culture of the Midwest, he thought, which held the ingredients of a "continuous, forming life" and the foundations of "a local character, a local literature" that could form a "regional culture" with deep roots and persisting traditions.[37] In contrast to the churning currents of culture in the farther American West, in other words, Stegner recognized the "healthy provincialism of Iowa," and he greatly admired its manifestations such as the Iowa- and Midwest-oriented literary magazine *The Midland*, which gave voice to midwestern regionalism during the early twentieth century.[38] Stegner would have shared the annoyance of those regionalists who were frustrated by, as the Iowan Herbert Quick said, "the great editors" of the East who failed to believe in the idea of the existence of an Iowa literature.[39] Stegner endorsed the effort, in keeping with Kent Ryden, to pay attention to the particularities of the history of the American Midwest, the unique interior region, one recognized a century ago as home to a people of a "different type," a region "far removed from the wild and dare-devil border" out "beyond the Rockies and the white-hot deserts of Arizona and New Mexico" and distinct from the "effete East."[40]

Underlying the call to recognize regionalism is a realization of the psychological costs of "alienation" and "rootlessness."[41] These are the dangers of, for example, California, which, as Pico Iyer argues, is "a society built on quicksand, where everyone is getting new lives every day."[42] The maladies associated with porous identities and physical displacement underscore the value of regionalism and attachments to particular landscapes, what Lucy Lippard calls the "lure of the local," or the "geographical component of the need to belong somewhere, one antidote to a prevailing alienation," or what Cleanth Brooks described as the "strength to be gained" from a "sense of belonging to a living community and the special focus upon the world bestowed by one's having a precise location in time and history."[43] This strength stems from the cultural power and psychological steadiness that accompany having a home where a person can feel placed and part of a community and be an active neighbor and citizen and engaged in civic affairs and in the lives of friends and family.[44] "Home," says the Iowa folk singer Greg Brown, "is where you know what's going on."[45]

Regional attachments can be tenuous, however, and unrealized. As Lawrence Durrell once explained, it can be difficult in the modern swirl of culture to detect the "hidden magnetic fields that the landscape is trying to communicate to the personality."[46] But these fields can be detected with a second effort and with more finely calibrated instruments if we, as Lippard suggests, "study the local knowledge that distinguishes every place from every other place."[47] This necessarily involves the revival of regional studies and overcoming the past indifference of scholars.[48] I urge more of my fellow historians and other scholars to undertake such studies and to focus on the American Midwest, a grossly understudied American region. Such studies could ultimately bolster the argument of a few scattered voices who have emphasized, against much opposition, that the regionalist impulse persists and recognize, as Cleveland-born Constance Rourke once noted, the "stubborn variety that seems to linger with us in spite of standardization."[49]

Regional attachments need not be limited to those with strong personal and historical connections to a place, although those connections can certainly deepen regionalist sentiments.[50] While the depth of connection for a relatively recent arrival to a new place may not be as intense as, say, the long-established presence of a peasant in the Black Forest, it can be no less real.[51] Yi-Fu Tuan recognizes the distinction between "rootedness" in a place that is historic and traditional and deep and that may not even be recognized consciously because it is so embedded and, alternatively, a "sense of place," which is more self-conscious and the product of learning, research, historical analysis, and the purposeful absorption of one's surroundings.[52] A sense of place, Tuan explains, "implies a certain distance between self and place that allows the self to appreciate a place."[53] The result is that regionalism is not the exclusionary category that some critics fear—people can learn to love or merely appreciate a place, even though they were initially foreign to it. All people can *find* a place, in other words, both those who are new to it and those who are products of it but not aware of their roots, and the search is valuable for both groups. It is good, said the Kansas-born poet William Stafford, to "welcome any region you live in or come to or think of, for that is where life happens to be—right where you are."[54]

To find a place, however, one must first see it, as John Brinkerhoff Jackson demonstrated, in part, through his attention to the small towns and rural spaces of the American interior.[55] The problem of "placelessness," Lippard argues, "may simply be place ignored, unseen, or unknown."[56] The Iowa regionalist Ruth Suckow once pointed to the "same old blindness" and the "colonial hang-over that has darkened, and still darkens" the realms of the creative mind and that limited the ability to see regions such as the Midwest.[57] This spirit of mitigating our blindness and widening our vision animates this book's call for closer attention to the Midwest and midwestern regionalism, and it can, I hope, serve as a nudge and help us to find more of the history of the Midwest, a region that, Michael Martone has explained, "is hard to see."[58] Its chapters can perhaps serve as "essays of place," as Kent Ryden calls them, which illuminate the "contours of the invisible landscape" and, as William Zeiger notes, "cultivate the habit of noticing."[59] To pay attention and to see, Wendell Berry argues, is to "come into the presence of a subject," to assign it some value, to recognize that some "attention is *owed*" to vast mental and physical territories that have been neglected and marginalized.[60]

This book represents some of the ways I have slowly started to find more of the Midwest in our history, but these realizations, I hasten to add, did not come rapidly and instead represent an incremental process of research and a somewhat unanticipated line of inquiry. Based on my own origins on a midwestern farm and in a small midwestern town and an interest in American history, culture, politics, and economic policy, I began researching the post–World War II economic problems that disrupted midwestern farming for a doctoral dissertation. Originally conceived as an economic history of the postwar "farm problem," I began to see how the worries over the declining number of midwestern family farms, in addition to being an economic question, also represented deeply rooted anxieties and legitimate fears about the passing of a distinct form of rural life in the Midwest and the loss of a core component of the Midwest's identity.[61] Through the process of viewing a midwestern U.S. Senate race up close during an era of drawing "red" versus "blue" state distinctions, I came to a greater realization of how particular places are unique and shaped by their own specific rhythms and heritage and socio-political contours.[62] Prompted by an obligation to teach a course on the history of South Dakota, I was led to explore how the foundational dynamics of a place determined and shaped a state's political culture and its regional orientation.[63] The resulting research and book led to a collaborative project with several other authors that produced a deeper exploration of South Dakota's politics, culture, and history and their interconnections.[64] Convinced of the value of such studies and how they can explain regions such as the Midwest, I began to explore a long-forgotten tradition of midwestern historical writing.[65] This trajectory led me to this book, which, I hope, can elucidate how and why the Midwest's fortunes declined so dramatically in intellectual and cultural circles during the past half century and how we might find the Midwest once again.

What this book seeks, most generally, is greater attention to a neglected region and a removal of the Midwest, in F. Scott Fitzgerald's ominous phrase, from the "ragged edge of the universe" and its placement closer to the center of our historical and cultural imagination. Greater attention, I hope, will yield a greater appreciation for and a semblance of balance in the treatment of the Midwest and spark a broader process of discovery, or rediscovery, perhaps best personified by St. Paulite Fitzgerald's most famous character. When the Minnesotan Nick Carraway dismissed the Midwest as a dull and remote "ragged edge" of modern life, he had just returned from years of dislocation and European war and so took his "restless" soul, his "provincial inexperience," his mind "full of interior rules," and his "provincial squeamishness" and sought more adventure in the East. Only later—after viewing the spectacular tumult and absurdity of jazz-age New York and the demise of his famous friend, "James Gatz of North Dakota," done in by the "constant, turbulent riot" of his heart and his break from the poor "farm people" of his youth, or his rootlessness—did Nick return, watching the "dim lights of small Wisconsin stations" pass by on the route to what Nick called "my Middle West." Only then did Nick recognize what he missed and how he was "subtly unadaptable to Eastern life," its "fantastic dreams," its "quality of distortion," its people who "smashed up things and creatures and then retreated back into their money or their vast carelessness." Nick's old Midwest—no longer dismissed as the "bored, swollen towns beyond the Ohio"—became for him the "warm center of the world." Nick saw, as Gatsby could not, what could be found "somewhere back in that vast obscurity beyond the city, where the dark fields of the republic rolled on under the night."[66] Nick could finally see his place and find his roots and can perhaps still help us all to see the Midwest as more than the ragged edge of a vast obscurity and to find its warm center, or at least some happy space in-between where, even if the spotlight often eludes the Midwest, it is no longer consigned to the shadows.

Fitzgerald's portrayal of Nick Carraway's momentary disconnection from the Midwest figures in the region's erasure from the popular imagination. One explanation for how the Midwest first came to be lost to the main currents of American thought is the abrupt turn in thinking about the region by the 1920s.[67] After the publication of some literary works that included some arguably unflattering assessments of the Midwest, an editor at *The Nation* suddenly pronounced the arrival of a "revolt from the village" school of thought in American writing that finally, it came to be believed, exposed the purported vices of midwestern small towns and broke the alleged monopoly previously held by apologists for the region. This characterization of events—which ignores the revelations of Nick Carraway and instead relies, mistakenly, on another strand of Fitzgerald's literary work—and the assumptions underlying it, despite their broad academic and popular acceptance and continual invocation, are deeply flawed and remain a persistent barrier to seeing and understanding the full complexity of the Midwest. The great influence of the flawed revolt thesis and its impact on the Midwest are explored in Chapter 1, "The Myth of the Midwestern 'Revolt from the Village.'"

One of the critical flaws in the revolt thesis is its focus on books that, at least according to some, were highly critical of the Midwest. But this focus is highly misleading and obscures a large body of work produced by midwestern regionalist writers who were neither alienated nor rebellious and who possessed a genuine affection for their home region. They staged what might be called a "revolt against the village revolt," but their efforts are largely forgotten while the popular understanding of the work of the village rebels lives on among literary scholars and historians and in the broader culture. The work and subsequent marginalization of these regionalist writers are explored in Chapter 2, "The Failed Revolt Against the Revolt."

During these same years, a group of midwestern historians met a similar fate. They actively chronicled their region during the early twentieth century and wrote important books with institutional support from within the

Midwest, but their fortunes quickly dimmed with the coming of World War II, new intellectual and cultural currents, and the final collapse of their organized efforts to study the Midwest. This regrettable turn, which left the Midwest largely voiceless in American historiography for a half century, is explained in Chapter 3, "The Decline of Midwestern History." From this declensionist narrative, one can better understand the erosion of midwestern regionalism and the migration of the American Midwest from the warm center of American consciousness to the ragged edge of our imagination.

Special thanks must be extended to Dr. Catherine Cocks at the University of Iowa Press and to Simpson College history professor Bill Friedricks (editor of the University of Iowa Press's Iowa and the Midwest Experience series) for their strong leadership and their peerless efforts to revive the study of the American Midwest. Their guidance, expertise, vision, and persistence over several years have been essential to my work on midwestern history and to the work of many others who are attempting to give the Midwest a stronger voice in academic discourse. It is also entirely fitting that the University of Iowa Press should publish this book given the University of Iowa's historic role in earlier iterations of midwestern regionalism.

This book is dedicated to the friendship and spirit of repartee of a group of men I came to know in graduate school at the University of Iowa, where some of this thinking began and which, a century ago, served as a center of regionalist thought and energy, a legacy largely in abeyance by my 1990s graduate school stint. Over coffee and eggs at Mickey's and Guinness pints at the Dublin Underground in Iowa City, Jason Duncan, Dave McMahon, Mark Milosch, and myself pondered the vanished world of Iowa regionalism and discussed Sinatra, the Hawkeyes, the implosion of Yugoslavia, the promise and perils of academia, politics, sports, and, most often, Irish history, which, as I later came to learn, once served as a model for some of the regionalist thinking of the early twentieth-century United States. This spirit of Irish dissidence—against the strong currents of popular culture and against academic fashion, in this case—and a respect for local cultures may hold one of the keys to reviving interest in the history of the Midwest.

Jon K. Lauck
Sioux Falls, July 2016

# CHAPTER ONE

# THE MYTH OF THE MIDWESTERN "REVOLT FROM THE VILLAGE"

When the twentieth century dawned, the American Midwest stood tall as the republic's ascendant and triumphant region—economically prosperous, politically formidable, culturally proud, and consciously regional. The Midwest, according to the geographer James Shortridge, "reached a pinnacle of self-confidence in the 1910s" when it was popularly viewed as the heartland of "morality, independence, and egalitarianism."[1] In quick succession, however, this popular conception was upended, and the region's standing embattled. In the years after World War I, vocal intellectuals recast the Midwest as a repressive and sterile backwater filled with small-town snoops, redneck farmers, and zealous theocrats or, in a more benign version, as a "colorless, flat spot in the middle of America."[2] This nascent interpretation was sparked by cultural rebels who had escaped their crimped upbringings in the region, unmasked its failings, and collectively, so it was argued, constituted a revolt from the village, or a cultural rebellion against the small-town and rural folkways of the Midwest. The "village revolt" interpretation won wide approval from the cultural elites of the era and was reinforced by a wider gathering of intellectual and political forces that were amenable to such a formulation; it fueled a spike in the number of attacks on the Midwest and, ultimately, a decline in attention to the region, despite the interpretation's deep flaws. To find the Midwest and its history, this flawed interpretation—which is still embraced by many intellectuals and still exerts great power in the American cultural imagination—must be dissected and amended so that a dated and one-sided but still common interpretive construction does not block the path

toward finding the history of the Midwest. "One reason to know our own histories," Lucy Lippard explains, "is so that we are not defined by others, so that
we can resist other people's images of our pasts, and consequently, our futures,"
and, as David Radavich argues, so that it is possible to combat the "cultural
silencing" that too often mutes the voices of the Midwest.[3]

The formative thrust of the revolt from the village interpretation came by
way of an essay penned by Carl Van Doren, a Columbia University English
professor and the literary editor of the increasingly radical magazine *The
Nation*, in *The Nation*'s fall book supplement of 1921.[4] Van Doren argued that,
for a half century, American literature had been "faithful to the cult of the village."[5] The "essential goodness and heroism" of the village had been a "sacred"
pillar of literature and had become a "doctrine" whose tenets included an
appreciation of little white churches, corner groceries, decent and wise ministers, faithful local doctors, diligent farmers, and picturesque country scenes.[6]
But then, as World War I was raging, a cadre of literary truth-tellers emerged
who revealed the realities of the "slack and shabby" village and exposed its
closeted skeletons, secrets, sexual escapades, degeneracy, "grotesque forms,"
"subterfuges," "pathos," "filth," "illusions," "demoralization," "rot," "compla-
cency," "stupidity," and "pitiless decorum which veils its faults" and obscured
an "abundant feast of scandal."[7] Van Doren celebrated, in particular, Edgar Lee
Masters's *Spoon River Anthology* (1915), Sherwood Anderson's *Winesburg, Ohio*
(1919), Sinclair Lewis's *Main Street* (1920), and F. Scott Fitzgerald's *This Side of
Paradise* (1920) and noted their embrace of a "formula of revolt" against "provincialism" that, after being consumed by the American reading public, would
finally undermine the "hazy national optimism of an elder style" and cause the
"ancient customs [to] break or fade."[8] The "bright barbarians" of Fitzgerald, for
example, "significantly illustrate[d] . . . the revolt from the village," according
to Van Doren, by breaking the "patterns" and "traditions which once might
have governed them" and then "laughing" and pursuing "their wild desires"
among "the ruins of the old."[9] Van Doren thus privileged Fitzgerald's conception of the Midwest as the ragged edge of the universe and ignored any vision
of the region as a warm center of communal and civic life.

Van Doren's interpretation was absorbed into subsequent historical treatments of the era. Frederick Lewis Allen's famous synthesis of the 1920s,
published soon after the close of the decade, set the tone by spotlighting the
"revolt of the highbrows" against boosters and Rotarians in "cities and towns

where Babbitry flourished" and by noting the "overwhelming" impact of authors such as Sinclair Lewis, who "revealed the ugliness of the American small town."[10] An early and influential interpreter of the era, Alfred Kazin, age twenty-three and writing from his kitchen table in Brooklyn as World War II approached, drew on Van Doren's formulation; cited the works of Masters, Lewis, Fitzgerald, and Anderson; and explained how the rebels "had revolted against their native village life in the Middle West" and attacked "provincialism" and the "ugliness" and "bitterness of small town life."[11] After World War II, in his well-known summary of American intellectual history, Henry Steele Commager included a chapter, "The Literature of Revolt," that argued it was "incontrovertible" that almost "all the *major* writers" of the 1920s were critical of American culture and commercialism and embraced the "revolt from the farm" theme.[12] When Mark Schorer's massive biography of Sinclair Lewis was released in 1961, Lewis was touted as the "great emancipator" of stunted souls from the Midwest's "smug provincialism" and "false sentiment and false piety."[13] In 1969, Anthony Channell Hilfer published a book essentially restating the revolt thesis for a new generation and arguing that the work of the cultural rebels of the 1920s could be revived and used by the rebellious students of the 1960s.[14] In another major synthetic treatment published during the 1970s, Richard Pells described the village rebels, who shared their "origins in rural and small-town America," as people who "found the village or farm claustrophobic" and "too constricting for individual creativity and self-expression."[15] Pells specifically points to Anderson, Lewis, and Fitzgerald and sees them as part of a broader movement among intellectuals who rejected American life during the 1920s for its "stupidity, aimlessness, and vulgarity."[16]

The working assumption that the Midwest was "culturally impoverished" and the critical focus on cultural rebellion have persisted in recent decades.[17] Citing Fitzgerald, Anderson, and Lewis, Lynn Dumenil's 1995 synthesis of the history of the 1920s specifically relies on the "theme that historians have called the revolt against the village."[18] In Christine Stansell's more recent treatment of the era, cultural "rebels" were drawn to Bohemia because, as one Greenwich Village resident said, they were "bored by some small place in the Middle West" and, as Stansell says, because they found the midwestern towns Sinclair Lewis described as "self-satisfied" and "mean-spirited."[19] Critics continue to see *Spoon River*, *Winesburg*, and *Main Street* as the "principal monuments of a phase of American fiction known as 'The Revolt from the Village.'"[20] In his comprehensive literary history of the Midwest, which tends to follow Van Doren's lead, Ronald Weber notes Van Doren's "celebrated 1921 article in *The Nation*" about the "revolt-from-the-village books."[21] Weber views 1920, which saw the publication of key works of revolt, as the "high-water mark" for "midwestern writing," giving the village rebels center stage in the literary history of the Midwest.[22] These supposed works of rebellion afforded privileged status to and, "conditioned by their early reception," provided "confirmation for what [critics] already believed" about the provincialism and monotony of the "American waste land" and the "plains and prairies that started west of the Hudson River"; this mode of thought has been consistently echoed by historians and other critics.[23]

These historians and critics have thus contributed to the entrenchment and institutionalization of Van Doren's original interpretation, which has also migrated into journalistic accounts of the era.[24] They have helped create what Maurice Beebe called the "revolt-from-the-village tradition," one shorn of any of the nuance Van Doren may have once recognized.[25] Anthony Channell Hilfer, who favored the writings of the village rebels, explained that the revolt from the village formulation had "become an accepted rubric of historical criticism."[26] The social and cultural criticisms in the alleged village rebels' books, which focused on the repression of thought and emotion and the conformity of small towns in places such as the Midwest, "gave the revolt unity."[27] When *Main Street* became a national "sensation," Hilfer explains, the "revolt from the village became official, public, almost *institutional*" and Van Doren's thesis proven beyond doubt.[28] Van Doren's "famous phrase," Gordon Hutner observes, became a "premise seemingly so true that it has never needed to be revisited."[29] As an entrenched and unquestioned force in American letters, one that tidily summarizes an important cultural moment, however, the revolt thesis—an interpretation based on one tossed-off magazine summary of a few works of literature, not on historical analysis—serves not as a useful and accurate shorthand. Instead, it functioned and still functions as a set of blinders, blocking out and distorting significant parts of the past.

The village revolt interpretation is simplistic and flawed, and its "institutionalization" within the annals of history clouds our vision of the midwestern past. The failure to account for the intellectual and cultural context of the revolt obscures the reason that the thesis took hold and persisted. Accounting for the intellectual and cultural forces that gave the revolt thesis currency explains why

it emerged to the exclusion of other emphases or more nuanced interpretations. The revolt thesis fails to fully comprehend other intellectual trends and
cultural forces that complicate and undermine its assumptions, and it remains
too stark and one-sided. It ignores, more specifically, regionalist or anti-rebel
voices. The revolt thesis is also premised on a one-sided interpretation of the
supposed rebels, who were more complicated than the thesis presumes. The
village revolt interpretation thus blurs our ability to properly see regions such
as the Midwest, which often served as the home of the rural areas, small towns,
and "villages" under assault. If the typical traditions of the small town were the
target of the purveyors of the village revolt thesis, as Hilfer notes, the "midwestern small town was doubly typical," and thus the Midwest's "hick towns"
were doubly the target of attack.[30] The works of Masters, Anderson, Lewis, and
others, Ronald Weber notes, made the Midwest a "convenient whipping boy"
and generated a "massive cultural resistance to the region."[31] The "Middle West
[became] a metaphor of abuse."[32] But if the dominant place of the revolt thesis
can be weakened and space can be created for more and varied voices from the
past, the Midwest can be more fully comprehended.

The inspiration for Van Doren's village rebel characterization can be traced
in part to the writings of the critic Van Wyck Brooks, who helps explain the origins of the revolt thesis and its effect upon the Midwest and, later, exposes its
central flaws.[33] Brooks grew up in New Jersey, the son of a failed and personally
distant businessman, and attended Harvard, where his professors emphasized
the coarseness of, inter alia, "the wilds of Ohio."[34] Brooks's first book, *The Wine
of the Puritans* (1908), blamed the continuing influence of the Puritan colonists
and the materialism of the Westward-moving pioneers for the supposed sterility and shallowness of American culture.[35] Brooks's second book, *America's
Coming of Age* (1915), was, according to Van Doren, highly influential and
"virtually the first book to voice the new age" complaints about the cultural
repressiveness and provincialism in the hinterlands that formed the basis of
the revolt thesis.[36] For Brooks, the pioneer and the Puritan were "our cultural
villains," and he specifically traced this villainy to the American Midwest.[37]
Brooks's third book, *The Ordeal of Mark Twain* (1920), which was published
the year before Van Doren's village revolt interpretation appeared, argued that
Twain's imagination was repressed by "puritanism and pioneering" because
he came from, as Brooks said, the "dry, old, barren, horizonless Middle West,"
"a desert of human sand!—the barrenest spot in all Christendom, surely, for

the seed of genius to fall in."[38] Brooks hoped for a day when "grotesque" places such as Sioux City, Iowa, and the "unlovable and ugly" towns of the American interior more generally would finally have culture and thus "dignity."[39]

When Van Doren published the revolt thesis while drawing on Brooks's intense criticism of American culture, Brooks was closely allied with H. L. Mencken, who exerted great influence over American intellectual life during the era and generally hated "Middle Western *Kultur*."[40] The keynoter of the cultural revolt of the 1920s, Frederick Lewis Allen concluded, was Mencken.[41] In 1927, Walter Lippmann called Mencken "the most powerful personal influence on this whole generation of educated people."[42] Mencken saw Americans as "provincial" and "stupid," and his "most articulate opponents were village editors, clubwomen, Fundamentalists, or conservative critics," who were often located in the Midwest.[43] Mencken focused on the "loneliness and hopelessness of the buried life of small towns" and directed his attacks at the "provincial American" and viewed the elements of American backwardness as an "essentially rural phenomena."[44] The Chicago writer James T. Farrell saw Mencken's writings as based on the "superiority of the values of the city over those of the rural areas."[45] Mencken attacked "yokel" farmers as "simian" and the source of, as Hilfer says, a "husbandry tyranny" over the nation.[46] Mencken was voicing a "well-worn vocabulary of condescension" among intellectuals that included "bumpkin, hick, yokel, hayseed, clodhopper."[47] Mencken belongs to "the 'revolt from the village' writers" and remains a valuable voice, as one *New Yorker* critic recently noted, because of "his campaign against provincialism."[48] In addition to having a broad impact on the intellectuals of the era, Mencken was, more specifically, a "central influence" on purported revolt books such as Sinclair Lewis's *Main Street*.[49] Although the themes of the revolt thesis and Mencken's attacks could be applied generally, the focus came to be on the American small town, which, Hilfer says, was "nicely adaptable" for articulating criticisms of repressiveness and conformity.[50] In Van Doren's formulation, the "villages of the Middle West" were particularly threatening because their "provincialism" could spread and thus present a wider danger.[51]

The intellectual heft of Brooks and the polemical firepower provided by Mencken's more popular media platforms gave voice to a broad intellectual attack on the alleged provincialism of American culture and were thought to signal and justify new literary themes. As Van Doren explained in his influential essay, it was crucial that intellectuals transcend and undermine an existing "cult of the village," or the ongoing respect for the traditions of small-town and rural life that persisted from the nineteenth century.[52] Broadly speaking, Brooks, Mencken, and Van Doren were seeking to undermine and overcome the persisting customs and values of nineteenth-century Victorian culture. The village revolt thesis both fueled and was bolstered by criticism of Victorian culture and thus was launched at a propitious time for its adoption and perpetuation. The purveyors of the revolt thesis found strong allies among the critics of Victorianism generally and, more specifically, among those who embraced the vogue of literary modernism.

Victorianism, as Daniel Joseph Singal explains, was the "culture against which the early Modernists rebelled."[53] Victorianism's American reign roughly stretched from the 1830s to the early twentieth century, and its "guiding ethos was centered upon the classic bourgeois values of thrift, diligence, and persistence and a recognition of the value of standards learned through education, religion, and manners that created a separation between stable communities and savagery."[54] Victorian ideals were especially strong in the rural areas and small towns of the Midwest, leaving the region vulnerable to the criticisms of the literary modernists.[55] If the decade prior to World War I was seen as the "last age of innocence," it was "a time in which simplicity and moral idealism still reigned supreme in the small towns and midwestern farmhouses."[56] Even as it began to erode in other areas, Victorian culture still lived on in small cities and towns and in the rural areas.[57] Citing the rural sociology literature of the 1920s, the historian James Shideler explained how rural people were "conservative and tradition-minded" and "rested patiently on a conventional certainty about good and evil, with staunch adherence to the values of hard work, thrift, and self-denial."[58] The famed Dr. Kennicott of *Main Street*, for example, adhered to the Victorian code of honest labor, moral uplift, community service, and patriotism.[59] It was these Victorian beliefs and cultural norms that came under assault, as Stanley Coben explains, by a "growing subculture of alienated intellectuals" that would form the basis of support for the village revolt thesis and contribute to what Paul Gorman deems the project of "breaking up the Victorian moral and cultural synthesis."[60] The revolt thesis, Barry Gross concluded, was invented and perpetuated by intellectuals "who themselves wanted to see the village revolted from, who were convinced that provincial life, especially in the Middle West, condemned America to the status of second-class culture."[61]

The influence of the intellectuals who led the criticism of Victorian culture was a new phenomenon in American life. While novelists, patrician writers, ministers, newspaper commentators, public speakers, political leaders, and others had always shaped American public discourse, the emergence of intellectuals as a "social type" was new.[62] More specifically, "alienated" intellectuals, or writers and thinkers who felt disconnected from the main traditions of American life and sought to criticize and reform them, rose to prominence. A dedication to "intellect" and the "life of the mind" was often set against an ingrained tendency toward the "[g]lorification of the small town" and the emphasis on "horse sense" and "simple honesty" out in the provinces such as the Midwest.[63] When the *New Yorker* was launched in the 1920s, it proclaimed its reverence for the serious and urbane intellectual life and its opposition to rural provincialism by announcing its motto as "Not for the old lady from Dubuque."[64] "From its superior vantage point in the citadel of New York, the *New Yorker* persistently in its early years deprovincialized the rest of America through ridicule and satire," Edward A. Martin explains, and the "most persistent debunking campaign of the early years involved ridicule of those regions of the country so unfortunate as to lie outside of New York."[65] A primary goal of the new "cosmopolitan" intellectual that the *New Yorker* would cater to, as David Hollinger has explained, was to oppose "parochialism" and "provincialism" and to "transcend the limitations of any and all particularisms" and to undermine Victorianism, patriotism, and "Puritanism."[66] These new intellectuals tended to privilege writers—including the "refugees from the Midwest" who provided the corpus of work that seemed to substantiate the village revolt thesis—who bolstered their critique of American life.[67]

A common enemy of the emergent intellectuals was the strictures of American Christianity. Van Doren included among the symbolic tenets of the cult of the village "the white church with tapering spire" and the "venerable parson." The prominence of New England and its Puritan tradition in American historical development, in particular, became a frequent target of criticism, causing one critic of the period to note the "present preoccupation with ecclesiastical muck-raking."[68] Frederick Hoffman has explained how the Puritan became "an unhistorical victim and villain" during the 1920s and how it became "fashionable" to attack religion and an invented form of Puritan history "in the attempt of the 1920s to justify its successful revolt against convention."[69] The Puritan, Hoffman argues, became a "convenient 'enemy'" for the cultural rebels of the 1920s and the emerging intellectual class, which sought to transform American culture.[70] Intellectuals believed that American religiosity, Warren Susman once explained, made it "impossible to have a decent art, architecture, and literature."[71] They venerated the freedom of Bohemian enclaves such as Greenwich Village as an escape from provincialism and the repressiveness of religious doctrine.[72] Intellectuals saw Greenwich Village as an "escape" and a "dream Mecca" for young spirits who "fled their Western villages" for the joy and freedom of a "stool in the Village Café."[73] One reason that American intellectual expatriates preferred living in France was its freedom from any stain of Puritanism, as in England, and because their images of France "clearly drew attention to many of the weaknesses of America."[74] The veneration of Greenwich Village and Paris complemented the assault on Puritanism and the interior villages and farm life in the Midwest because, as Walter Lippmann noted, the "deep and abiding traditions of religion belong to the countryside."[75] The influence of these assaults upon religiosity and provincialism was felt far beyond bohemia. As Malcolm Cowley recalled, there were people all over the country "who had never been to New York and yet were acting and talking like Greenwich Villagers."[76]

The critiques advanced by the emergent and alienated intellectuals and writers were both part of and bolstered by the rise of social science, especially anthropology, sociology, and psychology. Franz Boas and Ruth Benedict— both, like Van Doren, associated with Columbia, where, Van Doren said, "everybody seems to be reading" *Main Street*—and other anthropologists saw Victorian culture as backward and repressed when contrasted with foreign and primitive cultures.[77] The village rebels' attack on American Puritanism was supported by the anthropologists' praise of primitivism and their efforts "to point out the great happiness of people who were not brought up in terror of sex and who therefore lived a normal, happy, casual life."[78] Margaret Mead, a student of Benedict, believed that, in comparison to South Pacific cultures, "Victorian culture crippled Americans emotionally" and was the cause of their "neuroses."[79] Mead and other anthropologists embraced the cultural practices at work, for example, in Samoan and Mexican villages as superior to the American way of life.[80] These anthropologists, along with the village rebels and other emergent intellectuals, felt "estranged from the dominant values of their society" and thus were eager to find alternatives.[81]

Before a later division, anthropology and sociology had existed as one field of study and were focused on conducting studies of varying ethnographic groups. By the 1920s sociology had emerged as a prominent and independent field dedicated to "scientific" methods of analyzing society that often embraced "a model of modernizing society that suggested folk culture, and therefore communal order, was becoming extinct."[82] These methods shaped *Middletown* (1929), the "single most influential book by social scientists published during the 1920s."[83] *Middletown*, written by Robert and Helen Lynd, focused on the social inadequacies—the "lag of habits" caused by tradition—of the medium-sized midwestern city of Muncie, Indiana, and proved to be a popular interpretation with other intellectual and literary critics of the Midwest and provided a method of analysis borrowed by these critics.[84] Sinclair Lewis's *Main Street*, for example, has been viewed as "not only a sociological novel but a sociological event."[85] Lewis was known for his extensive research and for using research assistants and, as one biographer notes, went "into 'the field' like any cultural anthropologist."[86] Lewis's "meticulous" research in Minnesota and Kansas and other states made it possible for him to depict the "life of the new middle class, in Dakota villages and in the Cincinnatis and the Minneapolises."[87] The result was that *Main Street* has been interpreted as "a sociological caricature unmasking the small town."[88] With his extensive research and pseudo-scientific field work, Lewis was able, as E. M. Forster said, "to lodge a piece of a continent in our imagination" and to permanently shape the popular view of the Midwest.[89]

In addition to anthropology and sociology, the field of psychology had a pronounced effect on the intellectual life of the 1920s. Freud, as Alfred Kazin noted, "suddenly became the indispensable text."[90] The growth of Freudian psychology and its strong emphasis on the impacts of repressed emotions was directly linked to the "Puritan-baiting" of the era.[91] Freud's analyses were also connected to attacks on the pioneers for their "continuous suppression of desire."[92] The psychological focus on "personality," with its emphasis on soul-searching, personal liberation, and appealing to one's peers, began to replace Victorian "character," with its emphasis on self-reliance and moral restraint.[93]

Some intellectuals of the 1920s—whether writers, critics, anthropologists, sociologists, psychiatrists, or those in other fields—were tempted to take their criticism beyond the realm of intellectual discourse and into the field of active politics. While some were active in progressive causes, others were drawn to more radical politics and forms of Marxism, especially in the wake of the Russian revolution and its supposed accomplishments.[94] Lionel Trilling later recalled the "commitment that a large segment of the intelligentsia of the West gave to the degraded version of Marxism known as Stalinism" and the "belief that the Soviet Union had resolved all social and political contradictions and was well on the way toward realizing the highest possibilities of human life."[95] Sinclair Lewis talked of praying to the "spirit of Lenin" and noted the growing number of "good writers" in the Soviet Union.[96] In the late 1920s, Stalin called for the "intensification of the class war on the cultural front" that led, in 1929, to the formation of the John Reed Club in New York as a platform for promoting "proletarian artists" who could combat reactionary forces.[97] The club adopted the motto "Art is a Class Weapon."[98] Whether supporting the fledgling Communist movement or less-activist forms of politics, intellectuals often saw the rural and small-town traditions of the country as barriers to the political transformation they sought. Van Doren's assault on the "cult of the village" bolstered the case of those who thought that the enduring beliefs in the values of small towns were simply "propaganda" used by business to combat "centralized control" by government and that the "praise of the small town was a covert way of denying the need to think, a method of evading the admission that old formulas no longer served the new conditions."[99] The praise of the small town was viewed as a technique to "deny the bleaker realities" of America.[100] To the frustration of radicals, however, the belief in the value of small towns still held sway. In the 1928 presidential race, Herbert Hoover of Iowa was successfully billed as "a boy from a country village" during his landslide victory.[101]

In addition to critiquing small-town life and its effects on politics, Marxists also targeted the leading figure in the field of midwestern history. In 1933, Louis Hacker, a Marxist historian, also at Columbia, published the first major assault on Frederick Jackson Turner's views on American history in—like Van Doren—*The Nation*.[102] Hacker was a student of Charles Beard, whose highly influential and critical form of history sought to debunk much of what was once thought sacred in American history.[103] This included Turner's scholarship on the frontier, which had become a "major ideological force" in the country and thus in need of criticism and debunking.[104] Hacker viewed Turner as an obstacle to reform and viewed his own "scholarship as building a historical consciousness for the coming revolution."[105] Drawing on Van Wyck Brooks—who saw the frontier as an "almost totally negative" force—a new generation of historians came to believe that how one viewed the past determined how one operated in the present and how one should act in the future, and therefore, as Warren Susman explained, the "control over the interpretation of the nature of that past [became] a burning cultural issue."[106] It "became especially the function of the intellectual to find a useful past" that could "overthrow the official view" and therefore the "values and policies repellent to these intellectuals."[107] Turner understood the motivation of this new intellectual current. In a letter to Arthur Schlesinger Sr. in 1925, Turner argued that efforts to minimize the importance of the frontier were part of the "pessimistic reaction against the old America that followed the World War—the reaction against pioneer ideals, against distinctively American things historically in favor of Old World solutions," and the desire "to write in terms of European experience, and of the class struggle incident to industrialism."[108]

The critiques of an emergent group of scholars during the 1920s and the strong intellectual forces they represented provided lift to and substantiation for the revolt from the village interpretation and helped create a generally favorable intellectual climate for its perpetuation. The disillusionment with World War I and its intense moment of hyper-patriotism and the realization that the nation had become more urban than rural contributed further.[109] The mood fostered an urge to expose and discredit and created a ready audience for such treatments. It was an age when "debunking" became de rigueur and included not just assaults on the supposed myths of the small town and Turner's frontier but attacks on George Washington and Queen Victoria.[110] Rochelle Gurstein explains the "popularity of debunking" that "quickly became a staple of the party of exposure," or those who sought to unmask the hidden and ridicule the private and traditional.[111] In the new era of debunking, the "veil was removed from the small town," and the "debunkers turned with hostile joy against the staunch belief . . . in quiet country towns and hamlets."[112] One writer of the era noted that the ascendant intellectuals, "remembering bitterly the small towns they were brought up in," turned to "Puritan-baiting," Freudian analysis, and debunking.[113] Those who advocated the revolt from the village thesis were a part of this movement. Literature, as they saw it, needed to break free of the "obsolete dreams of the farm and village" and "destroy the myth of the village," which was "hostile to the imagination," and expose its "illusions and lies."[114]

The power of these combined intellectual forces during the 1920s had an impact on the way in which the supposed village rebels fashioned their writings. John T. Frederick, who was attempting to promote local writers in Iowa, noted the effect of outside influences on midwesterners. Frederick worried about what Ronald Weber calls the "harmful commercial influence" on writers caused by the concentration of the publishing industry in New York, which instilled what Frederick called a "tendency to false emphasis, distortion, in literary interpretations."[115] Frederick's attempts to provide midwestern writers a regional platform was a response to New York demands that the "midland artist warp his material to conform to a preconceived notion of what represented the Midwest, or that he burlesque his native soil for the amusement of the East."[116] Writers were "warped to the market," Hamlin Garland said, by the power of "New York publishers and managers" and the lure of financial gain.[117] "New York is Medusa," Edgar Lee Masters warned young writers.[118] Would-be writers noticed, of course, how authors such as Lewis were *being applauded* for exposing the small town in *Main Street* as being a place of repression and small-mindedness" and making money and becoming famous in the process.[119] Many of them recognized that Lewis was obsessed with marketing and publicity and finding clever methods to sell books and that his efforts paid handsomely.[120] Thomas McAvoy—a Notre Dame historian, priest, and native Indianan—noted the incentive for financial gain among the village rebels, choosing to exclude from his survey of the "midwestern mind" the "pessimistic view of the Midwest drawn up chiefly by the literary critics who went east to New York or west to Hollywood to reap the benefit of their midwestern origins."[121] McAvoy was arguing that certain ambitious writers in the Midwest were willing to "sell out" to those in the East who, given the intellectual forces of the era and the urban biases of the publishing industry, were eager to publish works critical of the Midwest, especially those by "insiders" who could write in a revelatory mode.[122] The "cultural coercions and imbalances" caused by eastern cultural dominance, in other words, created a strong market for the revolt from the village genre in the East and incentives for rebels to advance negative portrayals of the Midwest.[123] One University of Minnesota English professor chided midwestern writers who "derided their homeland for the edification of Manhattan."[124] The novelist Herbert Krause, a Minnesotan who was trained in Iowa and taught in South Dakota, grew weary of midwesterners too concerned with eastern tastes and too "in awe of dicta from beyond the Appalachians" and their attempts to "write as though their offices overlooked the Hudson River."[125]

However much the village rebels were influenced by the incentives of fame and fortune and failed to resist the gravitational pull of eastern cultural centers and publishing houses, the varied intellectual and political forces of the era certainly caused the revolt from the village thesis to be embraced and widely believed and afforded special status. Because some of the writings of the supposed village rebels were "usable" to the causes of prominent intellectuals, their writings were given the spotlight and canonized while the works of other authors that tended to dissent from the cause of cultural rebellion were derided or ignored.[126] The resulting bias in favor of the cultural rebels and famous expatriates yielded a distorted view of the events of the 1920s that persists in the historical literature.[127] The continuing awareness of the village rebels and the fame maintained by the "lost generation" and the attention afforded their "moveable feast" leaves far too much buried in the past, however, including regionalist works set in the small towns and on the farms of the Midwest. The rebels' and expatriates' great literary status abides while the rural Midwest remains stereotyped and marginalized. "The most celebrated literature about the Midwest has been written by those who left," notes Scott Russell Sanders when discussing Lewis and Anderson and others, "and who made a case for their leaving" a place "populated by gossips and boosters and Bible thumpers who are hostile to ideas, conformist, moralistic, utilitarian, and perpetually behind the times."[128]

In addition to leaving a residue of disdain behind that continues to obscure the view of the rural Midwest, privileging the cultural rebels and expatriates compels a privileging of urbanism and rural dislocation and a discounting of regional attachments. Still famous writers like Fitzgerald, for example, were strongly urban oriented, James Shideler once explained in a presidential address to the Agricultural History Society in Ames, and his "twilight fell over cocktails at the Biltmore."[129] Privileging the cultural radicals and expatriates necessarily meant privileging and favoring rootlessness and circumscribing regionalism. Malcolm Cowley recalled that the lives of the expatriates had involved a "long process of deracination" and how their early experiences were "involuntarily directed toward destroying whatever roots we had in the soil, toward eradicating our local and regional peculiarities, toward making us homeless citizens of the world."[130] The privileging of the rebels and ex-pats thus exalts themes of alienation, dislocation, and flashy flapper circles and overlooks the common life of people in areas such as the rural and small-town Midwest. As Sinclair Lewis's first wife Grace once asked, "Were the 1920s really the Jazz Age except for a few?"[131] While some of the ex-pats may, at times, have had nostalgic thoughts of home, these fleeting longings were seldom the subject of popular attention, which further highlights the favoritism displayed toward the narrative of rebellion against provincialism.

Because of the bias in favor of cultural rebellion, the "village revolt" writers were given great attention while others were ignored until they showed signs of joining the revolt. National praise and attention for midwestern writers, Sara Kosiba notes in a recent study, were generally limited to those who perpetuated stereotypes of the Midwest.[132] Van Doren's construction of the revolt thesis includes Zona Gale, for example, who was from Frederick Jackson Turner's hometown of Portage, Wisconsin. Gale received a much more positive treatment from national critics when she seemed to leave behind her positive "Friendship Village" stories and became more critical of the Midwest, a move that became a "positive turning point in Gale's career."[133] Interest in the "Chicago Renaissance"—or the burst of literary activity in Chicago about the time of World War I—also stemmed in part from its emphasis on critical realism or early modernist influences, its Bohemianism, and its role as a feeder system of writers who moved to New York, and because it was a distinctly unique outpost in the Midwest, seemingly removed from the agrarian and small-town traditions of the region and a haven for refugees of rural life.[134] Chicago is interesting to critics, in other words, because its writers were seeking a "cosmopolitan center *beyond* their seemingly small native worlds."[135]

If the village revolt school privileged certain writers to the exclusion of others, it also depended on a stark dualism. It relied on the image of a sanitized pre-revolt view of happy village life in the Midwest being overthrown by a later tradition of brilliant avant-garde cultural rebels speaking truth to sterile and oppressive traditions. But this simple dichotomy obscures a more complex history, one that included a pre-revolt tradition of both criticism and praise.[136] It is demonstrably untrue that prior to 1920 the Midwest was only portrayed with a warm and loving glow, as the early writings of Hamlin Garland and Willa Cather and other midwestern realists demonstrate.[137] Literary realism was a midwestern export, after all, a movement intended to dissent from the prevailing Victorianism of eastern literature. But Van Doren downplayed the tradition of critical writing about the Midwest that disproved his contention about the existence of a long-standing and monopolistic "cult of the village," a miscalculation that allowed his revolt from the village characterization to seem like a radical break in the flow of literary works about the Midwest.[138]

The fatal flaw in the revolt thesis—a flaw that fully exposes the mistaken enshrinement of the supposed village rebels as a representative group of intellectuals who stand for the wholesale rejection of the Midwest as a region—remains the rebels themselves. While the rebels were certainly critical of the Midwest at times, a fragment of thought Van Doren permanently burned into literary history, this is but a partial and misleading glimpse of the purported rebels' universe of thought. Edgar Lee Masters, for example, whom Van Doren cast as the revolutionary leader of the village revolt, vehemently rejected his inclusion in the revolt category and "never had any use" for Van Doren and saw him as a failed novelist.[139] Masters demanded that he not "be tied up with any one, with any group," and specifically rejected being lumped in with "the 'revolt-from-the-village' group."[140] But he went much further than rejecting Van Doren's theory and actually promoted his home region, a part of his life story that is rarely used to supplement or balance the use of *Spoon River*—which itself includes what Masters called its "joyous parts"—in treatments of American literary history.[141] Masters's "literary life" is pronounced dead in 1917, just after publication of the *Spoon River Anthology*, but such a pronouncement grossly misrepresents the overall character of Masters's body of work and severely limits the ability to see Masters's Midwest.[142] Masters protested the "horse mind" of simplistic critics, a "mind that has learned the road and follows it with blinders" and ignores evidence that fails to fit the preferred grand narrative.[143] Masters thought the critics were too wedded to pursuing theories: "Those fellows get a line going and they have to follow it."[144] When confronted, Masters said, critics too often protested that authors did something "unwittingly—not what he says *he* did but what *they* say he did."[145]

Masters's historical and biographical works, which mostly focused on his home region, are largely forgotten, along with his dedication to rural life and social and political decentralization and affection for the rural Midwest and its writers.[146] Masters was strongly inclined toward Jeffersonianism and saw Jefferson as the "genius of this republic."[147] Because of Masters's adherence to Jeffersonianism, agrarianism, and local control, his biography of Lincoln, *Lincoln, the Man* (1931), was critical of Lincoln's war-making and his tolerance of "centralists" and "monopolists."[148] Masters criticized the ugly side of life in urban Chicago—a city "full of demagogues, corruptionists, and egotists and snobs"—and New York but praised southern Illinois and its Jeffersonian qualities in works such as his last book, *The Sangamon* (1942), written for *The Rivers of America* series, a regionalist project that was inspired by Frederick Jackson Turner.[149] *The Sangamon* was a "celebration of the region of Masters' boyhood," Lois Hartley once noted; and his home country, Masters said, had a "magical appeal to me quite beyond my power to describe. I loved the people there then and I love their memory."[150] Masters endorsed Emerson's calls for "less government" and more "private character" and condemned modern poets because they had "no moral code and *no roots*."[151] He also loved the un-rebel James Whitcomb Riley and Riley's attention to "neighborhood flavor" and the "common life" of Indiana and how Riley "put Indiana as a place and a people in the memory of America, more thoroughly and more permanently than has been done by any other poet before or since his day for any other locality or people."[152]

In keeping with Masters's embrace of Riley and the Jeffersonianism of Riley's Indiana and Masters's southern Illinois, Sherwood Anderson was simi-larly concerned about the detachment from place, the growing rootlessness in the nation, the rise of technology, and the "terrible bigness of the country."[153] Anderson spent most of his childhood in Clyde, Ohio, and enjoyed piano, baseball, dancing, sleigh rides, and picnics; and, despite how the famed *Wines-burg* is often remembered, the "profoundest meaning of Clyde" for Anderson was "not alienation but communion."[154] Anderson was more focused on the old folkways of the rural Midwest, the legacies of "Jeffersonian yeomen," and "pastoral stillness" and breaking with boomtowns such as Chicago, which Anderson saw as a "strident wasteland, a nightmare of disorder, ugliness, and noise."[155] To break with Chicago, Anderson, as he wrote, put his "hope in the corn," or the old rural life of the Midwest.[156] Anderson was concerned, Lionel Trilling rightly recognized, that the "old good values of life have been destroyed," and Trilling explained how "the river, the stable, the prairie are very dear to him."[157] Trilling did not care for Anderson, but he recognized Anderson's belief in the "salvation of a small legitimate existence, of a quiet place in the sun and moment of leisurely peace."[158] One critic later noted that throughout his "career the *return to the village, not the revolt from it*, was to become the characteristic journey of Anderson's idealized self."[159] By the mid-1920s, Sherwood Anderson "had come almost full circle" from the impression left by *Winesburg* and confessed that he was "glad of the life on the farm and in small communities," and he ended, as his biographer David Anderson explained, "his enchantment with bohemian values and fraudulence."[160] Recognizing how his work had been misused, Sherwood Anderson said that New York boosters of his books such as *Winesburg* had "always a little misunderstood something in me" and explained that his goal was to explore the inner life of the Midwest, not to attack the region.[161] When Carl Van Doren insisted that Anderson's writing represented "weariness," "contempt," and "bitterness," Anderson responded by writing a letter to Van Doren to express his "confusion" about Van Doren's theories, to explain that Van Doren was touting "a weariness I do not feel," and to note that he preferred living in the Midwest to more trendy literary haunts such as France.[162] Anderson said he "always lived among these midwestern American people" and that "I do wish to stand by these people."[163]

The "limited attention" still given to Anderson remains focused on Anderson "rebelling against the village"—despite his own protests and the recognition of his complexity by some now-distant critics in some largely neglected criticism—and his other work is dismissed.[164] Anderson's career, Anthony Channell Hilfer asserted, "hit its peak with *Winesburg*," and then his novels became "banal," and, as a "mystagogue of cornfields, he became insufferable."[165] Anderson also suffered from the attacks launched by Irving Howe, who, along with Trilling, was a prominent part of the emerging and still-well-known community of writers and critics deemed the New York Intellectuals.[166] Given Howe's "exaltation of Western Europe and a slighting of the small town which was Anderson's origin and fertile field of operation," his rejection—in keeping with the New York Intellectuals—of life beyond the Hudson River as "arid, stultifying, crude, materialistic, isolated," and his rejection of Clyde, Ohio, which Anderson saw as a "fair and sweet town," Howe's attack on Anderson is entirely predictable.[167] Howe thought *Winesburg* was Anderson's "best work," written before his "downward curve" of the mid-1920s, and his judgment reflects the prevailing view of Anderson, who, if remembered much at all, is cast in the role of village rebel.[168]

Sinclair Lewis, perhaps the most famous of Van Doren's rebellious quartet during the 1920s and the author of the work most commonly cited as a critique of the Midwest, also, after a second look, defies categorization. Lewis's rebel designation is in part explained by his own intense commitment to marketing and publicity and making a literary splash.[169] Lewis understood that scandal sold, and he is remembered as a master entertainer. Lewis was also motivated in his early years by his sympathies for the intellectual left and was especially admiring of H. G. Wells, inclinations that helped him find favor among the prominent critics of the 1920s.[170] Some note that Lewis was at times unhappy as a child in Sauk Centre, Minnesota, and this caused him to seek revenge later.[171] One mentee noted that Lewis was "fiercely ugly," which, he thought, added to his bitterness.[172] Lewis's tendency to sensationalize to sell books, his interest in leftist social criticism and the support it generated for him, and perhaps some early grudges may partially explain his motivations and early literary bent and partially justify the village rebel label, but an exploration of Lewis should not end there. Lewis's other actions and statements also deserve consideration. While Lewis could be strange and petty and attack his friends, and while he drank to excess, he could also be kind and generous and mentor young writers.[173] This included midwesterners such as Zona Gale and Willa Cather.[174] Lewis also promoted and supported regionalists such as Ruth Suckow. After their early sojourns he noted that writers like Suckow had the "good sense" to return to the Midwest, and to young writers he "regularly preached the doctrine of remaining where their roots were."[175] Lewis said midwestern authors were "rough fellows but vigorous, ignorant of the classics and of Burgundy, yet close to the heart of humanity. They write about farmyards and wear flannel shirts."[176] Lewis also spent a considerable amount of time in the Midwest, perhaps hoping to deepen his rootedness too, but his restlessness and devotion to publicity and fame and rubbing shoulders with other literati meant that he could not stay put for long. When Lewis moved to Madison, Wisconsin, for a teaching stint, he said he wanted to "renew my knowledge of the Middle West. I find the country beautiful, open and stirring, with enough hills here to avoid stagnancy."[177] Although he acknowledged his affection for the Midwest, Madison was too boring for him, and he fled the scene by mid-semester, leaving his students in the lurch.[178]

Lewis's affection for the region could also be found in his famous works. Lewis's novels—as the often forgotten ambiguity of *Main Street* attests— were not merely assaults on the Midwest. In *Main Street*, Lewis portrays his famous character Carol Kennicott as "flighty" and frivolous, and one of his characters tells Carol that she is "so prejudiced against Gopher Prairie that you overshoot the mark. . . . Great guns, the town can't be all wrong!"[179] After publication, Lewis stressed the affirmative aspects of *Main Street* and confessed a "love of Main Street . . . a belief in Main Street's inherent power."[180] Lewis rejected Van Doren's attempt to cram him into the "village revolt" category while noting his affection for primary characters in *Main Street* such as Will Kennicott, Bea Sorensen, various farmers, and others.[181] Lewis rebuffed English jabs at America when discussing *Main Street* in London and said he "had intended *Main Street* as constructive criticism of his country."[182] Lewis said, "If I seem to have criticized prairie villages, I have certainly criticized them no more than I have New York, or Paris, or the great universities."[183] Lewis wrote to Mary Austin and asked, "If I didn't love Main Street would I write of it so hotly?"[184] Lewis also saw *Main Street* as a "tribute" to his decent, generous, and hard-working father, the doctor in Sauk Centre, Minnesota.[185] The ambiguities of Lewis's work extend beyond *Main Street*. In *Babbitt* (1922), George Babbitt happily returns to the normal life of Zenith.[186] In *Dodsworth* (1929), Lewis highlighted "midwestern virtues," and Sam Dodsworth sees Zenith as a place of "midwestern saneness."[187] John Updike, upon a re-reading of Lewis, concluded that the midwesterners in his novels were "basically decent folk."[188]

The literary historian John Flanagan noted that in later years Lewis "spoke nostalgically of his Sauk Centre days, of the friendliness of the people, and of the indelible memories of childhood," such as fishing, hunting, rafting, and hiking.[189] Lewis took pleasure in the civic institutions of Sauk Centre—the GAR hall, the Community Club, the Bryant Public Library, the Main Street Theater.[190] Of his early years in Sauk Centre, Lewis said, "It was a good time, a good place, and a good preparation for life."[191] Lewis "felt a very strong pull toward" Minnesota and praised its rural landscape and places such as the St. Croix Valley.[192] Lewis wrote that it "is an illusion that the haze and far-off hills is bluer and more romantic. In every state of the union, as in Minnesota, we have historical treasures small and precious and mislaid. It is admirable that we should excavate Ur of the Chaldees and study the guilds of Brabant, but for our own dignity, knowledge and plain tourist interest, we might also excavate Urbana of the Illinois."[193] Lewis was brought home from Italy after his death in 1951 and buried in Sauk Centre, proving, his brother thought, that "he had a lot of love for the old place."[194]

But Lewis's fondness for the Midwest is not what he is remembered for, which is partially explained by his own literary jabs, ambiguity, and personality flaws but also, more importantly, by how literary critics and intellectuals use his work. In 1920, *Main Street* perfectly fit the mood of many intellectuals, who were eager to assault small-town provincialism. *Main Street* became the best-selling book in the country during the first quarter of the twentieth century and sold because it featured "scandal, and scandal is always exhilarating," said the publisher Ernest Brace, and, Richard Lingeman says, because it "meshed with the postwar mood of cynicism among the intelligentsia and the young."[195] Lewis must be viewed through the village revolt prism, the critics say. Benjamin Schwarz opined in the *Atlantic Monthly* a decade ago that "Lewis can be rightly appreciated *only* by concentrating on his anomalous book *Main Street*," after which began his supposedly grim decline.[196] To read Lewis for "anything more" than a blip in "literary and cultural history" as a definer of small towns would be a mistake, Ronald Weber concludes.[197] After the 1920s, Alfred Kazin thought, Lewis went into "heart-breaking decline."[198] Lionel Trilling, perhaps the leading light of the New York Intellectuals, thought it was better for "the public" to be "confronted" with the Sinclair Lewis of 1919–1920 (and, he added, the Sherwood Anderson, then in his *Winesburg* phase)—back when Lewis "flamed across the sky with *Main Street*"—than the Lewis of 1940, when Lewis embraced the "belief that to be an American is a gay adventure."[199]

Critics' insistence that Lewis and other midwestern writers only be remembered for rebellion is why the fullness of the Midwest is now so hard to see and a great betrayal of what these writers intended. In the 1930s and 1940s, the Wisconsin regionalist writer August Derleth, who had vowed to remain close to his "roots" in Sauk City, Wisconsin, had several meetings with Masters, Anderson, and Lewis, and he published a now-forgotten account of these meetings in 1963.[200] Since Derleth was interested in regional writers and taught a course on regional literature through the College of Agriculture at Wisconsin, he naturally inquired about the revolt theory. In their conversations with Derleth, the supposed leading rebels—Masters, Anderson, and Lewis—all vehemently rejected the village revolt interpretation. Masters professed his love of the Midwest and his boyhood in Illinois, calling the time period the "best years of my life" and deeming the revolt interpretation as "just about as silly as you can get! . . . I didn't revolt against my village. . . . There never was anything to this revolt from the village business. We didn't do any such thing."[201] Masters said, "Carl Van Doren started [the revolt interpretation] and everybody else parroted him. . . . It was all nonsense, but they perpetuated it."[202] He dismissed literary critics who promoted the theory as "lice."[203] Anderson also rejected the view that his characters were only "hopeless and defeated" and laughed at the revolt thesis: "There wasn't anything to this revolting. I liked Clyde [Ohio]. . . . There's no such thing as 'revolting' or 'rebelling' or whatever it is they want to call it."[204] Critics who insisted on giving Anderson's work such a "point-of-view" were wrong.[205] Lewis said the revolt interpretation was "unsound, one of those theories put forth by critics who thereafter tend to look away from any evidence to the contrary."[206] Lewis dismissed Van Doren's "theories, unsupported by fact. The trouble with critics is that they like to create a horse and ride it to death."[207] Lewis thought critics were prone to "dig around and trump up a whole lot of motives and meanings the author never intended."[208] Lewis said he "loved" the characters in *Main Street*: "I didn't think it was rebellious then. I don't think it is now, either."[209]

Over the long term, critics have been far kinder to F. Scott Fitzgerald than to the other supposed rebels, but his inclusion in Van Doren's revolt rubric because of *This Side of Paradise* (1920) remains, perhaps, the most questionable of Van Doren's choices. Even though Van Doren believes Fitzgerald "had broken with the village" in *Paradise*, the book is focused not on the Midwest but on personal frustrations, drinking, sex, wealth, and self-absorption in the East and on exposing places such as Princeton, which Fitzgerald saw as the "pleasantest country club in America."[210] Edmund Wilson said *Paradise* was not "really *about* anything" and saw it as a "gesture of indefinite revolt."[211] Others viewed it simply as a "series of episodes" relating to the main character.[212] Barry Gross is more generous, finding the novel to be successfully focused on the theme of searching and finding personal meaning and spiritual guidance.[213] Others see it as a "college novel."[214] Whatever the case, *Paradise* does little to indict the rural and small-town Midwest. In his other fiction, it must be stressed, Fitzgerald is actually quite generous toward the Midwest or, at the worst, promotes a mixed picture. Most famously, in *The Great Gatsby*, Fitzgerald uses St. Paul to depict a "stable community of familiar names and places with traditional and personal qualities that contrast with the chaotic and indifferent elements of his Long Island experience."[215] For Nick Carraway, St. Paul symbolized a "city of the pastoral ideal not altered to an urban ash heap as was the eastern green breast of America," a "spiritual home," and a "place of continuity and consistent values."[216] Fitzgerald confessed "tremendous nostalgia" for St. Paul and wanted his daughter the playwright and composer to debut there.[217] In other short stories, Fitzgerald also notes some petty differences among St. Paul socialites and youth, so the image he presents is mixed.

But Fitzgerald was never focused on the rural and small-town Midwest—"the wheat or the prairies or the lost Swede towns"—he was focused on St. Paul, and then not very much, and, much more often, on the dalliances and drama and social climbing of the eastern seaboard.[218] Van Doren's classification of Fitzgerald should be discarded for a final reason—Fitzgerald's most famous character, Nick Carraway, finally returned to the Midwest, after all, and came to see it as the "warm center of the world."[219]

The weaknesses of the village revolt paradigm—its subservience to intellectual trends, its shallow understanding of midwestern culture, its bias in favor of cultural radicals, its misreading of or slanted approach to the supposed rebels' work, its imperviousness to any vision of the Midwest as a warm center of stability, calm, and community—were later revealed by Van Wyck Brooks, who did so much to launch Van Doren's interpretation and give the village revolt form.[220] Brooks had a mental breakdown in the late 1920s that brought him to the "brink of madness" and incapacitated him for five years, and, after his recovery, he spent less time, as he said, obsessing on "the dark side of our moon," and his studies led him "right out into the midst of the sunny side."[221] By the mid-1940s, Brooks thought, "[W]e are heading into a great half-century."[222] In contrast to Brooks's early denunciations of American culture, the Columbia University historian Casey Blake notes, a later Brooks and some other World War I–era critics now saw late nineteenth-century middle-class culture "with a fondness unimaginable in the 1910s and 1920s, when they had led the youthful revolt against Victorian gentility."[223] Brooks and others began to see the old "Victorian ethos"— which was particularly strong in the Midwest—as lending "a sense of place and of belonging to a wider culture" and as an alternative to the "individual rootlessness and bureaucratic organization they believed had supplanted Victorian self-reliance, pride in work, and loyalty to place and family."[224] He became annoyed with those who "could not seem to forgive the towns they were born in" and with their tales of "escape," and he thought his generation would be "remembered as the one in which everyone hated, often without visible reason, the town in which he was born."[225] In 1952, Brooks said, "What an ass I was at the age of 22!"[226] Of his famous book *America's Coming of Age* (1915), which inspired so much repetition and rebellion, he said, "It isn't right."[227] Brooks dismissed his earlier writing as "youthful levity" and rejected the work of the other writers of the era, believing that they had "ceased to be voices of the people" and were instead "poisoning one another with their despair and poisoning society" and that the "literary mind" had "lost its roots in the soil."[228] Brooks began to work against those writers he thought were trying to "kill off" the nation's cultural roots.[229] He also recognized midwestern regionalists for their work to give an interior voice to literature and admired their mission to "get in touch with the common life, with small-town life and rural life," and to "root oneself."[230]

Brooks largely failed to advance his new cause. As he told the Minnesota regionalist Frederick Manfred, his later work was "attacked and sneered at."[231] By mid-century he was considered "outmoded" and "out of fashion," and it had "been at least a decade since anyone concerned with literature took him very seriously."[232] Blake, similarly, cannot abide the new Brooks, as so many other critics could not recognize the positive portrayals of the Midwest advanced by the supposed village rebels or see the work of midwestern regionalists.[233] Blake dismisses Brooks's abandonment of a "critical voice" in favor of a "misty lyricism" and "antiquarianism" that would "alienate" him from cultural radicals attracted to his earlier attacks on American culture.[234] Blake fails to account for the cultural consequences of Brooks's early polemics and the fact that, as Bernard DeVoto noted, "for twenty years his false description had been a gospel to many writers whose careers consisted of preaching it to the dwellers in darkness."[235] Blake thus personifies, in the face of overwhelming contrary evidence, the chronic inability of intellectuals to finally dismantle the rickety framework of the revolt from the village thesis, despite its rotted foundations, and to break its persistent hold on the historical imagination.[236]

If Casey Blake is too resistant to the new Brooks, Blake's mentor, the midwesterner Christopher Lasch, born in Omaha, was more adept at finding value in Brooks's "spiritual conversion."[237] Lasch recognized the costs of a "wholesale repudiation of American life and a cult of alienation" that undergirded the revolt from the village thesis.[238] He regretted how the early twentieth-century forms of regionalism had been "abruptly 'brushed aside' in the 20s by the revolt against provincialism."[239] He recognized how the later Brooks came to find earlier precedents for the emergence of an "indigenous culture" in the provinces and how the work of earlier writers, as Brooks said, "destroyed the subservience of Americans to the local ideals of the motherlands—it broke the umbilical cord that attached them to Europe."[240] He also recognized Brooks's newfound opposition to the purported anti-village themes of Lewis,

Fitzgerald, and others that Brooks had made possible.[241] While recognizing Brooks's many inconsistencies, odd conversions, and intellectual "ordeal," Lasch correctly keys on the costs of the tendency—in the early Brooks and among other intellectuals—to "brush aside the past," the essential flaw in the enduring revolt from the village formulation, which obscures, among other things, the ability to see the Midwest and its history and to hear the voices of those who resisted the notion of a village revolt.[242]

# CHAPTER TWO

# THE FAILED REVOLT AGAINST THE REVOLT

The forces that propelled the village revolt thesis during the 1920s sustained their momentum throughout the 1930s and thereafter, and they persisted in edging the Midwest toward the margins of public consciousness. Despite a mild critical reprieve during the gloomiest days of the Great Depression and an upsurge of reflections upon the Midwest as a region during the early 1930s, this short-lived enthusiasm could not counter the broader forces driving in the other direction or lighten or alter a literary mood in which, as Van Wyck Brooks said, writers sought to "ridicule provinciality" and generally took "delight in kicking their world to pieces."[1] Older midwestern voices and those that counterbalanced the rebel school would ultimately be relegated to obscurity, but for several years an active group of writers sought to illuminate the recesses and contours of the midwestern world for a wider public. These mostly forgotten writers embraced the cause of regionalism and mounted a noble resistance against what proved to be more commanding cultural forces. Their defeat and ultimate disappearance from popular memory and the decline of the old midwestern social and cultural impulses they represented served as signposts along the broader path toward an eventual muting and dimming of midwestern regionalism and a wider and largely uncontested legitimacy for the village rebel thesis. "[I]t was a case of emphasizing the man-biting-dog business," as the Indianan R. Carlyle Buley noted: "The writers who did first-class stuff which had some relation to the American scene were not news."[2] Literary critics and historians, by choosing to invoke and by clumsily applying the village rebel framework to a complex course of events, continue to discount the

37

Midwest's older literary voices, silencing their once-proud attempts to assert a regional identity. In tandem with the ascendant social and political impulses of the World War II era, these forces conspired to hinder our collective ability to comprehend the fullness of the Midwest's history.

The still-prevalent critical attitudes toward certain midwestern voices, attitudes that are animated by the persistent force of the original village revolt thesis, keep the spotlight on one school of thought to the exclusion of another regional tradition. As the original revolt thesis rightly recognized, there once was another vigorous tradition of writing about the Midwest that was more sympathetic to the region and that the supporters of the revolt thesis sought to supplant. The broader cultural and political forces that gathered during the century's early decades gave great currency to the revolt thesis and the books it honored—a currency that bought precious space for many years in the American literary canon—to the exclusion of an earlier and arguably more vital body of work, one that was more vigilant in its attempts to perceive the Midwest as a region.[3] This bias, in retrospect, should not be shocking. Van Wyck Brooks, from whom so many cultural critics of the 1920s took their cues, was "painfully ignorant" of other traditions in his early work, and thus his criticism, Casey Blake notes, was less the indictment of American "cultural rootlessness" that Brooks intended than a prominent example of an alienated intellectual's failure to see and understand his nation's cultural roots, especially their regional dimensions, far from New York.[4] Only later did he come to see that his attacks on interior culture "came from a Harvard indoctrination and not from wide knowledge or actual investigation."[5] Among Brooks's "exciting discoveries" in later years was the essential belief "that we have an American tradition that is very rich, generous, liberal and humane."[6]

Along with Brooks, the westerner Bernard DeVoto, to his ultimate credit but also to his contemporary reputational detriment, became one of the few prominent critics of the era to recognize the shallowness of the village revolt thesis and its impoverished view of other cultural currents.[7] "The repudiation of American life by American literature during the 1920s signified that writers were isolated or insulated from the common culture," DeVoto argued in a series of lectures at Indiana University, and were "arrogant" toward and "ignorant" of American traditions.[8] DeVoto was exposing the village revolt school and its supporters for their willing disconnection from a more common American culture—what he saw as their obscurantism and their tendency to "isolate

and insulate themselves" and be "not only unrealistic but irresponsibly frivolous"—and highlighting the division between alienated intellectuals and other
Americans, who were more tightly bonded to local and regional cultures.[9] Too
many writers of the 1920s, DeVoto thought, took a "turn in abhorrence from
the village square to the High Place" to escape "the boobs, the suckers, the fall
guys, the Rotarians," the "inferior people who destroy individuality and break
the Artist's heart."[10] In keeping with other regionalists, DeVoto questioned, in
his private correspondence with the Minnesota regionalist writer Frederick
Manfred, the treatment of artists and writers "as of finer clay than us plain
folks, or as having experience superior to ours."[11] Writers were not above scrutiny, he thought, no matter how tortured or delicate or alienated they might
be. DeVoto was pointing to the differing sensibilities that divided the rebels
from the regionalists. Many of the abettors of the village revolt thesis "were different from other boys," as Malcolm Cowley later remembered in his literary
history of the era, and "hated [the] happy ones" who lived blissfully among
the contours of persisting cultural traditions and failed to see why those traditions should be attacked or to understand the necessity of revolt.[12] Cowley was
suggesting, albeit less forcefully than DeVoto, the existence of another line of
thought, one more rooted and less hostile to regional culture, but also one that
has largely elided collective memory.

The views of a leading set of critical intellectuals and their biases in favor
of a certain kind of writing encompassed by the revolt thesis left far too much
unsaid about the rebel school and, in particular, about other cultural currents
in the Midwest. The bias in favor of the village rebellion interpretation caused
its creator, Carl Van Doren, and subsequent critics to miss other midwestern
attempts to give voice to local and regional culture and to break the cultural
dominance of the East, efforts that were too frequently ignored because their
unfashionable products did not fit into a pattern of "usable" literary works.[13]
To contend that the intellectual and political forces of the 1920s and the weight
of scholarly opinion in subsequent decades privileged the cultural radicals and
the expatriates is to argue that other works were dismissed or deemphasized
or attacked, especially the several works that treated the Midwest with greater
benevolence, and that this critical selectivity yielded a long-lasting and distorted image of interwar literary currents. But far more midwestern writers,
Blair Whitney noted, praised their "home as a place of beauty, friendship, joy,
harmony, and peace" than embraced the purported denunciations of *Main*

*Street* or *Winesburg*.[14] Too many critics, however, see Van Doren's treatment, as Sara Kosiba notes, as "sufficient and fail to look at regional literature for the other characteristics it may contain."[15] The critics, Barry Gross once observed, missed "what the outsider always misses—the love, the affection, the ties that bind."[16]

Critics of the supposed cultural sterility of the early Midwest such as the early Van Wyck Brooks, to cite a central inspiration for the village rebellion school, failed to see the rich traditions of cultural and civic life that emerged in the youthful Midwest and instead insisted on viewing the region as "culture-less."[17] The painful ignorance underlying Brooks's cutting judgments during the 1920s, for example, included a failure to see the civic culture, folklore, and local literary traditions that "mediated between high and popular culture."[18] This "middlebrow" culture was especially strong in the Midwest and supported by the networks of civic clubs and cultural organizations that were active in the region and a source of social capital and thus a vital ingredient of midwestern democracy.[19] Joan Shelley Rubin explains that a modified form of the genteel tradition continued in the postwar years—remaining in place alongside the new modernist and mass culture trends—in the form of middlebrow culture, which was promoted by midwesterners such as Stuart Pratt Sherman.[20] Sherman was the first editor of the *New York Herald Tribune*'s supplement entitled *Books*, created in 1924.[21] Sherman was raised on an Iowa farm, taught English at Northwestern and the University of Illinois, and promoted a broad and democratic view of books and culture and supported literary and scholarly "generalizers."[22] Sherman criticized the new "Bohemians" and "radicals" and their works that attacked Puritan influences and endorsed traditional religious inclinations supporting "the inner check upon the expansion of impulse," which caused H. L. Mencken to attack Sherman, Rubin notes, as a "repressed and repressive enemy of art."[23] Sherman's views also caused him to lose the support of writers such as Carl Van Doren, whom Sherman had once taught at the University of Illinois.[24] Sherman grew frustrated with *The Nation*, to which he had earlier contributed, as it became more radical during the years Van Doren served as its literary editor and first pronounced the village revolt thesis.[25] When he took command of *Books*, Sherman emphasized the need to connect with a broad audience, and his "democratic leanings" constituted a "democratic resistance to the power of elites" to control culture.[26] Sherman opposed the dominance of "drawing room society" on literature

and promoted a broader, more popular, more midwestern conception of culture.[27] When seeking to expand the audience of *Books*, Sherman said that the
problem was "it is edited for Manhattan Island, which is as detached from the
rest of America as the Basques are detached from Europe. . . . What you need
is a link between the city and the provinces, which will show people out there
that you are thinking about them, are conscious, you know, that they exist."[28]
"Because of his years in the Midwest," Rubin concluded, "Sherman himself
was well suited to supply that link."[29]

In keeping with Sherman's thinking, a group of writers in the Midwest
attempted to promote literary regionalism during the early twentieth century,
a counter-tradition to the purported village rebellion that was given short
shrift in Carl Van Doren's famous treatment of the era and voices that were
"scarcely heard" over the "thunders of revolt."[30] Unlike the famous expatriates
and village rebels, another group of writers "stayed home" and tended to their
region and positioned themselves in opposition to the metropolitan and modernist currents in literature.[31] These regionalists were critical of the World War
I–era "cultural revolt" and, in Robert Dorman's felicitous phrase, engaged in a
revolt against that revolt.[32] The regionalists were critical of both the strictures
of genteel culture centered in the Northeast and the "emerging 'orthodoxy' of
modernism" and sought to promote a culture rooted in the midwestern soil.[33]
They constituted an "anti-expatriate movement" among midwesterners.[34] This
movement was given voice by John T. Frederick, who was an Iowa "farm boy"
taken in at the University of Iowa by C. F. Ansley, the head of the English department who had been "deeply influenced" by Josiah Royce's 1902 lecture at Iowa
on the virtues of a "higher provincialism."[35] "Cultivate [the province's] young
men," Royce had advised at the beginning of the century, "and keep them near
you. Foster provincial independence."[36] Frederick sought out authentic midwestern voices, "decried the standardization of literature imposed by New York
editors and publishers," and recognized the benefits of rural life and its harmo-
nious elements that "contrasted sharply with the alienation increasingly found
in the literature about urban America."[37] Frederick opposed the distortions
to writing caused by what Ronald Weber calls the "literary centralization of
Eastern publishing houses" and urged writers to stay close to home.[38] Toward
this end, Frederick launched the midwestern-oriented journal *The Midland* in
Iowa City in 1915, and the journal generally sought "to balance the drab rural
portraits" of the Midwest common to popular culture "with more positive

images of the Great Valley."[39] Regionalists in Iowa, according to E. Bradford Burns's study of the movement, recognized the positive aspects of family, farm, church, and school, which they saw as the "dominant institutions" within rural midwestern culture and which were the frequent targets of proponents of the village revolt thesis.[40]

Frederick discovered Ruth Suckow, published her first short story, and saw her work as "devoid of the hostility and resentment toward the Midwest that had led to the satires" of the 1920s and found it more "balanced" and defined by an "essential fairness."[41] Suckow regretted those souls lost to "rootless exile" in the 1920s and praised the advance of local culture among Iowans, who had lost their "cringing attitude," transcended the existing literary "caste," and "snatched" some ownership of literature for themselves and their region.[42] In contrast to the village revolt tradition, Suckow also did not attack religion and rejected the then "conventional" and "contemporary stereotype" of "stern" and "severe" Puritans constricting life in the Midwest and thus triggering youthful "rebellion."[43] She rejected an older form of literary stereotyping she deemed "Brontë-esque—that of a wild soul struggling against narrow bonds among the bleak midwestern moors."[44] Suckow was born in Hawarden, Iowa, the daughter of a Congregational minister, and remembered the Congregational church in Hawarden, in her father's words, as "like one big family."[45] Hawarden was a "real, acting democracy," and its churches "were the centers of this democratic life and spirit, as they were of the whole social life of the community."[46] Suckow's novel *Country People* (1924) places churches at the center of communal and civic obligation. For the German American immigrant farmer August Kaetterhenry in *Country People*, "[g]oing to church, and being steady and a good worker, and not drinking, and paying his bills and saving money, were all the same thing."[47] Despite brushes with H. L. Mencken and Sinclair Lewis during these years and even support from them, Suckow was "not strident in the de-bunking Mencken style."[48] Suckow focused on the common lives of those who peopled the midwestern interior section and made it a point to declare, "I have never . . . been a rebel or a satirist, in the Sinclair Lewis sense."[49] Suckow was remembered by her peers for her "quiet nobility," "democratic sentiments," "middle-class folkways," and—in great contrast to Lewis—aversion to "sensationalism."[50] Suckow, most importantly, remained conscious of regional differences: she praised the good land and hard-working farmers and the social stabilities and "more democratic basis of life" in the

Midwest and criticized, for example, the racial divisions in the South and the tendency of southern whites to treat honest work as "not a virtue but a humiliation."[51] Suckow's husband, the now-forgotten Iowa writer Ferner Nuhn, who embraced the motto "a man could grow wise in Omaha," bolstered Suckow's work and offered a moving defense of the "central ground" of the nation as against the literary domination of the East and the tendency of prominent writers to look to Europe for inspiration.[52]

Suckow's orbit of midwestern writers included the Iowa writer Herbert Quick, whose work she praised.[53] Quick was born on a farm near Steamboat Rock, Iowa, educated in a one-room country school, and worked on the family farm until he was twenty.[54] After reading law, Quick then served as an attorney in Sioux City for fifteen years starting in 1890 and became mayor before turning to writing full time and authoring eighteen books.[55] In contrast to the anti-regional slights by the New Yorker and other outlets that animated the village rebellion school, Quick, Wallace Stegner noted, "spoke of Dubuque and Waterloo without apology, as if they were as worthy a place in fiction as Paris or Versailles."[56] Quick's novel Vandemark's Folly (1922) "praised the pioneer past as heroic, epic, and somewhat idyllic" and explored the beauties and social rewards of rural life and farming.[57] Despite positive reviews from other critics, the inventor of the revolt thesis Carl Van Doren, not surprisingly, panned Vandemark's Folly.[58]

The work of Suckow and Quick was complemented by other writers such as Beth Streeter Aldrich, who moved from Iowa—not, as with so many of the rebels, to New York—to Nebraska, where she sympathetically chronicled rural and village lives and urged Nebraska writers to embrace their "native material."[59] She welcomed stories from Nebraskans about pioneer and farm life that could enrich her prose.[60] Against the cultural rebels, she argued that "a writer may portray some of the decent things of life around him and reserve the privilege to call that real life too."[61] She wanted people, especially the young, to have "some substantial tie . . . to the anchor of unchanging things."[62] Readers appreciated Aldrich's dissent from Mencken's corrosive cynicism and from the conventional readings of Main Street–type books.[63] The historian of the Midwest and Nebraska James C. Olson ranked Aldrich's A Lantern in Her Hand (1928) the second-most important depiction of life in Nebraska to date.[64]

Dorothy Canfield Fisher, born in Kansas in 1879, also published The Brimming Cup in 1921, which was seen as an "antidote" to Main Street and was the second-most purchased novel in the United States that year, just behind *Main Street*.[65] The novel portrays a young newlywed couple in a small village, the young wife's resistance to the advances of a sophisticated city man, and the "virtues of small town life."[66] Fisher had spent much of her youth in Lincoln, where she came to know Willa Cather and where her father served as chancellor of the University of Nebraska, which, in 1927, sponsored the formation of the journal *Prairie Schooner*—which was designed as a "medium for the publication of the finest writing of the prairie country"—and thus became the site of another outpost of midwestern regionalist writing and buttressed the work of Frederick's *Midland* in Iowa City.[67]

Among the allies of Suckow, Quick, Aldrich, and Fisher was Jay Sigmund, who was born on a farm near the Wapsipinicon River in eastern Iowa and forever claimed the area as his home. Sigmund attended country school, then dropped out of high school, and ultimately went to work at a life insurance company in Cedar Rapids and became heavily engaged in civic life and supporting the arts, local libraries, and the Episcopal church.[68] Sigmund also wrote poetry, which he refused to see as the exclusive province of "long-haired visionaries" or as a "strange, nebulous, misty thing," and told his fellow Iowans, "Poetry is not a thing of far places. You can see it, you can find it right at hand."[69] Sigmund commented to John Frederick that he relished Frederick's novel *Druida* (1923) because of its depictions of county fairs, farm bureaus, rural homes, and churches and its portrayal of the general "atmosphere of the middle western village," which Sigmund successfully sought to convey in his own work.[70] Sigmund focused on the "commonplace materials that lie at hand here in Iowa" and the "people here at home as they go about their every-day rounds," and he hoped others would enjoy his "little stories of the middle west."[71] His work included many poems on "Mississippi River Village Folk," and his story collections included the Iowa-oriented *Wapsipinicon Tales*.[72] For a time during the interwar years, Sigmund attracted the attention of more famous writers such as the regionalist Lewis Mumford, who praised Sigmund for his "sense of the mid-American earth."[73] The Illinoisan Carl Sandburg admired Sigmund's work, his attention to his home and region (his vision of the "color of earth as it sifts through the small town"), and his resistance to outside pressures that could turn his work in other directions.[74] Sandburg said Robert Louis Stevenson had voices such as Sigmund's in mind when he wrote, "To know what you prefer, instead of humbly saying Amen to what the world tells you you ought to prefer, is to keep your soul alive."[75] Sigmund continued to focus on the common life of the Midwest and questioned trendy "modern novels"—he doubted the need of literature to "reek with sex throughout," for example, and applied a lighter touch in his work—and regretted the fading of an older regional writing and of poets such as Longfellow and Whittier, whom, he recognized, it had "become fashionable to laugh at."[76]

Across the Mississippi River, into which Sigmund's Wapsipinicon emptied, the prolific writer August Derleth also took his stand and gave his voice and his robust energies to the Midwest. Derleth spent most of his life near Sauk City, Wisconsin, because he wanted to be close to his "roots."[77] Prizing a sense of regional "continuity," Derleth never left except to earn his degree in English from the University of Wisconsin and for a six-month stint as an editor in Minneapolis.[78] He cherished his "home milieu," and his niche of central Wisconsin became his Walden and the primary wellspring of his large literary ambitions.[79] Derleth's *Village Year* (1941), for example, offered an intense examination of nature and local social life and a microcosmic peek at a picturesque patch of Wisconsin featuring the pleasures of local apple groves and cane pole fishing with Prince Edward cans stuffed full of bait worms.[80] Derleth also wrote the history of the Wisconsin River for *The Rivers of America* series published by Farrar & Rinehart, which was originally conceived by Constance Skinner based on a suggestion by Frederick Jackson Turner, who was born and reared in nearby Portage, Wisconsin.[81] John Steuart Curry, who was then an artist in residence in Madison, traveled the Wisconsin River with Derleth and provided the illustrations for the book.[82] Derleth recognized in his Wisconsin River valley the "communal spirit of the towns," as did Suckow and other midwestern regionalists, and the "fundamental kinship of landsmen."[83] Derleth conceived of his collective output as part of a grand strategy to convey the "Sac Prairie" saga, to "tell the story of a typical middle western village from 1830 to 1950."[84] All the while, Derleth remained civically active in his little town—joining, for example, the Board of Education, the PTA, and a local social club and even serving as a local parole officer—and wrote and collected poems about Wisconsin and consistently promoted the general cause of midwestern history and writing.[85] Derleth stressed that the "writer of regional prose must know what has gone into the history of his region" and what gave life to its writers.[86] One result was Derleth's biography of Zona Gale, who was raised, like Turner, only thirty miles from Sauk City in Portage. Derleth recognized

Gale's rootedness, fondly recalling her "writing in her study overlooking the [Wisconsin] river where she might see always the broad stream, the islands, the blue Caledonia hills in the distance."[87] Late in his life, in 1961, Derleth published *Walden West*, a cumulative account of his enjoyment of nature, books, and the personalities of his "private Walden" in Sauk City and his belief that a "man belongs where he has roots" and is "part of a pattern," embedded in the traditions, landscape, and "soil and culture-stream from which he springs."[88]

Defying type, the supposed village rebels even supported Derleth. Sinclair Lewis—who said Derleth's "fictions rarely go farther from Sauk City than to Mackinac Island"—recognized that Derleth had "not trotted off to New York literary cocktail parties or to the Hollywood studios."[89] Derleth had "stayed home" and maintained a "modest pride" in his region and proved writers did not have "to write of the Bastille or of the mistresses of King Charles."[90] Lewis said Derleth could convey the "beauty and power of the earth" and saw Derleth as a "champion" of "regionalism" (but also criticized him for writing too much and urged him to more frequently use the "blue pencil" of revision).[91] Edgar Lee Masters confessed his admiration for Derleth's "steady adherence to your place and your daemon," wrote an introduction to one of Derleth's poetry collections, and said Derleth was as "familiar with the country about his town as Thoreau was with the environs of Concord."[92] Masters praised Derleth's journals *Village Year* and *Village Daybook* (1947) for capturing the "flavor and meaning of life in our villages out there": "That's the real middle west, Derleth!"[93] Masters admired Derleth's resistance to the demands of "any school" of thought and "absurd theories," was "tickled" that he was mining the "rich material of the MidWest," praised his poems as "right out of the soil, smelling of the moss and the roots of things," and concluded that Derleth "will make America love Wisconsin," which, Masters said, "deserves to be on the map."[94] Masters thought it would "take this kind of writing more and more to hold America from drifting beyond recall."[95] Such writings afforded readers a "definite identity," against the "welter" of "characterless" literature, despite being "mocked by the East."[96]

Just as the supposed village rebels were more supportive of regionalist voices than conventional wisdom would suggest, so too was Hamlin Garland, who matured on farms in Wisconsin, Iowa, and South Dakota but is typically remembered only for an early economic realism critical of the Midwest. After a long detour through other topics and regions, Garland returned to a midwestern focus in 1917 with *A Son of the Middle Border*, which William Dean Howells, an Ohioan and then prominent literary arbiter, praised for synthesizing the psychology, beauty, and arduous "conditions of the Middle West" and enlivening in "unsparing" detail the "farmlife of the Middle Border" and thus capturing a "whole order of American experience."[97] *Son* touched many readers and spurred Garland toward several more books about his midwestern experiences, including *A Daughter of the Middle Border*, which won the Pulitzer Prize in 1922.[98] The Wisconsinite Zona Gale praised Garland's new "epic," his "precious" commitment to his "section" of the country, and his "unashamed provincialism," which she saw not as a "defensive" stance or as one designed to "challenge" but simply as one that refused to be "apologetic" for its regional roots.[99] The one-time Illinois farm boy Allan Nevins judged *Son* the "best description of rural life in the Northwest ever written."[100]

Garland also returned to his earlier unease about the domination of the East over American writing and culture, noting that magazine editors and New York theater managers were "not friendly to plots laid in other, and especially inland, cities or towns."[101] Against these pressures, he counseled midwestern writers against "going Hollywood."[102] Garland regretted the loss of a "midwestern point of view," one that captured the midwesterners' "work-a-day world," one of labor, raising children, and enjoying one's neighbors, the world of "the folks" chronicled by Ruth Suckow.[103] Garland noted that he was the father of two daughters, feared the spread of "pornographic fiction" and "flippant" literary themes, and mourned the "sad egomania" of new writers, all of which were conveyed by the "atmosphere of Greenwich Village" and caused a lamentable "loss of decorum" and the diminution of "interior" voices from the "small towns of Ohio, Indiana, Illinois."[104] Garland appreciated the work of midwestern writers such as Booth Tarkington and Herbert Quick in part because they had not surrendered to cynicism, and he admired James Whitcomb Riley and favored, as Garland said, Riley's renditions of the "homely neighborliness of the mid-West."[105] The tendency of New York to dominate culture, he thought, caused the "villager and farm boy" to lose touch with his home culture and its "homely virtues," which prominent writers were making "taboo."[106] He recognized, of course, that his dissent was difficult to mount in the era of exalting village rebellion and would be dismissed with ease as the pining of "old fogies."[107] But Garland maintained his posture of dissent against the fashions of the period, and he made the case for preserving older traditions and virtues and did so by turning, in part, to the history of his home region, the Midwest, what he memorably called the "Middle Border."[108]

The collective force of these mostly forgotten midwestern voices—Sherman, Frederick, Suckow, Quick, Aldrich, Fisher, Sigmund, Derleth, and the late Garland—was directed, most notably, at resisting outside pressures and staying true to the unique vibrations of their home areas in the Midwest, which remained the central thrust of the regionalist ethos. They sounded a different tone than the proponents of the village rebel school, embraced a different set of values, and drew on different experiences. While mindful of the difficulties of midwestern life, especially the at-times arduous work of the farm, they focused on the workaday nature of such struggles, not in terms of victimization, but with the aim of giving voice to real lives, lessening the drawing-room orientation of an older literature and the cynicism of new writers, and maintaining a space for rooted midwestern voices in an era popularly defined by the themes of village rebellion. They also found succor and support in the social institutions of the rural and small-town Midwest, its local clubs, its churches, and its informal networks governed by village and agrarian mores, and they often resisted the calls of intellectuals and planners and other experts for stronger outside controls and a reliance on the federal state.[109] They conveyed the patterns of the region's history and honored the once-prized voices of the region that were increasingly met with skepticism or openly denigrated. They sought to explore and explain the social and civic communalism that contributed to the stabilities and continuities of life in the rural and small-town Midwest. This orientation of regionalist thought was alluded to and its regional nature highlighted by Randolph Bourne—he also recognized the "folksiness," the "warm social mixability," and the "excessive amiability" of the Midwest and the resulting "social stability" of the region—when he noted that the "East produces more skeptics and spiritual malcontents than the West," a recognition of the more grounded and non-rebellious nature common to the dominant form of midwestern regionalism.[110]

Bourne was recognizing the emphases and guiding characteristics that often shaped what the Minnesotan Meridel LeSueur called "the old regionalism."[111] If most midwestern regionalists tended to resist outside cultural or political pressures or focused primarily on capturing the rhythms of life in the small-town and rural Midwest, others, like LeSueur, who joined the Communist Party, took a different tack, one that attempted to fuse an existing regionalist orientation and the particulars of regional history to newer forms of radical protest.[112] When LeSueur made a case to Suckow for writing for the left-leaning journal *Midwest*, which attempted to provide a midwestern platform to regional writers inclined toward radicalism during the 1930s, she noted, in characteristic regionalist fashion, the "isolation of the midwestern artists" and the "difficulties of publication" for midwesterners disconnected from New York.[113] *Midwest* expired after only three issues, but LeSueur continued to work to combine regionalist themes and radical politics, and she published, among other works, her history of Minnesota and Wisconsin, *North Star Country*, in 1945.[114] LeSueur and the midwesterners who sympathized with her efforts were known—in a revealing display of midwestern regionalism—to dismiss and downplay the "party line" demands of others on the left and to promote instead a return to midwestern democratic traditions as a roadmap to reform.[115] The reliance on the "radicalism of tradition," LeSueur and her allies thought, would appeal to midwesterners and their regional loyalties much more effectively than foreign and constricting ideologies embraced by coastal intellectuals.[116] Despite LeSueur's pleas, many radicals during the 1930s saw such appeals to tradition as "backward" and counterproductive, and later scholars have tended to focus on a "single axis" of LeSueur's thought, especially its feminist and radical elements, obscuring its regionalist basis.[117] That LeSueur is not remembered for her promotion of regionalism highlights the later turns and emphases of the historical profession that obviated regional frames of reference and regionalist voices.[118]

Writers who adhered to an older form of regionalism also doubted LeSueur's radical approach.[119] Suckow, for example, was especially annoyed by the "young Communist bunch," who were too "iron-bound" and constricted by "purity" and "rule or definition" and who produced a "littleness" and a tendency to jump "on the next band wagon."[120] Suckow's criticism suggests that radical regionalism suffered from its focus on advancing radicalism in the moment and its tendency to be more radical than regional, a preference LeSueur endorsed in her celebration of the "important movement" of literature toward an "orientation with class instead of a region."[121] LeSueur favored transcending the "old regional sense" coupled to a deep historical consciousness in favor of the "dynamics of present" affairs.[122] The radicalism of LeSueur, who denounced the nation's "rotten bourgeois soil" and said she could "no longer breathe in [the] maggoty individualism of a merchant society," was simply more disconnected from her region's basic institutions than most midwestern regionalists.[123] But Suckow and her allies, who represented a more common form of midwestern regionalism, one resistant to "alien and internationalist and industrialist doctrines [that] ignored the saving, diversifying and decentralizing graces of place," remain relatively unknown in comparison to the LeSueur school given the later interest of American historians in the history of American radicalism.[124]

As the older regionalists and newer radical regionalists demonstrated, regionalism could take several forms, and, in the early 1930s, its various and divergent streams combined to help regionalism reach its high water mark. While "regional ideologies" ranged from left to right and regionalism, Michael Steiner has explained, entailed a "complex cluster of related ideas," its particular emphases on understanding and preserving a "basic America," one uncorrupted by outside interference; its recognition of the desirability of a "stable community identity"; its "reverence for the past" and attentiveness to history; its attachment to the land; and its dissent from the broader, homogenizing national culture and its promotion of a "buffer between the individual and the increasingly powerful nation state" afforded regionalist thought some orderly unifying qualities and were conducive to midwestern regionalism.[125] In this atmosphere, some once-cynical intellectuals who set out to "find" America and document it during the crises of the 1930s actually discovered a new appreciation of rural life.[126] Regionalist themes found favor in studies of folklore, in comic strips, in magazines, in country music, and in movies, which provided a respite from the more common "frenetic settings depicted in gangster, monster, gold-digger, and slapstick-comedy films."[127] The writing of midwestern farm novels peaked during this period and were authored by, as August Derleth called them, the "middle-west's soil novelists."[128] Artists such as Grant Wood, John Steuart Curry, Thomas Hart Benton, and Harvey Dunn also highlighted midwestern themes.[129] Wood wrote to Suckow that his few years abroad were "of value only to me in getting a perspective on my own country."[130] Wood, sitting in a Paris café one day with his fellow midwesterner William Shirer (a graduate of Coe College in Cedar Rapids, Iowa), realized, "[A]ll I really know is home. Iowa. Everything commonplace."[131] So he went home to Iowa and produced his famous regionalist art, which he saw as non-European and "anti-colonial" and as rooted in the Midwest.[132] Some New Deal programs also embraced a regionalist ethos and attempted to foster small-scale farming and a return to the land for displaced farmers, to promote economic decentralization, to preserve the viability of businesses on small-town main streets, and to spur regional writing.[133]

Regionalism's emphasis on roots and place also fostered and was reinforced by the study of midwestern history. Beginning with Frederick Jackson Turner's criticism of the dominance of the Northeast in historical writing and his call for more histories of the Midwest, a group of historians located at midwestern universities—and often products of midwestern farms and small towns—focused on the history of the region during the early twentieth century. Under the banner of the *Mississippi Valley Historical Review*, they explored the dominant themes of midwestern history, including the region's origins and its economic and political development, the primacy of farming, the history of Populism, and the region's commonplace "social history" as opposed to the more elite-oriented histories of political leaders, diplomats, and generals more common to the broader history profession at the time.[134] The attempt of *Books* under the leadership of Iowa-born Stuart Pratt Sherman to find writers out in the provinces extended to historians located in the Midwest, such as Frederic Logan Paxson at the University of Wisconsin.[135] Paxson had replaced Turner when Turner moved to Harvard (against the protest of some of his fellow midwesterners), and Paxson well-represented the faction of historians who were trying to bring greater focus to the Midwest and to lessen the Northeast's hold on the writing of history.[136] The historians of the Turner-Paxson school often bristled at the attacks on the region that stemmed from the village revolt thesis. The North Dakota–born historian James Malin, who taught for his entire career at Kansas, rejected the "literature of satire, sneer, and smear of such men as Mencken and the *American Mercury* group . . . in ridicule of the typical American, the common man, and his institutions."[137] The regionalist historian Walter Prescott Webb also thought that literary treatments had been too derogatory and sought to defend the nation's interior regions.[138] Bernard DeVoto, who is perhaps primarily remembered as a historian, also responded to the expatriates and rebels by arguing what "truly was bankrupt was not American civilization but the literary way of thinking about it."[139] DeVoto defended the Midwest, for example, in his book *Mark Twain's America* (1932), which sought to upend Van Wyck Brooks's curt dismissal of the nation's interior as a cultureless barren.[140]

While the 1930s did witness some welling regionalist energies, including some dedication to midwestern history, and the loosely constituted regionalist movement reached a high point by mid-decade, the larger cultural currents surging in the other direction were stronger.[141] In Michael Steiner's apt metaphor, regionalism existed as a fading "countercurrent" against the "often agitated and swollen mainstream of life."[142] As the decade wore on, the onrush of standardization, mass culture, urbanization, and nationally oriented government policies overwhelmed the regionalist enterprise.[143] The regionalist B. A. Botkin commented in 1938 that the "regionalism movement is almost played out."[144] Hamlin Garland wrote the same year that his works on the Midwest were "fading chronicles of a simpler time."[145] New York continued its magnetic draw for many writers, Edgar Lee Masters noted, where regionalist writing was a "closed book" to many intellectuals.[146] Suckow thought the literary scene was "full of little personalities" and was overtaken by the "little boys now on deck" who moved in "small circles" that cared little for regional themes.[147] Carey McWilliams, who carried a regionalist torch early in his career, recalled that "as the Depression deepened, regionalism was sort of pushed aside," and McWilliams, Michael Steiner explains, "renounced literary regionalism in favor of left-wing activism."[148]

Once-fertile fields of regionalist thought also dried up. If an important strand of midwestern regionalism was derived from rural rootedness and agrarian sentiment, it survived the interwar years increasingly ragged and frayed. When midwestern regional identity first took solid form in the years after the Civil War, the region was heavily agricultural.[149] In 1880, the census reported that Iowa was 85 percent "rural"; Minnesota 81 percent; Michigan 75 percent; Wisconsin 76 percent; Kansas 90 percent; Nebraska 87 percent; the Dakotas 93 percent; Indiana 81 percent; Missouri 75 percent; Illinois 69 percent; and Ohio 68 percent.[150] While urban centers were always present in the Midwest and served as hubs of economic activity and homes to regional writers, the rural Midwest bulked large and inspired much place-based writing about the region through the early twentieth century.[151] Rapid urbanization, however, greatly diminished the centrality of rural life in midwestern culture. The erosion of the old agrarian Midwest pained many Americans, who saw the city, in Jackson Lears's memorable summary, as "the source of corruption, dissipation, extravagance, and deception, a devil's playground swarming with painted women and confidence men," or, in William Leuchtenburg's portrayal, "as a great incubus sucking the life's blood of the countryside."[152] The rise of cities—by the 1920s urbanites became a majority of the nation's population—caused the rural interior to lose its former prominence, and the accompanying and growing prevalence of an "urban-cosmopolitan milieu" in intellectual life cut against regionalism.[153] The effort to juxtapose "the backward culture of the farm and the progressive culture of the cities" coupled with the cosmopolitan "skewering of rural life," both impulses that fueled the revolt thesis, were led by elites, Randall Patnode has explained, who "pressed the modernist urban agenda."[154] "Urbanism as a Way of Life," in the sociological parlance of the early decades of the twentieth century, helped to usher out the Midwestern Moment of regional writing.[155] The age of what Hal Barron deems a "pervasive hegemony of urban culture and mass society" was arriving.[156]

That Ohio and Illinois were less rural than other midwestern states indicated their place in the nineteenth-century urbanization and industrialization wave. Chicago, Decatur, Akron, Youngstown, Toledo, Pullman, and other cities became industrial centers and homes to factory workers, many of whom were recent immigrants.[157] The struggles of these new immigrants, the theme of "alienation" from the cold steel and concrete of the city's brutalist modernity, and the perils of urban exile became prominent literary foci as the themes of rural life rapidly faded.[158] The proletarian novels of Jack Conroy, James T. Farrell, and Nelson Algren began to edge out the work of older regionalists, and "proletarian literature" would become the "most visible and identifiable of genres in the Thirties."[159] This literature of the mean streets and pool rooms and neon-lit alleys and generalized urban gloom was defined, as Farrell wrote, by a "poverty of the senses" and a detachment from place, or at least a detachment from any place other than a despairing urban world featuring the "underdogs of sin, the small souls of corruption, the fools of poverty."[160] Nelson Algren's people were, as he said, the "nameless, useless nobodies who sleep behind the taverns."[161] In the modern urban crucible, as Algren wrote to his then-fellow Chicagoan Richard Wright, "we live here pretty much on the grim verge of ourselves," and regionalism meant little.[162]

Interchangeable and generically bleak urban environments decoupled from place increasingly, in the postwar era, abutted expanding suburban peripheries where regional attachments were weak while rural areas and small towns depopulated.[163] The postwar suburban boom was "one of the most momentous events of the latter half of the twentieth century."[164] By 1970 the number of Americans living in suburbs surpassed the number of both rural and urban dwellers, and prominent suburban dramas naturally followed, including Joyce Carol Oates's *Expensive People* (1968), which featured a migrating midwestern family, and the domestic ordeal of *Ordinary People* (1976), a novel set in the suburbs of Chicago, both of which, despite their setting, could have occurred in any suburb in the country.[165] The new literature of the suburbs emphasized blandness, alienation, insecurity, and a "cultureless" existence that was "uniformly unlocatable," "[u]nconstrained by region," and generally "against the grain of regional writing."[166] In contrast to the grounded nature of early twentieth-century midwestern regionalism and its attachments to place, the postwar suburbs were viewed as "nowhere."[167]

The burgeoning cities and suburbs dissolved the agrarian hegemony over midwestern life. By 1960, the states of the Midwest were much less rural than they had been during their formative decades: Iowa had dropped to 47 percent; Minnesota 38 percent; Michigan 27 percent; Wisconsin 36 percent; Kansas 39 percent; Nebraska 46 percent; South Dakota 61 percent; North Dakota 65 percent; Indiana 38 percent; Missouri 33 percent; Illinois 19 percent; and Ohio 27 percent.[168] The diminished status of rural life was revealed by the agricultural depression of the 1950s. In comparison to the farm crises of the 1890s and 1930s, the 1950s depression was of secondary importance to national politics and remains largely forgotten.[169] The "farm bloc" and the "farm vote" and the "farm problem," which still had some brief but fleeting currency during the 1956 election cycle, finally lost their once-prominent place in the headlines and their centrality to domestic politics.[170] After his election in 1960, the urbane President Kennedy told his advisor John Kenneth Galbraith, "I don't want to hear about agriculture from anyone but you, Ken. And I don't much want to hear about it from you, either."[171] During Kennedy's first year in office, the term "megalopolis" entered the American lexicon, highlighting the emergence of extreme forms of urbanization.[172] Farmers, who had once dominated midwestern life, were becoming, as the South Dakotan and agricultural historian Gilbert Fite wrote, "the new minority."[173] The resulting grief in the rural Midwest over the passing of the region's old agrarian order during the post–World War II era was intense and heartfelt.[174]

The eclipse of the traditional form of rural life was abetted by an urban-based mass culture, whose "standardizing and flattening processes" further eroded regional distinctions.[175] The midwestern rural and small-town culture of county fairs, Rotary clubs, and local churches faded as the primary means of socialization as mass circulation magazines and the prominence of radio and movies grew, and they "served to convey and reinforce the notion of a single, American national identity" and "to emphasize national commonalities over regional interests."[176] Famous sociological studies would examine how small-town cultures were overwhelmed by the outside forces of "mass society."[177] The cult of celebrity deepened with the rise of the "star system" in Hollywood during the 1920s, which selected and promoted particular celebrities, hailed urban and coastal glitter and glamor, and therefore reinforced images of small-town monotony and perceptions of the tediousness of rural life.[178] Regionalism and depictions of the common life of the Midwest were "neglected" in part and failed to "attract attention" because they lacked a "shock quality."[179] Regionalism suffered in comparison to celebrity-spiced Hollywood movies—Hamlin Garland dismissed movies as "a spectacle for morons of vitiated taste"—and pulp fiction because it was seen as "dull" and "mediocre."[180] Regional works were, critics thought, populated by "second-rate people not often revelatory of man's bravest potentiality" and suffered from a "drabness of style."[181] Hollywood producers focused on box-office income and what the "*national and world* audience wanted," and that, they determined, "was sex, sin, and sensation, set in a whipped-cream world of luxury and leisure."[182]

Regionalists could see the coming wave. In an early diagnosis of the emergence of an empty diva and celebrity culture and the spread of shallow urban happenings, Ruth Suckow praised hard-working midwesterners in comparison to "artistic" Manhattanites, saying she met twenty-five New Yorkers with "absurd and elaborate attitudes to one genuine person."[183] Suckow worried about Americans becoming too distracted by popular culture and "too afraid of settling" and rooting down in a locality for a long period so they could "leave a mark" and contribute something solid and enduring to the culture.[184] Sherwood Anderson thought people wanted "to be so big" because of the "terrible bigness of the country" and the spread of modern technology and the influence of mass-produced radio instead of "walking quietly and not asking much," a reprise of his long-running criticism of the "cult of the new" endlessly announced by those who "do not know of what they talk, but run about in circles, making noise and clamor."[185] People were yielding, he thought, to the "passion for success, power," which were "diseases that eat away peoples' lives."[186] Zona Gale's father, in a lonely gesture of dissent against the mass culture so detested by Anderson, had the radio removed from their Wisconsin home because, as he said, "it interrupts my thoughts."[187] Regionalists generally recognized that they had to compete with movies, radio, and the automobile and that such "modern inventions" worked in tandem with "metropolitan ideas" to produce a culture, one regionalist noted, that was "highly abstract and utterly unregional. . . . The moment a region swallows them, it becomes metropolitan in its mind."[188] The ascendance of television during the 1950s served as the "ultimate weapon" against older regionalist sentiments, one scholar noted, and "a weapon which irrevocably destroys all regional boundaries."[189] The mass popularity of the television quiz shows, which, as one midwestern historian observed, ultimately "revealed themselves to have been completely fraudulent," served as one famous form of mass distraction (and scandalized the brother of Carl Van Doren, creator of "The Revolt from the Village" thesis).[190] There came to be too much focus in American culture, said the Iowan Vernon Carstensen to the Nebraskan Merle Curti, on "Lucy or the BatMan," or a generic or national popular culture divorced from place.[191] In 1961, the midwesterner Newton Minow famously deemed television "a vast wasteland."[192]

Much of popular culture emerged out of California, which became the new home to millions of Americans during the war and postwar years and became increasingly influential as a trendsetter. As the case of the California boom indicated, the Midwest lost its former prominence to other emerging regions, especially the broadly defined "Sunbelt," which included southern California, and contributed to what Carl Abbott has deemed a profound "regional rebalancing" in the nation.[193] If the industrializing and populated and prosperous Midwest was the regional pacesetter in the late nineteenth century and at the beginning of the twentieth century, in the postwar era that honor fell to the "Sunbelt," a magnet for those departing the chilly and drab "Frost Belt" or, in later years, "Rust Belt."[194] The Sunbelt boom included the rise to prominence of the once-lowly and isolated and economically backward South. Greater urbanization, the attraction of new industry, halting progress on civil rights, and, perhaps most importantly, the coming of air conditioning remade the region.[195] The air conditioning "wave of the 1950s" transformed the region and significantly contributed to the loss of the region's uniqueness, and—in contrast to the loss of ten million people from 1910 to 1950—new residents began flocking to the South, including African Americans who had left during the early twentieth-century Great Migration.[196] The American West, including urban centers such as Seattle, San Francisco, and Denver, also began to develop.[197] In the late nineteenth century, the states of Iowa and Wisconsin by themselves had larger populations than all the states in the West *combined,* but during World War II and the postwar era the West emerged as a prominent industrial and commercial region and a recreation mecca.[198] Simultaneously, the one-time cultural influence of midwestern cities such as Chicago—once considered the nation's "second city" where all the railroads met and, in the early twentieth century, the "next great centre of literature, painting and sculpture"—faded in the glare of the burgeoning Sunbelt and the romantic draw of the American West.[199]

In addition to the growing prominence of placeless urbanism and mass culture and the sliding fortunes of the Midwest, many intellectuals—who by their primary nature tend toward stances of exile, removal, and alienation, or "unhousedness" and "extraterritoriality"—maintained a general posture of doubt and hostility toward regional thinking and saw it as simplistic and limiting, and they increasingly saw regions as "backward if not reactionary from the vantage point of the nation-state and urban elites."[200] Social scientists' embrace of modernization theory, which viewed the rural and traditional as ultimately doomed by progress in the form of urbanization and secularization, further obscured the view of regions and underscored their irrelevance.[201] These trends fueled an Othering dynamic catalyzed by the village revolt interpretation of the 1920s and an intellectual tendency to draw a line between the People of Culture on the coasts and those Out There, lost in the interior hinterlands, a tendency already strongly reinforced by the concentration of publishing in New York.[202] The label "regionalist" tended, more and more, to connote "provincial," "mediocre," "quaint," and "second-rate."[203] The writer Sanora Babb recalled that " '[r]egional' was the stinging word used by certain influential New York groups to try to keep writers outside of NY in their places. It was a patronizing put-down."[204] Some influential critics such as Mencken thought the "whole regional movement was largely imaginary," while recognizing the "great deal of damage" done to writers labeled "regional," a designation that left them in "pigeon-holes" from which they "find it difficult to struggle out."[205] One professor, when reviewing a midwestern manuscript for the University of Minnesota Press, pronounced it a "disservice" to students to "encourage them to intensive study of their own region" and thought they should be directed "toward far-flung 'realms of gold.' "[206]

Other intellectuals who turned to universalist doctrines such as Marxism

similarly showed little patience for regionalist appeals.[207] The regionalists'
focus on place offended both the broader group of cosmopolitan-oriented
intellectuals (who at times flirted with vague notions of Marxism) and the
newly active and more ideologically pure members of the Communist
Party (who embraced "internationalism" and saw the regionalists as "reactionary").[208] The "universal world culture" these intellectuals sought left little
room for old, rural, midwestern mores.[209] Marxism was premised on the overthrow of tradition and took an early stand against a reliance on the past—"the
tradition of the dead generations weighs like a nightmare on the minds of the
living"—and Marx could never "accept the intrusion of seemingly irrelevant
tradition" and thought it needed to be "swept away before the truly great historical accomplishments of revolutions could occur."[210] During the late 1920s
and early 1930s, American Communists, following instructions from Moscow,
made a concerted effort at "weaning [workers] from the bourgeois arts and
letters."[211] As the intellectuals of the left focused on what was "usable" to their
cause, older regionalist works suffered accordingly, and regionalists came in
for criticism.[212] Even the rather innocent midwestern art of Grant Wood was
denounced as fascistic.[213] Although the Soviet Union lessened its ideological
requirements in the late 1930s and sought to cater to "indigenous influences"
and "folk culture" during the Popular Front period, many intellectuals on the
left remained skeptical. Regionalists, too, bristled at such efforts and what they
considered foreign interference, the resistance to which had served as their
central operating principle.[214] Regionalists sought to escape "foreign 'isms' and
depend upon [their] native environment."[215] Edgar Lee Masters, in a characteristic regionalist protest, resisted the tendency to box and label his writing:
"These little men are all mixed up with ideologies—with abstracts; they want
to criticize your work on the basis of your social consciousness. Damned nonsense! The belief that you have to write about society, its economic phases, so
forth, is a wild obsession. As for -isms, I haven't any use for the lot of them."[216]
August Derleth rejected Communist poetry and thought "[p]ropaganda and
art don't mix, never will."[217] Sinclair Lewis rejected the Communists' attempts
to control the cause of anti-fascism and told them to "go to hell."[218] Lewis
counseled August Derleth to keep his distance from him because he was "one
of the chief objects of hatred of the whole Left Wing of literature."[219]

Despite the protests of some regionalists, the appeal of Marxism among
intellectuals remained strong during the 1930s and produced extensive debates

and discussions among the movement's various factions, shaped the decade's intellectual discourse, and highlighted another strand of thought contributing to the eclipse of regionalism. Namely, in New York, a prominent group of intellectuals emerged who were critical of Stalinism but sought to pursue Marxist analyses. These oft-studied New York Intellectuals were highly influential among cultural commentators; they were strong believers in "cosmopolitanism" and severely critical of small-town and rural culture. The New York Intellectuals gained their greatest strength in the left politics of the Depression and commonly found their voice in *Partisan Review*, which was originally founded in 1934 in New York as an organ of the Communist Party's John Reed Club and found little to love in the rural American interior.[220] As proponents of cosmopolitanism and, most often, advocates of socialism, they felt a "deep alienation" with American culture, which remained business-oriented and "insistently Christian."[221] The New York Intellectuals, according to Irving Howe, one of the group's leading lights (and an exacting critic of Sherwood Anderson), for the first time "did not acknowledge the authority of Christian tradition," and instead they looked for inspiration to European intellectuals and, in particular, to Marx and Lenin.[222] They "were unable to identify reflexively with an older America and to feel it to be genuinely their own," and this included an aversion to the interior small-town and agrarian tradition.[223] For the New York Intellectuals, Stephen Baskerville notes, the "America beyond the Hudson River remained a distant irrelevance into the 1940s, a shadowland of backwardness, superstition and myth."[224] The "marginality of their perspective," Baskerville thought, included their failure to take "little or no account of the political or cultural mainstream of American life, let alone of its sundry creeks and backwaters."[225] Moses Rischin concluded that the New York Intellectuals embraced a "New York parochialism, antirural bias, and knee-jerk distrust of western American traditions [that] locked them into a New York provincialism that did them no credit."[226]

Despite these criticisms, the influence of the New York Intellectuals—in the form of, to cite one example, the great impact of Richard Hofstadter on American historiography—did much to stymie interest in the American Midwest, except as a source of criticism or mockery.[227] Hofstadter firmly embraced Mencken and the popular readings of Masters, Anderson, and Lewis and their purported "portraits of the mean, stunted, starved lives, the sour little crabapple culture of the American small town, with its inhibitions and its tyrannies."[228] Many writers on the left, the regionalist B. A. Botkin conceded, thought regionalism, despite his and others' advocacy to the contrary, was "dead or phony stuff."[229] Such attitudes frustrated the western-born radical Carey McWilliams, Michael Steiner notes, who became "disillusioned with New York's intellectual scene, whose radicalism struck him as rootless, superficial, and infected with insufferable condescension toward anyone or anything west of the Hudson."[230] If McWilliams recognized the hostility of the eastern intelligentsia toward the West, he also found some regionalist impulses escapist and naïve, while other more strident intellectuals adhered to the "common 'regionalism equals fascism' equation" and the "regionalists-as-fascists story."[231] However curt the dismissal, the fortunes of regionalism would crash in a postwar era whose intellectual energies were cosmopolitan and universalist and devoted to global citizenship and international brotherhood and whose intellectuals were seized by the Plight of Modern Man and existential crises writ universal, not local, or regional.[232]

The tribulations of regionalism among intellectuals were largely mirrored in the political realm. While regionalism found some support in New Deal programs and during the 1930s more generally, the crosswinds of opposition were stronger, and the policy and politics of the era generally moved in a different direction. The extent of the economic calamity caused a firm embrace of the federal state and favored the general diminution of local control and autonomy and a focus on national solutions and a transcendence of parochial and small-scale policy approaches.[233] While the New Deal was makeshift and inconsistent and at times emphasized economic decentralization, antitrust campaigns, and aid to small business, its overall emphasis on federal regulation and reliance on the central administrative state, economic planning, and bureaucratic experts overshadowed its episodic regionalist gestures.[234] The more locally oriented policy approaches of midwestern political leaders, which once found favor, lost support. While the Iowan Herbert Hoover did attempt to promote administrative efforts to streamline and stabilize the economy from Washington, he remained wedded to his voluntary approach, skeptical of statist solutions, and highly critical of "spendthrifts," "socialists," and "totalitarians"; and as a result—given the gravity of the suffering during the Depression—his image of callousness and detachment grew, and his hands-off brand of policy making was popularly discredited.[235] Roosevelt's pledges of government activism helped him defeat three midwestern advocates of local control and opponents of New Deal statism (from Iowa, Kansas, and Indiana) in 1932, 1936, and 1940. These failed campaigns did reveal, however, how public skepticism of the New Deal remained strongest in the Midwest and underscored the region's persistent regional distinctiveness. In elections he won handily overall, Roosevelt lost Indiana, Michigan, Iowa, Nebraska, Kansas, and North and South Dakota in 1940 and lost Ohio, Wisconsin, Iowa, Indiana, Nebraska, Kansas, and North and South Dakota in 1944.[236] In both elections, Roosevelt's losses were concentrated in the Midwest (even the usually progressive Frederick Jackson Turner opposed Roosevelt).[237] This pattern added to the negative perception held by those critics who saw the Midwest as backward and regressive and a stronghold of political reaction, a place of growing "fascistic trends," according to Meridel LeSueur.[238]

To mitigate Roosevelt's political weaknesses in the Midwest, his advisors relied on the Iowa-born farm editor Henry Wallace. Wallace had left his father's GOP over Hoover's opposition to agricultural price-fixing plans, and he supported Al Smith in 1928 and therefore found favor with Rexford Tugwell, an original member of Roosevelt's "Brains Trust" who brought Wallace into FDR's inner circle with the hope of winning over skeptical midwestern voters (Wallace was awarded the Secretary of Agriculture cabinet post after the election).[239] After recruiting Wallace, the chief organizer of Roosevelt's new administration, Raymond Moley, sent Roosevelt a telegraph: "CORN BELT IN THE BAG."[240] Wallace was something of a "mystic" who drifted further to the left in his career, but perhaps because of his midwestern agrarian grounding he recognized, as he said, that "if government marched into the economic field decisively and directly at the top, the result can be regimentation of all types of activity in a manner completely abhorrent to the American temperament."[241]

In contrast to Wallace, who still maintained some "nostalgia for a Jeffersonian agrarian philosophy," Tugwell personified many intellectuals' embrace of the federal state.[242] Tugwell was a "staunch new nationalist and collectivist, a dedicated apostle of centralized economic planning" and, in a sign of the growing influence of the statists, crowded out Wallace for control of agricultural policy.[243] For Tugwell, the history of the nineteenth century and the creation of so many western states that were defined by small-scale agrarian economies and that sent similarly oriented representatives to Congress meant that the development of a properly "collective government" was stymied.[244] The "cult of feeble government," which originated with the American Revolution and became the entrenched American republicanism of the midwestern states, persisted into the 1920s and animated resistance to "federal interference," which Tugwell thought was essential to meeting the economic crisis of the 1930s.[245] Tugwell criticized the "weakening of government" during the 1920s under midwestern presidents such as Harding and Hoover, and he dismissed early progressivism as driven by the "desires of small property holders—after the Jeffersonian ideal—rather than [by] the very different aspirations of the 'proletariat.' "[246] He recalled that the growth of strong governments in urban areas had the greatest impact on the New Deal's embrace of a strong federal government. Most of the administrators of the New Deal state, Tugwell remembered, had "city backgrounds," and the "whole apparatus of municipal improvement came to Washington in 1933."[247] Tugwell, a New Yorker who found little to admire in the midwestern family farming tradition and "folk cultures" more generally, was eager to advance his plans aimed at "eliminating the small farmer," who had for too long stymied the growth of the federal state.[248]

Tugwell shaped Roosevelt's agenda-defining San Francisco Commonwealth Club speech during the 1932 campaign, which focused on the need to abandon old policy constraints, recognize the end of the agrarian frontier Turner had famously explained, and prepare for a new era of central government action.[249] The speech was designed to signal a major break from Hoover and the older politics of localism and individualism and to justify the use of the federal state and national planning.[250] The title of the original speech offered a contrast between an older "romantic" approach and a newer "realistic" one ("Individualism, Romantic and Realistic"), and its central thrust was to emphasize that the "old rural culture" was fading and that "rural attitudes were inadequate" to the present crisis.[251] This approach necessarily undermined the tenets of regionalism and reinforced a growing "tendency to see human collectivities in terms no smaller than the nation state."[252] Not surprisingly, midwestern historians objected to the use of Turner, who died in 1932, to advance Tugwell's plans to increase federal power.[253] But Tugwell and his line of thinking strongly influenced the broader intelligentsia. Writers paid by Tugwell's and other administrators' New Deal programs became less independent and more favorable toward federal approaches to social problems, and expatriate writers discovered when they returned from Europe that everyone was discussing economic planning, socialism, and Tugwell's ideas.[254]

A contrast to the increasingly influential ideas of Tugwell could be found among a second group of intellectuals who were also active during the New Deal and who represented a regional and midwestern mode of thought. FDR's Department of Agriculture, the sociologist Jess Gilbert explains, included two rival groups of reformers. The first, which included Tugwell, was comprised of easterners from privileged urban backgrounds with Ivy League degrees who were amenable to statist controls, collectivism, and technocratic planning. The second group was closely allied with the sentiments of midwestern regionalists and historians. They were midwestern farm kids who were raised in the Protestant reform tradition, were educated at state schools in the Midwest such as Wisconsin, and were attuned to midwestern culture. They understood the democratic and egalitarian rhythms of life in the rural Midwest, which Gilbert sees as a uniquely "one-class society" devoid of the sharp social stratification present in southern and western agriculture.[255] For these "midwestern farm boys," Gilbert concludes, "the regional dimension is significant."[256] In contrast to the statist planners and "urban outsiders" from the East or the rather obnoxious opponents of family farming such as Tugwell, Gilbert properly sees the midwestern farm boys as "organic intellectuals" who were deeply rooted in their region.[257] Milburn Lincoln Wilson—who was born in Atlantic, Iowa, in 1885 and earned degrees from Iowa State College and Wisconsin and went on to serve as a prominent New Deal economist—explained these regional bearings and confessed his uniquely midwestern point of view: "Everyone is a creature of his home environment, and as a child he develops in his mind stereotypes which he carries with him throughout his life. I was born in a community of corn belt farmers where the farms ranged from quarter to half-sections in size. Therefore, instinctively when I am talking about farmers, I am actually thinking about the kind of farmers and farm families that live on the farms that you look down upon when you fly over the Corn Belt."[258] The one-time centrality and consciousness of this Midwest and its regional tempo, however, were quickly wilting in a hothouse environment that included makeshift federal policy making during an exhausting and demoralizing economic depression, the gravity of which was compounded by unfolding international crises.

If the Depression and the New Deal strained the pillars of midwestern regionalism, World War II toppled them over. The war "engulfed the nation," Allan Winkler explained; and, after Pearl Harbor, "nothing would ever be the same."[259] The war became the "juggernaut that ran over American society," concluded one study, and, according to another, "radically altered the character of American society."[260] The national mood was dramatically transformed by what the regionalist Dorothy Canfield Fisher called the "sea-sick horror and disgust" over the war.[261] Many younger writers entered military service, a "cultural loss to the country," Edgar Lee Masters thought, which greatly reoriented the literary world.[262] The "country's headlong rush into yet another national war effort soon eclipsed" the efforts of the regionalists.[263] The war also brought a state-managed economy, a ratcheting up of federal power and bureaucratic controls, an entrenchment of the influence of urban-based labor unions, a dedication to large-scale "big science" projects such as the atomic bomb, and an "imperial presidency."[264] War-time production requirements caused corporations to burgeon in size and influence and contributed to what John Morton Blum called the "hardening pattern of bigness in American life."[265] The social shifts were also dramatic: fifteen million people moved during the war, California boomed, traditional family structures were disrupted, the farm population declined by nearly 20 percent, and mass culture in the form of popular movies and the music of Frank Sinatra and other celebrity crooners deepened its hold on the public.[266] The economic and social changes of the war era, it came to be recognized, "sounded the death knell for the traditional village-and-countryside kind of life" that midwestern regionalists prized.[267]

The war also upended the Midwest's once-distinctive views on foreign affairs. Prior to the war, the greatest bastion of resistance to foreign interventions was the Midwest—what New Yorkers, Carl Van Doren said, had long deemed the "peace-at-any-price Midwest"—where isolationist opinion makers and political leaders denounced coastal elites and the "war-mad metropolitan press" for edging the nation toward involvement in another European war.[268] When war finally came and the wisdom and necessity of intervention were widely and properly endorsed, one effect was to marginalize the previously pronounced voice of midwestern isolationism and to further discredit the region's political culture.[269] The midwestern-dominated America First Committee quickly dissolved.[270] Roosevelt's 1940 opponent—Wendell

Willkie, an Indianan who reproached Roosevelt for political centralization, reckless federal spending, and tilting toward intervention during the 1940 campaign ("If his promise to keep our boys out of foreign wars is not better than his promise to balance the budget, they're almost on the transports!")—ultimately became a chief proponent of the war and Roosevelt's personal diplomat, and he turned to "One World" internationalist thinking.[271] Willkie's *One World* (1943) was the "publishing phenomenon of the war," selling "faster than any book in publishing history."[272] In this atmosphere, Robert Dorman explains, regional sentiments and literary projects and lingering pockets of isolationism were "wiped out by the *nationalizing* requirements of wartime."[273] The casualties of the war included the once-popular isolationist views of midwestern leaders who became largely irrelevant or, like Willkie, changed their positions.[274] The latter included the midwestern regionalist and U.S. senator (and former Michigan newspaper editor) Arthur Vandenberg, who had first coined the phrase "return to normalcy," the battle cry of the isolationists of the interwar years.[275]

The war redirected the energies of intellectual circles. By discrediting isolationism, the war heightened the support for a new and expanded view of the nation's international role and made possible the embrace of treaties and alliances heretofore dismissed as dangerously "entangling" in the form of the United Nations charter, NATO, and other global military obligations.[276] Soon followed "global studies" and "area studies" programs designed to correspond with the nation's new international obligations that focused on "portions of the globe deemed strategic" and thus contributed to the obsolescence of an inward-looking American regionalism.[277] The war also brought scholars to the United States who became widely influential in the postwar years, gave rise to fields of study such as critical theory, and contributed to the postwar castigation of midwestern movements such as Populism.[278] Some novelists who wrote about the war were also critical of American soldiers, who were portrayed as "not nice guys, not emblems of a benign folk culture," treatments that would fuel the "ugly American" genre that generally denounced American parochialism and called for more cosmopolitan attitudes.[279]

The war also brought new social issues to the fore. The experience of women war workers—think Detroit's Rosie the Riveter—expanded their sphere of employment possibilities, eroded traditional gender roles, and became a strong basis of the later women's movement.[280] On a parallel plane, the war transformed race relations. Discrimination against African Americans, which Roosevelt did little to address during the 1930s, was starkly highlighted in a war against the Nazis that brought a greater focus to home-front racial injustices and slowly inched the nation toward addressing segregation and discrimination (as crystalized in the emerging view that "Lincoln freed the Negroes from cotton picking but 'Hitler was the one that got us out of the white folks' kitchen'").[281] Roosevelt's prohibition on racial discrimination in war industries in 1941 set the stage for the integration of the armed forces and the origins of the civil rights movement, which was often driven by African American veterans. [282] The demands of the Cold War, which necessitated the protection of the civil rights of minorities to counter Soviet criticism, further elevated the issue of race relations in civic affairs.[283]

The collective impact of these mid-century intellectual forces—the perpetuation of the revolt thesis, the failed attempt of midwestern regionalists to bend the curve of literary opinion, the broader dissipation of regional sentiments and the envelopment of mass culture, the doubts of cosmopolitan intellectuals and Marxists, national state making and war planning, and the new prominence of a transnational racial politics—was to lessen attention to and appreciation of the American interior. They also gave lift to intense studies of class dynamics, African American history and civil rights, gender, and foreign cultures and multiculturalism that would consume English and history departments in subsequent decades. Here lie the seeds of what Andrew Delbanco calls a later "dogma" that took hold in academia, which concentrated on the relationship of a myriad of topics to "race, class, gender" to the "exclusion of every other point of view," including categories of analysis such as regions, and tended to privilege cosmopolitan hybridity over staid provincialism and to dismiss interest in local culture as "false consciousness."[284] This critical enterprise underlies and nourishes what the Indiana-based writer Scott Russell Sanders calls the "dogma of rootlessness."[285] Midwestern writers, regionalists, and authors who once spoke to the broad American middle would suffer in this new atmosphere and under this new regime of academic emphases, Gordon Hutner notes, because their work would fall to "near the bottom of most revisionist agendas" in the postwar era.[286]

These scholarly trends left the village revolt construct frozen in place, unreformed. To the extent midwestern literature was discussed at all, the revolt thesis remained a prevailing theme and a tidy and convenient synopsis of an era, and it deterred deeper explorations of midwestern literature. Little elaboration seemed necessary. As the dominant interpretation, albeit one subject to sporadic but largely failed dissents, it remained entrenched and further amplified by repetition; and, in a not uncommon scholarly phenomenon, it served to "continually reinforc[e] a consensus about what information is important and what isn't."[287] The mid-century developments by which a broader understanding of the Midwest withered and the force of intellectual, cultural, and social trends began to suffocate literary regionalism also quickly came home to the field of midwestern history.

# CHAPTER THREE

# THE DECLINE OF MIDWESTERN HISTORY

T he high water mark of midwestern regionalism during the interwar era
was made possible, in part, by the emergence of a notable contingent
of midwestern historians who were dedicated to studying their region. These
historians, who formalized their efforts in the first decades of the twentieth
century, built a field of study premised on intraregional academic cooperation,
enlivened by a regional esprit de corps, unified by means of annual meetings
in midwestern cities, and equipped with an association, a scholarly journal,
and institutional support from midwestern universities. At the beginning of
the 1940s, one midwestern historian thought his field might be on the "verge
of a small boom."[1] Similar to the efforts of other midwestern regionalists,
however, the work of these early twentieth-century historians of the Midwest
and their organized movement was disrupted by World War II and the Cold
War, the transformation of the postwar university, academic trends, cultural
and intellectual forces that caused its diminishment and demise, and a final
loss of organizational coherence. Along with the persistence of the village
revolt school of thought and the resulting neglect of regional literary voices,
the collapse of midwestern history contributed to the sinking stature of the
Midwest, whose "nadir" came in the 1950s.[2] The demise of the midwestern
history project further relegated the Midwest to the margins of the American
historical imagination, and, given the transformation of the historical profession in the postwar era and its new priorities, the region had little chance of
recovering its once-prominent historical voice.

The father of the midwestern history movement was Frederick Jackson

Turner, a son of Wisconsin who moved to the East to earn his PhD at Johns Hopkins during the 1880s and recognized, quite quickly, the domination of the historical profession by those who focused on the eastern seaboard and Europe to the neglect of the American interior. Turner observed that historians had to date "come from the East, and as a result our history has been written from the point of view of the Atlantic coast."[3] Historians in the East, he thought, were "hardly aware of the country beyond the Alleghenies."[4] Turner's misgivings about the neglect of his region were embodied in the comment of one Brown University historian who simply pronounced that "Western history is stupid."[5] When he returned to Wisconsin after graduate school, Turner responded to this neglect and hostility by dedicating himself to studying his home region.[6] He wanted to "see American history considered more broadly than earlier writers, especially eastern writers, were disposed to treat it."[7] Turner also worked in tandem with the Wisconsin Historical Society, which provided critical institutional support for the study of the Midwest.[8] Other historical societies in the region, which emerged in the late nineteenth century as the Midwest's stature grew, also advanced the cause of chronicling the history of the region.[9] By studying the history of the nation's "great interior," said the Wisconsin-born and Wisconsin-trained historian Orin Libby from his post at the University of North Dakota, an "altogether different viewpoint" could be revealed.[10] It would be possible, said the then University of Iowa historian Allan Bogue to University of Kansas historian James Malin, to overcome "Ivy League prejudice" and the predominance of an eastern perspective on American history.[11] Grounded in such sentiments, the work of midwestern historians and the literary regionalists active during the early twentieth century greatly "complemented" one another and together served as sturdy and intertwined strands that bound and gave form to midwestern identity.[12]

Following Turner's leadership at the University of Wisconsin, other midwestern universities began to focus on midwestern history and—with the guidance of professors at the University of Iowa and the University of Illinois and staffers from the Nebraska Historical Society—in 1907 launched the Mississippi Valley Historical Association. Soon after, the MVHA launched its regionally oriented journal entitled the *Mississippi Valley Historical Review*, which focused on publishing historical research on the Midwest. Working collaboratively and through the MVHA and using the pages of the *MVHR*, a group of mostly midwestern-born and midwestern-raised historians—"nearly all of them came from rural or small-town backgrounds"—steadily advanced the study of the history of the Midwest.[13] The MVHA's "moral center was divided between Madison, shrine of the Turnerian mystique, and Lincoln, the locus of the 'Nebraska matriarchy,' " a reference to the Lincoln-based secretary of the MVHA, Clara Paine, who administered the organization for nearly a half century and whose husband first organized the MVHA.[14] The unified "spirit" of the MVHA was based, said the Iowa-born Benjamin Shambaugh, on the "common experiences and common interests" of its regionally oriented historians.[15] In keeping with the essential ingredients of the various artistic forms of regionalism, which were premised to a great extent on consciousness of regional history and a general "reverence for the past," these historians focused on the settlement and origins of the Midwest, land uses, farming, and the small details of the daily life of what Ruth Suckow called "the folks" on the prairie and less, following Turner's early criticism, on war, high diplomacy, politics, and the doings of eastern elites.[16] While committing themselves to the value of analyzing local, state, and regional history, they began the first focused studies of agrarian Populism, chronicled the economic development of midwestern towns, examined (without the scorn of the village rebel school) the role of religion in the Midwest (a "universally pervasive force" in the region), and generally attempted to give the Midwest a central place in the broader arc of American history.[17]

The efforts of midwestern historians peaked about the time of World War II, when midwestern history still benefitted from the leadership of historians at prominent midwestern universities. At the University of Iowa, Louis Pelzer—who earned his PhD at Iowa, had written several midwestern history books, and served as president of the MVHA—was editing the *MVHR*.[18] Pelzer was "closely identified" with Iowa and the Midwest—as an Iowa farm boy, Pelzer had "absorbed" the value of "hard work, loyalty, and integrity" and became devoted to his region—and in his historical work was "particularly concerned with the development of the Middle West."[19] At the University of Minnesota, the Minnesota-born and Minnesota-trained Theodore Blegen persisted in his regional history efforts and published a book making the case for the work of midwestern historians intended to rebuff the "taunt of provincialism, once so easily leveled at the champions of regionalism."[20] At Indiana University, John D. Barnhart—a product of Decatur, Illinois, who earned his PhD under Turner and taught in Minnesota and Nebraska but mostly at Indiana—maintained his "principal interest" in the "history of the Ohio Valley and the Old Northwest."[21] Barnhart's "magnum opus," *Valley of Democracy*, finally published in 1953, advanced a Turner-oriented history of the Midwest and reinforced the value of regionally oriented history emphasized in the recently published midwestern history tome written by R. Carlyle Buley.[22] As early as 1923, Buley, a native Indianan who earned his PhD at Wisconsin, had commenced work on his history of the Midwest.[23] He emphasized the basic details of midwestern life in his work but also cautioned against romanticizing the people of the region: "After all, they were just folks, doing their day's work, and caring little for the verdict of history."[24] Buley rejoiced when his extensive history of the Midwest, after years of struggle, was "finally taken in out of the cold, bitter winds of the gutters" and "adopted" for publication by the Indiana Historical Society, a sign of the strong collaboration between the midwestern historical societies and midwestern historians.[25] It won a Pulitzer Prize in 1951.[26] At the University of Wisconsin, the Missouri-born John D. Hicks, who held a Wisconsin PhD and held Turner's former post, promoted midwestern history. Merle Curti, who was Turner's last doctoral student and a product of rural Nebraska whose father was a Populist, replaced Hicks in 1943 and also maintained a keen interest in the region and "always retained his sympathetic understanding if not invariably his sense of identity with the Middle West."[27]

During the World War II era, the midwestern historians still benefitted from crucial institutional support for their efforts. Theodore Blegen migrated from the superintendency of the Minnesota Historical Society to serving as dean of the University of Minnesota graduate school in 1939, where, among his many initiatives, he strongly aided the new University of Minnesota Press, which actively sought to publish works about the Midwest.[28] To advance the regional cause, Blegen worked closely with the midwesterner Solon Buck (who was long active in the Minnesota Historical Society and the MVHA) and the president of the University of Minnesota (the midwesterner Guy Stanton Ford, who always maintained his regional allegiances and strongly advocated midwestern history).[29] Blegen also launched the University of Minnesota Regional Writing Fellowships to promote regional writing, especially in Wisconsin, Minnesota, Iowa, and the Dakotas, an initiative that led to several books published by the University of Minnesota Press.[30] The success of the University of Minnesota Press, which was formally launched in 1927, also inspired the creation of the University of Wisconsin Press.[31] In 1935, Wisconsin's president appointed John Hicks, who had recently returned to Madison from the University of Nebraska, to chair a committee and "start the ball rolling toward the establishment of a University of Wisconsin Press" based on the "success of the University of Minnesota Press."[32] Wisconsin also organized a conference on regionalism during the 1940s that became a book published by the University of Wisconsin Press.[33] Blegen and Hicks and other midwestern historians also continued to work closely with state historical societies in the region.[34] Into the late 1940s, the MVHA programs still made efforts to focus on the Midwest as a region.[35] In the late 1940s, the Newberry Library in Chicago—whose director recognized that the "character of the Midwest has been determined by the small town"—aided midwestern historians' efforts through fellowships designed to fund studies of the Midwest, organized an exhibition of prominent midwestern books, managed the production of a special issue of the *Chicago Sun's* book section dedicated to midwestern writing, and generally tried to encourage writing about the Midwest and recognize midwestern voices.[36]

These efforts to focus on the Midwest, which largely stemmed from an earlier organizational momentum and a sense of regional purpose grounded in an earlier era, proved to be the final efforts to systematically promote midwestern history and were overwhelmed by cross-currents that ushered in a new era of historical research and a transformed profession. The University of Minnesota Regional Writing Fellowships and the Newberry's midwestern studies fellowships, in harbingers of the era to come, both died by the early 1950s.[37] The greatest jolt to the midwestern history project, not surprisingly, came from World War II, which disrupted many academic careers and history departments.[38] At Iowa, Louis Pelzer lost two sons (Parker and Henry) to the war, and this "undoubtedly hastened the end of his own life."[39] Their death "was a blow from which he never recovered although he rarely disclosed his grief to the outside world."[40] Pelzer died in 1946 of a heart attack while serving as the editor of the *MVHR*.[41] During the war, surely adding to Pelzer's strains and grief, the *MVHR* struggled to find articles to publish.[42] John Hicks, who left Wisconsin for Berkeley during the war, reported back to Merle Curti on Hicks's remaining graduate students at Wisconsin whom Curti had inherited and said "practically all of them are in the army."[43] Hicks also reported that the "war is omnipresent" in Berkeley.[44] Curti noted that some of his colleagues went "to England to teach GIs" and that he had "lost [his] assistant to the War," not to be replaced.[45] The land historian Paul Gates was preoccupied with the thirteen hundred students in his "army-navy courses" and generally diverted from his studies by the "all-out war program."[46] Gates was so "swamped" by "army and navy trainees" that, he reported, "all research and writing is out."[47] Clarence Carter, an Illinois native with a PhD from Illinois, worried that the war would disrupt his studies of the early American territories in the Midwest and "stressed the necessity of preventing a break in the continuity of the cultural activities" such as his series.[48] At Indiana, R. Carlyle Buley noted the "war-time slump in enrollment."[49] At Kansas, James Malin reported that the "war is playing havoc with most considerations of long range planning" in the Kansas history department.[50] Universities often postponed the hiring of new professors until after the war.[51]

If the war disrupted the ongoing research efforts of midwestern historians, it also reoriented the general outlook of historians and fueled contempt for isolationist historians and the region, the Midwest, most often associated with strong currents of isolationism.[52] Howard K. Beale of Wisconsin, who was originally from Chicago, was opposed for an opening at Cornell because of his isolationist views.[53] Merrill Jensen, an Iowa-born isolationist who had taught high school in South Dakota and earned a PhD from Wisconsin and was teaching at Washington during the war, worried that his career would be undermined by his isolationism and by a senior professor and "belligerent interventionist" in the department.[54] The war also divided midwesterners—some of whom believed it must be fought, while others remained less aggressive. The Illinois-born writer Archibald MacLeish, for example, challenged Merle Curti, who embraced pacifism.[55] Curti was a supporter of his fellow midwesterner Charles Beard, who remained a fierce opponent of the war. Beard lashed out at wealthy internationalists in the East who, he thought, would endanger liberty at home by fighting wars abroad. As the nation's foreign commitments deepened and the "American Century" dawned, Beard and other politically active isolationists led what David Brown called a "midwestern resistance" to internationalism while the South, in stark contrast, led the charge to war.[56] Beard and Carl Becker, both of Republican backgrounds in Indiana and Iowa and leaders of the historical "relativism" cause of the 1930s (and loosely "social democrats"), were criticized as the war approached for clouding the nation's moral mission and diminishing the unity necessary for the war.[57] Intellectuals became increasingly critical of any "moral relativism" that would undermine the battle against the Axis and the need for "national mobilization," and they disparaged those interior leaders of isolationism who remained intransigent.[58]

The voices of isolation were also condemned by some midwestern historians, among whom the belief in the inevitability of war and the justness of the cause also spread. James Sellers of Nebraska prodded the MVHA to pass a resolution urging the U.S. Senate to support American rearmament and the aiding of Britain.[59] John Hicks, between conversations with his mentor Frederic Logan Paxson over the best method of deploying destroyers to help Great Britain, tried to "tilt" the 1941 program of the MVHA toward an interventionist position.[60] Hicks and his allies slowly won out. During the war, the MVHA maintained a more national focus and reflected a "growing sense of nationalism associated with the wartime experience and the nation's rise to world power."[61] Despite the potential for "screams of rage" from Beardians, Hicks lent his efforts to attacking Beard's "isolationist viewpoint."[62] The overwhelming necessity of and support for the war ultimately left Beard a "pariah" and an "unperson."[63] Beard told Curti he was "scalped by the vestal virgins in charge of the sacred altar and fire."[64] Historians of foreign policy "believed their most urgent task to be combatting the vestiges of isolationism" and advocated "internationalism" with great "tenacity."[65] The midwestern voices that personified isolationism before the war—Beard of Indiana, Charles Lindbergh of Minnesota, Senator Gerald P. Nye of North Dakota, Senator Arthur Vandenberg of Michigan, Colonel Robert McCormick and the *Chicago Tribune*, and the leaders of the midwestern-centered America First Committee—were increasingly dismissed as cranks.[66] Internationalism, most clearly enshrined in the newly created United Nations, which symbolized the embrace of entangling international commitments long fought by midwestern isolationists, became the vogue and helped fuel the collapse of regionalism.[67]

The ensuing Cold War had a doubly negative effect on the image of the Midwest. Not only did it further discredit an older midwestern isolationism in an era of international danger, but it also, in an odd coincidence of seemingly contradictory criticisms, linked the region with Cold War excesses that repulsed many intellectuals. The primary effect of the Cold War was to deepen the nation's outward commitments in response to the threat of Communism and to refocus political and cultural affairs on the widely assumed imminence of atomic war. The United States made heretofore unthinkably extensive military commitments in Europe and Asia, and the potentially ghastly implications of these commitments permeated the culture. Historians actively decided to move out of certain physical areas considered likely conflict zones if the Cold War turned hot and fears of nuclear war grew intense.[68] Paul Engle, writing to Sinclair Lewis in 1946 "from the corn country" of Iowa where he was directing the Iowa Writers' Workshop, said the "great word of the moment is atomic."[69] The Iowa-born historian Vernon Carstensen who was teaching at Wisconsin noted that Sears & Roebuck was distributing pamphlets on how to survive atomic bomb attacks and that one university president "told his faculty that in case of an atomic bomb attack, they will find safety in the concrete basements of the university buildings."[70] The mood was defined, Richard Pells explains, by the "sense of an approaching Armageddon."[71] The gallows humor included Christopher Lasch's jests about whether his building at the University of Iowa, Schaeffer Hall, could withstand a nuclear attack (he thought the drinking fountains were not up to the challenge).[72]

The Cold War necessarily affected scholarship. In order to combat Communism, diplomatic historians wrote books stressing the need to maintain an activist foreign policy and to prevent backsliding into the midwestern-led isolationism of the prewar years.[73] The head of the increasingly influential Social Science Research Council urged less attention be given to past divisions and conflict in the nation and more focus be placed on "union and co-operation," a directive that served to undermine an emphasis on regional distinctions.[74] American historians generally sought to lessen the focus on the "distinctiveness of American society," to "emphasize links with Europe" (in a reversal of Turner), and to focus on the history of the "Atlantic community" (which was frequently dubbed "NATO History") and the growth of "Western Civilization," which, after World War II, "became the most widely taught history course on American campuses."[75] At Iowa, "Western Civ" came to outpace the American survey class and the course on the American West, which were taught by the midwestern historian Allan Bogue, who had replaced Pelzer.[76] Programs in Russian history, a field that barely existed before World War II, grew especially rapidly because of the Cold War.[77] The Cold War spurred "International Affairs" and "Defense Studies" initiatives, including "area studies" programs designed to promote the understanding of zones of Cold War superpower contestation. By 1950, twenty-nine such programs had been launched at universities involving five hundred faculty members; and, by 1965, this initiative had grown to 153 programs involving four thousand faculty members who generally embraced modernization theory's assumption of the inevitable decline and disappearance of local and regional cultures.[78] Indiana launched an area studies program for the "Far East."[79] Wisconsin's history department began focusing on Latin America, Africa, and the Caribbean.[80] Merle Curti began teaching in India and Japan.[81] The Cold War also caused universities to place a great emphasis on science and math, especially during the post-*Sputnik* years.[82] The immediate needs of the Cold War, the reorientation of the postwar academy, and the muting of the Midwest's once-prominent isolationist voices all eroded the bases of regionalist thought during the early 1950s.

While regionalism withered, the extreme views of the anti-Communist cause came to be embodied by the World War II veteran and U.S. senator from Wisconsin Joe McCarthy, who brought further scorn to his region among intellectuals.[83] Eastern liberals, who had earlier denounced the Midwest as the land of reactionary isolationism, increasingly saw the rural Midwest as the home of a new kind of extremism. For critics of the Midwest, McCarthyism confirmed their image of the Midwest as a land of "ignorant biblical literalists, rednecks, and crypto anti-Semites," fascist and authoritarian undercurrents, and the generally darker aspects of democratic life.[84] While the Midwest was criticized for an older current of isolationism and the newer extremes of McCarthyism, it also was criticized for producing Henry Wallace, whose 1948 presidential campaign was widely attacked for a foolish and naïve accommodation of the Soviet Union and for being supported by Communists.[85] The region was whipsawed, then, by varying forms of criticism stemming from fears of the region's weak commitment to fighting the Cold War, whether based in 1930s-era conservative isolationism or 1940s-era leftist/Wallaceite appeasement, and from anger over McCarthy's overly vigorous pursuit of Communists.

Below the swirling currents of Cold War politics and inside the halls of academe, midwestern history also lost its former centrality. The massive boom in postwar higher education (spurred on by returning soldiers and postwar prosperity) and the deepening professionalization of history and new trends within the profession left midwestern history behind. These developments reinforced a long-standing tendency of historians—a tendency that first inspired the efforts of midwestern historians during the early twentieth century—to privilege the national over the regional. As Wisconsin historian William Hesseltine observed, historians had too often "seen politics from the perspective of the national government" and "surveyed cultural life from the offices of New York publishers."[86] Despite the existence of "infinite variations in American life" and "congeries of regions," the "nationalism" of historians persisted and "served primarily to advance the ends of controlling groups in urban districts of the northeastern region."[87] This nationalist tendency only intensified during the postwar era.

Earlier pockets of regional emphasis in history departments and their one-time regional loyalties were largely overwhelmed by the exponential growth in the discipline and its efforts to professionalize itself. In 1889 at Wisconsin, when Turner began his effort to reduce the influence of eastern historians who emphasized a "national" history, albeit one dominated by the development of the East, he was the only member of the Wisconsin faculty who taught history.[88] Before World War II, Wisconsin's history department still numbered less than ten faculty members, but by the 1960s its history department had grown to seventy members.[89] By that time, Wisconsin was training 650 graduate students in history and was awarding sixty PhDs a year.[90] Gone were the early years of the department when it was strongly oriented toward Turner and his work on the Midwest and the department was deemed the "Turnerverein."[91] The booming Wisconsin "multiversity" became too "huge" to maintain the old ways.[92] The influence of Turner and Wisconsin was also once strong in Berkeley because of the leadership of Herbert Bolton, who was from Wisconsin, had earned his B.A. at Wisconsin, and relied on Wisconsin for new PhDs to hire.[93] This influence continued into the 1930s, when Berkeley employed fifteen history faculty members, but it disappeared by the 1960s, when the Berkeley history department grew to sixty-five members and the Boltonian influence had long since vanished.[94]

Overall, the size of the history professorate grew five-fold from 1940 to 1970, and, in comparison to the 150 doctorates in history offered annually during the 1930s, by the 1960s it granted one thousand new PhDs annually, a vast expansion of the profession that fostered the creation of new journals and the growth of new subdisciplines.[95] Universities created fifty new doctoral programs in history during the postwar years.[96] Nearly half of the history PhDs awarded to that point in the entirety of American history were granted during the 1960s.[97] Where the once-small number of historians had caused the professional societies to fill their positions by "reaching down to small colleges and institutions of the second rank," the surplus of historians and larger departments after the war meant these positions were filled by historians from a "handful of major

universities" and thus caused a growing "elitism" within the profession.[98]
During this great boom, roughly a dozen schools came to dominate the history profession and tended to "monopolize the better jobs."[99] Because of the
rapid expansion, the large-scale postwar university had also become a "hopelessly impersonal institution, mired in bureaucracy and operating like a large
corporation."[100] Such changes caused a "decline of regional loyalties, a greater
'nationalization' of historical consciousness"; and, as Peter Novick explained
in his history of the profession, "regionalism could not survive the ridicule and
silent contempt of more cosmopolitan historians."[101] The "old guard" of the
MVHA lost out in the "general nationalization of consciousness among American historians" as its old midwestern-oriented organization faced growing
pressure from younger scholars to transform itself into a nationally oriented
association.[102] The vast expansion of historical subdisciplines was also premised on what Michael Kammen called the embrace of "cosmopolitanism"
and the transcendence of what Theodore Hamerow called the profession's
previous "provincialism."[103] A new "fragmentation and rootlessness" prevailed,
Hamerow noted, in place of the profession's former regional orientation.[104]

As the new profession was decoupled from any regional grounding, historians became less embedded in the local cultures where they taught. New
professional demands and new sources of funding changed the direction of
research and lessened local commitments. "Foundation grants to visit London
or Rome," Novick observed, "were in every way more rewarding than fees for
lectures to women's clubs or book reviews for newspapers."[105] The professionalization of hiring decisions resulted in the employment of fewer professors
with roots in their institution's region.[106] The formerly strong role of state historical societies diminished as more historians joined professional groups and
the historical societies chose their own paths, ultimately forming the American
Society for State and Local History.[107] The MVHA also abandoned its formerly
strong emphasis on working with local high school teachers and improving
high school history.[108] The "inward turn" in the profession deemphasized
"service" to the local community, emphasized "academic professionalization,"
and rewarded writing for a "strictly academic" audience instead of a broader
public.[109] The animus of professional historians was increasingly directed at
popular history writers, who were once active participants in midwestern history projects.[110] During World War II, efforts to recruit non-historians into the
MVHA "virtually ceased."[111] The rapid demise of the freelance historians was

protested by Allan Nevins, who found his "affection for history" as a "child in an Illinois farmhouse" and was educated at the University of Illinois.[112] Nevins had worked as a journalist, and then, in a turn of events that are astonishing in distant retrospect, he became a professor of history at Columbia and continued to write popular histories and protest against the prominence of "dryasdust monographers" who were "chiefly responsible for the present crippled gait of history in America."[113] Nevins made a persuasive case from a powerful platform, but it could not counteract the trends in the discipline. After World War II, the "academic boom swept away the last remnants of the amateur tradition."[114]

The swift growth and professionalization of academic history included a strong inclination toward social science and new subfields of historical inquiry, both of which tended to undermine the previous emphases of the midwestern historians. The rise of social science became attractive to many younger historians based on its perceived potential for original findings, its "scientific" basis, and its generous support by foundations.[115] Foundation grants determined academic research agendas and caused more academics to embrace foundation-favored social science projects that were considered "new" and methodologically innovative and aimed at promoting social reforms.[116] Some historians who were previously focused on the Midwest delved deeply into the social science arena.[117] They did so in part due to what Paul Gates recognized as an "increasing tendency to scoff at history," a discipline that was not known to engage in the large cooperative research projects such as those carried on by social scientists and funded by foundations (traditional historians continued to "function as lone wolves").[118] Ray Allen Billington and others worried that social sciences such as anthropology, sociology, and psychology were beginning to overshadow history, which was being "relegated to the background" of academia.[119] Those who failed to embrace social science techniques in their historical research were seen as "hacks, dullards, old fogies, and sticks-in-the-mud."[120] Those who embraced social science, however, were seen as bringing a "surge of cosmopolitanism" to the profession.[121] The fear of being left behind and seeming out-of-date and provincial only added to the long-standing fear among intellectuals, especially those who sympathized with the village rebellion school of thought, that they alone stood against the "threatening hordes of Babbitry" in the country.[122]

Social science also generated new historical themes aimed at undermining what had been key assumptions of midwestern history. Richard Hofstadter, for example, embraced social science and theories of status anxiety to completely overturn long-standing conclusions about the "myths of agrarian life" and the democratic and egalitarian nature of Populism and to emphasize the movement's irrationality, backwardness, and anti-Semitism as well as its "retrograde" and "vicious" elements.[123] No interpretive maneuver "reverberated more widely throughout the culture," Peter Novick argued, than the postwar assault on Populism, the effects of "which spread throughout the social sciences and the intellectual world at large."[124] The Populists "came to be portrayed as a backward-looking band of nativist book burners obsessed with imaginary grievances."[125] Many prominent intellectuals took to blaming "agrarian radicalism" and "provincial communities" and their alleged anti-intellectualism for the sins of McCarthy of Wisconsin, who personified "all the hostilities of the midwestern mind."[126] The "entire midwest Old Guard Republican wing" of the 1950s was seen as descending from the "Populist lunatic-fringers."[127] Other scholars, relying on the ascendant theories of the increasingly influential Frankfurt School, found in the Populists the basis for the "authoritarian personality" that made possible totalitarian regimes;[128] midwesterners such as John Hicks were left to defend the Populists.[129] Hicks thought that Hofstadter could understand urban America but had a "sophisticated New Yorker's lack of understanding of the rest of the country."[130] Such regionally based objections lost their influence, however, and Hofstadter's great popularity during the postwar years, along with the supportive work of his academic allies, allowed him to dominate the historical debate.

As the influence of the Frankfurt School suggested, Marxist theory also continued to animate scholarship and to enliven the debates of public intellectuals, but it also highlighted the double-sided nature of the attack on Turner during the postwar period that contributed to his work's declining fortunes. Some Marxist-oriented scholars, beginning in the 1930s, criticized Turner for his failure to highlight economic conflict, including Louis Hacker and Matthew Josephson;[131] midwestern historians rose to Turner's defense in response to these early attacks. Hicks, for example, was exasperated with "Hacker's eternal harping on the class struggle."[132] He rejected the attacks on Turner because Turner "did not bother to reconcile his every statement with the gospel according to Karl Marx."[133] Hicks similarly expressed his great annoyance with the Yale historian George Wilson Pierson's crusade against Turner.[134]

Pierson's anti-Turner book was billed as a critique of the "Foundations of the Middle Western Tradition."[135] Turner was also criticized by Benjamin Wright for being too "middle western" and "provincial" and for perpetuating a "myth" of midwestern development.[136] Curti thought Wright suffered from a "kind of snobbishness, a kind of Tory way."[137] In 1943, Edward E. Dale noted that the attacks on Turner were coming from "younger men, generally from the East, who knew Turner very slightly if at all, and whose knowledge of the changing West [was] purely academic."[138]

This early form of Marxist criticism of Turner persisted in some circles, but in the postwar period Turner was subjected to another line of criticism from a more prominent set of scholars that also undermined his work, especially its regionalist nature. Some historians argued that regional distinctions and more general divisions in American life had been exaggerated by historians such as Turner. This new "consensus" school held that conflict in the nation's past was largely superficial and that a broader adherence to essential principles had prevailed throughout American history. "No interpretative tendency of the 1950s was more typical" of the consensus movement, Novick concluded, than the attack on the Populists, who were simply seen by consensus scholars as business-oriented and property-seeking Americans, not as dissenters from the main currents of American political culture.[139] Similarly, no emphasis faded more quickly in the glare of the consensus school, John Higham argued, than regionalism and its focus on the nation's internal diversities.[140] Consensus history was the "antithesis," according to Laurence Veysey, of an "earlier accent upon regions and contrasts within America itself."[141] Turner's work was also frequently linked to Charles Beard—often quite clumsily—and other economic determinists, and they were collectively dismissed as part of a fading "progressive school" of history too wedded to a simplistic "The People v. The Interests" mode of interpretation.[142] The decline of progressive history, which found support at Wisconsin, and the rise of consensus thinking signaled the ascendance, as Wisconsin historian William Hesseltine argued, of the "Harvard-Columbia axis," at least for the moment, which afforded less credence to regional distinctions and interior-coastal conflicts.[143] Some critics of Turner's supposed embrace of progressive history and the proponents of the consensus school were not, it should be emphasized, enthusiastic about the American consensus that they thought had dominated American history, and they were critical of its dullness and its tendency to promote conformity, which they often saw as typified by the narrowness of life in the small-town Midwest, a line of criticism that had earlier taken the form of the village revolt but that was stretched into the postwar era to include the blandness of Eisenhower (an imagined Kansas rube who preferred to read Zane Grey novels and play golf) and suburban drones in grey flannel suits.[144]

If Marxist theory remained a current in intellectual discourse and fueled debates over economic policy and cultural politics, many historians, particularly those associated with the consensus school, remained standard-issue New Deal liberals, as suggested by the sighs of relief at the final passing of the Eisenhower era and the election of John Kennedy (when the more stylish Kennedy was elected president, young liberals such as Paul Gates could finally feel a "breath of fresh air . . . emanating from the White House").[145] They therefore tended to be supportive of the Roosevelt legacy and the continuation of his program and to be highly skeptical of his critics, who often took cues from prominent postwar politicians from the Midwest who had once embraced isolationism and remained pro-business and anti-statist, such as Senators Everett Dirksen of Illinois, Arthur Vandenberg of Michigan, and Robert Taft of Ohio.[146] "Many historians, almost certainly the majority of younger historians," Novick explained in his chronicle of the profession, "were either New Dealers or critics of Roosevelt from the left."[147] The lure of politics for historians, Theodore Hamerow also noted, was "almost always liberal, almost always Democratic."[148] In the years after World War II, as the large cadre of younger historians became increasingly critical of American society, the profession underwent a major shift to the left.[149] In one survey, 66 percent of historians called themselves "left" or "liberal."[150] During the 1964 presidential race, 90 percent of historians supported Johnson; and, in 1968, 80 percent supported Humphrey.[151] Older historians of a different stripe necessarily felt marginalized in this new era. James Malin of Kansas, for example, a historian who continued to focus on the Midwest and plains and who remained a critic of the New Deal, was deemed by younger historians as "off balance or more bluntly crazy."[152] Paul Gates, an activist liberal of a newer generation, was "continually shocked" by Malin's "conservative outlook, being quite in tune with that of Herbert Hoover in 1928."[153] Malin felt "censored" but said he did "not intimidate easily" and refused to "wear anybody's muzzle."[154] R. Carlyle Buley also resented younger and more liberal scholars who were attempting to change the focus of MVHA and end its midwestern orientation.[155]

The political preferences among historians and other intellectuals of the era were highlighted by their growing concerns over the "new right," a movement often associated with the American Midwest. While McCarthy of Wisconsin made the most noise and sparked many public recriminations from intellectuals that not infrequently redounded to his home region, there was also another more intellectual ripple of conservatism from the Midwest that drew public and scholarly interest and denunciations during the 1950s. In 1953, most prominently, a young professor in the Department of the History of Civilization at Michigan State University named Russell Kirk published *The Conservative Mind*.[156] Kirk, who was raised in rural Michigan, called for the preservation of place, for resistance to the growing power of the federal state, and for the preservation of older customs and forms of community, and he called himself a "Northern Agrarian" (he also criticized the rapid growth and bureaucratization of the postwar university).[157] Kirk's work grew out of his strong interest in the midwestern regionalist writer and humorist George Ade, who worked with other Indiana writers to advance regionalist themes, and Kirk formed the George Ade Society to preserve his legacy.[158] When Kirk began the organizational work necessary for a new conservative journal of thought during the 1950s, he argued strongly in favor of a plan to "place particular reliance upon writers and thinkers of the Middle West" and to "employ the talents available in the Middle West and the Lake States" in order to give the "Middle West some voice."[159] Kirk planned to publish the journal in the Midwest in order to counteract the "concentration of publishing in New York City" and its "tight circles of New York writers."[160] He thought a "profound misunderstanding of the temper and character of Middle Western life and opinion exists in the Eastern United States, and abroad, because serious thought in the heart of our country is represented only very fragmentarily, or not at all, in Eastern journals of opinion."[161] Despite Kirk's efforts, conservatism as an intellectual movement remained small and isolated and often ridiculed (the New York Intellectual Lionel Trilling said conservatives had no ideas, "just irritable mental gestures").[162] While Kirk found favor among a later generation of thinkers during the ascendance of political conservatism in the 1970s, his work was seldom considered in regional terms.

If historians during the 1950s—especially highly influential historians such as Hofstadter—tended to write from a posture of skepticism toward the old isolationist, small-town, agrarian, and anti–New Deal Midwest and this stance tended to marginalize the region, their newer fields of inquiry compounded the seclusion. In the rising field of American Studies, an area that at times seemed amenable to analyses of the older Midwest, one prominent work in particular proved problematic for the Turnerian school and the traditional understanding of the development of the rural Midwest.[163] In 1950, Henry Nash Smith published the still widely cited and popular *Virgin Land*, which sought to undermine the "myths" of the settlement of the agrarian Midwest.[164] Smith argued that Turner's views served to "divert attention" away from the nation's true problems, to foster isolationism, and to generally stymie social progress by privileging the "agricultural interior."[165] Smith privately confessed to an "irritation with the agrarian tradition generally which may owe something to the reactionary (or what seems to me reactionary) attitude of farmers up in this part of the world [Minnesota], who are pretty rockribbed in their allegiance to the more somber and dismal elements in the Republican Old Guard."[166] Smith purposely structured *Virgin Land* to give added emphasis to his attack on Turner and knew his book would raise the "blood-pressure of the historians" who still favored Turner.[167] *Virgin Land* "capped the assault on Turner" during the postwar period by relegating his work to the "ash heap of dead myths."[168] Hofstadter, naturally, praised *Virgin Land* and predicted its wide acceptance because it was "intellectually sophisticated," undermined Turner's "simpler formulas," revealed how the Midwest "nourished isolationism," and generally exposed the false tenets of midwestern agrarianism, and he relied on it heavily in his work.[169] Finally, for Hofstadter, the "pathology" of Turner's frontier was revealed.[170] Smith, whose work was largely an extension of the village revolt tradition, was also more generally hostile to regionalism, which he saw as simply the "fluttering of literary dovecotes," and thought "regionalism almost always succumbs to reactionary impulses";[171] midwestern historians such as Allan Bogue, R. Carlyle Buley, and Vernon Carstensen were, for obvious reasons, perturbed by Smith and *Virgin Land*.[172] The book remained a "sore spot" for Bogue, who thought Smith's cleverness and engaging "style" would "hide a multitude of sins," and he regretted that the "book won Smith much acclaim."[173] Such objections are largely forgotten, however, and *Virgin Land* still remains a widely praised staple of American historiography.[174]

If *Virgin Land* was critical of long-held assumptions about agrarianism and midwestern history and served as a rejection of Turner, other developing and rapidly growing subfields of history largely elided the older Midwest altogether. In the 1950s, for example, historians increasingly focused on cities.[175] Hofstadter pointed to, with relief, the entrance into the profession of a new generation of city kids for whom the "mystique of rural America" meant nothing.[176] Many of these young historians were far removed from the fading rural world of the Midwest and frontier notions of "rugged individualism" and "aggressive masculinity," and they largely found this heritage "overbearing."[177] Their predisposition was to see the city, as Paul Rosenfeld said, as "the rhythm of the age" and to dismiss rural life as backward and repressive, a stance in keeping with the village revolt thesis.[178] For younger historians and devotees of the revolt thesis, theirs was a revolt "from the village to the city, a city synonymous with art and culture, experience and sophistication, possibility and diversity, freedom and individualism, the new and the real."[179] The focus on cities and racial frictions in urban areas along with the rise of the civil rights movement also brought greater attention to African American history, slavery, and the South.[180] The history of racial discrimination, often written with an eye toward supporting the civil rights movement, became one of the great commitments of historians active during the 1950s.[181] Intellectual history also boomed in the years after World War II, and for a time it reigned as the "queen of the historical sciences," generated demand for courses in the field, and consumed the energies of historians such as Merle Curti.[182] Intellectual history necessarily reduced the focus on Ruth Suckow's "folks" and the details of the small-scale, workaday activities chronicled in the early social history written by midwestern historians. James Malin complained of the lessened attention to the "folk process" and the "little things" that concerned "little people" in some "particular time and place," and he noted the "rapid abandonment of local history" and "locality" in favor of "top down" treatments.[183]

In addition, midwestern historians lost some important allies to secession. From the time of the early work of Turner, most historical research on topics in the trans-Allegheny West was considered "western history" even though most of this work was concentrated on the Midwest and conducted at the ascendant and increasingly influential midwestern universities. But by the time of World War II, the far West was no longer the sparsely populated territory of an earlier era in which the universities tended to be weak.[184] As the work on midwestern history began to decline about the time of World War II and state universities and other schools in the far West became much stronger and began to focus on their region, western history began to be associated with the trans-Missouri West, and the Midwest faded from the once-broad formula of western history.[185] When the Western History Association was formed in 1961, it was premised on giving attention to the further West and designed to "fill a void" in the historical profession, drew support from the expanding universities of the trans-Missouri West, and, indeed, drew in some older historians who once focused on the Midwest as the field of midwestern history declined.[186] The California boom of the postwar era was as enticing to historians as to Americans at large and given added force by the institutional influence of the Huntington Library. Ray Allen Billington, who left the Midwest for the Huntington in 1963, lauded California as "out of this world. With perfect weather in the 70s daily, clear skies, mountains to gaze upon, palms and orange trees and camellias all about" and, speaking of the Huntington, a "library that has everything one needs or desires, life could not be sweeter."[187] During the postwar era, Berkeley also became a major force in American intellectual circles in part due to its vast graduate program, which made it the "largest in the world."[188] The rapid ascendance of California and the broader Santa Fe–ification of intellectual life—or the increasing trendiness of western space and natural beauty and deserts and Indian culture that began during the 1920s—drew further energy to the West. The rise of the Western History Association, the emergence of far western research centers and universities, and the drift of the Mississippi Valley Historical Association away from its regional roots increasingly left the history of the Midwest without a scholarly home.

These newer lines of emphasis among historians—whether top-down intellectual history, bottom-up analyses of African American history, or looks toward cities and away from rural life and toward the far West—highlighted the admirable broadening of the profession and its areas of inquiry and the introduction of new and powerful voices into the profession, but not ones that were particularly interested in the Midwest. These new voices took the profession in many new directions and hastened the decline of interest in more traditional areas of study, but they only did so, it must be emphasized, after years of neglect and exclusion, a pattern of discrimination that especially affected Jews. During World War II, in a then-common observation, Cornell historian Paul Gates recognized that a Jewish applicant's "race would not aid him here."[189] But finally—in the wake of World War II, the complete revelations of the European race war, and the wide public acknowledgment of the gas chambers, and in an atmosphere of growing civil rights activism—"anti-Semitism in the historical profession, as in society at large," was seen as an "embarrassing legacy to be exorcised."[190] During the 1950s, several Jewish historians were hired by prominent history departments.[191] These young Jewish historians brought a different set of urban experiences and outlooks and an alternative brand of politics, often radical, to the history profession, all of which contrasted, at times sharply, with the midwestern historians. They were often "New Yorkers with an inbred distaste for the hinterlands," and they led, for example, the criticism of the Populist tradition, which many midwestern historians had treated with appreciation but which some Jewish historians saw as a recipe for totalitarianism (for a less serious view of urban Jewish perceptions of how midwesterners saw Jews, recall the visit of Woody Allen's character to Wisconsin in the "Easter ham scene" of *Annie Hall*).[192]

One Wisconsin graduate student, Richard Schickel, who went on to become *Time* magazine's film critic, captured the differing styles and temperaments between those from the "small-town Midwest" and those from "Jewish leftist backgrounds."[193] He recalled that the midwesterners maintained a steady calm, "a sense that most crises were not terminal, that the seasons, the world, would roll on in their accustomed ways."[194] Graduate students from New York, however, shaped by the "nervous energy" of the metropolis and, in many cases, by their more radical roots and by living in the shadow of the holocaust, were far from sanguine. Schickel noted that while the "WASPs had a healthy sense of security about history's reliable course, the Jews had an equally healthy sense of its unreliability."[195] The perceptiveness of Schickel's observation surely applies to Turner, who was known for his camping and fishing trips to northern Wisconsin, his leisurely summers on the coast of Maine, and, not coincidentally, his low scholarly productivity. Turner said that while he had "found abundant opportunity for conflict with other men in the field," he never thought it "was worth while to get 'het up' over the matter."[196] Turner's measured mode of tweedy contemplation was imperiled in an age of extremes. During the crisis atmosphere of the war years, Willa Cather recognized in a letter to Sinclair Lewis that midwesterners were perhaps too naïve about the rise of evil regimes in Europe and were blinded by "incurable optimism and sweet trustfulness" and unable to understand Stalin and Mussolini: "I don't believe we'll waken up to the situation we've drifted into until the knife is at our throat."[197] She worried about those who "will tell you that 'things will come out all right,' just because they always have."[198] Overly rational or simplistic assumptions about the world during the crises of the 1940s increasingly became a target of criticism, and "innocence about history and human nature no longer seemed charming to the postwar intellectuals."[199]

The quiescence of the old Midwest could not survive the crisis atmosphere of the war years—nor, ultimately, could the one-time prominence of the region's historians—and the cultural currents of the 1950s further transformed an intellectual landscape that was already losing its conduciveness to midwestern studies. One moment in Lincoln, Nebraska, captured the coming storm. In 1957, Karl Shapiro, a World War II veteran from Baltimore who had landed in the University of Nebraska English department, received a manuscript in the mail and immediately sat down to read it. His student, Glenna Luschei, remembered Shapiro, after reading the enclosed manuscript in one sitting, concluding that it "will change our lives."[200] The manuscript, Allen Ginsberg's poem "Howl," signaled the coming of the counter-culture, more pronounced modes of rebellion, and more bitter forms of alienation.[201] Ginsberg and his fellow Beats were "strictly a-historical," engaged in a "ritual burning of the past," and viewed history as "an enemy, threatening man with a vicious traditionalism."[202] While some midwesterners rejected the notion of "Howl" as "literature" along with the whole idea of "the San Francisco Renaissance" from which it sprang, a post-"Howl" cultural revolt would nevertheless come, and it would leave some midwestern professors and "uptight Midwest kids" feeling "hopelessly square and 'out.' "[203] The 1960s would bring a greater emphasis on social activism, Marxism, political protest, and cultural rebellion and bring a definite "changing of the guard" in history departments and a quick and "sweeping repudiation of so-called consensus history," which held sway during the postwar years.[204] "Howl" spoke for the critics of conformity during the 1950s (who served as the "prophets of rebellion and the sires of the New Left") and some younger historians (whose "hunger for deviance" contrasted sharply with the "culturally straight" traditions of the midwestern historians of the early twentieth century).[205]

If the immediate postwar years brought one set of challenges to midwestern history—in the form of greater attention to foreign threats, urban areas, and intellectual history and a detour into and emphasis upon southern and western history, while at the same time on a broader intellectual and thematic plane, a general attenuation of regionality, and an emphasis on consensus and its perils—the 1960s brought another. A new generation of

Americanists included a growing contingent of leftist scholars who sparked a series of debates about making history "usable," the lessons of the American leftist tradition, the value of student protest, the failures of past scholarship, and the general need to transform a corrupt nation.[206] While some leftist historians promoted frontal attacks on "the system," others, such as the young and gifted historian Christopher Lasch, followed the revived writings of Antonio Gramsci, the Italian Communist jailed by Mussolini during the 1920s, and embraced a "long-term Gramscian strategy" of working within the university to fight on the "cultural front" to advance the creation of a new culture and "consciousness" more amenable to leftist social goals.[207] Expanding the influence of the left within the university, Lasch argued, was the wise and necessary step toward the "fundamental reform of American society."[208] At Wisconsin, where Turner's promotion of midwestern history had co-existed with a sometimes intertwined tradition of progressive history, the interest in progressive and Marxist history was revived while Turner's project rapidly dwindled.[209] The young historian William Appleman Williams inspired students with his critiques of American foreign policy as the Cold War, especially in intellectual circles, turned increasingly sour. Williams became the "godfather" of the new Wisconsin-based journal *Studies on the Left*, whose opening editorial was a plea to use historical research to advance the "reconstruction of society" and whose pages denounced American "empire."[210] The turn to the left was accelerated by the specter of the draft for many students and, as the war in Vietnam intensified, by what Vernon Carstensen called an already "ugly and despairing" mood during the 1960s.[211]

Any remaining sense of midwestern regionality was an immediate casualty, if its former presence was noticed much at all (the history of the Midwest is perhaps better remembered as an unknown soldier from this era of tumult). Williams's midwestern grounding, for example, was quickly lost in the fray. Williams had a Wisconsin PhD; was from rural Atlantic, Iowa, an admirer of the Populists, and an adherent of Beard's midwestern-oriented critique of the power of eastern capital; was generally sympathetic to an older reform tradition (he dubbed himself a "blue-eyed Iowa socialist"); and, unlike many of the younger and more secular radicals, considered himself a "committed *Christian* socialist" in search of a "Christian Commonwealth."[212] As one Wisconsin professor recalled, Williams "was always looking for the blond and blue-eyed Iowa Socialist, one who shared his own roots, which lay deep in the Iowa prairie."[213]

Williams embraced a "softer kind of Marxism, more idealistic and patriotic," not one grounded in a deep cultural "alienation."[214] Merle Curti recognized that Williams was "very patriotic" and could conceive of an "ideal America" against which he measured his criticisms.[215] Williams's criticism was not grounded in a belief in America as hopelessly corrupt and evil but aimed at pushing the nation toward its ideals. His energy came from what David Brown calls the "Gentile Populism/Progressivism" of the old Midwest and the rational reform efforts of the Populists as well as his fond memories of the family farm in Iowa and its conservative small-town agrarian traditions ("I'm just a little boy from Iowa," Williams said).[216] He was also a navy veteran of World War II with a Purple Heart, and thus his criticisms of foreign policy were more rooted in experience and less in alienation.[217] To Williams's consternation, antiwar and leftist activists dropped the midwestern regionalism out of his critiques of the bloated federal warfare state and his calls for a more decentralized economy in the Jeffersonian tradition.[218] Williams "deplored the extremism and anti-patriotic sentiments of the protesters," their violent tactics, and the embrace of "anti-Amerikanism"; and, while far from anti-Semitic, he was greatly chagrined by the "aggressiveness" of Jewish student rebels, so he finally fled Wisconsin in 1968 and decamped to the quietude of Oregon State University.[219] An older form of progressivism, one grounded in midwestern culture and combined with a more traditional form of regionalism that gave the Midwest a distinctive voice, was being defeated (as the case of Williams demonstrates) by a more generalized leftist tilt in the academy, even in a place such as Wisconsin that had once been strongly midwestern-oriented.

While Williams's work lost some of its regionalist nuance and his New Left followers took his critique in new directions and embraced other rationales for protest, other older emphases of midwestern historians also took on new forms. In the 1960s, a new form of social history began to displace an earlier body of work that was less strident and that had once received a strong emphasis from midwestern historians, including Arthur Schlesinger Sr., who advocated an early brand of social history at the University of Iowa during the 1920s, a social history that was linked to his early life in the Midwest.[220] Schlesinger had been raised in Xenia, Ohio, which he saw as part of the midwestern "valley of democracy," an experience his famous son remembered fondly as an "early immersion in Norman Rockwell–Andy Hardy country."[221] The "thriving rural community" of Xenia (from the Greek for "hospitality"),

Schlesinger Sr. recalled, had one policeman, a dozen churches, big yards, and lots of maples and elms; and, reflecting on his experience there, he thought his "boyhood could hardly have been pleasanter."[222] Schlesinger was educated at Ohio State University, mostly in traditional topics, but he became strongly interested, along with other midwestern historians, in nonelite history. When he returned to teach at Ohio State after graduate school, in an indication of the still-strong nexus between academic history and state historical societies, Schlesinger proposed and then chaired the Ohio Historical Commission, housed at the Ohio State Archaeological and Historical Society, which studied Ohio's role in World War I.[223] In 1919, Schlesinger accepted a generous offer from Dean Walter Jessup to serve as head of the University of Iowa history department.[224] With his new curricular freedom, Schlesinger began offering the nation's first course in social and cultural history to his Iowa students, who "typically came from farms or crossroads villages."[225] Schlesinger also traveled widely giving speeches in Iowa, and his department launched an annual Conference of Teachers of History and Social Studies to aid teachers and to afford them an opportunity to hear prominent speakers, including Hamlin Garland, whose recently published *A Son of the Middle Border* Schlesinger saw as a "minor American classic."[226] Schlesinger's courses and research interests pioneered new emphases on immigrants and African Americans and the extension of history "beyond its Anglo-Saxon base" and brought previously understudied groups into the American historical narrative.[227] After his new emphases were set forth in the book *New Viewpoints in American History* (1922), he then went to work on a multivolume collaborative social history of the United States that he launched with the help of Carl Becker, an Iowan, and edited with the local history oriented historian Dixon Ryan Fox, a project that became the *A History of American Life* series.[228] Schlesinger told his publisher that the project was designed to take American history beyond "party struggles, war and diplomacy," and it began a shift in the profession toward the history of women, African Americans, other ethnic groups, cities, and similarly neglected topics.[229]

In the 1960s, a "new social history" took flight, one much different from Schlesinger's early work, and it captured the scene in many history departments and was enlivened by the era's emphasis on the struggles of disadvantaged groups. Michael Kammen thought the rapidly rising new social history had "actually encircled its sibling disciplines," and its popularity caused older agricultural historians, who had earlier been strongly linked to the rural Midwest, to begin calling themselves social historians.[230] Social history, Robert Darnton noted at the time, "seemed to dominate research on all fronts."[231] By the 1970s the new social history had even overrun standard political history as the most popular field of study in the profession.[232] In contrast to the older form of midwestern social history, however, which had largely focused on describing the everyday lives of people on farms and in small towns or on the lives of common people more generally—or what Beverly Bond called the "prosaic details of a civilization founded upon corn and wheat, upon pigs and cattle, and upon hard, unremitting labor"—the new social history drew its inspiration and theoretical support from the then-popular work of English Marxists such as Eric Hobsbawm and E. P. Thompson and the older writings of Antonio Gramsci.[233] In keeping with the mood of the era, Hobsbawm and Thompson emphasized social revolts, resistance to established regimes, and the potential for revolution, and Gramsci's work, which saw a revival during the 1960s, emphasized how the "cultural hegemony" of dominant groups could be broken and revolution made possible; their disciples followed these themes and frequently emphasized elites' "social control" over nonelites.[234] When Lawrence Goodwyn published his new account of Populism in the 1970s, which criticized the Midwest for undermining the revolutionary potential of the movement, he relied heavily on E. P. Thompson's *The Making of the English Working Class.*[235] The new history was "implicitly subversive" and designed to serve as an "instrument of social reconstruction," and, in its advancement, older forms of history were dismissed as "hackneyed and old-fashioned."[236] Schlesinger's early volumes of social history were "regarded as an insult or a joke."[237] The new social history was written in a different tone and to serve a different purpose than the old midwestern social history, which was more explanative and divorced from instrumental ends and less directed at romanticizing the downtrodden and assigning their activities ideological meaning.[238] Schlesinger later rejected the notion that the "new social historians" of the 1960s had invented social history and criticized their hostility to integrating social history with the larger institutional structures and the political realm.[239] He criticized the new social history for being too technical, too theoretical, unreadable, and incapable of reaching a broader audience and for divorcing the popular public from their history, leaving people "disoriented and lost, not knowing where they have been or where they are going."[240] It was less an account of the lives of "the folks" and more of a search for models of rebellion.

Similar to the transformation of social history, the treatment of the natural world took a new form during the 1960s. Midwestern historians, starting with Turner, had always paid great attention to the impact of geography, nature, landscape, and environmental setting on the settlement experience and the subsequent history of midwestern farming. Place was also an essential component of regionalist writing generally. In the 1960s, however, treatments of nature and the natural setting of human communities became more tightly linked to the budding environmental movement. While midwestern historians had earlier focused on the Midwest as a "physical place," especially as it related to farming, they did not do so as a matter of ecology or necessarily as part of a "movement," although they certainly were interested in progressive-era conservation ideas such as those that created the national forests.[241] But, as Ian Tyrrell observes, "none of this was modern environmental history," which would develop in the 1960s and finally lead to the creation of the journal *Environmental History* in 1977 and be more closely linked to a "global awareness" of environmental problems and premised upon a different set of values, goals, and outlooks and less on particular regional settings.[242] If the early midwestern historians, many of whom were from farm families, focused on vegetation, soil, moisture, and the general natural landscape, it was often with an eye toward chronicling the innovativeness of farming techniques and efficient agricultural production and less with an eye toward the environmental despoliation caused by human activities or toward upholding a critical framework that highlighted and questioned settlers' "conquest" of nature.

All of the new historical themes of the postwar years, the large-scale changes in the postwar historical profession, and the overall diminishment of regionality finally came home to the MVHA, the original site of organized studies of the American Midwest. Soon after the war, a battle broke out within the MVHA over the question of abandoning the organization's regional roots and moving toward a nationally oriented organization. World War II was a "clear dividing line" between an earlier regional focus and a later broadening of the MVHA's conference topics and membership.[243] The nationalizing tendencies of World War II, more than any other force, "reduced the importance of place in the MVHA."[244] Younger, more liberal members of the MVHA spearheaded the charge toward the creation of a new organization and were led by

Ray Allen Billington and Paul Gates, who organized an attempt to change the MVHA's name in 1951.[245] Billington was a Michigan native who, after being kicked out of the University of Michigan for a student newspaper "caper," had been allowed into Wisconsin, where he studied with Frederic Logan Paxson and started attending MVHA meetings. At these meetings during the 1930s, he remembered, "[M]embers were drawn almost entirely from the Mississippi Valley" and "outlanders" were few.[246] Billington, who went on to earn his PhD at Harvard, styled himself as a young liberal reformer and thought the "MVHA programs in the past [had] been too often stocked by unknowns" and that the organization suffered from "mediocrity."[247] Billington praised the rise of the "sturdy young liberal" element in the profession, which, he thought, could challenge the reign of the "reactionaries" within the MVHA.[248] Billington complained, for example, about University of Nebraska historian James Sellers's resistance to change and also about the influence of the "Nebraska matriarchy," which was "strong among the ex-presidents on the board" of the MVHA who had earlier led the organization and maintained its regional orientation.[249] Billington fought the "plot" of these older members to resist changing the organization's name and adopting a national focus and thought newer members would need to "override the Nebraska matriarchy" because, "damn it, something must be done to save a hell of a good organization from the hands of that minority."[250] Gates agreed that the MVHA programs suffered from a narrow approach, showed "little imagination," and needed to become nationally oriented, and he thought the MVHA would remain professionally isolated if its "regional" traditions continued.[251] The organized effort, Billington recalled, to push for "reforms [was] manipulated by a small group led by" Billington and Gates and caused what Billington called the "Five Year War" of the 1950s.[252] The effort to change the MVHA's mission and name was at times conflated with a separate dispute over holding meetings in segregated cities (meetings in segregated cities ceased in 1952 under Merle Curti's leadership), and both operated to create a dualistic "old" versus "new" generational dynamic within the organization.[253]

Some midwesterners within the MVHA, against the swelling tides of the postwar years, sought to maintain a regional focus. In 1951, Indiana University historian R. Carlyle Buley noted to the University of Minnesota historian Philip D. Jordan that some of the "older members" of the MVHA were weary of the "attempt on the part of a few agitators to make something else out of the organization."[254] The "small group of agitators," Buley thought, were all "liberals" and "distinctly unhappy with anything which is a success whether it be the MVHA or the United States of America."[255] These liberals were "brought up" with an inflated sense of the importance of social science, were internationalists and adherents of "Willkie one-worldism," and had "no overlap with, respect for, or concept of the work of the Alvords, Turners, Thwaites's [sic], Quaifes, etc" who had built the MVHA.[256] Buley wrote Curti that he felt "sad" after returning from the spring 1951 MVHA meeting in Cincinnati: "somewhat as if I had lost, or was about to lose, a friend of long standing, that is the Mississippi Valley Historical Association."[257] The older members of the organization who understood its early twentieth-century growth, Buley believed, wanted to stick with the original regional focus of the MVHA.[258] They considered it a "breach of faith" with the founders to abandon their original mission and sought to uphold an "obligation to our guarantors who carried us through the early days and the hard years."[259] The long-time University of Minnesota historian Guy Stanton Ford thought more respect should be paid to the original mission of the MVHA's founders, who intended to study the nation's "whole inland empire, the history of whose settlement, institutions, and influence has been merely scratched."[260] Abandoning the original regional mission of the MVHA in favor of the potential for the national expansion of the organization or "in the interest of big enterprise for material growth," others thought, displayed the "spirit of the advertiser rather than the historian."[261] Others noted with pride the "appropriateness" of a major organization of American historians having "its origins in the great valley which many believe to be the heart of the nation."[262] Some older MVHA members, in keeping with Turner's vision of giving the Midwest a stronger voice in the historical profession, also thought the name change "would allow the eastern establishment to grab control."[263] Buley also did not think the MVHA should be distracted by the "Negro problem" or other social issues, which were more appropriately dealt with via other means: "Keeping an organization out of social reform, religious doctrine, and seventeen other things does not prevent individual members thereof from being interested in same."[264] In the end, the 1951 effort to change the name of the MVHA, an idea first floated during the war, was defeated by mail-in ballot by a vote of 530 to 236.[265] At the same time, the MVHA also "voted overwhelmingly against" attending meetings in segregated cities, a sign that the forces seeking to maintain the MVHA's regional grounding and those opposing segregation were the same, not separate, as suggested by some later accounts.[266]

The proponents of preserving the original mission of the MVHA were ultimately overwhelmed by the large number of younger historians who would enter the profession during ensuing years. In the early 1960s, the movement to change the MVHA's name and mission began again in earnest. The "rapid rate of growth" of the MVHA after the war led to the creation in 1962 of the ominous-sounding Committee on the Future, which was designed to plot a long-term course for the MVHA and determine whether the MVHA should remain "regional."[267] Billington personally chose the chairman and all of the members of the Committee on the Future, which, in keeping with Billington's long-time ambitions, would advance plans to transform the MVHA.[268] Billington, by then chairman of the MVHA Executive Committee (due to a nomination from fellow reformer Paul Gates), urged "hurried action" on a mission change before opponents such as James Olson at the University of Nebraska had a "volcanic eruption," and he believed the "small group of obstructionists centered about Lincoln must be over-ruled."[269] The "Nebraska people," according to the chairman of the Committee on the Future, would wage a "terrific fight" against changing the MVHA's mission.[270] In an opening effort to transform the larger MVHA based on a recommendation from the Committee on the Future, Billington engineered an Executive Committee–led name change of the *Mississippi Valley Historical Review* to the *Journal of American History* without the approval of the general membership.[271] Despite objections that the action was "unwise" and "improper," "was taken in haste" and "without a chance for discussion," and was procedurally inappropriate, Billington, based on a mail-in poll of the Executive Committee, ordered the name of the journal changed.[272] Billington recognized the maneuver as "devious" but said it was done in the name of "progress."[273] Some historians objected to the "parliamentary trickery" of the "hand-picked" and "high-powered futures committee" and criticized the "smoke-filled room deal" and "star chamber proceedings" that led to changing the name of the MVHA's journal.[274] Frederick Merk, a mild-mannered Wisconsinite who replaced Turner at Harvard, wrote Billington a "most ill-natured note . . . questioning the procedures and making it very clear that he considers this virtually a revolution."[275] Opponents recognized that changing the MVHA's journal's name made "inevitable" a name change for the MVHA.[276]

Bill Aeschbacher, a Nebraska PhD and the MVHA secretary-treasurer who had recently moved from Nebraska to become the director of the Eisenhower Library in Kansas, opposed a complete transformation of the MVHA but recognized its "eventual inevitability" despite the efforts of the "Lincoln contingent" to hold out.[277] Opponents of the mission change relied on the "ground of tradition" and "sentiment," but the "younger men feel the issue so strongly" that, Gates thought, the opponents were bound to lose.[278] Sensing the changing climate of opinion, old-timers recognized that "we have just about out-lived our usefulness" to the MVHA.[279] Aeschbacher allied himself with others who opposed changing the MVHA on the basis of "sentiment, tradition and association" but recognized that the "sentiment for a name change in the Association is substantial" and thought opponents would be condemned as "fuddy duddy, sanctimonious, pompous."[280] Aeschbacher noted a time when the MVHA placed a premium on holding meetings in the Midwest so its members could drive by car and routinely attend meetings, but, after World War II, he realized, the "revolution in transportation" and the "advent of the jet airplane in the 1960s" made this early priority obsolete.[281] Aeschbacher realized that the regional roots of the MVHA, both intellectual and physical, were dying.

Unlike the journal name change, the decision to transform the broader MVHA was put to a popular vote, and the rapid growth of the postwar history profession was evident in the final results. In October 1964 the mail-in ballots were counted, and the opponents of the name change were soundly defeated in a "landslide" vote of 2,595 to 661.[282] The quadrupling of the number of voting historians over the 1951 election reflected the rapid growth of the MVHA, the growing power of what Buley called the "great mass of younger historians," and the diminished stature of an older generation of historians with stronger regional loyalties.[283] In 1927 the organization had 921 mostly regional members, but by 1957 the MVHA had grown to 3,119 members and to over 8,000 by 1965.[284] Many of the new historians in the much larger postwar MVHA, Buley thought, simply did "not know the Middle West."[285] The older tradition of focusing on midwestern history by Buley and others was lost in later accounts of the MVHA mission change, which tended to focus on a generic triumph of the young and new over the old and stale. The reminiscences of the victorious reformers embraced a generic narrative of overcoming a "parochial," "provincial," and "regional" past with little recognition afforded to the earlier accomplishments of midwestern historians.[286] During the 1960s and after, the traditions of midwestern history kept alive by the MVHA were lost, and the old MVHA was increasingly "condemned for its provincialism and racial bigotry, or more commonly forgotten."[287] The end of the MVHA was a major blow to midwestern history because it had once "provided an institutional structure in which members could pursue a coherent research program" grounded in a region in contrast to the contemporary "indifference to place."[288]

The forces, considered collectively and in retrospect, that undermined the old school of midwestern history are not shocking, and their enumeration, it must be emphasized, is intended to serve not as a wholesale indictment of them or as a defense of isolationism or a rejection of professionalization or to render judgment on the other forces that caused midwestern history to decline, but simply as an explanation of what happened to a once-vigorous field of study, which is an essential first step toward a recovery of the midwestern past. The older form of midwestern history certainly had flaws and its practitioners could have limited visions and the vast new vistas of historical inquiry opened up in the postwar era and the new voices added to history departments surely improved the profession. The new profession would include what the Nebraskan Louis Hartz called "new fundamental categories" of thought and historical analyses that deserve applause, but it also abandoned, too hastily and with too little consideration, old ones.[289] To recall the one-time prominence of the field of midwestern history and the reasons for its demise is not to categorically reject the new but designed to serve, as John Higham once wrote, as an "appeal for cultivating inclusive sympathies."[290] It is to diagnose the cause of our current regional blindness, to call forth some forgotten voices of midwestern history, and to help broaden, once again, our field of vision to include the American Midwest.

# CONCLUSION

## AGAINST SUBORDINATION, TOWARD REVIVAL

That regionalism and its variants such as midwestern history have retreated so far into the recesses of the historical imagination fails to shock in an age of globalization and omnipresent mass culture stimuli and in an intellectual atmosphere shaped by scholars unconscious or dismissive of or even hostile to regionalist perspectives and values. The historian Robert Johnston, for example, argues that scholars should "radically subordinate" regionalism in their research because it causes them to lose sight of other, for Johnston, more critical trans-regional factors in American life and because the "regional" designation causes otherwise weighty historical research to be trivialized.[1] While Johnston wisely cautions against the dangers of overemphasizing regionalism, there remain meaningful regional dimensions to our lives that persist and that should, at a minimum, be recognized and, more ambitiously, be encouraged. Artificially suppressing these regional sentiments is at best imprudent and condescending and at worst mildly totalitarian, a move toward silencing an otherwise healthy component of American pluralism. Recognizing regionalist currents, finding regional voices to express them, preserving some capacity for the maintenance of regional cultures, protecting regionalism against the flood of outside generica and other sundry coercions, and acknowledging regionalism's invigorating effects on local community and political participation are all worthy goals for the civically inclined and those engaged in intellectual life— goals that might also appeal to a broader audience of prospective regionalists who are weary of the detached frivolousness of a hollow mass culture—and deserving of emphasis and focus, not suppression and subordination.[2] The challenge facing the proponents of these goals is glaringly illumined, however, by the call for regionalism not simply to be quashed, but "radically" so.

Exploring and appreciating worthy but neglected subfields of scholarship such as midwestern history can serve as one form of recognizing regionalism and resisting the urge to subordinate it to other priorities. To see midwestern history, if such a category of analysis is recognized at all, merely in terms of its role in revolting against small-town and rural folkways—or as part of the modernization narrative of the 1920s, which is the extent of the treatment of the region in many historical surveys—obscures more vital components and traditions of midwestern life. Solely focusing on the supposed midwestern village rebels only contributes to the further subordination of the region by spotlighting its alleged regressiveness and excluding more representative regionalist voices, both literary and historical. Listening, instead, to these voices can help locate another dimension of the Midwest that can be lost to other emphases and agendas. The Midwest—if distorting interpretative fogs and the clutter of other agendas are cleared away, and if forgotten midwestern regionalist voices are recalled and an older school of midwestern history is revived and put to work in the service of regionalism—can be found again.

A new midwestern history and regionalist movement will be different from the pre–World War II version, however. While a new effort should draw on the older forms of agrarian and small-town regionalism and seek to reintroduce them to a world that has long-since forgotten their one-time salience, it should also amplify some voices, including the African Americans who were first starting to become a significant presence in the Midwest in the pre–World War II era, and, in more recent years, Hispanics. It should also grapple with the long-run consequences of farm mechanization, industrialization, suburbanization, and other gathering forces of the early twentieth century that transformed the region. The amalgam of old and new, forgotten and to-be-discovered, and the collisions between them could make a compelling scholarly enterprise, and the early returns for the effort to revitalize the field and overcome decades of neglect are strong. The Midwestern History Working Group, formed in Wisconsin in 2013, became the Midwestern History Association in 2014, the same year the new journal *Middle West Review* was launched; it then was followed by the creation of *Studies in Midwestern History* in 2015.[3] Journals such as *Midwestern Gothic*, *Old Northwest Review*, and *The New Territory* have also been started to publish and study a new era's midwestern literature and advance long-form journalism and creative nonfiction.[4] Rust Belt Chic Press and *Belt Magazine* were launched to publish work focused on the industrial and urban Midwest.[5] The Hauenstein Center at Grand Valley State University in Grand Rapids, Michigan, also hosted midwestern history conferences in 2015, 2016, and 2017. All these developments bode well for a much-needed revival of midwestern studies, and the years ahead may prove to be a golden age for the field.[6]

The encouraging efforts to restore some vital infrastructure to the field of midwestern studies would be further bolstered by greater acceptance in the intellectual sphere. If those inclined toward regionalism and the revival of midwestern history are to resist "subordination"—either through neglect or by way of direct assault by intellectuals who are hostile to the idea of regional history or the region itself—it would be beneficial, for example, if more intellectuals and elites could control their fear of the local and see the benefits of regional perspectives.[7] The University of Minnesota historian Theodore Blegen once rightly noted the provincialism of the supposed cosmopolitan intellectuals and saw regionalism as its reverse, a vista from which to "view the region in relation to the nation and the world."[8] Blegen's fellow midwesterner, Frederick Jackson Turner, once jotted a similar note on his three-by-five card: "Westerners go east and so less provincial than easterners."[9] Regionalism, as Turner emphasized, placed people in a broader perspective, affording them a platform from which to see and interact with and contextualize the world.[10] The historian and cultural critic Christopher Lasch, who grew up in Nebraska, thought the neighborhood and small town were "more truly cosmopolitan than the superficial cosmopolitanism of the like-minded."[11] Lasch embraced the view of the small town as a space of "gregarious habits" that encourages "conversation, the essence of civic life," and as imbued with a "capacity to provide a window on the outer world."[12] Regionalism, in other words, encourages people to study other places as a function of understanding one's own region—"he knows not England who only England knows."[13]

In addition to providing a broader perspective on a complex world, regionalism can be a stronger basis for grounded citizenship. When endorsing the "cultivation of an intelligent provincialism," George Stewart noted that the "great majority of people are destined to be, in some sense, provincials—and so why not try to make them good provincials, not provincials by prejudice, but by knowing something about their own province for good or bad, and, therefore, better able to function also as citizens of the world."[14] As Robert Dorman has explained, regionalism is primarily an innocent and "soft" form of cultural identity that often takes the form of magazines, journals, art, works of history, museums, public forums, and civic inclinations, not the form of a politically rebellious, separatist, secessionist, or racialist movement, but one that respects American federalism and genuine intellectual pluralism and that seeks a place for all the nation's subcultures.[15] A mild regionalism is certainly preferable to the alternative. When Ruth Suckow discussed the colonialist attitudes of the cosmopolitans—whom she compared to "aesthetic nomads, a flock of cuckoo birds, always trying to make their homes in the nest that other birds have built"—versus the alleged provincialism of midwestern regionalists, she saw the colonialist mindset as "by far the more insidious of the two," one requiring from others a form of submission and an abdication of autonomy.[16]

The benefits of regionalism thus include a civic component related to the desire to avoid domination. "The overcentralization of so many phases of our culture is," Helen Clapesattle of the University of Minnesota Press observed while attempting to promote midwestern regional writing in the 1940s, "a truly unhealthy state of affairs." Clapesattle criticized the persisting power of a "few overdeveloped cultural centers"; rejected the attacks on regional attachments as "separatist sectionalism" and "provincialism" and rejected the insistence that Americans must embrace a "global point of view" at the expense of "home community"; and argued that regionalism's many foes "forget that trying to build a strong nation or a strong family of nations out of weak local communities is like adding a column of zeros; the result will be zero."[17] This was Turner's point about the happy crossroads of democracy and regionalism.[18] During the early twentieth century and in his work on midwestern history, Turner was sounding the themes of local citizenship, republicanism, civic engagement, anti-authoritarianism, and community activism and the ideals of Jeffersonian "independence," which, as Robert Dorman has explained, "resounded throughout regionalist discourse on the folk."[19] Confidence in and loyalty to regions and their traditions, in other words, foster democratic culture.[20]

Resisting charges of provincialism and respecting local and regional cultures involve developing some capacity for resistance to the flood of mass culture produced elsewhere. The early twentieth-century regionalists were especially alarmed at the growing influence of radio and movies and the rise of popular culture fads that episodically churned through the new forms of mass media.[21]

They feared a de-centered "bread and circuses" culture of popular distraction undermining regionalism, active citizenship, and participatory democracy and a mass culture that, as Josiah Royce remarked in his lecture about regionalism at the University of Iowa, produces a "monotonously uniform triviality of mind."[22] Finding a place for their region in the mass culture clatter is what animated midwestern regionalists such as Hamlin Garland, who felt his region and its voices were diluted and suppressed by the cultural domination of New York and Hollywood. As Dorman notes in his recent treatment of western regionalism, Garland and other regionalists "had no explicit concept of cultural hegemony such as we do today, but they knew a monopoly when they saw one."[23] Their anti-monopoly and Populist sentiments, as Christopher Lasch came to see, extended beyond superficial economic questions and were also grounded in their critique of culture and their felt need to mount a resistance to outside cultural domination.[24] They worried about the "continued subservience" of "writers in the hinterland" to New York and the coercive pressure "to write in the Manhattan manner," as one University of Minnesota professor explained in the 1930s, and they sought a "wholesome decentralization of publishing" and a greater "balance" of cultural forces and regional voices.[25] They sought a more open space for the voices of the heartland to be heard and a method of foiling the narrow views of those who thought, as one Harper's editor noted, that "only 'nobodies' lived west of the Alleghenies."[26]

The healthy and democratic urge to resist domination that shaped the work of earlier regionalists—a desire celebrated in many channels of present-day academic discourse, although in different forms and in other contexts—can provide succor and precedent to would-be regionalists in the present and a model for breaking with the mass culture monotony. The forgotten midwesterner Mary Austin, for example, developed her "regionalist sensibility" during her midwestern childhood in Macoupin County, Illinois, in the 1870s and 1880s and did not shy from protesting against the neglect of interior voices.[27] She criticized the "centralization of publishing trades in and around Manhattan" and the fact that most cultural criticism was nothing more than what "a small New York group thinks ought to be written and thought."[28] Iowa-born Frederick Manfred agreed with Austin about the domination of the literary sphere by "cliques, or schools of writing, or fashionable wit-gangs."[29] The Ohioan Louis Bromfield worried that the public believed that the work of the literary world was "conducted upon a pure and holy basis watched over by avenging muses" and was too "innocent of the tricks, the feuds, the cliques, the trading, the bartering that goes on in that world."[30] When John T. Frederick launched *The Midland* in 1915 in Iowa City, E. Bradford Burns explains, he did so out of recognition of the "publishing frustrations of the sons and daughters of the 'middle border.' "[31] Frederick wanted midwestern writers to put down roots in the region and not feel compelled to decamp to New York. "Scotland is none the worse for Burns and Scott," he said by way of comparison to another regional tradition, "none the worse that they did not move to London and interpret London themes for London publishers."[32]

Developing methods of resistance does not mean closing off outside cultural influences. While some prominent regionalist voices such as Lewis Mumford could speak in a "catastrophist" tone, instill a sense of hopelessness and doom in those seeking to keep the flame of local culture alive, and imply the need to build towering levies against the flood of mass culture, others embraced the principle of balance, seeking simply to find space and respect for regionalism by moving it further from the ragged edge of American culture and closer to the national center of thought.[33] Unlike the catastrophists, they believed that local and folk culture "persisted as a living, richly evolving worldview," albeit one under stress from outside pressures, and thought that the folk could be "active conservers and creators of their own culture."[34] People could appreciate local and regional culture, in other words, even as it evolved and recombined and took new forms amidst the cross-currents of mass culture. Folk elements could survive, as Turner said, in "memories, traditions, an inherited attitude toward life" and provide meaning and regional attachments even as the forces of popular culture were sifted through and absorbed or rejected.[35] A middle ground could be staked out between a surrender to mass culture and a self-imposed regional isolation, a space where regionalist thought and culture could breathe and thrive and avoid debilitating losses and total defeat, a form of resistance simply focused on peaceably yet firmly holding some hills and valleys, not on winning a culture war by defeating the invading forces of mass culture all along the line.

Seeking balance should not mean passivity or passionless plodding, how-ever, or quietly and submissively retreating to those aforementioned hills and valleys, a meek survivalism premised on acquiescence. Regionalism requires active agents of propagation. A bit more fire in the regionalist belly, in short, is in order. One of the sources of inspiration often cited by early twentieth-century regionalists, for example, was the revival of Irish culture during an age when Ireland sought its independence from England and freedom from centuries of subjugation.[36] Recognizing the regionalists' invocation of the Irish cause can be a source of fire, one used to spark regionalist sentiments generally and, more specifically, a revival of midwestern history. In his brilliant book on the Irish immigration to the American West, David Emmons explains how the Irish "forgot nothing and—since much of what happened to them was hard and cruel—forgave little."[37] This made the "Irish different from the Americans," whose "past was so much happier and more triumphant," and, more particularly, different from midwesterners, who, as Walter Havighurst once noted, enjoyed a "generally happy history."[38] The power of Irish memories stemmed from their "ability to tether one generation to those that came before it, to keep the past alive and lively."[39] So the "Irish looked downward to where they had been," while the Americans "looked outward toward where they were going."[40] The Americans at times chronicled the segments of their past, including the settlement of the Midwest, but they did so in a formal and serious way, producing a history that "did not need to be particularly memorable because it did not need to be remembered."[41] But now, after decades of decline, it does. We need to be a bit more Irish about the regionalist tradition and our midwestern history and treat them as causes worth fighting for, and the organizational efforts of early twentieth-century historians and writers and their institutional underpinnings may well serve as models of future action.[42]

Fighting to revive midwestern studies is a worthwhile cause not simply because of the Midwest's recent marginalization in the historical annals but also, as many scholars have noted, because there is much worth remembering and celebrating.[43] The early Midwest was the place that the first genuinely American tradition of democracy took root, after all, and where the democratic tradition expanded to include more of the republic's citizens and a functional ethnic pluralism took root.[44] Social critics such as John Dewey even recognized the civic and social value of the Midwest "prairie country" and saw it as the "solid element in our diffuse national life" that "held things together and [gave] unity and stability," a region Ruth Suckow deemed "the solid center, the genuine *interior*," or what Diane Johnson sees as a "calm center," indifferent or resistant to the "shifting values and faddish self-doubts of coastal America."[45] Dan Guillory sees in the Midwest "a reassuring sobriety and decency in human relations, a sense of moderation and social optimism that sustains even the smallest transactions and accounts for generosity on a heroic scale."[46] When Wallace Stegner pointed to the successes of midwestern regionalism, he high-lighted, for example, the "stability and conservatism" of Iowa and saw it as "solid cultural earth for [Iowa] artists to dig in."[47] Princeton sociologist Robert Wuthnow, who was born on a Kansas wheat farm, has recently updated this assessment and noted the continuing strength of the region's civic institutions in the decades after World War II.[48] These treatments are cited not with the intention of arguing that the Midwest is inherently superior or flawless but to bolster the justification for taking the Midwest and its history seriously once again. While some intellectuals and exiles from the region may have lost the thread and come to see the Midwest as the "ragged edge of the universe," in the words of Fitzgerald, there exists an important counter-tradition that includes those who saw it and still see it as the "warm center of the world" and worthy of a history and a presence in the main channels of academic and popular thought.

If democratic and civic energies are made stronger by regionalism and, in particular, by midwestern regionalism, they might also gain from a corre-sponding leavening of the corrosive cynicism that pervades contemporary culture. To understand or even appreciate a region is to afford some commit-ment to it, to elevate it, if only slightly, and even to protect it from degrading clichés and the realm of easy cynicism, or to recognize some qualities long associated with the Midwest. One early twentieth-century reporter from New York noted of the Midwest an "absence . . . of that temper and spirit of 'smart-ness' and flippancy so noticeable in the East. . . . Every man who approaches a stranger is taken to be honest until he proves to be otherwise."[49] This was a posture toward the world that contrasted with the popular leader of the anti-midwestern mindset, H. L. Mencken, who "had grown too hard to pity anyone foolish enough to believe in anything."[50] Mencken may have once been considered edgy and smart, but the social costs of his cynicism now abound, and, after a century, his protests seem entirely unnecessary. When intellectuals started assaulting the Midwest and making claims for the village revolt, there was a strong cultural and social tradition to assault. But as Cynthia Ozick has remarked, by the 1970s "no question remained that was forbidden in polite society, and no answer either; there was little left of the concept of polite society altogether. . . . Babbitt and H. L. Mencken's booboisie were routed."[51] The assault on the supposed repressiveness of interior small towns and social codes that animated American intellectual life for decades was in the later twentieth century "reduced to a pointless game," as Daniel Joseph Singal explained, and by the 1960s was already "becoming overripe and starting to caricature itself."[52] Ozick worries about the old American writers and traditions simply becoming "toys for our irony" and the new tendency to "value irony more than dignity."[53] She dares to suggest the wisdom of recovering some older traditions and strains of thought and the need to seek relief from the "irony, satire, condescension, and the always arrogant power of the present to diminish the past."[54]

If a regionalist consciousness is to dampen our cynicism and bolster community participation and the rudiments of democracy in places such as the Midwest, however, the elements of regionalism must be revived and brought to a broader audience. One crucial element of this consciousness is a sense of regional history, which has been sadly neglected in the Midwest for a half century. This history can be found again if scholars can break the cycle of neglect, overcome decades of inertia, combat persisting stereotypes, tap an older tradition of historiography, and combat the unhealthy urge to subordinate regionalism. If they can, American pluralism and the democratic tradition will be more robust, and the stories of regions such as the Midwest will be heard again, not as distant echoes from the ragged edge, but in the form of rooted voices from the solid center of the nation.

# NOTES

INTRODUCTION

1   Kenneth Winkle, "'The Great Body of the Republic': Abraham Lincoln and the Idea of a Middle West," in *The Identity of the American Midwest: Essays on Regional History* (Bloomington, Indiana University Press, 2001), 113 (quotations); David D. Anderson, "The Dimensions of the Midwest," *MidAmerica* vol. 1 (1974), 7–8; Jon K. Lauck, "Why the Midwest Matters," *Midwest Quarterly* vol. 54, no. 2 (Winter 2013), 171–73.

2   Bernard DeVoto, *The Literary Fallacy* (Boston, Little, Brown, 1944), 157.

3   Oscar Lovell Triggs (ed), *Selections from the Prose and Poetry of Walt Whitman* (Boston, Small, Maynard & Company, 1898), 194–95.

4   Albert Bushnell Hart, "The Future of the Mississippi Valley," *Harper's Magazine* vol. 101 (February 1900), 413. On the region's prominence during this era, see also Cameron Blevins, "Space, Nation, and the Triumph of Region: A View of the World from Houston," *Journal of American History* vol. 101, no. 1 (June 2014), 129.

5   Anderson, "A New Testament," *Little Review* vol. 6, no. 6 (October 1919), 6. The *Little Review* was founded in Chicago by Margaret Anderson, who was from Columbus, Indiana.

6   Turner to Carl Becker, March 10, 1916, in Wilbur Jacobs, *The Historical World of Frederick Jackson Turner* (New Haven, Yale University Press, 1968), 143 (quotation); Turner, "Significance of the Mississippi Valley in American History," *Proceedings of the Mississippi Valley Historical Association* vol. 3 (1909–1910),

159–84. Turner's work was "widely recognized at the time as a formal proc-
lamation that the Middle West had reached cultural maturity and must
henceforth be taken into account in the world of art and ideas as well as in the
world of business and politics." Henry Nash Smith, "The West as an Image of
the American Past," *University of Kansas City Review* vol. 18 (1951), 36.

7    See chapters 2 and 3 in Jon K. Lauck, *The Lost Region: Toward a Revival of
Midwestern History* (Iowa City, University of Iowa Press, 2013).

8    Peter Y. Paik, "Introduction," in Marcus Paul Bullock and Peter Y. Paik (eds),
*Aftermaths: Exile, Migration, and Diaspora Reconsidered* (New Brunswick, Rutgers University Press, 2008), 3 (uprootedness); Anne Firor Scott, "On Seeing
and Not Seeing: A Case of Historical Invisibility," *Journal of American History*
vol. 71, no. 1 (June 1984), 8 (vision, unseen); Michael O'Brien, "On Observing
Quicksand," *American Historical Review* vol. 104, no. 4 (October 1999), 1202
(etiolated); Edward Watts, "The Midwest as a Colony: Transnational Regionalism," in Timothy R. Mahoney and Wendy J. Katz (eds), *Regionalism and
the Humanities* (Lincoln, University of Nebraska Press, 2008), 168. On the
"lack of a vocabulary" or a "critical category" for understanding regionalism
in contrast to the categories of race, class, and gender, the academic "zoning
restrictions" that inhibit regional studies, and how a regional focus can be a
"kiss of death" for writers, see Michael Kowaleski, "Writing in Place: The New
American Regionalism," *American Literary History* vol. 6, no. 1 (Spring 1994),
174–76 (quotations); Alvin Kernan, *In Plato's Cave* (New Haven, Yale University Press, 1999), 246–50. On how the training of professional historians
"inculcates an indifference to place," see David Glassberg, *Sense of History:
The Place of the Past in American Life* (Amherst, University of Massachusetts
Press, 2001), 112 (quotation); John A. Jakle, *My Kind of Midwest: Omaha to
Ohio* (Chicago, The Center for American Places, 2008), 47.

9    Herbert Krause, "A Note on the Possibilities of South Dakota Writing" [1955],
in Arthur R. Huseboe (ed), *Poems and Essays of Herbert Krause* (Sioux Falls,
Center for Western Studies, 1990), 208; James McManus, "Your What Hurts?"
in Becky Bradway (ed), *In the Middle of the Middle West: Literary Nonfiction
from the Heartland* (Bloomington, Indiana University Press, 2003), 15. There
has been, Michael Rosen says, "no cachet to being a midwestern writer."
Michael J. Rosen, "Is There a Midwestern Literature?" *Iowa Review* vol. 20,
no. 3 (Fall 1990), 100. Edward Watts argues that midwesterners are "written
out" of scholarship, owing to the "self-referentiality of the coastal cultural,

academic, and publishing centers of the nation." Watts, "Re-centering the Center," *American Literary History* vol. 21, no. 4 (Winter 2009), 860. On intellectuals who feel "stuck" in the Midwest, see Robert Hellenga, "Rural Writers," in Bradway (ed), *In the Middle of the Middle West*, 200.

10   Willa Cather, *On Writing: Critical Studies on Writing as Art* (New York, Alfred A. Knopf, 1949), 94.

11   August Derleth, *Three Literary Men: A Memoir of Sinclair Lewis, Sherwood Anderson, Edgar Lee Masters* (New York, Candlelight Press, 1963), 33 (quoting Anderson).

12   Ben Zimmer, " 'Bicoastalism': A Long Flight to 'Mad Men,' " *Wall Street Journal*, April 18, 2014. See Diane Johnson, *Flyover Lives: A Memoir* (New York, Viking, 2014); Jon K. Lauck, "Born in a Small Town," *Claremont Review of Books* (Summer 2014), 1–3; Cary W. de Wit, "Flyover Country," in Andrew Cayton, Richard Sisson, and Christian Zacher (eds), *The American Midwest: An Interpretive Encyclopedia* (Bloomington, Indiana University Press, 2007), 66–68; Matthew Wolfson, " 'Flyover Country' Is an Insult to Midwesterners Like Me. So Is 'Heartland' Sentimentality," *New Republic*, March 22, 2014; Luke Rolfes, *Flyover Country* (Georgetown, Kentucky, Georgetown Review Press, 2015); Cheryl Unruh, *Flyover People: Life on the Ground in a Rectangular State* (Emporia, Quincy Press, 2011) and *Waiting on the Sky: More Flyover People Essays* (Emporia, Quincy Press, 2014); Will Weaver, "Midwestern Voice: Still Listening," *Middle West Review* vol. 2, no. 1 (Fall 2015), 123–28.

13   David D. Anderson, "Notes toward a Definition of the Mind of the Midwest," *MidAmerica* vol. 3 (1976), 9. Anderson, an Ohio native, found the cartoon "peculiarly unfunny."

14   Robert L. Dorman, *Hell of a Vision: Regionalism and the Modern American West* (Tucson, University of Arizona Press, 2012), 13–14 (resistance); Frederick Jackson Turner, "Is Sectionalism in America Dying Away," *American Journal of Sociology* vol. 13, no. 5 (March 1908), 661–62; Donald G. Holtgrieve, "Frederick Jackson Turner as a Regionalist," *Professional Geographer* vol. 17 (May 1974), 159–65; Donald Davidson, *The Attack on Leviathan: Regionalism and Nationalism in the United States* (Chapel Hill, University of North Carolina Press, 1938), 13–17; Richard W. Etulain, *Re-imagining the Modern West: A Century of Fiction, History, and Art* (Tucson, University of Arizona Press, 1996), 107; David M. Wrobel, "Beyond the Frontier-Region Dichotomy," *Pacific Historical Review* vol. 65, no. 3 (August 1996), 420, 426.

15  Turner to Theodore Blegen, March 16, 1923, FF Turner, 1923, Box 6, Blegen Papers, University of Minnesota Archives.

16  Josiah Royce, "Provincialism," in *Race Questions, Provincialism, and Other American Problems* (Freeport, New York, Books for Libraries Press, Inc., 1967 [1908]), 57–108; John T. Frederick, "Ruth Suckow and the Middle Western Literary Movement," *English Journal* vol. 20, no. 1 (January 1931), 3; Morton and Lucia White, *The Intellectual versus the City: From Thomas Jefferson to Frank Lloyd Wright* (Cambridge, Harvard University Press, 1962), 179–83; Dorman, *Hell of a Vision*, 9, 64; Michael C. Steiner and David M. Wrobel, "Many Wests: Discovering a Dynamic Western Regionalism," in *Many Wests: Place, Culture, and Identity* (Lawrence, University Press of Kansas, 1997), 1 (on the "long series of death knells for the West and other American regions"); Jay B. Hubbell, "The Decay of the Provinces," *Sewanee Review* vol. 35 (1927), 486; Joan Shelley Rubin, *The Making of Middle Brow Culture* (Chapel Hill, University of North Carolina Press, 1992), 29.

17  Royce, "Provincialism," 74; Tremaine McDowell, *American Studies* (Minneapolis, University of Minnesota Press, 1948), 83–84.

18  "Phi Beta Kappa Address; Provincialism The Cure for Mob Spirit; Professor Royce of Harvard Discusses Interesting Problems in Scholarly Manor," *Daily Iowan*, June 12, 1902; E. Bradford Burns, *Kinship with the Land: Regionalist Thought in Iowa, 1894–1942* (Iowa City, University of Iowa Press, 1996), 25; Robert V. Hine, "A Centennial for Josiah Royce," *California History* vol. 66, no. 2 (June 1987), 90, 93; Robert V. Hine, "The Western Intellectual Josiah Royce," *Montana: The Magazine of Western History* vol. 41, no. 3 (Summer 1991), 71; Stow Persons, *The Decline of American Gentility* (New York, Columbia University Press, 1973), 250–52.

19  Robert L. Dorman, *Revolt of the Provinces: The Regionalist Movement in America, 1920–1945* (Chapel Hill, University of North Carolina Press, 1993), 17 (quotations); Mary Austin, "New York: Dictator of American Criticism," *The Nation*, July 31, 1920.

20  Robert Loerzel, "The Origins of the Society of Midland Authors," in Jon K. Lauck (ed), *The Midwestern Moment: The Forgotten World of Early Twentieth-Century Midwestern Regionalism* (Hastings, Nebraska, Hastings College Press, 2018).

21  David M. Wrobel, *Global West, American Frontier: Travel, Empire, and Exceptionalism from Manifest Destiny to the Great Depression* (Albuquerque, University of

New Mexico Press, 2013); Michael C. Steiner, "Regionalist Thought in the Midwest," paper presented at the First Annual Midwestern History Conference, Grand Valley State University, Grand Rapids, Michigan, April 2015; Benjamin T. Spencer, "Regionalism in American Literature," in Merrill Jensen (ed), *Regionalism in America* (Madison, University of Wisconsin Press, 1951), 231–38.

22  Walter Lippmann, *A Preface to Morals* (New York, Macmillan Company, 1929), 8; Lynn Dumenil, *Modern Temper: American Culture and Society in the 1920s* (New York, Hill and Wang, 1995), 148.

23  Dorman, *Revolt of the Provinces*, xii (source of quotation), 19.

24  A. T. Volwiler to L. C. Wimberly, April 17, 1943, FF 2, Box 1, Wimberly Papers, University of Nebraska Archives (cow); Martin Severin Peterson, "Regional Magazines," *Prairie Schooner* vol. 3, no. 4 (Fall 1929), 295; Lowry Charles Wimberly, "The New Regionalism," *Prairie Schooner* vol. 6, no. 3 (Summer 1932), 214, 220–21; Kathleen A. Boardman, "Lowry Charles Wimberly and the Retreat of Regionalism," *Great Plains Quarterly* vol. 11 (Summer 1991), 143–56. Wimberly was part of the "midwestern circles" of regionalists discussed by Robert Dorman. Dorman, *Revolt of the Provinces*, 45.

25  Edward Hoagland, "But Where Is Home?" *New York Times Book Review*, December 23, 1973.

26  Kent C. Ryden, *Mapping the Invisible Landscape: Folklore, Writing, and the Sense of Place* (Iowa City, University of Iowa Press, 1993), 294; Lucy R. Lippard, *The Lure of the Local: Senses of Place in a Multicentered Society* (New York, The New Press, 1997), 25. Wilbur Zelinsky notes that regions live on despite the "virtually universal" belief to the contrary. Zelinsky, *Not Yet a Placeless Land: Tracking an Evolving American Geography* (Amherst, University of Massachusetts Press, 2011), 1–2.

27  George R. Stewart, "The Regional Approach to Literature," *College English* vol. 9 (April 1948), 372; Raymond D. Gastil, *Cultural Regions of the United States* (Seattle, University of Washington Press, 1975); Colin Woodard, *American Nations: A History of the Eleven Rival Regional Cultures of North America* (New York, Viking, 2011); Jim Wayne Miller, "Anytime the Ground Is Uneven: The Outlook for Regional Studies and What to Look For," in William E. Mallory and Paul Simpson-Housely (eds), *Geography and Literature: A Meeting of the Disciplines* (Syracuse, Syracuse University Press, 1987), 2–3, 10; Martin Ridge, "The American West: From Frontier to Region," *New Mexico Historical Review* vol. 64, no. 2 (April 1989), 136, 140. For mid-twentieth-century evidence that

the "minority culture of the province is making its commentary upon the dominant rootless civilization," see Cleanth Brooks, "Regionalism in American Literature," *Journal of Southern History* vol. 26, no. 1 (February 1960), 36.

28  Robert D. Kaplan argues that "we all need to recover a sensibility about time and space that has been lost in the jet and information ages" or face greater foreign policy challenges from the "revenge of geography." Kaplan, *The Revenge of Geography: What the Map Tells Us about Coming Conflicts and the Battle against Fate* (New York, Random House, 2012), xix, 28. See also David Brooks, "Tribal Lessons," review of Jared Diamond, *The World until Yesterday: What Can We Learn from Traditional Societies* (New York, Viking, 2012), in *New York Times Book Review*, January 10, 2013.

29  See regional historian Andrew Cayton's warning to urban historians about the "danger of homogenizing the past, of flattening the very real regional and local idiosyncrasies of nineteenth-century America by making Chicago, Boston, and New Orleans relatively interchangeable settings for fairly predictable dramas." Cayton, "On the Importance of Place, or, a Plea for Idiosyncrasy," *Journal of Urban History* vol. 24, no. 1 (November 1997), 81.

30  In keeping with more recent headlines, the regionalist Lewis Mumford found the origins of regionalism and a "deep-rooted counter-movement to modernism" in places such as Catalonia, Provence, and Brittany during the eighteenth and nineteenth centuries. John L. Thomas, "Lewis Mumford: Regionalist Historian," *Reviews in American History* vol. 16, no. 1 (March 1988), 166 (quotations); Donald Davidson and Theresa S. Davidson, "Regionalism," *Modern Age* vol. 37, no. 2 (Winter 1995) (originally written in 1955), 102–15; Celia Applegate, "A Europe of Regions: Reflections on the Historiography of Sub-national Places in Modern Times," *American Historical Review* vol. 104, no. 4 (October 1999), 1157.

31  Jon K. Lauck (ed), *The Interior Borderlands: Regional Identity in the Midwest and Great Plains* (Sioux Falls, Center for Western Studies Press, forthcoming in 2018); Kim Ode, "Does Minnesota's Region Have an Identity Crisis? What If Minnesota Gave the Cold Shoulder to the Midwest? A Panel Explores Ways to Forge and Reflect Regional Identity, with a Nod to the North," *Star Tribune*, November 20, 2014; Kent Blaser, "Where Is Nebraska, Anyway?" *Nebraska History* vol. 80 (1999), 3–14; James D. McLaird, "From Bib Overalls to Cowboy Boots: East River / West River Differences in South Dakota," *South Dakota History* vol. 19, no. 4 (Winter 1989), 455–91;

Soo Oh and Ryan Mark, "Which States Do You Think Are in the Midwest?" *Vox*, January 27, 2016 ("No topic provokes as much of an impassioned [and polite] discussion from our dear midwestern friends and colleagues as which states are part of the Midwest"). A 2016 poll found that 82 percent of Missourians thought that Missouri was in the Midwest while 13 percent thought it was in the South. "Trump Leads in Missouri," Public Policy Polling, July 15, 2016.

32    Bill Holm, "Is Minnesota in America Yet?" in Mark Vinz and Thom Tammaro (eds), *Imagining Home: Writing from the Midwest* (Minneapolis, University of Minnesota Press, 1995), 178.

33    Stegner, *The American West as Living Space* (Ann Arbor, University of Michigan Press, 1987), 22.

34    Wallace Stegner and Richard Etulain, *Stegner: Conversations on History and Literature* (Reno, University of Nevada Press, 1996, revised edition), xv. Stegner said, "The Middle West is there from the eastern edge of Indiana clear to the Rocky Mountains, practically—at least clear to the Missouri—all one homogenous thing . . . [b]ut the West is several different regions." Stegner and Etulain, *Stegner*, 155–56. In contrast to other regions, the midwestern historian Frederic Logan Paxson once noted that the Midwest "induced a settled habit." Frederic Logan Paxson, *When the West Is Gone* (New York, Henry Holt and Company, 1930), 85.

35    Burns, *Kinship with the Land*, 25.

36    Stegner and Etulain, *Stegner*, 148; Stegner, *American West as Living Space*, 69–73.

37    Stegner and Etulain, *Stegner*, 148.

38    Stegner and Etulain, *Stegner*, 190 (healthy); Stegner to John T. Frederick, December 8, 1942, John T. Frederick Papers, University of Iowa Archives; Stegner, "The Trail of the Hawkeye," *Saturday Review of Literature*, July 30, 1938, 16–17.

39    Suckow, "Middle Western Literature," 175.

40    Hildegarde Hawthorne, "A Middle West Chronicler," *New York Times Book Review*, July 30, 1922.

41    Carl Jung noted the costs of losing touch with one's home, including "alienation" and "rootlessness," and others recognized the "acute sense of psychic damage" that attended the loss of traditional places. Leonard Lutwak, *The Role of Place in Literature* (Syracuse, Syracuse University Press, 1984), 214

(alienation, rootlessness), 216 (acute). See also William Leach, *Country of Exiles: The Destruction of Place in America* (New York, Pantheon Books, 1999), which is dedicated to the memory of Christopher Lasch, who embraced this theme late in his life. See Jon K. Lauck, "The Prairie Populism of Christopher Lasch," *Great Plains Quarterly* vol. 32, no. 3 (Summer 2012), 183–205. Recent social science research indicates that a critical ingredient of psychological health is a knowledge of one's family history and roots. Bruce Feiler, "The Stories That Bind Us: Children Who Know Their Family's History Are Better at Facing Challenges," *New York Times*, March 17, 2013. See also Emily Esfahani Smith, "Relationships Are More Important than Ambition: There's More to Life than Leaving Home," *Atlantic Monthly*, April 16, 2013.

42  Pico Iyer, *The Global Soul: Jet Lag, Shopping Malls, and the Search for Home* (New York, Alfred A. Knopf, 2000), 5. On the "psychic cost of moving," see Louise DeSalvo, *On Moving: A Writer's Meditation on New Houses, Old Haunts, and Finding Home Again* (New York, Bloomsbury, 2009), 4. For a thorough review, see Edward Relph, *Place and Placelessness* (London, Pion Limited, 1976).

43  Lippard, *Lure of the Local*, 7; Brooks, "Regionalism in American Literature," 36; Jon K. Lauck, "Finding the Rural West," in David Danbom (ed), *Bridging the Distance: Common Issues in the Rural West* (Salt Lake City, University of Utah Press, 2015), 7–34.

44  For a brilliant treatment of feelings of homesickness and rootlessness from a historical perspective, see Susan Matt, *Homesickness: An American History* (New York, Oxford University Press, 2011) and "Home, Sweet Home," *New York Times*, April 19, 2012.

45  Brown quoted in Mary Swander, "The Roosting Tree," in Vinz and Tammaro (eds), *Imagining Home*, 41. In contrast to Brown's local focus, John Dewey once noted the "languid drooping interest" in national and international news. John Dewey, "Americanism and Localism," *The Dial*, vol. 68 (1920), 684.

46  Lawrence Durrell, "Landscape with Literary Figures," *New York Times*, June 12, 1960. See also Nathan Glazer, "Foreword," in Gastil, *Cultural Regions of the United States*, viii; Steiner and Wrobel, "Many Wests," 6–7; Liisa Malkki, "National Geographic: The Rooting of People and the Territorialization of National Identity among Scholars and Refugees," *Cultural Anthropology* vol. 7, no. 1 (February 1992), 26; Elizabeth Raymond, "Learning the Land: The Development of a Sense of Place in the Prairie Midwest," *MidAmerica* vol. 14

(1987), 31; Mary Austin, "Regionalism in American Fiction," *English Journal* vol. 21, no. 2 (February 1932), 97.

47  Lippard, *Lure of the Local*, 7.

48  Even geographers have difficulty seeing regional distinctions within the country, according to D. W. Meinig, "American Wests: Preface to a Geographical Interpretation," *Annals of the Association of American Geographers* vol. 62, no. 2 (June 1972), 159. For University of Minnesota geographer John Fraser Hart's attempt to persuade geographers to focus less on theory and statistics and more on region and place in the face of much professional resistance, see John Fraser Hart, "The Highest Form of the Geographer's Art," *Annals of the Association of American Geographers* vol. 72, no. 1 (March 1982), 1–29. Hart's efforts to "pump life into a dying corpse" were in vain and resulted in a "dull thud," and, as a result, regional geography "has now fallen into desuetude." Hart to author, August 20 and 22, 2013. See also Anssi Paasi, "Region and Place: Regional Identity in Question," *Progress in Human Geography* vol. 27, no. 4 (2003), 11 (explaining how "regional geography narratives have lost their validity in academic research"). On the disappearance of regional sociology, see John Shelton Reed, "Sociology and the Study of American Regions," *Appalachian Journal* vol. 7, no. 3 (Spring 1980), 171.

49  Constance Rourke, "The Significance of Sections," *New Republic*, September 20, 1933, 150 (stubborn); Ruth Suckow, "The Folk Idea in American Life," *Scribner's Magazine* vol. 88 (September 1930), 246; Wendy J. Katz and Timothy R. Mahoney, "Regionalism and the Humanities: Decline or Revival?" in Katz and Mahoney (eds), *Regionalism and the Humanities* (Lincoln, University of Nebraska Press, 2008), ix (impulse); Dorman, *Hell of a Vision*, 15; Reed, "Sociology and the Study of American Regions," 175–77; Ira Sharkansky, *Regionalism in American Politics* (Indianapolis and New York, The Bobbs-Merrill Company, Inc., 1970), 5; Karen Halttunen, "Groundwork: American Studies in Place," *American Quarterly* vol. 58, no. 1 (March 2006), 1–15 (noting recent attention to regionalism).

50  The Royal Commission on Local Government in England and Wales found that one's attachment to one's "home area" was stronger the longer a person lived there and was strongest if it was one's birthplace. Relph, *Place and Placelessness*, 31.

51  Relph, *Place and Placelessness*, 18, 30. Relph notes that an "outsider can in some senses see more of a place than an insider." On the one extreme, Relph notes

an "existential outsideness" or complete placelessness more common in the twentieth century, a "selfconscious and reflective uninvolvement, an alienation from people and places, homelessness, a sense of the unreality of the world, and of not belonging" in comparison to a "full range of possible awareness [of place], from simple recognition for orientation, through the capacity to respond emphatically to the identities of different places, to a profound association with places as cornerstones of human existence and individual identity." *Place and Placelessness*, 51, 62–63.

52   Yi-Fu Tuan, "Rootedness versus Sense of Place," *Landscape* vol. 24 (1980), 3–8; Steiner, "Regionalism in the Great Depression," 434. A new arrival has the benefit of seeing a place with fresh eyes but also, as James Wood notes, must overcome the "light veil of alienation thrown over everything" caused by some degree of displacement. Wood, "On Not Going Home," *London Review of Books* vol. 36, no. 4 (February 20, 2014), 5.

53   Tuan, "Rootedness versus Sense of Place," 4. Place, according to Karen Halttunen's rendering of Tuan's work, "is about being-in-the-world, about pausing and resting, belonging and becoming involved." Halttunen, "Groundwork," 5. Relph adds that place can be found "by association with local events and the development of local myths and by being lived in," such as American settlers who "were making a place authentically through their own labour and through a commitment to a new way of life." Relph, *Place and Placelessness*, 71.

54   Stafford, "Regionalism, Localism, and Art," *South Dakota Review* vol. 13 (1975), 47.

55   Jackson first started to record regional differences after "seeing the American countryside with fresh eyes" after having battled his way across Europe with the American army during World War II, according to Helen Lefkowitz Horowitz, "J. B. Jackson and the Discovery of the American Landscape," in John Brinckerhoff Jackson, *Landscape in Sight: Looking at America* (New Haven, Yale University Press, 1997) (edited by Horowitz), xix. Jackson said, "I *see* things very clearly, and I rely on what I see. . . . And I see things that other people don't see, and I call their attention to it." Horowitz, "J. B. Jackson and the Discovery of the American Landscape," in Jackson, *Landscape in Sight*, xxiv (Jackson quotation and italics in original). Tuan's essay, quoted above, was published in *Landscape*, a journal Jackson founded in 1951. Horowitz, "J. B. Jackson and the Discovery of the American Landscape," in Jackson, *Landscape in Sight*, xx. On the process of observing the small towns of the American

interior, see Jackson's essay "The Almost Perfect Town," in *Landscape in Sight*, 31–42. For one professor's finding of the Midwest, see Dan Guillory, "Being Midwestern," in Bradway (ed), *In the Middle of the Middle West*, 191–99. See also Scott Russell Sanders, *Staying Put: Making a Home in a Restless World* (Boston, Beacon Press, 1993), xiv.

56  Lippard, *Lure of the Local*, 9. On the "invisibility" of the Midwest, see David Radavich, "Midwestern Dramas," in Bradway (ed), *In the Middle of the Middle West*, 188–89.

57  Ruth Suckow, "Middle Western Literature," *English Journal* vol. 21, no. 3 (March 1932), 176. For an attempt to cure this blindness and help others to see the "invisible landscape" around them, see Ryden, *Mapping the Invisible Landscape*. On how such blindness affects the view of the Midwest, see Michael Martone, "The Flatness," in *A Sense of Place: Essays in Search of the Midwest* (Iowa City, University of Iowa Press, 1988), 29–30.

58  Michael Martone, "The Flyover," in Vinz and Tammaro (eds), *Imagining Home*, 7; Janet Wondra, "Mid: One Tentative Taxonomy of a Region," in Bradway (ed), *In the Middle of the Middle West*, 53.

59  Ryden, *Mapping the Invisible Landscape*, 211; Zeiger, "The Personal Essay and Egalitarian Rhetoric," in Chris Anderson (ed), *Literary Non-fiction: Theory, Criticism, Pedagogy* (Carbondale, Southern Illinois University Press, 1989), 237–38; Scott Russell Sanders, "Landscape and Imagination," *North American Review* vol. 274, no. 3 (September 1989), 63. On "not merely looking at a place, but *seeing* into and appreciating the essential elements of its identity," see Relph, *Place and Placelessness*, 54 (italics in original).

60  Wendell Berry, "Writer and Region," *Hudson Review* vol. 40, no. 1 (Spring 1987), 26 (italics in original).

61  Jon K. Lauck, *American Agriculture and the Problem of Monopoly: The Political Economy of Grain Belt Farming, 1953–1980* (Lincoln, University of Nebraska Press, 2000).

62  Jon K. Lauck, *Daschle v. Thune: Anatomy of a High Plains Senate Race* (Norman, University of Oklahoma Press, 2007).

63  Jon K. Lauck, *Prairie Republic: The Political Culture of Dakota Territory, 1879–1889* (Norman, University of Oklahoma Press, 2010).

64  Jon K. Lauck, John E. Miller, and Don Simmons (eds), *The Plains Political Tradition: Essays on South Dakota Political Culture*, 2 vols. (Pierre, South Dakota State Historical Society Press, 2011 and 2014).

65    Lauck, *Lost Region*.

66    F. Scott Fitzgerald, *The Great Gatsby* (New York, Charles Scribner's Sons, 1925), 3, 49, 59, 98–99, 17–18, 181–82. In *My Ántonia*, Jim Burden also felt, at first, that he had passed "over the edge" of the world upon arriving in Nebraska but came to appreciate its beauty and value. Willa Cather, *My Antonia* (New York, Barnes & Noble Classics, 2003 [1918]), 11. For a review of psychological advantages of finding and knowing one's home, see Glassberg, *Sense of History*, 113–15.

67    James R. Shortridge, "The Emergence of 'Middle West' as an American Regional Label," *Annals of the Association of American Geographers* vol. 74, no. 2 (1984), 218.

CHAPTER ONE

1     James R. Shortridge, *The Middle West: Its Meaning in American Culture* (Lawrence, University Press of Kansas, 1989), 8.

2     Phil Stong, "The U.S. in the Middle," *Saturday Review of Literature*, September 17, 1938.

3     Lucy R. Lippard, *The Lure of the Local: Senses of Place in a Multicentered Society* (New York, The New Press, 1997), 85; David Radavich, "Midwestern Dramas," in Becky Bradway (ed), *In the Middle of the Middle West: Literary Nonfiction from the Heartland* (Bloomington, Indiana University Press, 2003), 187.

4     Van Doren typescript "Three Worlds," 137, Box 7, FF 7, Van Doren Papers, Princeton University. *The Nation* was one of the "most admired vehicles for shaping literary opinion during the decade." Gordon Hutner, *What America Read: Taste, Class, and the Novel* (Chapel Hill, University of North Carolina Press, 2009), 52. Van Doren taught English at Columbia from 1911–1930 and called himself an "unbeliever, a scholar and a skeptic." Gloria Lubar, "Carl Van Doren Is Storehouse of Americana," *Washington Post*, December 2, 1945 (quotation); "Carl Van Doren, 64, Noted Author, Dies," *New York Times*, July 19, 1950. In his autobiography, Van Doren confessed to "snobbishness." Van Doren, *Three Worlds* (New York, Harper & Brothers, 1936), 1.

5     Carl Van Doren, "Contemporary American Novelists X. The Revolt from the Village: 1920," *The Nation* vol. 113, no. 2936 (October 12, 1921) (Fall Book Supplement), 407. The essay was reprinted in Van Doren, *The American Novel*,

*1789–1939* (New York, Macmillan, 1940). See also Van Doren, *Three Worlds*, 152. Clayton Holaday noted that the "antivillage view" or revolt thesis was not "precisely identified" until Van Doren's essay. Holaday, review of Anthony Channell Hilfer, *The Revolt from the Village, 1915–1930* (Chapel Hill, University of North Carolina Press, 1969), in *American Literature* vol. 42, no. 2 (May 1970), 262. The narrative of "heroic" writers attacking "ferociously smug" small towns has become a "powerful" force in American literary history, according to Gordon Hutner, *What America Read*, 21. See also Van Doren's chapter entitled "On Hating the Provinces," in *The Roving Critic* (Port Washington, New York, Kennikat Press, Inc., 1923), 83–86.

6 Van Doren, "Revolt from the Village," 407.

7 Van Doren, "Revolt from the Village," 407.

8 Van Doren, "Revolt from the Village," 408–10. In *Main Street*, Nicolas Witschi notes, "contemporary critics such as Van Doren saw nothing less than a wholesale rejection of the fantasy of a livable small-town ethos." Witschi, "Sinclair Lewis, the Voice of Satire, and Mary Austin's Revolt from the Village," *American Literary Realism* vol. 30, no. 1 (Fall 1997), 78. Van Doren wrote to Lewis that *Main Street* was "fearfully truthful," but he also believed that "towns a little bigger than Gopher Prairie seem to me a good deal better than the 3000-population towns." Carl Van Doren to Sinclair Lewis, November 22, 1920, Box 49, FF 630, Lewis Papers, Beinecke Library, Yale University; Mark Schorer, *Sinclair Lewis: An American Life* (New York, McGraw-Hill, 1961), 285.

9 Van Doren, "Revolt from the Village," 412.

10 Frederick Lewis Allen, *Only Yesterday: An Informal History of the 1920s* (New York, Harper & Row, 1964 [1931]), 191, 196; Burl Noggle, "The Twenties: A New Historiographical Frontier," *Journal of American History* vol. 53, no. 2 (September 1966), 300; Charles W. Eagles, "Urban-Rural Conflict in the 1920s: A Historiographical Assessment," *Historian* vol. 49, no. 1 (November 1986), 31; William L. Burton, "'Yesterday' Revisited," *Illinois Quarterly* vol. 36, no. 1 (1973), 49–64. David M. Kennedy concluded that "[m]ore than any other single work, [*Only Yesterday*] has for longer than half a century shaped our understanding of American life in the 1920s," and he saw its "spiritual heart" as "The Revolt of the Highbrows" section. Kennedy, "Revisiting Frederick Lewis Allen's *Only Yesterday*," *Reviews in American History* vol. 14, no. 2 (June 1986), 309, 312. Allen's interpretation coincided "precisely with a vision of the twenties that found great currency during the thirties and that has helped to distort

the history of American fiction." Hutner, *What America Read*, 55. In addition to Allen, the "best example of the revolt against the village is" the essay collection by Harold Stearns, *Civilization in the United States: An Inquiry by Thirty Americans* (New York, Harcourt Brace, 1922). Lynn Dumenil, *Modern Temper: American Culture and Society in the 1920s* (New York, Hill and Wang, 1995), 325 (quotation); Charles C. Alexander, *Here the Country Lies: Nationalism and the Arts in Twentieth Century America* (Bloomington, Indiana University Press, 1980), 90–92; Arthur A. Ekirch Jr., *Ideologies and Utopias: The Impact of the New Deal on American Thought* (Chicago, Quadrangle Books, 1969), 12. One of the "chief themes" of the book, Stearns announced, was that the "most moving and pathetic fact in the social life of America to-day is emotional and aesthetic starvation." Stearns, *Civilization in the United States*, vi–vii. Stearns said that the new intellectuals disliked "almost to the point of hatred and certainly to the point of contempt, the type of people dominant in our present civilization." James H. Shideler, " 'Flappers and Philosophers,' and Farmers: Rural-Urban Tensions of the Twenties," *Agricultural History* vol. 47, no. 4 (October 1973), 289 (quoting Stearns). Stearns and others "left an enduring picture of a barren, neurotic, Babbitt-ridden society." Henry F. May, "Shifting Perspectives on the 1920's," *Mississippi Valley Historical Review* vol. 43, no. 3 (December 1956), 409. Stearns dramatically boarded a ship to Europe as soon as he finished *Civilization* and said he would never return. Richard Lingeman, *Sinclair Lewis: Rebel from Main Street* (New York, Random House, 2002), 180. Although he died before its completion, the revolt thesis was also outlined for the planned final volume of Vernon Parrington's literary history trilogy *Main Currents of American Thought*. See "Addenda" in Parrington, *The Beginnings of Critical Realism in America, 1860–1920* (New York, Harcourt, Brace & World, Inc., 1930), 323–86. On page 373, Parrington notes, "A revolt of the young intellectuals against the dominant middle class—its Puritanism, its Victorianism, its acquisitive ideals: represented by Sinclair Lewis." In 1931, Russell Blankenship offered a similar treatment in *American Literature as an Expression of the National Mind* (New York, Henry Holt, 1931) (note section on "The Attack").

11    Alfred Kazin, *On Native Grounds: An Interpretation of Modern American Prose Literature* (San Diego, A Harvest Book: Harcourt Brace & Company, 3rd edition, 1995 [1942]), 192–94, 197, 205. Merle Curti's *The Growth of American Thought* (New York, Harper & Brothers, 1943) also includes a section on "The Revolt Against the Genteel Tradition," 710–14. See also Granville Hicks, *The*

*Great Tradition: An Interpretation of American Literature since the Civil War* (New York, Biblio and Tannen, 1967 [1935]), 231; and Arthur Moore, "There's Ink in Black Soil," *Chicago Sun Book Week*, May 4, 1947. In an early warning about this line of thought, Bernard DeVoto noted in 1944 that historians were being too accepting of the ascendant literary treatment of the 1920s. DeVoto, *The Literary Fallacy* (Boston, Little, Brown, 1944), 22–23.

12   Henry Steele Commager, *The American Mind: An Interpretation of American Thought and Character since the 1880s* (New Haven, Yale University Press, 1954), 247 (italics added). Richard Hofstadter also included a chapter entitled "The Revolt Against Modernity" in his book *Anti-intellectualism in American Life* (New York, Knopf, 1962), which interpreted an "older, rural and small-town America" as "now fully embattled against the encroachments of modern life." See page 122. In a later book, Hofstadter argued that intellectuals began an "assault on national pieties" that "culminated in the unconstrained frontal attack of the 1920s" and that included a "war" of "metropolitan minds against the village mind." Hofstadter, *The Progressive Historians: Turner, Parrington, Beard* (New York, Knopf, 1968), 86–87. For another prominent historian who was critical of the 1920s, see William E. Leuchtenburg, *The Perils of Prosperity, 1914–1932* (Chicago, University of Chicago Press, 1958), which David Danbom sees as grounded in an "approach which seemed to elevate the satire of H. L. Mencken and Sinclair Lewis to established historical fact." David B. Danbom, "The Professors and the Plowmen in American History Today," *Wisconsin Magazine of History* vol. 69, no. 2 (Winter 1985/1986), 108. Catherine McNicol Stock similarly notes that in place of actual social history too many historians rely on the "uniformly uncomplimentary images of the 'village rebels.'" Stock, *Main Street in Crisis: The Great Depression and the Old Middle Class on the Northern Plains* (Chapel Hill, University of North Carolina Press, 1992), 4. For another invocation of the "drabness of small town midwestern life" and its "provincialism," see Arthur S. Link, *American Epoch: A History of the United States since the 1890's* (New York, Alfred A. Knopf, 1959), 325. For yet another use of the "flatness of small town life" theme, see Samuel Eliot Morison, *The Oxford History of the American People* (New York, Oxford University Press, 1965), 911. See also Robert Spiller et al., *The Literary History of the United States* (New York, Macmillan, 1948), 1181; and Arthur Hobson Quinn, *The Literature of the American People: An Historical and Critical Survey* (New York, Appleton-Century, 1951), 868–86 (on the "Analysts of Decay").

13   *Book-of-the-Month Club News*, September 1961 (featuring the Schorer biography as the cover story and noting that Book-of-the-Month Club books reflected "the unanimous choice" of the board), FF Mark Schorer, August Derleth Papers, Wisconsin Historical Society (WHS); Mark Schorer, *Sinclair Lewis*.

14   Hilfer, *Revolt from the Village*, 251.

15   Richard H. Pells, *Radical Visions and American Dreams: Culture and Social Thought in the Depression Years* (New York, Harper & Row, 1973), 35.

16   Pells, *Radical Visions and American Dreams*, 23, 35.

17   See James M. Cox, "Regionalism: A Diminished Thing," in Emory Elliott (ed), *Columbia Literary History of the United States* (New York, Columbia University Press, 1988), 773.

18   Lynn Dumenil, *Modern Temper: American Culture and Society in the 1920s* (New York, Hill and Wang, 1995), 151–53. In 1992, Gore Vidal also perpetuated the conventional view of the revolt, placing Lewis among the group of writers who were "brought up in similar towns in the Middle West and *every last one of them* was hell-bent to get out." Gore Vidal, "The Romance of Sinclair Lewis," *New York Review of Books* (October 8, 1992) (emphasis added).

19   Christine Stansell, *American Moderns: Bohemian New York and the Creation of a New Century* (New York, Metropolitan Books, 2000), 44, 46.

20   Jerome Loving, "Introduction," in Edgar Lee Masters, *Spoon River Anthology* (New York, Penguin Books, 2008 [1915]), x.

21   Ronald Weber, *The Midwestern Ascendancy in American Writing* (Bloomington, Indiana University Press, 1992), 85, 224 (noting the declining attention to the Midwest as a region and concluding that the "Midwest as a place is more than ever in danger of vanishing completely").

22   Weber, *Midwestern Ascendancy*, 81; Ed Piacentino, "Challenging the Canon: Other Southern Literary Lives," *Southern Literary Journal* vol. 38, no. 2 (Spring 2006), 146; Danbom, "Professors and the Plowmen," 124–28 (noting the intense "anti-rural bias" and the "gratuitous insults" directed toward rural Americans in histories of the 1920s).

23   Barry Gross, "The Revolt That Wasn't: The Legacies of Critical Myopia," *CEA Critic* vol. 30, no. 2 (January 1977), 4–5.

24   Wes D. Gehring, "The Henpecked Hustler," *USA Today*, November 2006; Joan Acocella, "On the Contrary," *New Yorker*, December 9, 2002; Benjamin Schwarz, "Sheer Data," *Atlantic Monthly*, February 2002; Morris Dickstein,

"The Complex Fate of the Jewish-American Writer," *The Nation*, October 4, 2001; Robert Brustein, "The War on the Arts," *New Republic*, September 7 and 14, 1992; Richard Lingeman, "Home Town, USA," *Washington Post*, January 29, 1978; John Blades, "An Age of Innocence Recalled," *Chicago Tribune*, July 2, 1971; Gerald Carson, "Our Towns," *New York Times*, November 15, 1964; Nobuo Abiko, "Revolt from the Village," *Christian Science Monitor*, September 19, 1962.

25  Maurice Beebe, review of David D. Anderson, *Sherwood Anderson: An Introduction and Interpretation* (New York, Holt, Rinehart and Winston, 1967), in *American Literature* vol. 40, no. 4 (January 1969), 571; Hilary Hallet, "Based on a True Story: New Western Women and the Birth of Hollywood," *Pacific Historical Review* vol. 80, no. 2 (May 2011), 207; David Davis, "Regional Criticism in the Era of Globalization," *Modern Fiction Studies* vol. 54, no. 4 (Winter 2008), 847; Evan Brier, "The Accidental Blockbuster: *Peyton Place* in Literary and Institutional Context," *Women's Studies Quarterly* vol. 33, no. 3–4 (Fall 2005), 53; Martha Carpenter, "Susan Glaspell's Fiction: *Fidelity* as American Romance," *Twentieth Century Literature* vol. 40, no. 1 (Spring 1994), 98; Nicolas Witschi, "Sinclair Lewis, the Voice of Satire, and Mary Austin's Revolt from the Village," 79.

26  Hilfer, *Revolt from the Village*, 3.

27  Hilfer, *Revolt from the Village*, 29.

28  Hilfer, *Revolt from the Village*, 158 (italics added).

29  Hutner, "The 'Good Reader' and the Bourgeois Critic," *Kenyon Review* vol. 20, no. 1 (Winter 1998), 23–24; Barry Gross, "In Another Country: The Revolt from the Village," *MidAmerica* vol. 4 (1977), 101–11; Gross, "Revolt That Wasn't," 4–8; David D. Anderson, "Notes toward a Definition of the Mind of the Midwest," *MidAmerica* vol. 3 (1976), 8–10; Marcia Noe, "The Revolt from the Village," *Dictionary of Midwestern Literature* (Bloomington, Indiana University Press, 2016); Abigail Tilley, "*Winesburg, Ohio*: Beyond the Revolt from the Village," *Midwestern Miscellany* (Fall 2003), 44–52. On the growth, more generally, of a "literary genre" that is premised on "condescension and retribution toward one's origins," see Wendell Berry, "Writer and Region," *Hudson Review* vol. 40, no. 1 (Spring 1987), 23.

30  Hilfer, *Revolt from the Village*, 4 (doubly); George F. Day, "The Midwest," in *A Literary History of the American West* (Fort Worth, Texas Christian University Press, 1987), 636 (hick). The "'village' has in nearly all cases been a

small town in the vast agricultural areas of the Middle West." R. T. Prescott, "Ruth Suckow," *Prairie Schooner* vol. 2, no. 2 (Spring 1928), 138. The critics who embraced the revolt thesis "were convinced that provincial life, *especially in the Middle West*, condemned America to the status of second-class culture." Gross, "Revolt That Wasn't," 4.

31  Weber, *Midwestern Ascendancy*, 196–97.

32  Frederick J. Hoffman, *The Twenties: American Writing in the Postwar Decade* (New York, Macmillan, 1949), 369.

33  Van Doren typescript "Three Worlds," 181, Box 7, FF 7, Van Doren Papers, Princeton University.

34  Christopher Lasch, "The Ordeal of Van Wyck Brooks," 3 (source of quotation), manuscript located in Lasch Papers, Rush Rhees Library, University of Rochester; Malcolm Cowley, "Van Wyck Brooks: A Career in Retrospect," *Saturday Review of Literature* (May 25, 1963), 17–18; William Wasserstrom, *Van Wyck Brooks* (Minneapolis, University of Minnesota Press, 1968), 13–14; Casey Nelson Blake, *Beloved Community: The Cultural Criticism of Randolph Bourne, Van Wyck Brooks, Waldo Frank, and Lewis Mumford* (Chapel Hill, University of North Carolina Press, 1990), 17–19.

35  Brooks, *The Wine of the Puritans: A Study of Present-Day America* (London, Sisley's, 1908); Bernard Smith, "Van Wyck Brooks," in Malcolm Cowley (ed), *After the Genteel Tradition: American Writers, 1910–1930* (Carbondale, Southern Illinois University Press, 1964), 59; James R. Vitelli, *Van Wyck Brooks* (New York, Twayne Publishers, Inc., 1969), 79–80; Gorham B. Munson, "Van Wyck Brooks: His Sphere and His Encroachments," in William Wasserstrom (ed), *Van Wyck Brooks: The Critic and His Critics* (Port Washington, New York, Kennikat Press, 1979), 47–48; Daniel Aaron, *Writers on the Left: Episodes in American Literary Communism* (New York, Octagon Books, 1974 [1961]), 10; Paul R. Gorman, *Left Intellectuals and Popular Culture in Twentieth-Century America* (Chapel Hill, University of North Carolina Press, 1996), 56; Blake, *Beloved Community*, 102–5; Joan Shelley Rubin, *Constance Rourke and American Culture* (Chapel Hill, University of North Carolina Press, 1980), 44–49; Jan C. Dawson, "Puritanism in American Thought and Society, 1865–1910," *New England Quarterly* vol. 53, no. 4 (December 1980), 508.

36  Brooks, *America's Coming of Age* (New York, B. W. Huebsch, 1915), 8–15; Van Doren to Brooks, March 13, 1934 (confessing his pleasant memories of discovering the book at Columbia Library and describing how he "read it through

NOTES TO PAGES 15-16

standing on my excited feet") (virtually); and Van Doren to Brooks, March 6, 1934, Folder 2963, Brooks Papers, Annenberg Library, University of Pennsylvania; Richard Ruland, *The Rediscovery of American Literature* (Cambridge, Harvard University Press, 1967), 3, 5, 8; David M. Wrobel, *The End of American Exceptionalism: Frontier Anxiety from the Old West to the New Deal* (Lawrence, University Press of Kansas, 1993), 107–10; Hilfer, *Revolt from the Village*, 113; Kim Townsend, *Sherwood Anderson: A Biography* (Boston, Houghton Mifflin Company, 1987), 118; DeVoto, *Literary Fallacy*, 45, 48, 57; Oscar Cargill, "The Ordeal of Van Wyck Brooks," *English Journal* vol. 35, no. 9 (November 1946), 472; Dayton Kohler, "Van Wyck Brooks: Traditionally American," *English Journal* vol. 30, no. 4 (April 1941), 264. On Brooks's call for revolution, his turn to socialism, and his attraction to Bohemianism, see Casey Nelson Blake, *Beloved Community*, 52–63.

37   Hilfer, *Revolt from the Village*, 114 (villains); Blake, *Beloved Community*, 134; John Patrick Diggins, *The Rise and Fall of the American Left* (New York, W. W. Norton, 1992), 139. On Brooks's view of the "innate depravity and barbarity of the frontier influence," see Donald Davidson, *The Attack on Leviathan: Regionalism and Nationalism in the United States* (Chapel Hill, University of North Carolina Press, 1938), 14. Some critics like Brooks "eagerly awaited" the decline of frontier influences because they saw them as "culturally regressive." David M. Wrobel, "Beyond the Frontier-Region Dichotomy," *Pacific Historical Review* vol. 65, no. 3 (August 1996), 415. The writers in Stearns's influential collection *Civilization in the United States* also criticized the pioneer. See Stearns, "The Intellectual Life," and Van Wyck Brooks, "The Literary Life," 135–50, 183. But, Malcolm Cowley noted, Stearns's writers "knew nothing about vast sections of the country" and were "city men." Cowley, *Exile's Return: A Literary Odyssey of the 1920s* (New York, Penguin Books, 1994 [1951, 1934]), 74.

38   Brooks, *The Ordeal of Mark Twain* (New York, Dutton, 1920), 30, 38. Brooks asked "how can we compare the fertile human soil of any spot in Europe with that dry, old, barren, horizonless Middle West of ours? How was Mark Twain to break the spell of his infancy and find a vocation there? Calvinism itself had gone to seed: it was nothing but the dead hand of custom; the flaming priest had long since given way to the hysterical evangelist." Brooks, *Ordeal of Mark Twain*, 30. See also DeVoto, *Literary Fallacy*, 40–41, 60; DeVoto, *Mark Twain's America* (New York, Little, Brown, 1932), 41. The metaphor is not uncommon. Diane Dufva Quantic notes how the revolt caused critics to

condemn "that intellectual desert, the Middle West." Quantic, "The Revolt from the Village and Middle Western Fiction, 1870–1915," *Kansas Quarterly* vol. 5 (1973), 6.

39  Van Wyck Brooks, *Sketches in Criticism* (New York, E. P. Dutton, 1932), 130 (unlovable); Blake, *Beloved Community*, 104 (grotesque; dignity).

40  Terry Teachout, *The Skeptic: A Life of H. L. Mencken* (New York, HarperCollins, 2002), 178 (kultur; italics in original); Hilfer, *Revolt from the Village*, 121.

41  Allen, *Only Yesterday*, 191.

42  Allen, *Only Yesterday*, 193.

43  Kazin, *On Native Grounds*, 200–201.

44  Hilfer, *Revolt from the Village*, 122, 125, 127.

45  Hilfer, *Revolt from the Village*, 127.

46  Hilfer, *Revolt from the Village*, 129; Don S. Kirschner, *City and Country: Rural Responses to Urbanization in the 1920s* (Westport, CT, Greenwood Publishing, 1970), 17; Shideler, "'Flappers and Philosophers,' and Farmers," 289; Robert Wuthnow, *Red State Religion: Faith and Politics in America's Heartland* (Princeton, Princeton University Press, 2012), 155.

47  Shideler, "'Flappers and Philosophers,' and Farmers," 289 (quotations); Mencken, "The Husbandman," *Prejudices: Fourth, Fifth, and Sixth Series* (New York, Library of America, 2010), 23–33.

48  Joan Acocella, "On the Contrary," *New Yorker*, December 9, 2002. "Never in all history, as Edmund Wilson said, did a literary generation so revile its country; and never, as Mencken proved so unforgettably, was the abuse so innocent or so enjoyable." Kazin, *On Native Grounds*, 192. Mencken's biographer Terry Teachout makes the ironic observation that Mencken had "seen comparatively little of his native land" and suggests that he was "as much of a philistine as the philistines." Teachout, *Skeptic*, 202.

49  Stephen L. Tanner, "Sinclair Lewis and the New Humanism," *Modern Age* vol. 33, no. 1 (1990), 33–35 (quoting Lewis's 1922 statement, "If I had the power, I'd make Henry Mencken the pope of America"); Hilfer, *Revolt from the Village*, 162 (central). Mencken wrote to a friend about Lewis's *Main Street*: "That idiot has written a masterpiece." Teachout, *Skeptic*, 177; Benjamin Schwarz, "Sheer Data," *Atlantic Monthly*, February 2002.

50  Hilfer, *Revolt from the Village*, 29.

51  Van Doren, "Revolt from the Village," 410.

52  Van Doren, "Revolt from the Village," 407.

53  Daniel Joseph Singal, "Towards a Definition of Modernism," *American*

*Quarterly* vol. 39, no. 1 (Spring 1987), 9; James Gilbert, "Many Modernisms," *Reviews in American History* vol. 29, no. 2 (June 2001), 265.

54  Singal, "Towards a Definition of Modernism," 9 (ethos); Daniel Walker Howe, "American Victorianism as a Culture," *American Quarterly* vol. 27, no. 5 (December 1975), 521.

55  Howe, "American Victorianism as a Culture," 515.

56  Hilfer, *Revolt from the Village*, 111.

57  Stanley Coben, "The Assault on Victorianism in the Twentieth Century," *American Quarterly* vol. 27, no. 5 (December 1975), 605.

58  Shideler, "'Flappers and Philosophers,' and Farmers," 286.

59  Jon K. Lauck, "Finding Solace in the Midwest Where It Isn't Supposed to Be," *Flyover Country Review*, vol. 2, no. 2 (April 2015).

60  Coben, "The Assault on Victorianism in the Twentieth Century," 605; Gorman, *Left Intellectuals*, 5; Diggins, *Rise and Fall of the American Left*, 97.

61  Gross, "Revolt That Wasn't," 4.

62  Christopher Lasch, *The New Radicalism in America: The Intellectual as a Social Type* (New York, Knopf, 1965); F. W. Dupee, "The Americanism of Van Wyck Brooks," in Robert Wooster Stallman (ed), *Critiques and Essays in Criticism, 1920–1948* (New York, The Ronald Press Company, 1949), 463; Stow Persons, *The Decline of American Gentility* (New York, Columbia University Press, 1973), 266; Teachout, *Skeptic*, 189 (on the rise of "the adversary culture"). Lionel Trilling called them a "gradually cohering body of dissenters from the orthodoxies of American life." Quoted in Fred Siegel, *The Revolt Against the Masses* (New York, Encounter Books, 2013), 3.

63  Hilfer, *Revolt from the Village*, 30 (source of quotation); Danbom, "Professors and the Plowmen," 106; Russell Lynes, "Intellectuals vs. Philistines," *New York Times*, July 10, 1949 (noting Carlyle's definition of the Philistine as "a man without sentiment, who cares naught for moonlight and music. A low, practical man who pays his debts. I hate him").

64  Allen, *Only Yesterday*, 196; Aram Bakshian Jr., "The *New Yorker* Casts Its Ballot," *National Interest* no. 123 (January/February 2013), 83. The *New Yorker* "reflected [Greenwich] Village's values by flying in the face" of conventional publications. Peter Watson, *The Modern Mind: An Intellectual History of the 20th Century* (New York, HarperCollins, 2001), 217. Lasch also notes the decline of "provincial culture" and the "concentration of cultural life in the city of New York," including the emergence of the *New Yorker*, as a sign of the emergence of a new "intellectual class." Lasch, *New Radicalism in America*, 319–20.

65  Edward A. Martin, *H. L. Mencken and the Debunkers* (Athens, University of
    Georgia Press, 1984), 186. For the debunkers' attacks on midwestern ser-
    vice clubs, see Jeffrey A. Charles, *Service Clubs in American Society: Rotary,
    Kiwanis, and Lions* (Urbana, University of Illinois Press, 1993), 86–89. For the
    view that the debunkers were targeting the Midwest and midwestern service
    clubs, see Thomas S. Hines Jr., "Echoes from 'Zenith': Reactions of American
    Businessmen to *Babbitt*," *Business History Review* vol. 41, no. 2 (Summer
    1967), 127–30 (one *New York Times* interviewee commented, "What gets me
    is why, when these literary fellahs want to get funny about America, they
    always pick on the Middle West"). One Rotary Club president protested
    that his organization was simply about "good fellowship" and working for the
    "good of the community." Schorer, *Sinclair Lewis*, 434. For a review, by the
    midwestern writer Booth Tarkington, of the trendy criticism of Rotary, see
    Tarkington, "Rotarian and Sophisticate," *World's Work* vol. 58 (January 1929),
    42–44, 146.

66  David A. Hollinger, "Ethnic Diversity, Cosmopolitanism, and the Emergence
    of the American Liberal Intelligentsia," *American Quarterly* vol. 27, no. 2 (May
    1975), 133, 135–37. *The Smart Set* was launched in 1900, *Vanity Fair* in 1914, *The
    American Mercury* in 1924, and *The New Yorker* in 1925. Joan Acocella, "On the
    Contrary," *New Yorker*, December 9, 2002. These larger circulation periodi-
    cals were supplemented by various low-circulation "little magazines." Hutner,
    *What America Read*, 52; Frederick J. Hoffman, Charles Allen, and Carolyn F.
    Ulrich, *The Little Magazine: A History and a Bibliography* (Princeton, Princeton
    University Press, 1946).

67  Frederick J. Hoffman, "Philistine and Puritan in the 1920s: An Example of the
    Misuse of the American Past," *American Quarterly* vol. 1, no. 3 (Autumn 1949),
    253.

68  Hutner, *What America Read*, 88 (source of quotation); Rochelle Gurstein,
    *The Repeal of Reticence: America's Cultural and Legal Struggles over Free Speech,
    Obscenity, Sexual Liberation, and Modern Art* (New York, Hill and Wang, 1996),
    128–34; Aaron, *Writers on the Left*, 7–8; Robert T. Handy, "The American Reli-
    gious Depression, 1925–1935," *Church History* vol. 29, no. 1 (March 1960), 6–7.

69  Hoffman, "Philistine and Puritan in the 1920s," 247; Cowley, *Exile's Return*,
    61; Diggins, *Rise and Fall of the American Left*, 139; DeVoto, *Literary Fallacy*,
    35, 52–53; Paul A. Carter, *Another Part of the Twenties* (New York, Columbia
    University Press, 1977), 43–44; Richard H. Pells, *The Liberal Mind in a*

*Conservative Age: American Intellectuals in the 1940s and 1950s* (Wesleyan, Wesleyan University Press, 1989), 118; John Higham, "The Rise of American Intellectual History," *American Historical Review* vol. 56, no. 3 (April 1951), 466. For the Midwest, moreover, the "Puritan" influence was but a fraction of the religious influence in the region, which included large numbers of Catholics, Lutherans, Methodists, and other denominations. Jon Gjerde, *The Minds of the West: Ethnocultural Evolution in the Rural Midwest, 1830–1917* (Chapel Hill, University of North Carolina Press, 1997), 5.

70 Hoffman, "Philistine and Puritan in the 1920s," 263; Teachout, *Skeptic*, 125; Kazin, *On Native Grounds*, 196. On the advantages of having a convenient enemy and, more specifically, the need for a new, more "usable past," Van Wyck Brooks wondered in 1918 if "we might even invent one?" Brooks, "On Creating a Usable Past," *Dial*, April 11, 1918. Brooks's ally Randolph Bourne said, "If there were no puritans we should have to invent them." Hilfer, *Revolt from the Village*, 66.

71 Warren I. Susman, "History and the American Intellectual: Uses of a Usable Past," in Lucy Maddox (ed), *Locating American Studies: The Evolution of a Discipline* (Baltimore, Johns Hopkins University Press, 1999), 31. On Susman's work with Hoffman and his forays into midwestern history, including a possible dissertation entitled "The Middle West: Image and Reality (1890–1930)," see Paul Murphy, "The Last Progressive Historian: Warren Susman and American Cultural History," *Modern Intellectual History* (September 2016), 14.

72 Aaron, *Writers on the Left*, 10–12; Hoffman, "Philistine and Puritan in the 1920s," 252; Edward Abrahams, *The Lyrical Left: Randolph Bourne, Alfred Stieglitz, and the Origins of Cultural Radicalism in America* (Charlottesville, University Press of Virginia, 1986), 6–11; John Strausbaugh, *The Village: 400 Years of Beats and Bohemians, Radicals and Rogues: A History of Greenwich Village* (New York, Ecco, 2013).

73 Harlan Hatcher, *Creating the American Novel* (New York, Farrar & Rinehart, 1935), 77.

74 Warren I. Susman, "A Second Country: The Expatriate Image," *Texas Studies in Literature and Language* vol. 3, no. 2 (Summer 1961), 174, 183; Diggins, *Rise and Fall of the American Left*, 140.

75 Shideler, " 'Flappers and Philosophers,' and Farmers," 294 (Lippmann quote). In *Main Street*, a suffrage leader instructs Carol that the "Middlewest is double-Puritan—prairie Puritan on top of New England Puritan." Sinclair

Lewis, *Main Street* (New York, New American Library, Signet Classics, 2008 [1920]), 462.

76 Cowley, *Exile's Return*, 10.

77 Carl Van Doren to Sinclair Lewis, November 22, 1920, Box 49, FF 630, Lewis Papers, Beinecke Library, Yale University; Coben, "Assault on Victorianism in the Twentieth Century," 606; Richard Handler, "Boasian Anthropology and the Critique of American Culture," *American Quarterly* vol. 42, no. 2 (June 1990), 252–53; Gorman, *Left Intellectuals*, 97.

78 Hoffman, "Philistine and Puritan in the 1920s," 252; James Atlas, *Bellow: A Biography* (New York, Random House, 2000), 50. For a critique of intellectuals' and cultural rebels' exultation of the "primitive" and the neglect of the common life of the Midwest, see Ruth Suckow, "The Folk Idea in American Life," *Scribner's Magazine* vol. 88 (September 1930), 245–55.

79 Coben, "Assault on Victorianism in the Twentieth Century," 606–7; Watson, *Modern Mind*, 277–81; Derek Freeman, *Margaret Mead and Samoa: The Making and Unmaking of an Anthropological Myth* (New York, Penguin Books, 1986).

80 Gorman, *Left Intellectuals*, 99; Michael C. Steiner, "Regionalism in the Great Depression," *Geographical Review* vol. 73, no. 4 (October 1983), 433.

81 Gorman, *Left Intellectuals*, 98.

82 Gorman, *Left Intellectuals*, 91 (model); May, "Shifting Perspectives on the 1920's," 407; Celia Applegate, "A Europe of Regions: Reflections on the Historiography of Sub-national Places in Modern Times," *American Historical Review* vol. 104, no. 4 (October 1999), 1158; Vicente L. Rafael, "Regionalism, Area Studies, and the Accidents of History," *American Historical Review* vol. 104, no. 4 (October 1999), 1209; Michael Kammen, *American Culture, American Tastes: Social Change and the 20th Century* (New York, Knopf, 1999), 140; Nathan Glazer, "The 'Alienation' of Modern Man: Some Diagnoses of the Malady," *Commentary* vol. 3, no. 4 (April 1947), 378–79; Gorman, *Left Intellectuals*, 100; Morton White, *Social Thought in America: The Revolt Against Formalism* (New York, Viking Press, 1949), 180–202. Sociological theory privileged the triumph of the "modern" over the "backward folk." Mary Neth, "Seeing the Midwest with Peripheral Vision: Identities, Narratives, and Region," in *The Identity of the American Midwest: Essays on Regional History* (Bloomington, Indiana University Press, 2001), 836.

83 Coben, "Assault on Victorianism in the Twentieth Century," 608 (quotation); Hutner, *What America Read*, 90–91; Watson, *The Modern Mind*, 212–15;

Christopher Shannon, *Conspicuous Criticism: Tradition, the Individual, and Culture in American Thought, from Veblen to Mills* (Baltimore, Johns Hopkins University Press, 1996), 27.

84  Henry F. May, "Shifting Perspectives on the 1920's," *Mississippi Valley Historical Review* vol. 43, no. 3 (December 1956), 408 (lag). Although often viewed as supporting the village revolt thesis, some sociologists embraced themes supportive of the regionalists' critique of the social costs of a declining rural culture and the growth of urban life. They recognized the costs of breaking away, as one sociologist said, "from home ties, from church affiliations, from moral obligations." Gorman, *Left Intellectuals*, 90. While the prominent sociologist Louis Wirth thought there was relatively "little in the way of sociological study of midwestern towns," he noted that Chicago was "one of the most intensively studied cities in the world." Wirth to Stanley Pargellis, June 27, 1947, NL 03/05/06, Box 2, FF 46, Pargellis Papers, Newberry Library.

85  Hilfer, *Revolt from the Village*, 158 (quotation); Thomas D. Horton, "Sinclair Lewis: The Symbol of an Era," *North American Review* vol. 248, no. 2 (Winter 1939/1940), 381. By seeming sociological, the work thus had a larger impact on historical interpretation. Ronald M. Grosh, "Provincialism and Cosmopolitanism: A Re-assessment of Early Midwestern Realism," *Midwestern Miscellany* vol. 21 (1993), 16; Stephen S. Conroy, "Sinclair Lewis's Sociological Imagination," *American Literature* vol. 42, no. 3 (November 1970), 348–62.

86  Hilfer, *Revolt from the Village*, 159 (quoting Mark Schorer); Weber, *Midwestern Ascendancy*, 147.

87  Schwarz, "Sheer Data."

88  Hilfer, *Revolt from the Village*, 160.

89  Schwarz, "Sheer Data."

90  Kazin, *On Native Grounds*, 194; Lionel Trilling, *The Liberal Imagination: Essays on Literature and Society* (New York, Charles Scribner's Sons, 1950), 34; Cowley, *Exile's Return*, 61; Roderick Nash, *The Nervous Generation: American Thought, 1917–1930* (Chicago, Ivan R. Dee, 1970), 47–49; Watson, *Modern Mind*, 273; Carter, *Another Part of the Twenties*, 38–39; Theodore S. Hamerow, *Reflections on History and Historians* (Madison, University of Wisconsin Press, 1986), 188; Hoffman, Allen, and Ulrich, *Little Magazine*, 170–88; Lawrence R. Samuel, *Shrink: A Cultural History of Psychoanalysis* (Lincoln, University of Nebraska Press, 2013); Frederick Hoffman, *Freudianism and the Literary Mind* (Baton Rouge, Louisiana State University Press, 1957, 2nd edition [1945]),

52–58; C. B. Stendler, "New Ideas for Old: How Freudism Was Received in the United States from 1900–1925," *Journal of Educational Psychology* (April 1947), 202 (connecting the popularization of Freud to the postwar mood and the "*revolt* against the accepted American order" and social mores) (italics added).

91  Hoffman, "Philistine and Puritan in the 1920s," 249.

92  Hoffman, "Philistine and Puritan in the 1920s," 250.

93  Blake, *Beloved Community*, 50–51.

94  Aaron, *Writers on the Left*, 62–64; Ekirch, *Ideologies and Utopias*, 59–61; Dimitri von Mohrenschildt, "American Intelligentsia and Russia of the N.E.P. [1921–1928]," *Russian Review* vol. 6, no. 2 (Spring 1947), 59–60.

95  Trilling, *Liberal Imagination*, vii; Gorman, *Left Intellectuals*, 110; Paul Hollander, *Political Pilgrims: Western Intellectuals in Search of the Good Society* (New York, Oxford University Press, 1980), 76–77; Pells, *Liberal Mind*, 33; and Diggins, *Rise and Fall of the American Left*, 106-7; Hoffman, Allen, and Ulrich, *Little Magazine*, 148–69.

96  Lingeman, *Sinclair Lewis*, 151.

97  Carl Van Doren noted that by 1932 "many of the younger writers in New York were communists or inclined to communism" (he had originally written "most," not "many"). Van Doren typescript "Three Worlds," 286, Box 7, FF 9, Van Doren Papers, Princeton University; Gorman, *Left Intellectuals*, 117 (intensification; proletarian).

98  Gorman, *Left Intellectuals*, 117. Attacks on the middle class were common among intellectuals and writers of the era, and the "great question for many critics was to determine the revolutionary potential" of literary works. Hutner, *What America Read*, 6. The village revolt tradition gave the politically inclined "literary support for theories of sovereignty which assumed that the people were fools and the institutions of a foolish people must be corrupt and contemptible." DeVoto, *Literary Fallacy*, 46.

99  Hilfer, *Revolt from the Village*, 30 (quotation). Van Doren thought the "best American literature has always inclined toward the left." Van Doren, "To the Left: To the Subsoil," *Partisan Review & Anvil* vol. 3, no. 1 (February 1936), 9.

100  Hilfer, *Revolt from the Village*, 31.

101  Hilfer, *Revolt from the Village*, 165.

102  Louis M. Hacker, "Sections—or Classes," *The Nation*, July 26, 1933; Scott C. Zeman, "Historian Louis M. Hacker's 'Coincidental Conversion' to the Truth,"

*Historian* vol. 61, no. 1 (Fall 1998), 89; Diggins, *Rise and Fall of the American Left*, 152; Allan G. Bogue, *Frederick Jackson Turner: Strange Roads Going Down* (Norman, University of Oklahoma Press, 1998), 446–47; Hacker, "Frederick Jackson Turner: Non-economic Historian," *New Republic*, June 5, 1935.

103  Zeman, "Historian Louis M. Hacker's 'Coincidental Conversion' to the Truth," 87; Warren I. Susman, "History and the American Intellectual: Uses of a Usable Past," *American Quarterly* vol. 16, no. 2 (Summer 1964), 258.

104  Susman, "History and the American Intellectual," 254; Wrobel, *End of American Exceptionalism*, 127.

105  Zeman, "Historian Louis M. Hacker's 'Coincidental Conversion' to the Truth," 91.

106  Blake, *Beloved Community*, 134 (negative quote); Susman, "History and the American Intellectual," 256.

107  Susman, "History and the American Intellectual," 258.

108  Turner quoted in Gerald D. Nash, *Creating the West: Historical Interpretations, 1890–1990* (Albuquerque, University of New Mexico Press, 1991), 21, n. 29.

109  The "urban experience" in places such as Greenwich Village served as a contrast with the "revolt from the village that energized many leading figures of the rebellion." Leslie Fishbein, review of Adele Heller and Lois Rudnick (eds), *1915, the Cultural Moment: The New Politics, the New Woman and New Psychology, the New Art, and the New Theatre in America* (New Brunswick, Rutgers University Press, 1999), in *Journal of American History* vol. 79, no. 4 (March 1993), 1648; Danbom, "Professors and the Plowmen," 107.

110  Allen, *Only Yesterday*, 196; Morison, *Oxford History of the American People*, 910; Oscar Handlin, *Truth in History* (Cambridge, Harvard University Press, 1979), 98; Susman, "History and the American Intellectual," 258.

111  Gurstein, *Repeal of Reticence*, 134.

112  Martin, *H. L. Mencken and the Debunkers*, 12, 88.

113  Gurstein, *Repeal of Reticence*, 135.

114  Hilfer, *Revolt from the Village*, 26.

115  Weber, *Midwestern Ascendancy*, 177. Roderick Nash notes how "eager" publishers were to find writers who could muse on life in Paris during the 1920s and how publishers believed the "public appetite for the fabulousness of the 1920s to be unsatiated." Nash, *Nervous Generation*, 18, 20. Welford Dunaway Taylor also notes how the "tastes of the publishing industry have been largely shaped by the native New York ambience." Taylor, "Anderson and the Problem

of Belonging," in David D. Anderson, *Sherwood Anderson: Dimensions of His Literary Art* (Lansing, Michigan State University Press, 1976), 63.

116  Hoffman, Allen, and Ulrich, *Little Magazine*, 8 (quotation); Frederick Manfred, "Milton, Manfred, and McGrath: A Conversation on Literature and Place," *Dacotah Territory* nos. 8/9 (Fall/Winter 1974–1975), 22.

117  Hamlin Garland, "Current Fiction Heroes," *New York Times Book Review*, December 23, 1923. Garland also noted the ratchet effect of fashion on authors and how, to seem edgy, "each must go a little further than his predecessor." Garland, "Current Fiction Heroes." For a scholarly treatment of this warping, see Richard H. Brodhead, *Cultures of Letters: Scenes of Reading and Writing in Nineteenth-Century America* (Chicago, University of Chicago Press, 1993), 115–41.

118  Masters to August Derleth, January 15, 1939, Derleth Papers, WHS.

119  Sara A. Kosiba, "A Successful Revolt? The Redefinition of Midwestern Literary Culture in the 1920s and 1930s" (PhD dissertation, Kent State University, 2007), 100 (italics added); Hutner, *What America Read*, 42; Tremaine McDowell, "Regionalism in American Literature," *Minnesota History* vol. 20, no. 2 (June 1939), 112. Joseph Wood Krutch argued that the "social situation" and the "cultural climate" made Lewis's early books "perfectly apropos" and "strongly favored him." Krutch, "Sinclair Lewis," *The Nation*, February, 24, 1951. By the time Lewis and Anderson published their most remembered village revolt works, Edward A. Martin notes, "contempt for life in the provinces was a fashionable attitude." Martin, *H. L. Mencken and the Debunkers*, 8. On authors who wanted "to sell many copies of a book" by being sensational and the mistake of interpreting this to reflect the wider beliefs of a culture, see Bruce Kuklick, "Myth and Symbol in American Studies," *American Quarterly* vol. 24 (October 1972), 444.

120  *Main Street* was "the most sensational publishing event in twentieth-century American publishing history" in part because of Lewis's marketing. Schwarz, "Sheer Data"; Eileen Power, "New Novels," *New Statesman*, February 4, 1933 (calling Lewis a "publicist rather than an artist"). R. T. Prescott said the revolt "crescendoed in a pyrotechnical detonation in Sinclair Lewis." Prescott, "Ruth Suckow," 138. August Derleth recognized how Lewis's career "throve on adversity." August Derleth to Sinclair Lewis, October 5, 1937, Box 46, FF 488, Lewis Papers, Beinecke Library, Yale University. Hemingway, whose family had deep midwestern roots, thought Lewis was "exploiting" his topic. Weber,

*Midwestern Ascendancy*, 161; James Nagel, "The Hemingways of Oak Park, Illinois: Background and Legacy," in Nagel (ed), *Ernest Hemingway: The Oak Park Legacy* (Tuscaloosa, University of Alabama Press, 1996), 3–12. Lewis was intense about publicity, shrewdly business-like with editors, insistent on the broad distribution New York publishing houses could provide, and willing to browbeat writers such as Frederick Manfred about abandoning a St. Paul publisher—a lowly "Midland outfit"—in favor of New York outlets. "Got to have a big house in the East," Lewis said, or "you're writing in a wilderness, in a vacuum. To nobody." Frederick F. Manfred, "Sinclair Lewis: A Portrait," *American Scholar* vol. 23, no. 2 (Spring 1954), 179–82; Lewis to Frederick Manfred, February 10, 1946, and Manfred to Van Wyck Brooks, May 6, 1946, Box 13, Manfred Papers, Upper Midwest Literary Archives, University of Minnesota; Manfred, "Some Notes on Sinclair Lewis' Funeral," *Minnesota Review* vol. 3, no. 1 (Fall 1962), 89; Nancy Bunge, "The Minnesota School: Sinclair Lewis's Influence on Frederick Manfred," *North Dakota Quarterly* vol. 70 (Winter 2003), 118. When choosing the name for his novel *Babbitt*, Lewis made his choice carefully and correctly believed that "two years from now we'll have them talking of Babbittry." Weber, *Midwestern Ascendancy*, 165. On Lewis's obsession with marketing, publicity, and winning prizes and his attempts to disguise such ambitions, see Martin Light, "A Further Word on Sinclair Lewis' Prize-Consciousness," *Western Humanities Review* vol. 15 (Autumn 1961), 368–71. Gore Vidal noted that as "a careerist, Lewis was an Attila. In his pursuit of blurbs, he took no prisoners." Vidal, "Romance of Sinclair Lewis," 16. Brooke Allen also noted Lewis's "insatiable need for attention." Brooke Allen, "Sinclair Lewis: The Bard of Discontents," *Hudson Review* (Spring 2003), 193. On the intense marketing of the cultural rebels generally, see Kevin J. H. Dettmar and Stephen Watt, "Introduction," in Dettmar and Watt (eds), *Marketing Modernisms: Self-Promotion, Canonization, Rereading* (Ann Arbor, University of Michigan Press, 1996), 6–9 and essays in same. When commenting on the village rebels, John T. Frederick said a "good way to become famous is to attack something." Frederick, "Ruth Suckow and the Middle Western Literary Movement," *English Journal* vol. 20, no. 1 (January 1931), 5.

121  Thomas T. McAvoy, "What Is the Midwestern Mind?" in *The Midwest: Myth or Reality?* (Notre Dame, Indiana, University of Notre Dame Press, 1961), 54.

122  Grosh, "Provincialism and Cosmopolitanism," 17. On the branding and marketing of a midwestern writer, the forces of consumerism during the 1920s,

the use of a "national literary network," and how a career is "strategically marketed," see Guy Reynolds, "Willa Cather's Case: Region and Reputation," in Timothy R. Mahoney and Wendy J. Katz (eds), *Regionalism and the Humanities* (Lincoln, University of Nebraska Press, 2008), 79–81, 84. Another commentator noted how much better northeastern writers were at "literary politics" and charming the "community of editors and publicists and review specialists." Edward Hoagland, "But Where Is Home?" *New York Times Book Review*, December 23, 1973.

123   Edward Watts, "The Midwest as a Colony: Transnational Regionalism," in Mahoney and Katz (eds), *Regionalism and the Humanities*, 172 (coercions). On the "dearth of publishing centers" in the middle of the country and the resulting "bottleneck of publishing" in New York, see Joseph A. Brandt, "A Pioneering Regional Press," *Southwest Review* vol. 26 (Autumn 1940), 26.

124   McDowell, "Regionalism in American Literature," 114. McDowell was the first professor of American literature at the University of Minnesota and promoted the creation of the school's American Studies program. John T. Flanagan, *Theodore C. Blegen: A Memoir* (Northfield, Minnesota, Norwegian-American Historical Association, 1977), 78.

125   Krause, review of Roy W. Meyer, *The Middle Western Farm Novel in the Twentieth Century* (Lincoln, University of Nebraska Press, 1965), in *Minnesota History* vol. 39, no. 7 (Fall 1965), 293 (source of quotation); Robert C. Steensma, " 'Our Comings and Goings': Herbert Krause's *Wind Without Rain*," in Arthur R. Huseboe and William Geyer (eds), *Where the West Begins: Essays on the Middle Border and Siouxland Writing, in Honor of Herbert Krause* (Sioux Falls, Center for Western Studies Press, 1978), 14. Early in her career, the Iowa regionalist Ruth Suckow, in a characteristic concern, worried about being "so far away from the centers of writing" and asked, is "there any hope for one who is not in Chicago or New York?" Leedice McAnelly Kissane, *Ruth Suckow* (New York, Twayne Publishers, Inc., 1969), 22. Speaking to the literary scene of the South, Cleanth Brooks noted the aggressive critiques of southern fiction by over-compensating southerners "who meant to show that they were just as emancipated as the critics of New York." Brooks, "Regionalism in American Literature," *Journal of Southern History* vol. 26, no. 1 (February 1960), 37.

126   On the impact of "antibourgeois prejudice permeating literary academe," see Hutner, *What America Read*, 6. Hutner notes that if "history is written by the victors, so too is literary history." His book attempts to highlight the literary

works of the 1920s that are not part of the "rebellion" genre. Hutner, *What America Read*, 6, 42–50.

127  Nash, *Nervous Generation*, 1–32.

128  Scott Russell Sanders, "Writing from the Center," *Georgia Review* vol. 48, no. 4 (Winter 1994), 735.

129  Shideler, " 'Flappers and Philosophers,' and Farmers," 283.

130  Cowley, *Exile's Return*, 27. Cowley was, in effect, making an argument for a stronger grounding in regionalism and goes on to chide Harvard for its efforts to shed any "regional or economic ties." Cowley, *Exile's Return*, 29. Cowley also criticizes the "life-is-a-circus type of cynicism rendered popular by the *American Mercury*: everything is rotten, people are fools; let's all get drunk and laugh at them." Cowley, *Exile's Return*, 35. Cowley's strong turn to rootedness is perhaps linked to his rather extended—in comparison to other writers—flirtation with radicalism. See Christopher Benfey, "The Revisionist: The Literary Glory and Political Disgrace of Malcolm Cowley," *New Republic*, March 3, 2014.

131  Schwarz, "Sheer Data." Fitzgerald later said that the "jazz age" only applied to the "upper tenth of [the] nation." Nash, *Nervous Generation*, 3.

132  Kosiba, "A Successful Revolt?" 54.

133  Zona Gale, "The American Village Defended," *New York Times Magazine*, July 19, 1931; Kosiba, "A Successful Revolt?" 54–55 (turning); Hilfer, *Revolt from the Village*, 136; Leon T. Dickinson, "America's Main Street," *Chicago Sun Book Week*, May 4, 1947. Van Doren praised Gale for abandoning her "sweet and dainty" and "sugary" early works, which he saw as "dull and petty." Van Doren, "Revolt from the Village," 410–11. I want to thank Robert Dorman for first highlighting the implications of Gale's transition to me.

134  Irving Howe thought the Chicago Renaissance "worked on the assumption that in America there was no cultural tradition either valuable or accessible" and that its participants understood that "they were trapped in the Midwest's dead-end as a sectional culture." Howe, *Sherwood Anderson* (New York, William Sloane Associates, 1951), 65, 74. He also thought the Chicago writers were too limited to succeed at literature because they were provincial "townsmen." Howe, *Sherwood Anderson*, 60. Robert M. Crunden also focuses on the Chicago scene's modernism and its writers' interest in socialism, psychoanalysis, and sexual liberation and their belief that religion was a "fraud" and that "small towns repressed" the soul and Anderson's role in the "revolt of Americans

against their village upbringing." Crunden, *American Salons: Encounters with European Modernism, 1885–1917* (New York, Oxford University Press, 1993), 122, 124. The Chicago Renaissance was also known as the "Chicago Liberation" for what it "represented: a release from the restraints of outmoded Victorianism and Puritanism." David D. Anderson, "Midwestern Writers and the Myth of the Search," *Georgia Review* vol. 34, no. 1 (Spring 1980), 138 (quotations); Richard Lingeman, *Small Town America: A Narrative History 1620–The Present* (New York, G. P. Putnam's Sons, 1980), 366–67, 376; n.a., "The Second Annual Newberry Library Conference on American Studies," *Newberry Library Bulletin* 2nd series, no. 1 (October 1952), 25–29.

135 Timothy B. Spears, *Chicago Dreaming: Midwesterners and the City, 1871–1919* (Chicago, University of Chicago Press, 2005), xvii (italics added). Spears, drawing on Van Doren's revolt thesis and Raymond Williams's Marxism, points to what he sees as Chicago's surprisingly strong "bohemian work— radical politics, the talk and practice of free love, and the commitment to avant-garde representations." Spears, *Chicago Dreaming*, 209–10.

136 Grosh, "Provincialism and Cosmopolitanism," 9–18; Quantic, "Revolt from the Village," 5–16.

137 Although written after Van Doren's essay, the title of the final chapter in O. E. Rolvaag's *Giants in the Earth* (New York, Harper & Brothers, 1927) sufficiently makes the point: "The Great Plain Drinks the Blood of the Christian Men and Is Satisfied."

138 While Van Doren did recognize the earlier critical work of E. W. Howe, for example, he believed that such earlier works failed to dethrone the "sacred" nature of the "cult of the village." Van Doren, "Revolt from the Village," 407. In *The Midwestern Ascendancy in American Writing*, Ron Weber correctly emphasizes the ambivalence and complexity of writing about the Midwest, but he also tends to find the negative portrayals more satisfactory. For a critique of the tendency to miss earlier, pre-revolt works that included criticism of the Midwest, see Quantic, "Revolt from the Village," 5–16; and Margaret D. Stuhr, "The Safe Middle West: Escape to and Escape from Home," *MidAmerica* vol. 14 (1987), 18–27. On Howe, his son Gene A. Howe wrote "My Father Was the Most Wretchedly Unhappy Man I Ever Knew," *Saturday Evening Post*, October 25, 1941, which explains that Howe became embittered after his preacher/father had an extramarital affair and abandoned his family.

139 Masters to Derleth, December 15, 1944, Derleth Papers, WHS (never); Robert Van Gelder, "An Interview with Mr. Edgar Lee Masters," *New York Times*, February 15, 1942. In contrast to Masters's rejection of his designation as a village rebel, Van Doren, in the revolt thesis, "found the Masters poem the *genesis of all the literature of protest against village life* that appeared between 1915 and the early 1920s." Schorer, *Sinclair Lewis*, 296 (emphasis added).

140 Robert Van Gelder, "An Interview with Mr. Edgar Lee Masters," *New York Times*, February 15, 1942.

141 Masters to Derleth, December 31, 1939, Derleth Papers, WHS; Edgar Lee Masters, "The Genesis of Spoon River," *American Mercury* vol. 28 (January 1933), 39 (joyous); Ernest Earnest, "A One-Eyed View of Spoon River," *CEA Critic* (November 1968), 3–4; Weber, *Midwestern Ascendancy*, 101; Donald Davidson, "Sectionalism in the United States," *Hound & Horn* vol. 6 (July–September 1933), 578. Masters emphasized that there were "poems in my *Spoon River* books about faithful and loving hearts, about kind and generous and hopeful people." August Derleth, *Three Literary Men: A Memoir of Sinclair Lewis, Sherwood Anderson, Edgar Lee Masters* (New York, Candlelight Press, 1963), 42. Masters noted that he had "written much beside the *Spoon Rivers*" and that he had "stood for that side of man which hopes and toils in spite of the biting insects that infest this bank and shoal of time." Masters to Derleth, December 31, 1939, Derleth Papers, WHS. Of the people of his home "Sangamon river neighborhood," Masters said they "were hospitable, warm-hearted and generous beyond any people I have known, and full of the will to live." Masters said he wrote *Spoon River* to "awaken that American vision, that love of liberty which the best men of the Republic strove to win for us, and to bequeath to time." Masters, "Genesis of Spoon River," 39, 41, 55.

142 Loving, "Introduction," in Masters, *Spoon River Anthology*, xviii. Masters is remembered as a "one-book author." Ronald Primeau, *Beyond Spoon River: The Legacy of Edgar Lee Masters* (Austin, University of Texas Press, 1981), x. Aside from Masters's *Spoon River*, critics thought, the "rest of his work merited only a speedy oblivion," and they "disregard his large output as insignificant and consider his one important book as somewhat of a literary accident." John T. Flanagan, "The Spoon River Poet," *Southwest Review* vol. 38, no. 3 (Summer 1953), 227, 237. Masters thought his work faded, in part, due to his hostility to the "experiments" and "driveling idiocies" of the "modernists." Masters to Derleth, September 13, 1943, Derleth Papers, WHS.

143  Masters to Derleth, December 31, 1939, Derleth Papers, WHS.

144  Derleth, *Three Literary Men*, 42.

145  Derleth, *Three Literary Men*, 42 (emphasis in original).

146  Masters to Derleth, March 22, 1938, Derleth Papers, WHS; Lois Hartley, "Edgar Lee Masters: Biographer and Historian," *Journal of the Illinois State Historical Society* vol. 54, no. 1 (Spring 1961), 57. Masters said his "heart is with the prairies, and for that matter with Wisconsin and Michigan." Masters to Derleth, September 14, 1941, Derleth Papers, WHS. For a similar Jeffersonianism from another once-prominent and now-forgotten midwestern writer who was rejected by critics by the time of World War II, see David D. Anderson, *Louis Bromfield* (New York, Twayne Publishers, 1964), 173–79. Anderson concludes that in "all his works Bromfield is very much a midwesterner and an agrarian romantic." Anderson, *Louis Bromfield*, 175. Bromfield wrote that the "'revolt' was the product of the excitable young men who issued manifestos, created riots in theatres and launched new revues." Bromfield, "The Novel in Transition," in Oliver M. Sayler, *Revolt in the Arts: A Survey of the Creation, Distribution and Appreciation of Art in America* (New York, Brentano's, 1930), 288. By the time of the war, Bromfield was dismissed by Edmund Wilson as not simply a "second-rate" writer but a "fourth rank" writer. Wilson, "What Became of Louis Bromfield," *New Yorker*, May 13, 1944.

147  Lois Hartley, "Edgar Lee Masters, Political Essayist," *Journal of the Illinois State Historical Society* vol. 57, no. 3 (Autumn 1964), 252, 259 (source of quotation); Robert Van Gelder, "An Interview with Mr. Edgar Lee Masters," *New York Times*, February 15, 1942; Gross, "Revolt That Wasn't," 5.

148  Masters to Derleth, April 10, 1938, Derleth Papers, WHS; Masters, *Lincoln, the Man* (New York, Dodd, Mead, 1931); Hartley, "Edgar Lee Masters: Biographer and Historian," 61–65 (source of quotations). Perhaps because of Masters's decentralist views, Masters voted for Willkie in 1940. Derleth, *Three Literary Men*, 31. Masters saw Lincoln as a "Hamiltonian clothed as a country rube." Masters to Derleth, September 17, 1941, Derleth Papers, WHS. See also Matthew D. Norman, "An Illinois Iconoclast: Edgar Lee Masters and the Anti-Lincoln Tradition," *Journal of the Abraham Lincoln Association* vol. 24, no. 1 (2003), 43–57.

149  Masters manuscript, "Survey of the Country," July 21, 1939, Derleth Papers, WHS (quotation); Masters, *The Sangamon* (New York, Farrar & Rinehart, 1942); Primeau, *Beyond Spoon River*, 168–69; Hartley, "Edgar Lee Masters:

Biographer and Historian," 77–82; Hilfer, *Revolt from the Village*, 147; William F. Thompson, "Introduction," in August Derleth, *The Wisconsin: River of a Thousand Isles* (Madison, University of Wisconsin Press, 1985 [1942]), xi–xii. Masters thought Chicago was the "most ridiculous city in the country." Masters to Derleth, October 25, 1943, Derleth Papers, WHS.

150 Hartley, "Edgar Lee Masters," 83; Ronald Primeau, " 'Awakened and Harmonized': Edgar Lee Masters' Emersonian Midwest," *MidAmerica* vol. 5 (1978), 42–43. In Van Doren's estimation, by contrast, Masters could "hate as no other American poet does." Van Doren, "Revolt from the Village," 408.

151 Hartley, "Edgar Lee Masters, Political Essayist," 251; Robert Van Gelder, "An Interview with Mr. Edgar Lee Masters," *New York Times*, February 15, 1942 (roots) (italics added). Ronald Primeau concluded that Masters was "a 'regionalist' to the end." Primeau, *Beyond Spoon River*, 183.

152 Masters, "James Whitcomb Riley: A Sketch of His Life and an Appraisal of His Work," *Century Magazine* (October 1927), 704–15. Masters said that Riley "never lost perspective upon himself" and "did not get the idea that his success entitled him to leave Indiana" for Boston or New York. Masters, "James Whitcomb Riley." See also John E. Miller, "The Funeral of Beloved Poet, James Whitcomb Riley," *Studies in Midwestern History* vol. 2, no. 6 (July 2016), 70–78. Masters also praised the midwestern poet Vachel Lindsay and in a biography concluded that "Lindsay's ancestry, his education, his religion, his morals, his tastes were Middle West." Masters, *Vachel Lindsay: A Poet in America* (New York, Charles Scribner's Sons, 1935), vii.

153 Anderson to Derleth, January 17, 1940, Derleth Papers, WHS.

154 Walter B. Rideout, *Sherwood Anderson: A Writer in America* (Madison, University of Wisconsin Press, 2005), 46, 48 (source of quotation); Howe, *Sherwood Anderson*, 15–16; Lauck, "Finding Solace."

155 Glen A. Love, "*Winesburg, Ohio* and the Rhetoric of Silence," *American Literature* vol. 40, no. 1 (March 1968), 38–40 (quotation); Love, "Horses or Men: Primitive and Pastoral Elements in Sherwood Anderson," in Hilbert H. Campbell and Charles E. Modlin (eds), *Sherwood Anderson: Centennial Studies* (Troy, New York, Whitson Publishing Co., 1976), 235–45.

156 Love, "*Winesburg, Ohio* and the Rhetoric of Silence," 41; Brom Weber, *Sherwood Anderson* (Minneapolis, University of Minnesota Press, 1964), 20; Tony Hiss, *The Experience of Place* (New York, Alfred A. Knopf, 1990), xv. Instead of keeping *Winesburg* trapped inside the "village revolt" rubric, John Ferres

explores its much deeper agrarian sympathies in Ferres, "The Nostalgia of *Winesburg, Ohio,*" *Newberry Library Bulletin* vol. 6, no. 8 (July 1971), 235–42.

157 Lionel Trilling, "Sherwood Anderson," *Kenyon Review* vol. 3, no. 3 (Summer 1941), 297–98.

158 Trilling, "Sherwood Anderson," 297–98, 301; Weber, *Sherwood Anderson,* 30.

159 Love, "*Winesburg, Ohio* and the Rhetoric of Silence," 43 (italics added).

160 Robert L. Dorman, *Revolt of the Provinces: The Regionalist Movement in America, 1920–1945* (Chapel Hill, University of North Carolina Press, 1993), 279 (full circle quotation); David D. Anderson, "Sherwood Anderson and the Coming of the New Deal," *Bulletin of the Midwest Modern Language Association* vol. 5, no. 2 (1972), 92.

161 Weber, *Midwestern Ascendancy,* 115 (source of quotation). Anderson also thought that Twain "belonged out here in the Middle West" and had "lost something of his innocence" when under the influence of easterners. Howard Mumford Jones, *Letters of Sherwood Anderson* (Boston, Little, Brown and Company, 1953), 31. Anderson was also misunderstood because of his quirkiness and what one critic called "typical Andersonian nebulousness." Ralph Cianco, "'The Sweetness of the Twisted Apples': Unity of Vision in *Winesburg, Ohio,*" *PMLA* vol. 87, no. 5 (October 1972), 994; Brom Weber, "Anderson and 'The Essence of Things,'" *Sewanee Review* vol. 59, no. 4 (Autumn 1951), 682.

162 Van Doren, "Accusation," *Nation,* November 23, 1921; Anderson to Van Doren, November 22, 1921, FF 4, Box 14, Van Doren Papers, Princeton University.

163 Anderson to Van Doren, November 22, 1921, FF 4, Box 14, Van Doren Papers, Princeton University.

164 Maurice Beebe, review of David D. Anderson, *Sherwood Anderson: An Introduction and Interpretation* (New York, Holt, Rinehart and Winston, 1967), in *American Literature* vol. 40, no. 4 (January 1969), 570.

165 Hilfer, *Revolt from the Village,* 156.

166 Brom Weber notes the "excessive personal animus directed against Anderson by Howe." Weber, "Anderson and 'The Essence of Things,'" 681.

167 Howe, *Sherwood Anderson*; Weber, "Anderson and 'The Essence of Things,'" 683 (source of quotation). Susan Sontag also found Sherwood Anderson, according to David D. Anderson, "almost laughable." Anderson, "Introduction," in *Sherwood Anderson: Dimensions of His Literary Art* (Lansing, Michigan State University Press, 1976), xi. Anderson, from the "unfashionable Midwest," was seen as "strange if not downright outlandish" by New York

critics. Welford Dunaway Taylor, "Anderson and the Problem of Belonging," in Anderson, *Sherwood Anderson*, 63.

168 Howe, "American Moderns," in Arthur M. Schlesinger Jr. and Morton White (eds), *Paths of American Thought* (Boston, Houghton Mifflin Company, 1963), 311; Howe, *Sherwood Anderson*, 75, 197–213.

169 Joseph Wood Krutch opined that "Sinclair Lewis loved notoriety almost as much as he loved fame." Krutch, "Sinclair Lewis," *The Nation*, February 24, 1951, 179.

170 Hilfer, *Revolt from the Village*, 34; Weber, *Midwestern Ascendancy*, 152; Richard Lingeman, "Sinclair Lewis Arrives," *New England Review* vol. 23, no. 1 (Winter 2002), 39; Barnaby Conrad, "A Portrait of Sinclair Lewis: America's 'Angry Man' in the Autumn of His Life," *Horizon* (March 1979), 42; Lingeman, *Sinclair Lewis*, 51–53, 104, 484; Vidal, "Romance of Sinclair Lewis," 14. Joseph Wood Krutch argued that the "social situation" and the "cultural climate" made Lewis's early books "perfectly apropos" and "strongly favored him." Krutch, "Sinclair Lewis," 179. On the strong influence of Wells and his call for a "revolt of the competent" against the provincial, see Fred Siegel, "The Godfather of American Liberalism," *City Journal* (Spring 2009). Lewis named his son Wells after H. G. Wells. Mary Austin to Sinclair Lewis, December 17, 1920, Box 48, FF 447, Lewis Papers, Beinecke Library, Yale University.

171 John J. Koblas, *Sinclair Lewis: Home at Last* (Bloomington, MN, Voyageur Press, 1981), 14, 16; Weber, *Midwestern Ascendancy*, 146–47, 150. Van Doren thought Lewis had "revenges to take upon the narrow community in which he grew up." Van Doren, "Revolt from the Village," 410. On Lewis's many personal foibles and family difficulties, see the account by his ex-wife Dorothy Thompson, "The Boy and Man from Sauk Centre," *Atlantic Monthly* vol. 206 (November 1960), in which Thompson minimizes the claims of Lewis's bitterness and opines that the sports, hunting, and outdoor activities of rural Minnesota created an "environment which was not uncongenial but whose demands [Lewis] could not meet." August Derleth also downplayed Lewis's supposed resentment. Derleth, *Three Literary Men*, 11.

172 Conrad, "A Portrait of Sinclair Lewis," 42 (ugly). Gore Vidal said Lewis "was gargoyle ugly: red-haired, physically ill-coordinated, suffered from acne that was made cancerous by primitive X-ray treatments." Vidal, "Romance of Sinclair Lewis," 14. Frederick Manfred also noted that Lewis was "incredibly ugly" but that after a half hour of conversation with Lewis "males forget about

it." That Manfred thought females did not may explain why Manfred thought Lewis was "tremendously suspicious of women." Frederick Manfred to Van Wyck Brooks, May 6, 1946, Box 13, Manfred Papers, Upper Midwest Literary Archives, University of Minnesota. On this point, James McManus condemns those writers who lack the "emotional intelligence to stop associating their pimply emotional frustration with where it took place." McManus, "Your What Hurts?" in Becky Bradway (ed), *In the Middle of the Middle West: Literary Nonfiction from the Heartland* (Bloomington, Indiana University Press, 2003), 15. On Conrad's final completion of an assignment Lewis gave him, see Adam Nagourney, "After 60 Years, a Promise Kept to Sinclair Lewis," *New York Times*, January 26, 2011.

173  Frederick Manfred to Mark Schorer, October 23, 1953, Box 16, Manfred Papers, Upper Midwest Literary Archives, University of Minnesota; Conrad, "A Portrait of Sinclair Lewis," 40–51; Allen, "Sinclair Lewis," 192. Lewis extended great praise, for example, to the University of Minnesota's regional fellowship program designed to "encourage youngsters in regional writing." Helen Clapesattle to Theodore Blegen, May 15, 1944, FF Fellows, Box 5, Blegen Papers, UM Archives. When Barnaby Conrad and Mark Schorer were discussing Schorer's extensive biography of Lewis at Trader Vic's in San Francisco in 1960, Schorer remarked on studying Lewis: "I like him less every day, every week, every month, every year." Conrad, "Arts & Letters," *Wilson Quarterly* (Spring 2002), 114. Schorer worked on his massive Lewis biography for a decade and was greatly relieved at "being free of the thing at last." Mark Schorer to August Derleth, June 27, 1960, Derleth Papers, WHS. Gore Vidal marveled at how Schorer's critical biography of Lewis "could effectively eliminate a popular and famous novelist" from the cultural scene. Vidal, "Romance of Sinclair Lewis," 14. Schorer was born in Sauk City, Wisconsin, and collaborated with the Wisconsin regionalist August Derleth, who was also from Sauk City. Derleth noted Lewis's assistance to budding writers and criticized Schorer's biography for neglecting this aspect of his career. Derleth, *Three Literary Men*, 13. In a 1937 speech to the Wisconsin Education Association, Lewis strongly advocated Derleth's work, especially the various books of his "Sac Prairie Saga." Derleth, *Three Literary Men*, 16. Derleth remained an advocate of Lewis and rejected the idea that he revolted from the village, while Schorer thought that "Lewis did revolt from the village," "lied" about and obscured his unhappy youth, and tried to make his youth seem "normal." Schorer thought Lewis's

revolt had failed and that Lewis "did always remain a provincial, stuck to the end in Sauk Centre but unable to endure it." Mark Schorer to August Derleth, September 30, 1958, Derleth Papers, WHS. When considering the work of Schorer, one should remember that he "came to loathe his subject." Atlas, *Bellow*, x. On Schorer's grudge against Lewis, see Kenneth B. Grant, "Novelists and Biographers: The Sinclair Lewis, August Derleth, and Mark Schorer Triangle," *MidAmerica* vol. 27 (2000), 11–21.

174 Zona Gale to Lewis, March 22, 1921, Box 47, FF 503, and Willa Cather to Lewis, April 14, [1920s?], Box 46, FF 470, both in Lewis Papers, Beinecke Library, Yale University; Weber, *Midwestern Ascendancy*, 146. Cather noted to Lewis that "[w]e have managed to hang together, though there are a good many people who would like to see us claw each other." Cather to Lewis, September 2, [1938?], Box 46, FF 470, Lewis Papers, Beinecke Library, Yale University.

175 Weber, *Midwestern Ascendancy*, 175. Lewis hoped the Iowan Wallace Stegner, for another example, would "get away from all the cultural quacks" at Harvard and "go back to Utah and Iowa, and put on the mantle of greatness that is awaiting him." Lewis, "Fools, Liars and Mr. DeVoto," *Saturday Review*, April 15, 1944, 11.

176 Lewis, "Minnesota, the Norse State" (1923), reprinted in Sally E. Parry (ed), *The Minnesota Stories of Sinclair Lewis* (St. Paul, Borealis Books, 2005), 14.

177 Lingeman, *Sinclair Lewis*, 450. In 1944, when living in Duluth and visiting Two Harbors and Grand Marais, Minnesota, Lewis wrote to Van Doren that "[a]s always, I'm fascinated by the Middlewest" and praised the beauty of fall on the North Shore of Lake Superior. Schorer, *Sinclair Lewis*, 716.

178 William Holtz, "Sinclair Lewis, Rose Wilder Lane, and the Midwestern Short Novel," *Studies in Short Fiction* vol. 24, no. 1 (Winter 1987), 46; Lingeman, *Sinclair Lewis*, 452. Rumors circulated that Lewis was planning to write a novel about the Wisconsin faculty. Derleth, *Three Literary Men*, 20–21. Van Doren commented that what Lewis "doesn't realize is that in order to have friends, one must be willing to suffer a little boredom, and Red has never learned that, and he has almost no friends left." Lingeman, *Sinclair Lewis*, 519. On Lewis's "passion for novelty and excitement" that prevented him from settling, see John T. Flanagan, "A Long Way to Gopher Prairie: Sinclair Lewis's Apprenticeship," *Southwest Review* vol. 32 (August 1947), 405. Lewis said he had "to combine being settled and working with having a taste of new lands." Lewis to Stuart Pratt Sherman, July 7, 1923, Box 2, Sherman Papers, University Archives,

University of Illinois. An acting president of Iowa State University scotched a position for Lewis because he was viewed as a drunk and because of *Babbitt*, which had "misrepresented the American businessman and encouraged Middle Western students in their inferiority complex." Lingeman, *Sinclair Lewis*, 449.

179 Lewis, *Main Street*, 69, 304; Weber, *Midwestern Ascendancy*, 159; Lauck, "Finding Solace."

180 Weber, *Midwestern Ascendancy*, 164; Richard Lingeman, "Home Town, USA," *Washington Post*, January 29, 1978; Schorer, *Sinclair Lewis*, 320; Lingeman, *Sinclair Lewis*, 185; G. Thomas Tanselle, "Sinclair Lewis and Floyd Dell: Two Views of the Midwest," *Twentieth Century Literature* vol. 9, no. 4 (January 1964), 180, 182; Weber, *Midwestern Ascendancy*, 164; Perry Miller, "The Incorruptible Sinclair Lewis," *Atlantic Monthly* (April 1951), 33.

181 Van Doren, *Three Worlds*, 153–59; Weber, *Midwestern Ascendancy*, 164; Schorer, *Sinclair Lewis*, 320. Richard Lingeman says that Lewis "hit the roof" when he read Van Doren's revolt thesis. Lingeman, *Sinclair Lewis*, 185. William Allen White appreciated such characters but also thought *Main Street* focused too much on "the shady side of Main Street." Lingeman, *Sinclair Lewis*, 159. See also Schorer, *Sinclair Lewis*, 285. The editor of the Sauk Centre *Herald* also wrote that "Sauk Centre is proud of Sinclair Lewis, but we've felt that in *Main Street* he only told one side of the story, missed the fun of the small town." Schorer, *Sinclair Lewis*, 435.

182 Lingeman, "Sinclair Lewis Arrives," 35. Lewis's bristling at European criticism calls to mind his ex-wife's comments about his Minnesota roots: "He was as American as ham and eggs and strawberry shortcake, and always distinguishably so." Thompson, "Boy and Man from Sauk Centre."

183 Koblas, *Sinclair Lewis*, 15 (source of quotation); Sally E. Parry, "Gopher Prairie, Zenith, and Grand Republic: Nice Places to Visit, But Would Even Sinclair Lewis Want to Live There?" *Midwestern Miscellany* vol. 20 (1992), 15–19.

184 Dorman, *Revolt of the Provinces*, 18–19. Lewis wrote in another letter that "[m]ind you, I like G. P. [Gopher Prairie], all the G. P.'s; I couldn't write about them so ardently if I didn't." Schorer, *Sinclair Lewis*, 301. Austin often saw herself at the other "end of the rainbow" from supposed critics such as Lewis. Witschi, "Sinclair Lewis, the Voice of Satire, and Mary Austin's Revolt from the Village," 77.

185 John T. Flanagan, "The Minnesota Backgrounds of Sinclair Lewis's Fiction,"

*Minnesota History* vol. 37, no. 1 (March 1960), 3. Lewis's father was a "staid Victorian" and Congregationalist and opposed the cultural rebellion and was not impressed with *Main Street*. Koblas, *Sinclair Lewis*, 5, 10, 19.

186  Jon K. Lauck, "Reading *Babbitt* in Cancun," *Old Northwest Review* (Fall 2015), 117–34; Weber, *Midwestern Ascendancy*, 168.

187  Weber, *Midwestern Ascendancy*, 171.

188  John Updike, "Exile on Main Street," *New Yorker* (May 17, 1993), 96. George Douglas similarly found, upon an earlier re-reading, that *Main Street* did not fit "our working stereotypes" and noted Lewis's "nostalgic attachment to and belief in the freedom and cleanliness of midwestern life." He concluded that *Main Street* had "become beclouded by our stereotypes of Lewis as heckler and village atheist." George H. Douglas, "*Main Street* after Fifty Years," *Prairie Schooner* vol. 44, no. 4 (Winter 1970/1971), 340–41.

189  Flanagan, "Minnesota Backgrounds of Sinclair Lewis' Fiction," 2; C. Rath, "On the Occasion of Sinclair Lewis' Burial," *South Dakota Review* vol. 7 (1969), 46.

190  Koblas, *Sinclair Lewis*, 11. On the Bryant Public Library, see Wayne A. Wiegand, *Main Street Public Library: Community Places and Reading Spaces in the Rural Heartland, 1876–1956* (Iowa City, University of Iowa Press, 2011), 11–46.

191  Flanagan, "Minnesota Backgrounds of Sinclair Lewis's Fiction," 13.

192  Flanagan, "Minnesota Backgrounds of Sinclair Lewis's Fiction," 3.

193  Koblas, *Sinclair Lewis*, xxi.

194  Rath, "On the Occasion of Sinclair Lewis's Burial," 44.

195  Lingeman, "Sinclair Lewis Arrives," 28. It was "scandal," Van Doren thought of *Spoon River*, that "spread its fame." Van Doren, "Revolt from the Village," 407.

196  Schwarz also notes the "literary community's consistent dismissal" of Lewis after his early work and how the "literary tastemakers" lost interest in a "hopelessly dated" Lewis. Schwarz, "Sheer Data." On the privileging of Lewis's negative works and the tendency to ignore his positive portrayals, see Kenneth H. Wheeler, *Cultivating Regionalism: Higher Education and the Making of the American Midwest* (DeKalb, Northern Illinois University Press, 2011), 99–101.

197  Weber, *Midwestern Ascendancy*, 173.

198  Alfred Kazin, "Mark Schorer," *Book-of-the-Month Club News*, September 1961, 6, available in FF Mark Schorer, August Derleth Papers, WHS.

199  Lionel Trilling, "Mr. Lewis Goes Soft," *Kenyon Review* vol. 2, no. 3 (Summer 1940), 364, 366.

200 Derleth, *Three Literary Men*, 13.

201 Derleth, *Three Literary Men*, 42, 49; Masters to Derleth, December 31, 1939, Derleth Papers, WHS.

202 August Derleth, "Masters and the Revolt from the Village," *Colorado Quarterly* vol. 8, no. 2 (Autumn 1959), 164.

203 Derleth, *Three Literary Men*, 48. Masters also called editors the "scum of the earth," "whimsical as whores, and as corrupt." Masters to Derleth, July 17, 1940, Derleth Papers, WHS.

204 Derleth, *Three Literary Men*, 34; Anderson to Derleth, January 4, 1940, Derleth Papers, WHS.

205 Derleth, *Three Literary Men*, 35. Anderson rejected, for example, Ima Honaker Herron's *The Small Town in American Literature* (Durham, Duke University Press, 1939). Anderson to Derleth, January 17, 1940, Derleth Papers, WHS. Herron's book included contrasting sections on "The Battle of the Village" and the "Village Apologists."

206 Derleth, *Three Literary Men*, 12.

207 Derleth, *Three Literary Men*, 12.

208 Derleth, *Three Literary Men*, 23.

209 Derleth, *Three Literary Men*, 13. Van Doren also included Floyd Dell, who had grown up in small-town Illinois and Davenport, Iowa, in his village rebel taxonomy because of Dell's novel *Moon-Calf* (1920), which was released just before *Main Street*. Dell later protested in his autobiography that it was "ridiculously untrue" to deem *Moon-Calf* a part of, as Ronald Weber says, an "exposé of the Midwest." *Moon-Calf* was dedicated to Dell's young Minnesota wife and the Midwest's "hospitality" toward the young. Dell also saw *Main Street* as an "exposé" not of the midwestern small town but of Carol Kennicott's urban pretensions and abuse of the fictional Gopher Prairie, and he told Lewis that he was "too cruel to the . . . Middle West." Van Doren, "Revolt from the Village," 410–11; Weber, *Midwestern Ascendancy*, 85 (exposé), 160 (cruel); Tanselle, "Sinclair Lewis and Floyd Dell," 175–78 (hospitality); Spears, *Chicago Dreaming*, 219; Lingeman, *Sinclair Lewis*, 150–51; Schorer, *Sinclair Lewis*, 277; DeVoto, *The Literary Fallacy*, 99.

210 Van Doren, "Revolt from the Village," 412; Fitzgerald, *This Side of Paradise*, 35; Fitzgerald, "Early Success" (1937), in Edmund Wilson (ed), *The Crack-Up* (New York, New Directions, 1993), 88.

211 Edmund Wilson, "Fitzgerald before *The Great Gatsby*," in Alfred Kazin (ed), *F. Scott Fitzgerald: The Man and His Work* (New York, Collier's, 1966), 79 (italics in original).

212 Clinton S. Burhans, "Structure and Theme in *This Side of Paradise*," *Journal of English and Germanic Philology* vol. 68, no. 4 (October 1969), 605, n. 1.

213 Barry Gross, "*This Side of Paradise*: The Dominating Intention," *Studies in the Novel* vol. 1 no. 1 (Spring 1969), 51–59.

214 Jeffrey Hart, "Rediscovering Fitzgerald," *Sewanee Review* vol. 112, no. 2 (Spring 2004), 194.

215 Patricia Kane, "F. Scott Fitzgerald's St. Paul," *Minnesota History* vol. 45, no. 4 (Winter 1976), 141.

216 Kane, "F. Scott Fitzgerald's St. Paul," 142.

217 Weber, *Midwestern Ascendancy*, 212.

218 F. Scott Fitzgerald, *The Great Gatsby* (New York, Charles Scribner's Sons, 1925), 177; Kane, "F. Scott Fitzgerald's St. Paul," 142–48. Fitzgerald grew weary of the farm novels of Garland, Cather, and others. Weber, *Midwestern Ascendancy*, 206.

219 Fitzgerald, *Great Gatsby*, 3.

220 Van Doren himself actually recalled his early years on a farm and in a small town in Illinois in such a tender manner that it significantly undercuts his later promotion of a revolt against midwestern backwardness. See Van Doren typescript "Three Worlds," Box 7, FF 7, Van Doren Papers, Princeton University.

221 Glenway Wescott, "Van Wyck Brooks," *New York Times*, December 14, 1964; Cowley, "Van Wyck Brooks," 18; Blake, *Beloved Community*, 239–40 (quotations). Brooks's breakdown is recounted in Van Wyck Brooks, *Days of the Phoenix: The Nineteen-Twenties I Remember* (New York, E. P. Dutton, 1957).

222 Van Wyck Brooks to Frederick Manfred, June 28, 1945, Box 13, Manfred Papers, Upper Midwest Literary Archives, University of Minnesota.

223 Blake, *Beloved Community*, 11.

224 Blake, *Beloved Community*, 11. Brooks had earlier recognized, as he said, "that a man without a country could do nothing of importance, that writers must draw sustenance from their own common flesh and blood and that their deracination also meant ruin." Cowley, "Van Wyck Brooks," 1963.

225 Van Wyck Brooks, *On Literature Today* (New York, E. P. Dutton, 1941), 21. It was fashionable, Brooks noted, to feel "that our towns were peculiarly damned. . . . I cannot count the number of my friends who complained of the human 'sinks' and 'dumps' in which their lines were cast." "Just to escape from these towns and tell the world how ugly, false and brutal they were seemed to be almost the motive of these writers in living." Brooks, *The Opinions of Oliver Allston* (New York, E. P. Dutton, 1941), 265, 270 (Allston was a pseudonym for Brooks).

226 Blake, *Beloved Community*, 40. In 1937, three decades after his casual denunciations of the rural interior, Brooks told Hamlin Garland that he was finally
turning in a serious way to the "growth of the Western mind and the literary
feeling for the Western scene." Brooks to Garland, January 17, 1937, Box 1150,
Hamlin Garland Papers, University of Southern California. On Brooks's
regrets for his earlier attacks and his admission that "he had read American
history wrongly," see James Hoopes, *Van Wyck Brooks: In Search of American
Culture* (Amherst, University of Massachusetts Press, 1977), 234–35. See also
T. J. Jackson Lears, *No Place of Grace: Anti-modernism and the Transformation
of American Culture, 1880–1920* (Chicago, University of Chicago Press, 1981),
256–57. Louis Hacker, who began the assault on Frederick Jackson Turner
in keeping with the directives of Brooks and others, also changed his mind
and gave "credence to the Turnerian viewpoint." Zeman, "Historian Louis M.
Hacker's 'Coincidental Conversion' to the Truth," 94; Hacker, *The Shaping
of the American Tradition* (New York, Columbia University Press, 1947), xv.
Lewis Mumford later admitted that his circle's critique of the United States
was "so relentless, so unsparing, so persistently negative that it was often
grossly unjust, as I was in my ruthless denigration of the saving virtues of the
. . . Pioneer." Dorman, *Revolt of the Provinces*, 86.

227 Harvey Breit, "Talk with Van Wyck Brooks," *New York Times*, January 13, 1952.

228 Lasch, "Ordeal of Van Wyck Brooks," 9 (levity quote). For other Brooks
quotes, see DeVoto, *Literary Fallacy*, 26.

229 Thomas, "Uses of Catastrophe," 245 (kill). For Brooks's later assessment of
midwestern writing, see Brooks, *The Times of Melville and Whitman* (New
York, E. P. Dutton & Co., 1947), 73–97.

230 Brooks, *Opinions of Oliver Allston*, 258, 262. The popularization of Brooks's
early views by way of Carl Van Doren's thesis should also be tempered by
the important fact that Van Doren, in contravention of the conventional
wisdom, confessed to great fondness for his youth on a farm and in a small
town in Illinois and great admiration for his father and only later became
"morose" and felt "superior" to that way of life. Van Doren typescript "Three
Worlds," 41, 44, 70–74, 164, Box 7, FF 6, Van Doren Papers, Princeton University. Van Doren noted to friends that he had a "happy childhood" despite
the "common" literary tendency to "abuse families." Van Doren typescript
"Three Worlds," 44, Box 7, FF 6, Van Doren Papers, Princeton University.
The "revolt," Van Doren said, was prompted by "early irritations" (he had

deleted the phrase "out of hatred"), and the "villain" was "dullness." Van Doren typescript "Three Worlds," 165, 284, Box 7, FF 7, Van Doren Papers, Princeton University. In Van Doren's literary world, "Youth . . . was always right," and the old was "death," and so he sought to "revise the canon." Van Doren typescript "Three Worlds," 184, 210, Box 7, FF 7, Van Doren Papers, Princeton University. In perhaps an allusion to his doubts about the notion of a revolt from the village, Van Doren's original manuscript was subtitled "Revolt from the Village?"; but this subtitle was deleted from the later book. Van Doren typescript "Three Worlds," title page, Box 7, FF 6, Van Doren Papers, Princeton University.

231  Brooks to Frederick Manfred, December 9, 1947, and December 15, 1947 (sneered), Box 14, Manfred Papers, Upper Midwest Literary Archives, University of Minnesota. For criticism of Brooks from the New York Intellectuals, see Lionel Trilling, "Family Album," *Partisan Review* vol. 15, no. 1 (January 1948), 106 (arguing that the later Brooks appealed "only to the Philistine" and was "impossible to take seriously"); Van Wyck Brooks to Frederick Manfred, January 21, 1948, Box 14, Manfred Papers, Upper Midwest Literary Archives, University of Minnesota (telling Manfred to note the attacks on Brooks's work). Brooks also told Manfred, for another example, that his *The Opinions of Oliver Allston* was "pretty generally disliked and abused." Brooks to Frederick Manfred, March 4, 1946, Box 13, Manfred Papers, Upper Midwest Literary Archives, University of Minnesota.

232  William H. Prichard, "Not to Write Was Not to Be Alive," *New York Times Book Review*, November 1, 1981.

233  On the collapse of Brooks's reputation caused by his "nostalgia," see Joseph Epstein, *Plausible Prejudices: Essays on American Writing* (New York, W. W. Norton, 1985), 258. "If Brooks continues to be read," claimed Anthony Hilfer, a proponent of the revolt thesis, it would only be because of the role of *America's Coming Age* in helping writers create the village rebellion school of thought. Hilfer, *Revolt from the Village*, 157.

234  Blake, *Beloved Community*, 240, 247.

235  DeVoto, *Literary Fallacy*, 66.

236  For the attacks on the later Brooks as a totalitarian and fascist, see Hoopes, *Van Wyck Brooks*, 236–37.

237  Lasch, "Ordeal of Van Wyck Brooks," 11.

238  Lasch, "Ordeal of Van Wyck Brooks," 1; Jon K. Lauck, "The Prairie Populism

of Christopher Lasch," *Great Plains Quarterly* vol. 32, no. 3 (Summer 2012), 183–205.

239 Lasch, "Ordeal of Van Wyck Brooks," 2. On Brooks's later criticism of intellectuals who inhabited a "small closed world, walled in from the common world," see Brooks, "Reflections on the Avant-Garde," *New York Times Book Review* (December 30, 1956).

240 Lasch, "Ordeal of Van Wyck Brooks," 9.

241 Lasch, "Ordeal of Van Wyck Brooks," 10.

242 Lasch, "Ordeal of Van Wyck Brooks," 15.

## CHAPTER TWO

1   Van Wyck Brooks, *On Literature Today* (New York, E. P. Dutton, 1941), 23, 15.

2   Buley to Bernard DeVoto, May 24, 1944, FF 160–162, Box 8, DeVoto Papers, Stanford University.

3   "The literature of the rebels and renegades has survived and has come to be taken as a complete picture" of the 1920s, Malcolm Cowley observed, and did not include the portrayals of the nation's "smiling parts, the broad farmlands, the big Sunday dinners after coming home from church." Cowley, "In Defense of the 1920s," *New Republic*, April 24, 1944.

4   Casey Nelson Blake, *Beloved Community: The Cultural Criticism of Randolph Bourne, Van Wyck Brooks, Waldo Frank, and Lewis Mumford* (Chapel Hill, University of North Carolina Press, 1990), 143.

5   Edward Krickel, "The Study of the Expatriates," *South Atlantic Bulletin* vol. 35, no. 3 (May 1970), 30–31.

6   Brooks to Frederick Manfred, March 4, 1946, Box 13, Manfred Papers, Upper Midwest Literary Archives, University of Minnesota.

7   Bernard DeVoto, *The Literary Fallacy* (Port Washington, New York, Kennikat Press, Inc., 1944), 30, 42.

8   DeVoto, *Literary Fallacy*, 150; Wallace Stegner, *The Uneasy Chair: A Biography of Bernard DeVoto* (Salt Lake City, Peregrine Smith Books, 1988), 182–83, 251–59. DeVoto's criticism was first set forth in a series of six lectures at Indiana University in 1943 and then published collectively as *The Literary Fallacy* in 1944. R. Carlyle Buley to John T. Flanagan, January 10, 1947, Flanagan Papers, University of Illinois; Richard Lingeman, *Sinclair Lewis: Rebel*

*from Main Street* (New York, Random House, 2002), 474. Sinclair Lewis attacked DeVoto in response to his book (and surely in response to DeVoto's earlier criticism of Lewis), and Van Wyck Brooks, still friendly with the then much less rebellious Lewis, applauded Lewis's "masterpiece of demolition." Lewis, "Fools, Liars and Mr. DeVoto," *Saturday Review of Literature*, April 15, 1944; Brooks to Sinclair Lewis, April 23, 1944, Box 46, FF 462, Lewis Papers, Beinecke Library, Yale University; Bernard DeVoto, "Sinclair Lewis," *Saturday Review of Literature*, January 28, 1933; Mark Schorer, *Sinclair Lewis: An American Life* (New York, McGraw-Hill, 1961), 712. On DeVoto's largely forgotten critique, see Fred Siegel, "The Anti-American Fallacy," *Commentary* (April 2010). Henry Nash Smith (see chapter 3), a critic of Frederick Jackson Turner and midwestern agrarian "myths," "violently" hated DeVoto's *The Literary Fallacy*. Smith to Copley Morgan, November 9, 1949, FF 17, Box 1, Smith Papers, Bancroft Library. Also note, in conjunction with DeVoto's critique, Archibald MacLeish's criticism of intellectuals for abandoning the "common culture." "The Irresponsibles," *Nation* (May 18, 1940), 618–23; *The Irresponsibles: A Declaration* (New York, Duell, Sloan & Pearce, 1940). MacLeish, born in Glencoe, Illinois, was considered, in part, a "poet of the Midwest." Graham Hutton, "Hawkeye, Huck Finn and an English Boy," *Chicago Sun Book Week*, May 4, 1947. Irving Dillard of the *St. Louis Post-Dispatch* highlighted MacLeish as a "native of Illinois." Dillard to Stanley Pargellis, February 15, 1947, NL 03/05/06, Box 2, FF 46, Pargellis Papers, Newberry Library. On MacLeish's criticism of intellectuals during the 1930s, see Eleanor M. Sickels, "Archibald MacLeish and American Democracy," *American Literature* vol. 15, no. 3 (November 1943), 226–27. Van Wyck Brooks agreed with MacLeish that the writers of the era had been "drugged by fatalism." Scott Donaldson, *Archibald MacLeish: An American Life* (Boston, Houghton Mifflin, 1992), 335.

9  DeVoto to Van Wyck Brooks, August 2, 1943, Folder 743, Brooks Papers, Annenberg Library, University of Pennsylvania.

10  Bernard DeVoto, "They Turned Their Backs on America: Writers of the Twenties Missed the Real Meaning of the Times," *Saturday Review of Literature*, April 8, 1944.

11  DeVoto to Frederick Manfred, May 8, 1953, Box 16, Manfred Papers, Upper Midwest Literary Archives, University of Minnesota. As a writer, Manfred saw himself as a "Midlander with Midland American themes." Manfred to Brooks,

March 21, 1953, Box 16, Manfred Papers, Upper Midwest Literary Archives, University of Minnesota.

12   Malcolm Cowley, *Exile's Return: A Literary Odyssey of the 1920s* (New York, Penguin Books, 1994 [1951, 1934]), 16. For an entertaining exchange between Cowley and the regionalist writer Frederick Manfred about whether Cowley understood the Midwest and its democratic sensibilities, see letters in Box 17, Manfred Papers, Upper Midwest Literary Archives. Despite his later reputation, Theodore Dreiser of Indiana counted himself as a lover of the farms and towns of the Midwest and its "really happy people." His pessimism stemmed from the fact that he "had seen Pittsburgh." Van Wyck Brooks, *The Confident Years: 1885–1915* (New York, E. P. Dutton, 1952), 70–71.

13   Warren I. Susman, "History and the American Intellectual: Uses of a Usable Past," *American Quarterly* vol. 16, no. 2 (Summer 1964), 258. On the more recent "neglect of regionalists (usually dismissed as 'local color writers') by the credentialed custodians of American literary culture," see David R. Pichaske, "Dave Etter: Fishing for Our Lost American Souls," *Journal of Modern Literature* vol. 23, no. 3/4 (Summer 2000), 393.

14   Blair Whitney, "A Portrait of the Author as Midwesterner," *Great Lakes Review* vol. 1, no. 2 (Winter 1975), 33.

15   Sara A. Kosiba, "A Successful Revolt? The Redefinition of Midwestern Literary Culture in the 1920s and 1930s" (PhD dissertation, Kent State University, 2007), 1–2.

16   Barry Gross, "The Revolt That Wasn't: The Legacies of Critical Myopia," *CEA Critic* vol. 30, no. 2 (January 1977), 8.

17   Robert L. Dorman, *Revolt of the Provinces: The Regionalist Movement in America, 1920–1945* (Chapel Hill, University of North Carolina Press, 1993), 86, 91 (cultureless).

18   Blake, *Beloved Community*, 143.

19   Dwight Macdonald, memorably, attacked "midbrow's nostalgia for small town life" as part of the "tepid, flaccid Middlebrow Culture that threatens to engulf everything in its spreading ooze." Paul R. Gorman, *Left Intellectuals and Popular Culture in Twentieth-Century America* (Chapel Hill, University of North Carolina Press, 1996), 182. On the assault on middlebrow literature and the "canonization of modernism" during this era, see Tom Perrin, *The Aesthetics of Middlebrow Fiction: Popular US Novels, Modernism, and Form, 1945–75* (New York, Palgrave Macmillan, 2015), 6.

20  Joan Shelley Rubin, *The Making of Middle Brow Culture* (Chapel Hill, University of North Carolina Press, 1992), xvii–xviii. Rubin has also chronicled the "faded" efforts of Constance Rourke, a midwesterner, to respond to the "critique of America as culturally barren, materialistic, and provincial." Rubin, *Constance Rourke and American Culture* (Chapel Hill, University of North Carolina Press, 1980), xii. Van Wyck Brooks recognized the error of his early criticism after reading Rourke, who, he noted, had "deep roots in the Middle West," when he wrote the preface for her posthumous book *The Roots of American Culture and Other Essays* (New York, Harcourt, Brace, 1942), vi.

21  Rubin, *Making of Middle Brow Culture*, 42.

22  Rubin, *Making of Middle Brow Culture*, 43, 47–48.

23  Carl Van Doren to Stuart Pratt Sherman, August 6, 1923, Box 4, Sherman Papers, University Archives, University of Illinois; Rubin, *Making of Middle Brow Culture*, 55–56; Richard Ruland, *The Rediscovery of American Literature* (Cambridge, Harvard University Press, 1967), 14. Sherman "was the constant butt of Mencken's criticism." Schorer, *Sinclair Lewis*, 361 (butt); Ruland, *Rediscovery of American Literature*, 137–65. On Sherman's reluctance to attack the Puritan tradition, see Floyd Dell to Sherman, n.d. (probably 1921), Box 1, Sherman Papers, University Archives, University of Illinois.

24  Van Doren typescript "Three Worlds," 87–90, Box 7, FF 6, Van Doren Papers, Princeton University; Rubin, *Making of Middle Brow Culture*, 47–48, 55.

25  Carl Van Doren to Stuart Pratt Sherman, February 6, 1916, Box 4, Sherman Papers, University Archives, University of Illinois; Van Doren typescript "Three Worlds," 146–47, 161, Box 7, FF 7, Van Doren Papers, Princeton University; Rubin, *Making of Middle Brow Culture*, 59–60. *The Nation*, Alfred Kazin explained, "suddenly in 1918 veered from its austere and intellectual conservatism and went over to the new writers" of cultural radicalism. Alfred Kazin, *On Native Grounds: An Interpretation of Modern American Prose Literature* (San Diego, A Harvest Book: Harcourt Brace & Company, 3rd edition, 1995 [1942]), 194. Van Doren explained that "*The Nation* had turned from Sherman to Mencken." Van Doren, *Three Worlds* (New York, Harper & Brothers, 1936), 149.

26  Rubin, *Making of Middle Brow Culture*, 70.

27  Sherman quotation from 1924 newspaper clipping, Box 28, FF 1440, Sherwood Anderson Papers, Newberry Library. Because of Sherman's midwestern democratic leanings and his support for midwestern writing, he also broke

with the New Humanists of the 1920s, who sought a focus on high culture. Ruland, *Rediscovery of American Literature*, 68; Stephen L. Tanner, "Sinclair Lewis and the New Humanism," *Modern Age* vol. 33, no. 1 (1990), 41, n. 52.

28  Rubin, *Making of Middle Brow Culture*, 77 (Manhattan); Ruland, *Rediscovery of American Literature*, 62. On the "critical bias against middle-class readers and their so-called middlebrow taste," see Gordon Hutner, *What America Read: Taste, Class, and the Novel* (Chapel Hill, University of North Carolina Press, 2009), 2. On the privileging of any "foreign" culture products that are "abstruse," see Tad Friend, "The Case for Middlebrow," *New Republic*, March 2, 1992. "In the culture guardians' claret nightmares middlebrow is exemplified by a grandmother rocking on a porch somewhere near Decatur, Illinois." Friend, "Case for Middlebrow."

29  Rubin, *Making of Middle Brow Culture*, 78. Sherwood Anderson recognized Sherman's "strength in the outlying country." Anderson to Sherman, n.d. (probably 1921), Box 1, Sherman Papers, University Archives, University of Illinois. By the 1960s, Sherman was already forgotten and "seldom mentioned and rarely read." Ruland, *Rediscovery of American Literature*, xi.

30  R. T. Prescott, "Ruth Suckow," *Prairie Schooner* vol. 2, no. 2 (Spring 1928), 138. The works of these regionalists, E. Bradford Burns notes, "complemented the ideas" of Frederick Jackson Turner and other midwestern historians who were seeking a broader audience for midwestern history. E. Bradford Burns, *Kinship with the Land: Regionalist Thought in Iowa, 1894–1942* (Iowa City, University of Iowa Press, 1996), 53; Jon K. Lauck, *The Lost Region: Toward a Revival of Midwestern History* (Iowa City, University of Iowa Press, 2013), 29–52.

31  Ronald Weber, *The Midwestern Ascendancy in American Writing* (Bloomington, Indiana University Press, 1992), 175. Frederick Manfred contrasted the regionalists who stayed close to their roots to the "bright children of restlessness who leave Toledo or Des Moines and go to New York," and he generally saw it as a "tragedy for midland brains to go to New York." Frederick Manfred to Van Wyck Brooks, March 7, 1947, Box 14, Manfred Papers, Upper Midwest Literary Archives, University of Minnesota. On Van Wyck Brooks's view that the "young Western boys, fresh from the prairie," were manipulated by their elders in Paris during the interwar years, see Brooks, *The Opinions of Oliver Allston* (New York, E. P. Dutton, 1941), 240.

32  Dorman, *Revolt of the Provinces*, 115.

33  Dorman, *Revolt of the Provinces*, 115–16.

34  Milton M. Reigelman, *The Midland: A Venture in Literary Regionalism* (Iowa City, University of Iowa Press, 1975), 41. On the "fascination" with the expatriates and how "literary scholars have written endlessly" about them, see Krickel, "Study of the Expatriates," 29.

35  Josiah Royce, "Provincialism," in *Race Questions, Provincialism, and Other American Problems* (Freeport, New York, Books for Libraries Press, Inc., 1967 [1908]), 57–108; Frederick J. Hoffman, Charles Allen, and Carolyn F. Ulrich, *The Little Magazine: A History and a Bibliography* (Princeton, Princeton University Press, 1946), 141; Thomas Stritch, *My Notre Dame: Memories and Reflections of Sixty Years* (Notre Dame, University of Notre Dame Press, 1991), 59–61; Edward Fischer, *Notre Dame Remembered: An Autobiography* (Notre Dame, Indiana, University of Notre Dame Press, 1987), 51–58; Weber, *Midwestern Ascendancy*, 176; C. F. Ansley to Frederick, November 11, 1914, John T. Frederick Papers, University of Iowa Archives.

36  Reigelman, *Midland*, 3.

37  Burns, *Kinship with the Land*, 41.

38  Weber, *Midwestern Ascendancy*, 177. For a recognition of Frederick's "anti-hegemonic resistance to the cultural center" and a defense against Frederick's critics, see Tom Lutz, "The Cosmopolitan *Midland*," *American Periodicals* vol. 15, no. 1 (2005), 80.

39  Martin Severin Peterson, "Regional Magazines," *Prairie Schooner* vol. 3, no. 4 (Fall 1929), 293 (quotation); Wallace Stegner to John T. Frederick, December 8, 1942, John T. Frederick Papers, University of Iowa Archives; Burns, *Kinship with the Land*, 9; Wallace Stegner, "The Trail of the Hawkeye," *Saturday Review of Literature*, July 30, 1938, 16; Weber, *Midwestern Ascendancy*, 177. When it was launched, *The Midland* was the only "general literary magazine published between the Alleghenies and the Rockies." Sargent Bush Jr., "The Achievement of John T. Frederick," *Books at Iowa* vol. 14 (April 1971). *The Midland* was seen as the "perfect embodiment of the literary spirit of the Middle West." Statement by Edward J. O'Brien in John T. Frederick Papers, University of Iowa Archives. Half of the stories published in *The Midland* were written by midwesterners or about the Midwest. Hoffman, Allen, and Ulrich, *Little Magazine*, 144. Frederick also directed the Illinois guide during the New Deal, and his "enthusiasm for the midwestern country gave the book much of its quality." Jacob Scher manuscript, 1947, located in NL 03/05/06, Box 2, FF 46, Pargellis Papers, Newberry Library. In a sign of the complexity of Sherwood Anderson's

writings and in a recognition of his warm views of the Midwest, the regionalist Frederick sought him out and brought him to Iowa City to talk to an audience of hundreds. Frederick to Anderson, November 23, 1925, Box 20, FF 983, Anderson Papers, Newberry Library. *The Midland*, after a move to Chicago, was "killed" by the Great Depression, Frederick later said. Frederick to Society for the Study of Midwestern Literature, April 2, 1971, reprinted in *Midwestern Miscellany* vol. 29 (Spring 2001), 12. The Iowa Writers' Workshop was not able to save *The Midland* from the Depression. Norman Foerster to Frederick, May 8 and 26, 1933, John T. Frederick Papers, University of Iowa Archives. On the efforts of Norman Foerster at the Iowa Writers' Workshop to promote regional writing in keeping with Frederick Jackson Turner's focus on regions, see Richard W. Etulain, "The American Literary West and Its Interpreters: The Rise of a New Historiography," *Pacific Historical Review* vol. 45 (August 1976), 318–19.

40  Burns, *Kinship with the Land*, xi. For other examples of the literary regrets about the decline of farm life that contrast to the village rebel interpretation, see Robert H. Walker, "The Poet and the Rise of the City," *Mississippi Valley Historical Review* vol. 49, no. 1 (June 1962), 85–99; and Morton and Lucia White, *The Intellectual versus the City: From Thomas Jefferson to Frank Lloyd Wright* (Cambridge, Harvard University Press, 1962).

41  Frederick to Ruth Suckow, April 27, 1920, John T. Frederick Papers, University of Iowa Archives; Weber, *Midwestern Ascendancy*, 179 (source of quotations). Suckow admired Frederick's novel *Green Bush* (New York, Knopf, 1925) and fought off other patrons at the Dubuque library to get a copy. Ruth Suckow to John T. Frederick, September 29, 1925, John T. Frederick Papers, University of Iowa Archives.

42  Suckow, "Iowa" (1926), reprinted in John T. Flanagan (ed), *America Is West: An Anthology of Middlewestern Life and Literature* (Minneapolis, University of Minnesota Press, 1945), 612–16.

43  Suckow, *Some Others and Myself: Seven Stories and a Memoir* (New York, Rinehart & Company, 1952), 169–74; Jon K. Lauck, "Finding Solace in the Midwest Where It Isn't Supposed to Be," *Flyover Country Review* vol. 2, no. 2 (April 2015).

44  Suckow, *Some Others and Myself*, 170.

45  Suckow, *Some Others and Myself*, 176; Ruth Suckow, "The Folk Idea in American Life," *Scribner's Magazine* vol. 88 (September 1930), 247; Margaret Matlack Kiesel, "Iowans in the Arts: Ruth Suckow in the Twenties," *Annals of Iowa* vol. 45 (1980), 262; Burns, *Kinship with the Land*, 61.

46  Suckow, *Some Others and Myself*, 176. Frederick Manfred, who grew up in

nearby Doon, Iowa, also noted how "[p]eople work at the job of being democratic out here." Frederick Manfred to Malcolm Cowley, January 28, 1956, Box 16, Manfred Papers, Upper Midwest Literary Archives (quotation); Manfred to Bernard DeVoto, March 24, 1953, FF 325, Box 16, DeVoto Papers, Stanford University.

47  Suckow, *Country People* (New York, Alfred A. Knopf, 1924), 155; Kosiba, "A Successful Revolt?" 70. Even Mencken, surprisingly, admired *Country People*. Mencken to Suckow, April 11, 1923, Series 1, Box 2, Suckow Papers, University of Iowa Archives. In a measure of his complex views of the Midwest and his support of younger midwestern writers, so did Lewis. Clifton Fadiman, Sinclair Lewis, and Carl Van Doren (eds), *The Three Readers* (New York, The Readers Club, 1943), 173–77. See also William Holtz, "Sinclair Lewis, Rose Wilder Lane, and the Midwestern Short Novel," *Studies in Short Fiction* vol. 24, no. 1 (Winter 1987), 41–44.

48  Kiesel, "Iowans in the Arts," 280. Mencken took an interest in Suckow because, as he said, he thought the "Anglo-Saxon stock in America is played out" and he was looking for new voices and noticed Suckow's Germanic background, which she shared with Mencken. Mencken asked her in an early letter: "What are you racially?" Kiesel, "Iowans in the Arts," 276–77. Mencken wondered if Suckow was "Wendish" and whether her ancestors were from Prussia and commented that there was more "artistic activity" from the "peoples of later immigration." Mencken to Suckow, August 16, 1922, Series 1, Box 2, Suckow Papers. Mencken published Suckow's essay about her German grandfather. Suckow, "A German Grandfather," *American Mercury* (November 1927), 280–84. On Mencken's pro-German views, see Terry Teachout, *The Skeptic: A Life of H. L. Mencken* (New York, HarperCollins, 2002); and Fred Siegel, *The Revolt Against the Masses* (New York, Encounter Books, 2013), 25–26. Mencken's treatment of Cather seems more in character. Mencken said of Willa Cather: "I don't care how well she writes, I don't give a damn what happens in Nebraska." R. Douglas Hurt, "Midwestern Distinctiveness," in *The Identity of the American Midwest: Essays on Regional History* (Bloomington, Indiana University Press, 2001), 163. In a probable allusion to Mencken, Cather also noted a "New York critic" who had said "I simply don't care a damn what happens in Nebraska, no matter who writes about it." Cather, *On Writing*, 94. Mencken did, however, recognize the emergence of strong midwestern writing during the era and said "Greenwich Village is simply a collection of frauds" who produced "trivial

and even infantile" work. Mencken to Suckow, August 16, 1922, Series 1, Box 2, Suckow Papers.

49  Kiesel, "Iowans in the Arts," 286. For Suckow's criticisms of Hollywood and celebrity culture, see Suckow, "Hollywood Gods and Goddesses," *Harper's* vol. 173 (July 1936).

50  H. W. Reninger, "Spoken at the Memorial Service for Ruth Suckow Nuhn," *Midwest* vol. 3 no. 2 (1960), 13.

51  Suckow to Frederick, October 30, 1935, Series 1, Box 2, Suckow Papers.

52  Nuhn focused on Henry James, Henry Adams, and T. S. Eliot and their orientation "to Mother England, to Mother Church, to twelfth-century France." He regretted that "many bright American boys know instantly more about movements abroad than they do about life at home. It is not that they dislike their own history and culture; they do not know it." Nuhn, *The Wind Blew from the East* (New York, Harper & Brothers Publishers, 1940), 38, 86, 262; John Dewey to Nuhn, June 16, 1942, Series 1, Box 3, Suckow Papers; Randall Stewart, review of *Wind Blew*, in *American Literature* vol. 15, no. 2 (May 1943), 205 (Omaha). Edgar Lee Masters similarly regretted the dominance of "Anglophile culture." Masters to Derleth, May 12, 1940, Derleth Papers, WHS. The "British influence is powerful. It dominates [New York] where the magazines are published, and the books, and where the money is." Masters to Derleth, September 17, 1941, Derleth Papers, WHS. Carl Van Doren also recognized the "appetite of the Atlantic seaboard for any English author . . . and brings to mind some of the nasty things the nastier Germans say about us." Carl Van Doren to Stuart Pratt Sherman, February 6, 1916, Box 4, Sherman Papers, University Archives, University of Illinois.

53  Kiesel, "Iowans in the Arts," 284.

54  Burns, *Kinship with the Land*, 58.

55  Allan Bogue to James Malin, July 14, 1969, Mss. Coll. 183, Malin Papers, Kansas State Historical Society; Allan G. Bogue, "Herbert Quick's Hawkeye Trilogy," *Books at Iowa* vol. 16 (April 1973). For Masters's similar experience making the transition from lawyer-to-writer, see Charles E. Burgess, "Edgar Lee Masters: The Lawyer as Writer," in John E. Hallwas and Dennis J. Reader (eds), *The Vision of This Land: Studies of Vachel Lindsay, Edgar Lee Masters, and Carl Sandburg* (Macomb, Western Illinois University, 1976), 55–73.

56  Stegner, "The Trail of the Hawkeye," *Saturday Review of Literature*, July 30, 1938, 4.

57  Herbert Quick, *Vandemark's Folly* (New York, A. L. Burt, 1922); Burns, *Kinship with the Land*, 3 (source of quotation); Allan G. Bogue, "Herbert Quick's Hawkeye Trilogy," *Books at Iowa* vol. 16 (April 1973).

58  Van Doren, "The Roving Critic," *The Nation* vol. 114 (March 15, 1922), 319; Bogue, "Herbert Quick's Hawkeye Trilogy."

59  Aldrich, "Mid-Western Writers," *Prairie Schooner* vol. 1, no. 1 (January 1927), 81 (native); James C. Rosse, "Bess Streeter Aldrich," *Prairie Schooner* vol. 3, no. 3 (Summer 1929), 226–29.

60  In a radio address on Nebraska's KFAB in 1926, for example, Aldrich asked Nebraskans to send her their stories, which they did. See Box 1, Aldrich Papers, Nebraska State Historical Society.

61  Aldrich, "Why I Live in a Small Town," *Ladies Home Journal* (June 1933). In the same article, Aldrich said, "There are fiction writers who would have us believe that just three types of people inhabit small midwestern towns. There are those who are discontented, wanting to get away; there are those who are too dumb to know enough to want to get away; and the rest are half-wits."

62  Aldrich, "Why I Live in a Small Town."

63  Helen G. Masters to Aldrich, May 12, 1928, and Mrs. Theodore Roosevelt Jr. to Aldrich, February 13, 1928, both in Box 1, Aldrich Papers, Nebraska State Historical Society. For letters relating to Aldrich's defense of the Nebraska Writers' Guild and local writing generally, see letters from spring 1928 in Box 1, Aldrich Papers, Nebraska State Historical Society.

64  Aldrich, *A Lantern in Her Hand* (New York, Appleton-Century, 1928); James C. Olson to Stanley Pargellis, March 27, 1947, NL 03/05/06, Box 2, FF 46, Pargellis Papers, Newberry Library. Olson had been asked to provide a list of the ten best books about Nebraska by Newberry Library director Stanley Pargellis for a special issue of the *Chicago Sun* book review focused on midwestern literature. For precursors of Aldrich, see James C. Olson, "The Literary Tradition in Pioneer Nebraska," *Prairie Schooner* vol. 24, no. 2 (Summer 1950), 161–68.

65  Mark J. Madigan, "Dorothy Canfield Fisher, 1879–1958," *Legacy* vol. 9, no. 1 (1992), 51; Irving Dillard to Stanley Pargellis, February 15, 1947, NL 03/05/06, Box 2, FF 46, Pargellis Papers, Newberry Library.

66  Madigan, "Dorothy Canfield Fisher," 52 (*The Brimming Cup* was set in Vermont).

67  Front matter, *Prairie Schooner* vol. 1, no. 1 (January 1927); Madigan, "Dorothy Canfield Fisher," 54. On Fisher's father, James H. Canfield, who worked on

railroads in Minnesota and Iowa and had a democratic approach to education and a "face well bronzed by prairie sun," see Laurence R. Veysey, *The Emergence of the American University* (Chicago, University of Chicago Press, 1965), 111.

68  Sigmund describes his upbringing in "An Announcement of Distinction," a clipping from *Cedar Rapids Republican*, no date, in Box 1, Sigmund Papers, University of Iowa. Sigmund's story is reminiscent of the career of Ted Kooser, who worked as an insurance executive in Nebraska while writing poetry.

69  N.a., "Poetry Is for All of Us, Iowa Business Man Holds; Jay Sigmund Presents This View in Talk at School of Business Here," *Mason City Globe-Gazette*, November 20, 1934 ("long-haired visionaries" is newspaper's description; remaining quotes from Sigmund).

70  Sigmund to Frederick, February 7, 1923, Box 1, Sigmund Papers.

71  N.a., "An Announcement of Distinction," clipping from *Cedar Rapids Republican*, no date, in Box 1, Sigmund Papers, University of Iowa.

72  Jay Sigmund, *Land O'Maize Folks* (New York, James T. White and Co., 1924) ("village folk" poems); Sigmund, *Wapsipinicon Tales* (Cedar Rapids, The Prairie Publishing Company, 1927).

73  Mumford to Sigmund, December 7, 1931, Box 1, Sigmund Papers.

74  Sandburg to Sigmund, June 30, 1936, Box 1, Sigmund Papers.

75  Sandburg to Sigmund, November 24, 1925, Box 1, Sigmund Papers. See generally Allan C. Carlson, "Bard of the Wapsipinicon: An Assessment of Jay G. Sigmund," *Modern Age* vol. 55, no. 1 (Fall 2013), 31–46; and Zachary Michael Jack, *The Plowman Sings: The Essential Fiction, Poetry, and Drama of America's Forgotten Regionalist Jay G. Sigmund* (Lanham, Maryland, University Press of America, 2008). Sigmund also aided the young Cedar Rapidian Paul Engle, who went on to direct the Iowa Writers' Workshop from 1941–1965 and whose early work included regional themes. But Engle later turned away from Iowa and toward the international scene and founded the University of Iowa's International Writing Program (and edited *Poems of Mao Tse-tung*). On Engle's warm recollections of his youth in Iowa, see Engle, *A Lucky American Childhood* (Iowa City, University of Iowa Press, 1996). On the decline in the workshop's regional emphasis, see Eric Bennett, *Workshops of Empire: Stegner, Engle, and American Creative Writing during the Cold War* (Iowa City, University of Iowa Press, 2015).

76  Sigmund to Frederick, February 7, 1923, Box 1, Sigmund Papers (modern,

reek); Sigmund to Frank Luther Mott (Director of the University of Iowa school of journalism), April 12, 1935, Box 1, Sigmund Papers (laugh).

77  August Derleth, *Three Literary Men: A Memoir of Sinclair Lewis, Sherwood Anderson, Edgar Lee Masters* (New York, Candlelight Press, 1963), 13. The basement of the public library in Sauk City includes a "Derleth room" featuring a wide range of Derleth's writings and other materials about Derleth's life. Sinclair Lewis's biographer Mark Schorer was also from Sauk City. Derleth to Stanley Pargellis, May 6, 1947, NL 03/05/06, Box 2, FF 46, Pargellis Papers, Newberry Library. Derleth and Schorer studied with Helen White at Wisconsin, who took courses from Frederick Jackson Turner and saved her notes from Turner's famous classes. Vernon Carstensen to Merle Curti, November 5, 1966, Box 8, FF 18, Curti Papers, WHS.

78  Derleth, *The Wisconsin: River of a Thousand Isles* (Madison, University of Wisconsin Press, 1985 [1942]), xiv.

79  Derleth, *The Wisconsin*, xiv–xv.

80  Derleth, *Village Year: A Sac Prairie Journal* (New York, Coward-McCann, 1941), 34, 47.

81  William F. Thompson, "Introduction," in Derleth, *The Wisconsin*, xi–xii; Earl Rovit, "The Regions versus the Nation: Critical Battle of the Thirties," *Mississippi Quarterly* vol. 8 (1960), 91. Clifford Lord of the Wisconsin Historical Society listed *The Wisconsin* as first on his list of the ten "best books" about Wisconsin. "Ten Best Books about Wisconsin," NL 03/05/06, Box 2, FF 46, Pargellis Papers, Newberry Library. Masters, who wrote the book on the Sangamon River for the series, praised *The Wisconsin*, in Masters to Derleth, October 13, 1942, Derleth Papers, WHS. For a list of the other twenty-three books in the series, see front matter, Walter Havighurst, *Upper Mississippi: A Wilderness Saga* (New York, Rinehart and Co., 1937).

82  Derleth, *Three Literary Men*, 20; William F. Thompson, "Introduction," in Derleth, *The Wisconsin*, xvii. Derleth surveyed river islands, discussed Curry's health, and mused about the Wisconsin River with the Iowan turned University of Wisconsin professor Aldo Leopold. Leopold to Derleth, May 27 and June 8, 1943, and Leopold to Louis A. Clas, July 9, 1943, Derleth Papers, WHS.

83  Derleth, *The Wisconsin*, 321.

84  Derleth, *Three Literary Men*, 10–11. For a complete list of Derleth's "Sac Prairie Saga" books, see front matter, Derleth, *Walden West* (New York, Duell, Sloan and Pearce, 1961).

85   Garland to Derleth, November 10, 18, and 25, and December 4, 1936, Derleth
     Papers, WHS; Derleth, *Three Literary Men*, 27; Thompson, "Introduction," in
     Derleth, *The Wisconsin*, xv–xvi. Derleth also taught a class at the University of
     Wisconsin on regional literature and served as the literary editor of the Mad-
     ison *Capital Times* for two decades. Derleth dedicated *The Wisconsin* to Louise
     Phelps Kellogg, the prominent historian of Wisconsin and the Midwest.
     Derleth, *The Wisconsin*, 337. Derleth also wrote a history of the development
     and prominent figures of Sauk City. Derleth, *Restless Is the River* (New York,
     Charles Scribner's Sons, 1939).

86   Thompson, "Introduction," in Derleth, *The Wisconsin*, xviii.

87   Derleth, *Still Small Voice: The Biography of Zona Gale* (New York, D. Appleton-
     Century, 1940); Derleth, *The Wisconsin*, 323. On Garland's fondness for Gale,
     see Hamlin Garland to Derleth, July 2, 1939, Derleth Papers, WHS. Garland
     thought Gale "remained loyal to Portage as [William Allen] White is to
     Emporia [Kansas]." Garland to Derleth, January 22, 1940, Derleth Papers,
     WHS. Gale, in keeping with Derleth's description, described her environs
     for Garland: "the river is open, the hills are blue, the grass is faintly greening,
     robins and blackbirds are in their places, wild geese honk at night, and the
     call of the bluebirds is in the air." Gale to Garland, St. Patrick's Day [n.d.],
     1921, Box 1825, Hamlin Garland Papers, University of Southern California. On
     Garland's comparison of Gale to William Allen White, note White's focus on
     the Midwest as a region during the 1920s, in Charles E. Delgadillo, " 'A Pretty
     Weedy Flower': William Allen White, Midwestern Liberalism, and the 1920s
     Culture War," *Kansas History* vol. 35, no. 3 (Autumn 2012), 187–90. On White's
     focus on the American middle, see Edward Gale Agran, *"Too Good a Town":
     William Allen White, Community, and the Emerging Rhetoric of Middle America*
     (Fayetteville, University of Arkansas Press, 1998).

88   Derleth, *Walden West*, 64–65 (quotations); Schorer to Derleth, October 20,
     1961, Derleth Papers, WHS; Vivian Kawatzky, "Our Own Thoreau's Major
     Effort," *Milwaukee Sentinel*, November 26, 1961.

89   Derleth, *Three Literary Men*, 25.

90   Derleth, *Three Literary Men*, 25.

91   Derleth, *Three Literary Men*, 16, 25–26. In 1939 a *Time* reviewer also noted the
     extreme levels of productivity by the "indefatigable" Derleth that had by then
     already resulted in fourteen books and one thousand stories. "Horn Tooter,"
     *Time* vol. 34, no. 18 (October 30, 1939). Masters also thought it possible for

Derleth "to produce faster than [his] audience can read [him]." Masters to Derleth, May 8, 1939, Derleth Papers, WHS. See also Masters to Derleth, April 5 and November 15, 1940, Derleth Papers, WHS.

92   Masters to Derleth, December 6, 1939, Derleth Papers, WHS (adherence); Derleth, *Three Literary Men*, 51 (Concord).

93   Derleth, *Three Literary Men*, 53–54.

94   The sources of all quotations except "roots" and "deserves" are located in Masters to Derleth, April 2 and 6, 1938, Derleth Papers, WHS; Masters to Derleth, September 29, 1939, Derleth Papers, WHS (roots); Masters to Derleth, August 20, 1939, Derleth Papers, WHS (deserves). Masters frequently attacked the "dogmatic suggestions" of critics and praised Derleth for pursuing his own course. Masters to Derleth, September 17, 1941, Derleth Papers, WHS.

95   Masters to Derleth, September 17, 1941, Derleth Papers, WHS.

96   Masters to Sherwood Anderson, December 21, 1935, Box 24, FF 1213, Anderson Papers, Newberry Library.

97   Garland, *A Son of the Middle Border* (New York, Macmillan, 1917); Howells, "An Appreciation," *New York Times Review of Books*, August 26, 1917 (Howells combined "farm life" into "farmlife"). Garland confessed in *Son* that his early critical writings were written "in a mood of bitter resentment," a mood he chose not to "defend" in *Son*. Garland, *Son of the Middle Border*, 319. On his early "bleak" depictions, Garland understood that "no one considered it so in those days" and recognized the easing of the difficulties of early frontier life. Garland to George Ade, October 17, n.d. (probably 1917), Box 809, Hamlin Garland Papers, University of Southern California.

98   (New York, Macmillan, 1921). On the "hundreds of letters" to Garland from pioneer families thanking Garland for telling the story of their midwestern settlement experiences, see Garland to Leland Case, June 18, 1938, Box 1269, Hamlin Garland Papers, University of Southern California.

99   Zona Gale, "National Epics of the Border," *Yale Review* vol. 11 (1922), 852; Gale to Garland, n.d., Box 1825, Hamlin Garland Papers, University of Southern California.

100  Allan Nevins, "Garland and the Prairie," *Literary Review* vol. 2, no. 50 (August 19, 1922), 882 ("To any one who was reared on a farm of the upper Mississippi Valley [Garland] brings back the sights, the odors, the sounds, the people, and the work, with more than the fullness of life"). Non-midwestern and Marxist critics found Garland's new focus on the Midwest deadened by "dullness" and

"prolixity" and "self-satisfied, fastidious, undemocratic, out of sympathy with every vital movement in contemporary life." Granville Hicks, "Garland of the Academy," *Nation* vol. 133 (October 21, 1931), 435–36. For similar criticism of regionalism, see also Hicks, *The Great Tradition: An Interpretation of American Literature since the Civil War* (New York, Macmillan, 1933), 145–46, 278 (calling Garland's later career "pure tragedy" and regionalism "merely antiquarian"); Julia Mickenberg, "'Revolution Can Spring Up from the Windy Prairie as Naturally as Wheat': Meridel LeSueur and the Making of a Radical Regional Tradition," in Michael C. Steiner (ed), *Regionalists on the Left: Radical Voices from the American West* (Norman, University of Oklahoma Press, 2013), 29. Granville Hicks was one of the Communist Party's "premier literary critics in the 1930s." Richard H. Pells, *The Liberal Mind in a Conservative Age: American Intellectuals in the 1940s and 1950s* (Wesleyan, Wesleyan University Press, 1989), 318 (premier); Daniel Aaron, *Writers on the Left: Episodes in American Literary Communism* (New York, Octagon Books, 1974 [1961]), 174, 194–95, 262; Neil Jumonville, *Henry Steele Commager: Midcentury Liberalism and the History of the Present* (Chapel Hill, University of North Carolina Press, 1999), 210.

101  Hamlin Garland, "Current Fiction Heroes," *New York Times Book Review*, December 23, 1923. In response to Garland's article, Fred Lewis Pattee counseled Garland to "cease growling," to return to the West, and to counter prevailing literary trends with his own strong writing. Pattee, "The Fiery Radicals of Yesteryear," *New York Times Book Review*, February 24, 1924.

102  Garland to Derleth, April 16, 1938, Derleth Papers, WHS. Garland favored publishing efforts that might "promote Chicago and the Midwest as a publishing center." Keith Newlin, "Why Hamlin Garland Left the Main-Travelled Road," *Studies in American Naturalism* vol. 1, nos. 1 and 2 (Summer and Winter 2006), 80.

103  Garland, "Current Fiction Heroes"; Suckow, "Folk Idea in American Life."

104  Garland to Stuart Pratt Sherman, February 8, n.d. (probably early 1920s), Box 2, Sherman Papers, University Archives, University of Illinois; Garland, "Current Fiction Heroes" (quotations); Garland, "An Un-American Art," *New York Times*, March 2, 1925. Garland was "saddened" that fiction had become "pre-occupied with the animal side of sex life" and that "virtuous women no longer interest novelists or dramatists." Garland to Derleth, April 16, 1938, Derleth Papers, WHS (quotations); Garland, *Back-Trailers from the Middle Border* (New York, Macmillan, 1928), 95; and *Roadside Meetings* (New York,

Macmillan, 1930), 135. Garland was disappointed in "any writer who limited himself to the evil and ugly aspects of life." John T. Flanagan, *James Hall: Literary Pioneer of the Ohio Valley* (Minneapolis, University of Minnesota Press, 1941), 157. On Garland's early advocacy for midwestern voices in American letters and his later opposition to what he called the "vogue" for modernism, which he saw as "pornographic" and driven by commercial motives, see Keith Newlin, *Garland in His Own Time: A Biographical Chronicle of His Life, Drawn from Recollections, Interviews, and Memoirs by Family, Friends, and Associates* (Iowa City, University of Iowa Press, 2013), xxv–xxvi. Van Wyck Brooks recalled a 1938 letter from Garland expressing his displeasure with "this age of nudity and jazz." Brooks, "From *An Autobiography* (1965)," in Newlin, *Garland in His Own Time,* 224. See also Charles Fenton, "The American Academy of Arts and Letters vs. All Comers: Literary Rags and Riches in the 1920s," *South Atlantic Quarterly* vol. 58, no. 4 (1959), 581. Brooks also found the "obscenity and profanity of many of our writers" to be "childish." Brooks, *On Literature Today,* 20. DeVoto also found it "immature." DeVoto to Frederick Manfred, May 8, 1953, Box 16, Manfred Papers, Upper Midwest Literary Archives, University of Minnesota.

105 Garland, "Current Fiction Heroes"; Weber, *Midwestern Ascendancy,* 49 (quoting Garland), 52. On the "disappearance" of Tarkington from the academic discussion, see Hutner, *What America Read,* 26–27. For a recent and aggressive dismissal of Tarkington, see Thomas Mallon, "Hoosiers: The Lost World of Booth Tarkington," *Atlantic Monthly* (May 2004). Edgar Lee Masters thought Riley was "regional" and "wrote very beautiful poems about his own country of Indiana, making it magical and beloved" but recognized that he had become "neglected." Masters to Derleth, February 3, 1940, Derleth Papers, WHS. Masters noted Riley's attention to region and his influence "bringing writers in other regions to write about theirs." Masters to Derleth, February 7, 1940, Derleth Papers, WHS. William Dean Howells saw Riley as "the poet of our common life," but James Woodress notes how later critics "dealt severely" with Riley. James Woodress, *Booth Tarkington: Gentleman from Indiana* (New York, Greenwood Press, 1954), 18.

106 Garland, "Current Fiction Heroes."

107 Garland, "Current Fiction Heroes."

108 Keith Newlin, *Hamlin Garland: A Life* (Lincoln, University of Nebraska Press, 2008), 327–48. Garland worked with the South Dakotan Leland Case, the

brother of future U.S. Senator Francis Case, to organize a collection of mid-western books at the Case brothers' alma mater, Dakota Wesleyan University, that became the Friends of the Middle Border Museum. Leland Case to Garland, June 21, 1938, Box 1269, Hamlin Garland Papers, University of Southern California; Jarvis Harriman, *The Man from the Hills: A Biography of Leland Davidson Case* (Oklahoma City, Westerners International, 1994), 73–76.

109 Regionalists tended to be agrarian, "conventionally religious," suspicious of outside planning and controls, and resistant to foreign prescriptions and pseudo-sciences such as Marxism and Freudianism. Rovit, "Regions versus the Nation," 96.

110 Randolph Bourne, "A Mirror of the Middle West," *The Dial*, November 30, 1918, 480. On the Midwest's "easy friendliness not found in Eastern cities," see Donald Davidson, *The Attack on Leviathan: Regionalism and Nationalism in the United States* (Chapel Hill, University of North Carolina Press, 1938), 189.

111 LeSueur quotation from Julia Mickenberg, "Writing the Midwest: Meridel LeSueur and the Making of a Radical Regional Tradition," in Sherrie A. Inness and Diana Royer (eds), *Breaking Boundaries: New Perspectives on Women's Regional Writing* (Iowa City, University of Iowa Press, 1997), 149. On B. A. Botkin's attempts to distinguish a newer radical regionalism from an older, less political regionalism, see Hirsh, "Theorizing Regionalism and Folklore from the Left," in Steiner, *Regionalists on the Left*, 135, 137.

112 The influence of an "old regionalism" and the limited appeal of a newer radical regionalism are suggested by LeSueur's concern that the "Midwest's population was becoming increasingly conservative." One LeSueur correspondent cast doubt on the search for a radical tradition in the region and saw the Midwest as defined by "bitterness" and populated by "God fearing people." Mickenberg, "Revolution Can Spring Up," 33, 39.

113 Meridel LeSueur to Suckow, August 16, 1936, Series 1, Box 2, Suckow Papers; LeSueur to Sherwood Anderson, August 19, 1936, Box 23, FF 1156, Anderson Papers, Newberry Library. Although smaller-scale radical little magazines existed in the Midwest, prior to *Midwest* "no centralized vehicle had yet emerged to combine efforts of writers across the region." Mickenberg, "Revolution Can Spring Up," 32.

114 LeSueur, *North Star Country* (New York, Duell, Sloane & Pearce, 1945). In Iowa during the New Deal, the staffers of the state's Federal Writers' Project located in Des Moines also launched the small magazine *Hinterland*, which

was similar to *Midwest*, under the auspices of what they called the Midwest Literary League using FWP time and resources, causing friction with administrators in Washington. *Hinterland* ceased publication in 1939. Julia Mickenberg, "Left at Home in Iowa: 'Progressive Regionalists' and the WPA Guide to 1930s Iowa," *Annals of Iowa* vol. 56 (Summer 1997), 243–45, 264. The primary product of the FWP in Iowa was *Iowa: A Guide to the Hawkeye State* (Iowa City, State Historical Society of Iowa, 1938). See Don Farron, "The Federals in Iowa: A Hawkeye Guidebook in the Making," *Annals of Iowa* vol. 41 (1973), 1190–96. During the 1930s, other radical little magazines in the Midwest included *Hub*, *Left*, *The Dubuque Dial*, *Left Front*, and *New Quarterly*. Mickenberg, "Left at Home in Iowa," 239; Hoffman, Allen, and Ulrich, *Little Magazine*, 155.

115 Mickenberg, "Revolution Can Spring Up," 30–31; Douglas Wixson, *Worker-Writer in America: Jack Conroy and the Tradition of Midwestern Literary Radicalism, 1898–1990* (Urbana, University of Illinois Press, 1994), 248; Mickenberg, "Left at Home in Iowa," 241, n. 15, 256–57.

116 Mickenberg, "Writing the Midwest," 145, 148. Craig Jackson Calhoun highlights the false choice between rationality and tradition first bestowed by the Enlightenment and describes a "radicalism of tradition," one grounded not in a tradition of monarchy and old-world feudalism, for example, but in a tradition of "everyday social practice," an emphasis similar to Suckow's focus on "the folks." Craig Jackson Calhoun, "The Radicalism of Tradition: Community Strength or Venerable Disguise and Borrowed Language?" *American Journal of Sociology* vol. 88, no. 5 (March 1983), 888.

117 Mickenberg, "Writing the Midwest," 145–46; Mickenberg, "Revolution Can Spring Up," 26–27. On the denunciation of regionalism by radicals, see Steiner, "Preface," xi, and Steiner, "Introduction," 8, in Steiner, *Regionalists on the Left*. After the 1935 American Writers' Congress, LeSueur "recalled fierce attacks on regionalism by Communist Party members." B. A. Botkin's 1937 address to the American Writers' Congress similarly fell flat with the "audience of predominantly urban leftists." Radical regionalists were "rejected by the leftist literary movement they were committed to, by fellow leftists who could only see regionalism as reactionary." Hirsh, "Theorizing Regionalism and Folklore from the Left," 150–51. Michael Steiner explains how regionalists were "pummeled from the center and the left of the political spectrum." Steiner, "Carey McWilliams, California, and the Education of a Radical Regionalist,"

in Steiner (ed), *Regionalists on the Left*, 357. See also Wixson, *Worker-Writer in America*, 390–92.

118 Steiner similarly notes how Carey McWilliams's early regionalism is forgotten in favor of his later radicalism. Steiner, "Carey McWilliams, California, and the Education of a Radical Regionalist," 356.

119 Mickenberg stresses that the "progressive regionalists" were only "one faction" of the regionalist movement of the decade. Mickenberg, "Left at Home in Iowa," 237. The midwestern-born historian John D. Hicks, who wrote a pioneering treatment of agrarian Populism, echoed other midwesterners who saw Communism as "something vastly different from our home-grown varieties of radicalism, or liberalism, whatever we may choose to call them." John Hicks to DeWitt Wallace, April 20, 1948, FF Correspondence April 1948, DB 14, John D. Hicks Papers, Bancroft Library.

120 Suckow to Frederick, October 30, 1935, Series 1, Box 2, Suckow Papers, University of Iowa.

121 Wixson, *Worker-Writer in America*, 394.

122 LeSueur to Sherwood Anderson, August 19, 1936, Box 23, FF 1156, Anderson Papers, Newberry Library.

123 Aaron, *Writers on the Left*, 279.

124 Dorman, *Revolt of the Provinces*, 23.

125 Michael C. Steiner, "Regionalism in the Great Depression," *Geographical Review* vol. 73, no. 4 (October 1983), 430, 432–33, 441–42; Steiner, "Region, Regionalism, and Place," in Joan Shelley Rubin and Scott E. Casper (eds), *Oxford Encyclopedia of Cultural and Intellectual History* (New York, Oxford University Press, 2013), 275–88; William B. Hesseltine, "Regions, Classes, and Sections in American History," *Journal of Land and Public Utility Economics* vol. 20 (February 1944), 35–44.

126 Richard H. Pells, *Radical Visions and American Dreams: Culture and Social Thought in the Depression Years* (New York, Harper & Row, 1973), 199; Mickenberg, "Left at Home in Iowa," 238.

127 Steiner, "Regionalism in the Great Depression," 438–40; Susman, "The Culture of the Thirties," in *Culture as History: The Transformation of American Society in the Twentieth Century* (Washington, D.C., Smithsonian Books, 2003), 164.

128 August Derleth to Sinclair Lewis, October 5, 1937, Box 46, FF 488, Lewis Papers, Beinecke Library, Yale University; Roy W. Meyer, *The Middle Western*

*Farm Novel in the Twentieth Century* (Lincoln, University of Nebraska Press, 1965), 4–5.

129 The "American scene" group of Wood, Curry, Benton, and others was "primarily, but not exclusively, a phenomenon of the Middle West" and "not an art of mountains, clouds or the sea." Alfred Frankenstein, "Paul Sample," *Magazine of Art* vol. 31 (July 1938), 387 (quotation); Michael C. Steiner, "Grant Wood and the Politics of Regionalism," *Middle West Review* vol. 3, no. 1 (Fall 2016), 71–95. Benton rejected Marxism and modernism and the other "factors inimical to indigenous art—colonialism, highbrowism, the make-believes and snobberies of the wealthy circles." Dorman, *Revolt of the Provinces*, 118. It was Benton's "pictures of rural America that particularly separated him from the left." Erika Doss, *Benton, Pollock, and the Politics of Modernism: From Regionalism to Abstract Expressionism* (Chicago, University of Chicago Press, 1991), 124. After Van Wyck Brooks's change of direction, Benton wished him well "turning the colonial tide" and helping others "survive the current political pressure from the East." Benton to Brooks, October 8, 1944, Folder 258, Folder 1637, Brooks Papers, Annenberg Library, University of Pennsylvania.

130 Wood to Suckow, December 7, 1931, Series 1, Box 2, Suckow Papers.

131 Richard Lingeman, *Small Town America: A Narrative History 1620–The Present* (New York, G. P. Putnam's Sons, 1980), 382. On Shirer and his "Midwestern Beginnings," see Ken Cuthbertson, *A Complex Fate: William L. Shirer and the American Century* (Montreal, McGill-Queen's University Press, 2015), 7–26.

132 James M. Dennis, *Renegade Regionalists: The Modern Independence of Grant Wood, Thomas Hart Benton, and John Steuart Curry* (Madison, University of Wisconsin Press, 1998), 6, 53.

133 Steiner, "Regionalism in the Great Depression," 433. One product was the "American Guide" series to various states. Arthur A. Ekirch Jr., *Ideologies and Utopias: The Impact of the New Deal on American Thought* (Chicago, Quadrangle Books, 1969), 168–69. Some radical regionalists, frustrated by their rejection by the left, found a home in the Federal Writers Project. The Oklahoma regionalist B. A. Botkin, for example, became the National Folklore Editor of the FWP. Hirsh, "Theorizing Regionalism and Folklore from the Left," 151. John Frederick of *The Midland*, while not a radical, directed the Illinois Guide. See also Ian Tyrrell, "Public at the Creation: Place, Memory, and Historical Practice in the Mississippi Valley Historical Association," *Journal of American History* vol. 94, no. 1 (June 2007), 43.

134  See chapter 3; Lauck, *Lost Region*; Jon K. Lauck, "The Prairie Historians and the Foundations of Midwestern History," *Annals of Iowa: A Quarterly Journal of History* vol. 71, no. 2 (Spring 2012), 137–73.

135  Rubin, *Making of Middle Brow Culture*, 80.

136  Paxson was seen as one of the "optimistic historians of the twenties." Henry F. May, "Shifting Perspectives on the 1920's," *Mississippi Valley Historical Review* vol. 43, no. 3 (December 1956), 422, n. 45. Paxson's trilogy on World War I included *Postwar Years: Normalcy, 1918–1923* (New York, Cooper Square, 1966 [1948]), which did not discuss the alleged revolt from the village.

137  James C. Malin, *Essays on Historiography* (Lawrence, KS, James C. Malin, 1946), 109.

138  Gerald D. Nash, *Creating the West: Historical Interpretations, 1890–1990* (Albuquerque, University of New Mexico Press, 1991), 115.

139  May, "Shifting Perspectives on the 1920's," 418.

140  Bernard DeVoto, *Mark Twain's America* (New York, Little, Brown, 1932), 225 (rebutting, inter alia, Brooks's *The Ordeal of Mark Twain* [New York, Dutton, 1920] and finding Brooks "ignorant of the America about which he writes," including the "Middle Western Border"); Ruland, *Rediscovery of American Literature*, 139; Anthony Channell Hilfer, *The Revolt from the Village, 1915–1930* (Chapel Hill, University of North Carolina Press, 1969), 65. DeVoto explained in *Mark Twain's America* that the frontier was, in Robert Dorman's phrase, "far from being a death march of culture." Dorman, *Revolt of the Provinces*, 90. DeVoto openly confessed to Brooks that he planned to "attack your books" and declined invitations to socialize lest his critical faculties be constrained. DeVoto to Van Wyck Brooks, August 2, 1943, Folder 743, Brooks Papers, Annenberg Library, University of Pennsylvania.

141  Steiner, "Regionalism in the Great Depression," 430.

142  Steiner, "Regionalism in the Great Depression," 436.

143  Rovit, "Regions versus the Nation," 93.

144  Hirsh, "Theorizing Regionalism and Folklore from the Left," 153.

145  Garland to August Derleth, April 16, 1938, Derleth Papers, WHS.

146  Masters to August Derleth, January 15, 1939, Derleth Papers, WHS. By 1940, Masters also said (when discussing Mencken's views) the "magazines were now in the hands of young morons." Masters to Derleth, May 12, 1940, Derleth Papers, WHS.

147  Suckow to John T. Frederick, October 30, 1935, Series 1, Box 2, Suckow Papers.

148 Steiner, "Carey McWilliams, California, and the Education of a Radical Regionalist," 357.

149 Michael C. Steiner, "The Origins of Regionalist Thought in the Midwest," paper delivered at the First Annual Midwestern History Association Conference, Grand Rapids, Michigan, April 2015, in author's possession.

150 *Fifteenth Census of the United States: 1930: Population vol. II; General Report, Statistics by Subjects* (Washington, D.C., U.S. Department of Commerce, 1933), 14.

151 Richard C. Wade, *The Urban Frontier: The Rise of Western Cities, 1790–1830* (Cambridge, Harvard University Press, 1959) (explaining the origins of Cincinnati and St. Louis and other midwestern cities); Benjamin T. Spencer, "Regionalism in American Literature," in Merrill Jensen (ed), *Regionalism in America* (Madison, University of Wisconsin Press, 1951), 220–39.

152 Jackson Lears, *Rebirth of a Nation: The Making of Modern America, 1877–1920* (New York, Harper, 2009), 134; William E. Leuchtenburg, *The Perils of Prosperity, 1914–32* (Chicago, University of Chicago Press, 1958), 225, 227 (incubus); Charles W. Eagles, *Democracy Delayed: Congressional Reapportionment and Urban-Rural Conflict in the 1920s* (Athens, University of Georgia Press, 1990) (on rural resistance to increasing urban control of politics); Charles W. Eagles, "Urban-Rural Conflict in the 1920s: A Historiographical Assessment," *Historian* vol. 49, no. 1 (November 1986), 26–48 (reviewing historians' attention to urban-rural conflict and noting historians' anti-rural bias); Steven Conn, *Americans against the City: Anti-Urbanism in the Twentieth Century* (New York, Oxford University Press, 2014), 20 (deeming Frederick Jackson Turner's writings "an anti-urban romance, played out in the Midwest"); Walker, "Poet and the Rise of the City," 85–99; Don Kirschner, *City and Country: Rural Responses to Urbanization in the 1920s* (Westport, CT, Greenwood Press, 1970), 14 (noting the view that "cities were threatening to destroy the old rural society"). Kirschner was a graduate student at the University of Iowa who was originally a "student of [Samuel] Hays' working on urban-rural conflicts in three mid-western states in the 1920s" but became an advisee of Christopher Lasch at Iowa. Lasch to William Leuchtenburg, March 23, 1961, William Leuchtenburg Papers, UNC-Chapel Hill. On Lasch's later appreciation of the rural Midwest, see "The Prairie Populism of Christopher Lasch," *Great Plains Quarterly* vol. 32, no. 3 (Summer 2012), 183–205.

153 Doss, *Benton, Pollock, and the Politics of Modernism*, 125 (milieu); George E.

Mowry, *The Urban Nation, 1920–1960* (New York, Hill and Wang, 1965), 2–3. On the absence of regional settings and distinctions in urban studies, see Raymond A. Mohl, "City and Region: The Missing Dimension in U.S. Urban History," *Journal of Urban History* vol. 25, no. 1 (November 1998), 3–21; James Connolly, "Bringing the City Back In: Space and Place in the Urban History of the Gilded Age and Progressive Era," *Journal of the Gilded Age and Progressive Era* vol. 1, no. 3 (July 2002), 258–78; Andrew Cayton, "On the Importance of Place, or, a Plea for Idiosyncrasy," *Journal of Urban History* vol. 24, no. 1 (November 1997), 81; and David R. Goldfield, "The New Regionalism," *Journal of Urban History* vol. 10, no. 2 (February 1984), 176. On changes to rural social institutions, see James H. Madison, "Reformers and the Rural Church, 1900–1950," *Journal of American History* vol. 73, no. 3 (December 1986), 645–68. The new interstate highway system built during the 1950s would also focus on connecting urban centers, elevating their importance further. Earl Swift, *The Big Roads* (New York, Houghton Mifflin, 2011).

154   Randall Patnode, " 'What These People Need Is Radio': New Technology, the Press, and Otherness in 1920s America," *Technology and Culture* vol. 44, no. 2 (April 2003), 298.

155   Larry Lyon, *The Community in Urban Society* (Prospect Heights, IL, Waveland Press, 1989), 21–22.

156   Hal S. Barron, "And the Crooked Shall Be Made Straight: Public Road Administration and the Decline of Localism in the Rural North, 1870–1930," *Journal of Social History* vol. 26, no. 1 (Autumn 1992), 81; Jason Weems, *Barnstorming the Prairies: How Aerial Aviation Shaped the Midwest* (Minneapolis, University of Minnesota Press, 2015), xxii–xxiii. See chapter 1, "Rise of the Urban Mass Mind," in Mowry, *Urban Nation*, 1–34.

157   David R. Meyer, "Midwestern Industrialization and the American Manufacturing Belt in the Nineteenth Century," *Journal of Economic History* vol. 49, no. 4 (December 1989), 922 (explaining that the Midwest's share of national manufacturing output grew from 14 percent in 1860 to 26 percent by 1900); Philip Scranton, "Multiple Industrializations: Urban Manufacturing Development in the American Midwest, 1880–1925," *Journal of Design History* vol. 12, no. 1 (1999), 45–63; Brian Page and Richard Walker, "From Settlement to Fordism: The Agro-Industrial Revolution in the American Midwest," *Economic Geography* vol. 67, no. 4 (October 1991), 296–304.

158   Lyon, *Community in Urban Society*, 96–97; Roger A. Salerno, *Landscapes of*

*Abandonment: Capitalism, Modernity, and Estrangement* (Albany, State University of New York Press, 2003), 157–58, 163.

159  David Madden, "Introduction," in Madden (ed), *Proletarian Writers of the Thirties* (Carbondale, Southern Illinois University Press, 1968), xvi (visible); Walter B. Rideout, *The Radical Novel in the United States, 1900–1954: Some Interrelations of Literature and Society* (Cambridge, Harvard University Press, 1956), 171; Barbara Foley, *Radical Representations: Politics and Form in U.S. Proletarian Fiction, 1929–1941* (Durham, Duke University Press, 1993), 66 (noting Conroy's quite midwestern/pragmatic comment that "to me a strike bulletin or an impassioned leaflet are of more moment than three hundred prettily and faultlessly written pages about the private woes of a society gigolo"); James E. Murphy, *The Proletarian Moment: The Controversy over Leftism in Literature* (Urbana, University of Illinois Press, 1991).

160  Joseph Warren Beach, *American Fiction, 1920–1940* (New York, Russell & Russell, 1960), 274 (Farrell quotation); Maxwell Geisman, *American Moderns: From Rebellion to Conformity* (New York, Hill and Wang, 1958), 191 (underdogs); Frederick J. Hoffman, *The Modern Novel in America* (Chicago, Regnery Co., 1951), 156.

161  Algren quoted in Malcolm Cowley, "Nelson Algren's Chicago," *Nation*, February 20, 1982, 210 (nobodies); "Rough Stuff," *Time*, May 28, 1956 (deeming Algren the "poet laureate of Skid Row").

162  Algren to Wright, February 18, 1939, quoted in David A. Taylor, "Literary Cubs, Canceling Out Each Other's Reticence," *American Scholar* vol. 78, no. 2 (Spring 2009), 139.

163  Jon C. Teaford, *Cities and Suburbs: The Political Fragmentation of Metropolitan America* (Baltimore, Johns Hopkins University Press, 1979); Heather Barrow, *Henry Ford's Plan for the American Suburb: Dearborn and Detroit* (DeKalb, Northern Illinois University Press, 2015); Ann Durkin Keating, *Building Chicago: Suburban Developers and the Creation of a Divided Metropolis* (Urbana, University of Illinois Press, 2002); and Elaine Lewinnek, *The Working Man's Reward: Chicago's Early Suburbs and the Roots of American Sprawl* (New York, Oxford University Press, 2014); Jane Adams (ed), *Fighting for the Farm: Rural America Transformed* (Philadelphia, University of Pennsylvania Press, 2003).

164  Robert A. Beauregard, *When America Became Suburban* (Minneapolis, University of Minnesota Press, 2006), 23 (momentous); William Sharpe and

Leonard Wallock, "Bold New City or Built-Up 'Burb? Redefining Contemporary Suburbia," *American Quarterly* vol. 46, no. 1 (March 1994), 1.

165 Oates, *Expensive People* (New York, Modern Library, 2006 [1968]), 8–9, 14, 23 (set in one of the thousands of identical homes of a generic midwestern suburb named "Fernwood"); Judith Guest, *Ordinary People* (New York, Viking, 1976); Evan S. Connell, *Mrs. Bridge* (New York, Viking, 1959) (set in Kansas City).

166 Catherine Jurca, *White Diaspora: The Suburb and the Twentieth-Century American Novel* (Princeton, Princeton University Press, 2001), 14 (unlocatable and grain), 17, 137, 160 (unconstrained); Margaret Marsh, "Historians and the Suburbs," *OAH Magazine of History* vol. 5, no. 2 (Fall 1990), 44; Marsh, "Reconsidering the Suburbs: An Exploration of Suburban Historiography," *Pennsylvania Magazine of History and Biography* vol. 112, no. 4 (October 1988), 582–83; Samuel Zipp, "Suburbia and American Exceptionalism," *Reviews in American History* vol. 36, no. 4 (December 2008), 600; Sharpe and Wallock, "Bold New City or Built-Up 'Burb?" 2.

167 James Howard Kuntsler, *The Geography of Nowhere* (New York, Free Press, 1993). For a call for scholars to move beyond "mere literary reiterations of prevailing postwar social and cultural critiques" of the suburbs, see Keith M. Wilhite, "Framing Suburbia: U.S. Literature and the Postwar Suburban Region, 1945–2002" (PhD dissertation, University of Iowa, July 2007), 7.

168 U.S. Census, Table 13, Urban and Rural Population; Earliest Census to 1980 (Washington, D.C., U.S. Department of Commerce, 1980), 1-52-54.

169 See Jon K. Lauck, *American Agriculture and the Problem of Monopoly: The Political Economy of Grain Belt Farming, 1953–1980* (Lincoln, University of Nebraska Press, 2000); and Robert Wuthnow, *Remaking the Heartland: Middle America since the 1950s* (Princeton, Princeton University Press, 2010).

170 N.a., "Play to the Farm Vote," *Time*, April 16, 1956; n.a., "Farm Revolt Again in '56?—Five State Report," *New York Times*, September 9, 1956; Jimmye S. Hillman, "Whatever Happened to the Farm Problem?" *Gastronomica* vol. 11, no. 4 (Winter 2011), 86–90. On the decline of farming culture and the rise of "agribusiness" in the 1950s, see Shane Hamilton, "Agribusiness, the Family Farm, and the Politics of Technological Determinism in the Post–World War II United States," *Technology and Culture* vol. 55 (July 2014), 560–90.

171 G. Scott Thomas, *A New World to Be Won: John Kennedy, Richard Nixon, and the Tumultuous Year of 1960* (Santa Barbara, Praeger, 2011), 66 (agriculture); Pells, *Liberal Mind in a Conservative Age*, 57.

172 Michael B. Katz, "What Is an American City?" *Dissent* vol. 56, no. 3 (Summer 2009), 20.

173 Gilbert C. Fite, *American Farmers: The New Minority* (Bloomington, Indiana University Press, 1981).

174 Jon K. Lauck, "'The Silent Artillery of Time': Understanding Social Change in the Rural Midwest," *Great Plains Quarterly* vol. 19, no. 4 (Fall 1999), 245–55; Patnode, "What These People Need Is Radio," 289; Dennis S. Nordin and Roy V. Scott, *From Farmer to Prairie Entrepreneur: The Transformation of Midwestern Agriculture* (Bloomington, Indiana University Press, 2005), 151–53.

175 Mark Storey, "Country Matters: Rural Fiction, Urban Modernity, and the Problem of American Regionalism," *Nineteenth-Century Literature* vol. 65, no. 2 (2010), 194.

176 Steve Craig, "'The More They Listen, the More They Buy': Radio and the Modernizing of Rural America, 1930–1939," *Agricultural History* vol. 80, no. 1 (Winter 2006), 3 (quotations); J. Steven Smethers and Lee B. Jolliffe, "Singing and Selling Seeds: The Live Music Era on Rural Midwestern Radio Stations," *Journalism History* vol. 26, no. 2 (Summer 2000), 61–70 (explaining how radio first emphasized local and regional talent but by the 1950s embraced national and generic programming); Patnode, "What These People Need Is Radio," 285–305; Claude S. Fischer and Glenn R. Carroll, "Telephone and Automobile Diffusion in the United States, 1902–1937," *American Journal of Sociology* vol. 93, no. 5 (March 1988), 1153 (noting faster usage rates in the Midwest, which had "many well-off, independent farmers [who] were relatively quick adopters," unlike the South); Mowry, *Urban Nation*, 5 (explaining how movie companies sought "to reach for the widest possible audience and therefore to tailor the product as closely as possible to the taste of the masses").

177 Arthur J. Vidich and Joseph Bensman, *Small Town in Mass Society: Class, Power and Religion in a Rural Community* (Princeton, Princeton University Press, 1958); Lyon, *Community in Urban Society*, 13–14.

178 Mowry, *Urban Nation*, 5; Rovit, "Regions versus the Nation," 93, n. 4.

179 Rovit, "Regions versus the Nation," 97 (quotations); Patnode, "What These People Need Is Radio," 296.

180 Garland, *Afternoon Neighbors* (New York, Macmillan, 1934), 459; Bernard DeVoto, "Regionalism or the Coterie Manifesto," *Saturday Review of Literature*, October 31, 1936 (dull); H. W. Janson, "The International Aspects of Regionalism," *College Art Journal* vol. 2, no. 4, part 1 (May 1943), 110 (mediocre). Carl Van Doren, creator of the revolt thesis, thought Lewis's "slashing

portrait of Gopher Prairie" was launched "against all villages" for the crime of "being dull." Carl Van Doren, "Contemporary American Novelists X. The Revolt from the Village: 1920," *The Nation* vol. 113, no. 2936 (October 12, 1921) (Fall Book Supplement), 410.

181  Hoffman, Allen, and Ulrich, *Little Magazine*, 129, 135.

182  Mowry, *Urban Nation*, 18 (italics added).

183  Suckow to Frederick, December 8, 1924, Series 1, Box 2, Suckow Papers. Sherwood Anderson criticized one literary huckster for writing bad scripts for Hollywood studios and then turning around and "writing a book making very clever fun of Hollywood life." Anderson to Derleth, January 30, 1940, Derleth Papers, WHS.

184  Suckow to Frederick, March 8, 1930, Series 1, Box 2, Suckow Papers.

185  Anderson to August Derleth, January 17, 1940, Derleth Papers, WHS (big, terrible, walking); Anderson, "The New Note," *Little Review* vol. 1 (March 1914), 23 (cult, circles).

186  Anderson to August Derleth, January 17, 1940, Derleth Papers, WHS.

187  Zona Gale to Hamlin Garland, n.d., 1929, Box 1825, Hamlin Garland Papers, University of Southern California. To make Mr. Gale's point, see Bruce Lenthall, *Radio's America: The Great Depression and the Rise of Modern Mass Culture* (Chicago, University of Chicago Press, 2007), 17–52.

188  Dorman, *Revolt of the Provinces*, 288. On the older Victorian concern over the flood of mass culture, see Daniel Walker Howe, "American Victorianism as a Culture," *American Quarterly* vol. 27, no. 5 (December 1975), 511.

189  Rovit, "Regions versus the Nation," 97. On the impact of television and mass culture on the Midwest, see Thomas T. McAvoy, "What Is the Midwestern Mind?" in *The Midwest: Myth or Reality?* (Notre Dame, Indiana, University of Notre Dame Press, 1961), 62; and John D. Hicks, *My Life with History: An Autobiography* (Lincoln, University of Nebraska Press, 1968), 42. In 1948, one hundred thousand television sets were in use in the United States. By the end of the 1950s, fifty million were in use. Wilbur Schramm, Jack Lyle, and Edwin B. Parker, "Television in the Lives of Our Children," in Derek L. Phillips (ed), *Studies in American Society* (New York, Thomas Y. Crowell, 1965), 54. Schramm was a midwesterner who created the Iowa Writers' Workshop.

190  Carstensen to Curti, November 1, 1959, FF 18, Box 8, Curti Papers, WHS (revealed); "Carl Van Doren, 64, Noted Author, Dies," *New York Times*, July 19, 1950.

191 Carstensen to Curti, April 10, 1966, Box 8, FF 18, Curti Papers, WHS. The Wisconsin regionalist August Derleth also was diverted into the growing world of science fiction. Peter Viereck to Derleth, February 4, 1953, Derleth Papers, WHS.

192 On Minow's speech, see Minow, "How Vast the Wasteland Now?" *Bulletin of the American Academy of Arts and Sciences* vol. 45, no. 5 (February 1992), 16–30.

193 Carl Abbott, "Urbanizing the Sunbelt," *OAH Magazine of History* vol. 18, no. 1 (October 2003), 12 (rebalancing); Abbott, *The New Urban America: Growth and Politics in Sunbelt Cities* (Chapel Hill, University of North Carolina Press, 1981); Michelle Nickerson and Darren Dochuk, *Sunbelt Rising: The Politics of Space, Place, and Region* (Philadelphia, University of Pennsylvania Press, 2011); Michael Steiner, "The Sunbelt, the Midwest, and Versions of American Regionalism," *Middle West Review* vol. 2, no. 2 (Spring 2016), 219–23.

194 David Goldfield, "Writing the Sunbelt," *OAH Magazine of History* vol. 18, no. 1 (October 2003), 5; Edward L. Glaeser and Kristina Tobio, "The Rise of the Sunbelt," *Southern Economic Journal* vol. 74, no. 3 (January 2008), 611.

195 James C. Cobb, *The Selling of the South: The Southern Crusade for Industrial Development, 1936–1990* (Urbana, University of Illinois Press, 1993); Bruce J. Schulman, *From Cotton Belt to Sunbelt: Federal Policy, Economic Development, and the Transformation of the South, 1938–1980* (New York, Oxford University Press, 1991).

196 Raymond Arsenault, "The End of the Long Hot Summer: The Air Conditioner and Southern Culture," *Journal of Southern History* vol. 50, no. 4 (November 1984), 599 (quoting the *New York Times* explaining how the "air conditioner, the airplane and television" made the country "much less regionally diverse"), 604 (noting, by the World War II era, the anti-regional combination of air-conditioned movie theaters in the South), 613 ("wave"), 616, 618. In 1960, the Air Conditioning Institute promoted the idea that its product had "broken down regional barriers." Arsenault, "End of the Long Hot Summer," 619, n. 114. On the resulting diminishment of Southern distinctiveness, see Christopher A. Cooper, "Declining Dixie: Regional Identification in the Modern American South," *Social Forces* vol. 88, no. 3 (March 2010), 1083–1101.

197 Carl Abbott, *The Metropolitan Frontier: Cities in the Modern American West* (Tucson, University of Arizona Press, 1993).

198 Earl Pomeroy, *The American Far West in the Twentieth Century* (New Haven, Yale University Press, 2008), 2.

199 Hildegarde Hawthorne, "A Record of Vanished America," *New York Times Book Review*, January 15, 1922 (centre); Thomas Dyja, *The Third Coast: When Chicago Built the American Dream* (New York, Penguin Press HC, 2013).

200 Jim Wayne Miller, "Anytime the Ground Is Uneven: The Outlook for Regional Studies and What to Look For," in William E. Mallory and Paul Simpson-Housely (eds), *Geography and Literature: A Meeting of the Disciplines* (Syracuse, Syracuse University Press, 1987), 4–5 (quotations); Vicente L. Rafael, "Regionalism, Area Studies, and the Accidents of History," *American Historical Review* vol. 104, no. 4 (October 1999), 1208; Ian Buruma, "The Cult of Exile," *Prospect*, March 2001, 23–27.

201 Celia Applegate, "A Europe of Regions: Reflections on the Historiography of Sub-national Places in Modern Times," *American Historical Review* vol. 104, no. 4 (October 1999), 1158; Mary Neth, "Seeing the Midwest with Peripheral Vision: Identities, Narratives, and Region," in *The Identity of the American Midwest: Essays on Regional History* (Bloomington, Indiana University Press, 2001), 46–47; Michael E. Latham, *Modernization as Ideology: American Social Science and "Nation Building" in the Kennedy Era* (Chapel Hill, University of North Carolina Press, 2000); Nils Gilman, *Mandarins of the Future: Modernization Theory in Cold War America* (Baltimore, Johns Hopkins University Press, 2007), 1–23.

202 Miller, "Anytime the Ground Is Uneven," 3. On regions as a new Other, see Applegate, "Europe of Regions," 1164.

203 Rovit, "Regions versus the Nation," 90; Larry Woiwode, *Words Made Fresh: Essays on Literature and Culture* (Wheaton, IL, Crossway, 2011), 24.

204 Steiner, "Introduction," 8–9. Donald Davidson wrote in 1938 that critics invoked "regionalism" as a "catch-word which they use almost as a formula of dismissal for tendencies that they do not bother to take seriously." Davidson, *Attack on Leviathan*, 228.

205 Mencken to August Derleth, May 5 (imaginary) and 13 (pigeon-holes), 1941, Derleth Papers, WHS; William Stafford, "The Fiction of Not Being Local," *South Dakota Review* vol. 13 (1975), 47–48.

206 D. Tyler to Margaret Harding, January 7, 1944, FF Flanagan-America is West, University of Minnesota Press Archives (referencing, presumably, "On First Looking into Chapman's Homer" [1816] by John Keats).

207 Connolly, "Bringing the City Back In," 272. On the "influential Communist line in the arts and letters of the 1930s" and the "significant number of

American writers and artists [who] joined the political Left," see Gorman, *Left Intellectuals*, 5, 110. In the 1930s, it was "fashionable to be a Communist or to support radical causes." Kosiba, "A Successful Revolt?" 152.

208 Dorman, *Revolt of the Provinces*, 23; David P. Peeler, *Hope among Us Yet: Social Criticism and Social Solace in Depression America* (Athens, University of Georgia Press, 1988), 2.

209 Doss, *Benton, Pollock, and the Politics of Modernism*, 124.

210 Marx's "dead generations" quote is from his 1852 commentary on the 1848 revolution in France, "The Eighteenth Brumaire of Louis Bonaparte." Calhoun, "Radicalism of Tradition," 887 (intrusion, swept).

211 Gorman, *Left Intellectuals*, 111.

212 Warren I. Susman, "History and the American Intellectual: Uses of a Usable Past," in Lucy Maddox (ed), *Locating American Studies: The Evolution of a Discipline* (Baltimore, Johns Hopkins University Press, 1999), 30; Newton Arvin, "Quebec, Nebraska and Pittsburgh," *New Republic*, August 12, 1931; Lingeman, *Small Town America*, 380; Pells, *Radical Visions and American Dreams*, 153; Doss, *Benton, Pollock, and the Politics of Modernism*, 124.

213 Dennis, *Renegade Regionalists*, 15, 69; H. W. Janson, "Benton and Wood, Champions of Regionalism," *Magazine of Art* vol. 39 (May 1946), 186; Janson, "The International Aspects of Regionalism," 114. Dennis explains that "urban viewers of art, and especially those who write about it, look down upon farm folk, people working the land, as little more than quaint." Dennis, *Renegade Regionalists*, 16. On the continuing critiques of Wood, see Lawrence W. Levine, *Highbrow Lowbrow: The Emergence of Cultural Hierarchy in America* (Cambridge, Harvard University Press, 1988), 1.

214 Gorman, *Left Intellectuals*, 123, 128. On the Communist Party's opposition to regionalism prior to the Popular Front, see Wixson, *Worker-Writer in America*, 377–81. The use of indigenous culture by the Communist Party during the Popular Front period was "condemned by anti-Stalinist Marxists as counterrevolutionary." Mickenberg, "Revolution Can Spring Up," 28.

215 H. W. Janson, "The International Aspects of Regionalism," *College Art Journal* vol. 2, no. 4, part 1 (May 1943), 110. The midwesterner Constance Rourke "attacked doctrinaire Marxist critics, in particular, for dismissing older vernacular literature while they attempted to create proletarian forms." Gorman, *Left Intellectuals*, 131. Rourke thought local culture "could serve as a viable basis for revolution." Mickenberg, "Revolution Can Spring Up," 29.

216  Derleth, *Three Literary Men*, 41.

217  Derleth to Sinclair Lewis, October 5, 1937, Box 46, FF 488, Lewis Papers, Beinecke Library, Yale University.

218  The "Communist-dominated League of American Writers" did approve of Lewis's *It Can't Happen Here* (1935), a critique of Huey Long's populism and demagoguery. Brooke Allen, "Sinclair Lewis: The Bard of Discontents," *Hudson Review* (Spring 2003), 198 (hell); Deming Brown, "Sinclair Lewis: The Russian View," *American Literature* vol. 25, no. 1 (March 1953), 9–11. Lewis, who took his jabs at "hobohemia," tended to be, especially in his later career, skeptical of radical causes and remained, Ronald Weber argued, in an "older tradition of small-town outsiders and scoffers." Weber, *Midwestern Ascendancy*, 151–52.

219  Lewis to Derleth, February 9, 1938, Derleth Papers, WHS. Lewis was concerned about the growth of federal power and was highly critical, for example, of Roosevelt's court-packing plan. Arthur Vandenberg to Sinclair Lewis, February 10, 1937, Box 49, FF 629, Lewis Papers, Beinecke Library, Yale University.

220  "Editorial Statement," *Partisan Review* vol. 1, no. 1 (February/March 1934); Aaron, *Writers on the Left*, 280–81, 297; Gorman, *Left Intellectuals*, 138. *Partisan Review* privileged an "intellectual" approach grounded in "European Marxism" over a "crude," "vulgar," and "populist" "folk tradition." Wixson, *Worker-Writer in America*, 397–98. On the anti-rural and anti-regional focus of *Partisan Review*, see Terry A. Cooney, "Cosmopolitan Values and the Identification of Reaction: *Partisan Review* in the 1930s," *Journal of American History* vol. 68, no. 3 (December 1981), 582–84.

221  Gorman, *Left Intellectuals*, 140–41.

222  Moses Rischin, "When the New York Savants Go Marching In," *Reviews in American History* vol. 17, no. 2 (June 1989), 289. Howe, in a common formulation of the era and one that undermined regionalism, said that an "exciting . . . intellectual life" required a "break from the small town into the roominess of the city" and "bohemia." Howe, "This Age of Conformity," *Partisan Review* vol. 21, no. 1 (January–February 1954), 9–10.

223  Rischin, "When the New York Savants Go Marching In," 297.

224  Stephen Baskerville, review of Terry A. Cooney, *The Rise of the New York Intellectuals: Partisan Review and Its Circle, 1934–1945* (Madison, University of Wisconsin Press, 1986), in *Journal of American Studies* vol. 22, no. 1 (April 1988), 161; James Atlas, *Bellow: A Biography* (New York, Random House,

2000), 182. The leading New York Intellectual Philip Rahv accepted the idea
of "rural idiocy." Atlas, *Bellow*, 300.

225 Baskerville, review of Cooney, *Rise of the New York Intellectuals*, 162. One of
the ironies of their focus on the problem of alienation was the inability to
see midwestern regionalists attempting to combat the condition via the focus
on their regional roots. On the general condition, see Nathan Glazer, "The
'Alienation' of Modern Man: Some Diagnoses of the Malady," *Commentary*
vol. 3, no. 4 (April 1947), 378–85.

226 Rischin, "When the New York Savants Go Marching In," 292.

227 David S. Brown, *Richard Hofstadter: An Intellectual Biography* (Chicago, University of Chicago Press, 2006), 99–119; David B. Danbom, "The Professors
and the Plowmen in American History Today," *Wisconsin Magazine of History*
vol. 69, no. 2 (Winter 1985–1986), 108. The editor of *The New York Times Book
Review*, after the release of David Brown's biography, pronounced Hofstadter
"probably this country's most renowned historian" and mentions Hofstadter's
treatment of "midwestern rubes." Sam Tanenhaus, "The Education of Richard Hofstadter," *New York Times Book Review*, August 6, 2006; Kenneth H.
Wheeler, *Cultivating Regionalism: Higher Education and the Making of the American Midwest* (DeKalb, Northern Illinois University Press, 2011), 102–3 (noting
the impact of Hofstadter's negative views of the Midwest on historians).

228 Richard Hofstadter, *Anti-intellectualism in American Life* (New York, Knopf,
1962), 411.

229 Hirsh, "Theorizing Regionalism and Folklore from the Left," 154.

230 Michael C. Steiner, "Carey McWilliams, California, and the Education of a
Radical Regionalist," in *Regionalists on the Left*, 363.

231 Steiner, "Introduction," 11 (fascism); Steiner, "Carey McWilliams, California,
and the Education of a Radical Regionalist," 364; and Hirsh, "Theorizing
Regionalism and Folklore from the Left," 144—all in Steiner, *Regionalists on
the Left*.

232 Mark Greif, *The Age of the Crisis of Man: Thought and Fiction in America,
1933–1973* (Princeton, Princeton University Press, 2015) (especially chapter
3); Richard Wright, "Introduction," in St. Clair Drake and Horace R. Cayton,
*Black Metropolis: A Study of Negro Life in a Northern City* (revised and enlarged
edition, University of Chicago Press, 1993 [1945]), 23.

233 On intellectuals' embrace of executive power, see Pells, *Liberal Mind in a Conservative Age*, 10–26.

234 On the growth of large-scale bureaucracies and top-down hierarchical organizations, see Louis Galambos, "Technology, Political Economy, and Professionalization: Central Themes of the Organizational Synthesis," *Business History Review* vol. 57, no. 4 (Winter 1983), 471–93.

235 Ellis W. Hawley, "The New Deal and Business," in John Braeman, Robert H. Bremner, and David Brody (eds), *The New Deal: The National Level*, vol. 1 (Columbus, Ohio State University Press, 1975), 55–56.

236 W. Stull Holt also emphasized that FDR's victories came because of large majorities in urban areas that canceled out the votes from the large blocks of rural counties. Holt, *Historical Scholarship in the United States and Other Essays* (Seattle, University of Washington Press, 1967), 168–69.

237 Turner's biographer Ray Allen Billington noted how Turner, despite being a "progressive through most of his life," was a "strong supporter of Hoover in 1932," which "came as a shock" to Billington. He was "even more shocked" to read Turner's letter to Hoover "praising the latter's book on 'Individualism' as one of the greatest works in our history." Billington to Gates, May 21, 1971, Gates Papers, Cornell University. Hamlin Garland also supported Hoover in 1932. Hicks, *Great Tradition*, 146. On resistance to New Deal statism in the prairie Midwest, see Catherine McNichol Stock, *Main Street in Crisis: The Great Depression and the Old Middle Class on the Northern Plains* (Chapel Hill, University of North Carolina Press, 1992).

238 LeSueur to Sherwood Anderson, August 19, 1936, Box 23, FF 1156, Anderson Papers, Newberry Library.

239 Ekirch, *Ideologies and Utopias*, 109.

240 Raymond Moley, *The First New Deal* (New York, Harcourt Brace, 1966), 78.

241 James Holt, "The New Deal and the American Anti-statist Tradition," in John Braeman, Robert H. Bremner, and David Brody (eds), *The New Deal: The National Level* (Columbus, Ohio State University, 1975), 44; Thomas W. Devine, *Henry Wallace's 1948 Presidential Campaign and the Future of Postwar Liberalism* (Chapel Hill, University of North Carolina Press, 2013).

242 Ekirch, *Ideologies and Utopias*, 114.

243 Ekirch, *Ideologies and Utopias*, 114. Tugwell held a PhD from the University of Pennsylvania, where he studied under Simon Patten, a pioneer in the field of economic planning. Tugwell, who taught economics at Columbia, was tapped to join Roosevelt's "brains trust" by fellow Columbia professor Raymond Moley, who personally brought Tugwell to Roosevelt. Moley, *First New Deal*, 15–16; Ekirch, *Ideologies and Utopias*, 77, 115.

244 Rexford G. Tugwell, *In Search of Roosevelt* (Cambridge, Harvard University Press, 1972), 64. On the turn toward "collectivism," Tugwell's visit to the Soviet Union, and his embrace of Soviet planning, see Ekirch, *Ideologies and Utopias*, 60, 63, 68.

245 Tugwell, *In Search of Roosevelt*, 64.

246 Tugwell, *In Search of Roosevelt*, 90, 63.

247 Tugwell, *In Search of Roosevelt*, 91.

248 Moley, *First New Deal*, 356, 358; Michael V. Namorato, *Rexford G. Tugwell: A Biography* (New York, Praeger, 1988), 3, 60, 62. Tugwell sought "collectivist economic remedies" and the "reorganization and reform of agriculture along industrial lines." Sidney Baldwin, *Poverty and Politics: The Rise and Decline of the Farm Security Administration* (Chapel Hill, University of North Carolina Press, 1968), 74, 88; Richard S. Kirkendall, *Social Scientists and Farm Politics in the Age of Roosevelt* (Columbia, University of Missouri Press, 1966), 42, 96; Rexford Tugwell, "The Place of Government in a National Land Program," *Journal of Farm Economics* vol. 16, no. 1 (January 1934), 55–69. Jess Gilbert sees Tugwell as a "high modernist" who advocated statist planning and disdained the rural family farm traditions and "folk cultures" that agrarian midwesterners supported. Gilbert, "Agrarian Intellectuals in a Democratizing State: A Collective Biography of USDA Leaders in the Intended New Deal," in Catherine McNicol Stock and Robert D. Johnston (eds), *The Countryside in the Age of the Modern State: Political Histories of Rural America* (Ithaca and London, Cornell University Press, 2001), 238; Bernard Sternsher, *Rexford Tugwell and the New Deal* (New Brunswick, Rutgers University Press, 1964), 364; Jess Gilbert, "Eastern Urban Liberals and Midwestern Agrarian Intellectuals: Two Group Portraits of Progressives in the New Deal Department of Agriculture," *Agricultural History* vol. 74, no. 2 (Spring 2000), 174, 176; Pells, *Liberal Mind in a Conservative Age*, 271.

249 Tugwell, *In Search of Roosevelt*, 173; Ekirch, *Ideologies and Utopias*, 83. Hoover, of course, rejected the premises of the Commonwealth Club speech. Ekirch, *Ideologies and Utopias*, 84. The Commonwealth Club was considered the "most distinguished audience of its kind on the Coast." Frederic Logan Paxson to John D. Hicks, August 5, 1942, FF Correspondence June–August 1942, DB 10, John D. Hicks Papers, Bancroft Library.

250 Tugwell, *In Search of Roosevelt*, 176.

251 Tugwell, *In Search of Roosevelt*, 178.

252 Miller, "Anytime the Ground Is Uneven," 5.

253 James Malin said the New Dealers were "creating a Turner to suit their particular purpose." James C. Malin, "Space and History: Reflections on the Closed-Space Doctrines of Turner and Mackinder and the Challenge of Those Ideas by the Air Age," Part 1, *Agricultural History* vol. 18, no. 2 (April 1944), 73. Malin thought New Dealers were using Turner's idea of the closing frontier to promote a "popular argument in justification of the totalitarian tendency toward regimentation and social planning—an alleged substitute for the frontier." Malin, *Essays on Historiography*, 36 (quotation); Howard R. Lamar, "Regionalism and the Broad Methodological Problem," in Glen E. Lich (ed), *Regional Studies: The Interplay of Land and People* (College Station, Texas A & M University Press, 1992), 37; Tugwell, *In Search of Roosevelt*, 173; Richard Hofstadter, *The Progressive Historians: Turner, Beard, Parrington* (New York, Knopf, 1968), 90; Nash, *Creating the West*, 33, 41–42; Curtis Nettels, "Frederick Jackson Turner and the New Deal," *Wisconsin Magazine of History* vol. 17, no. 3 (March 1934), 258, 261–64; Steven Kesselman, "The Frontier Thesis and the Great Depression," *Journal of the History of Ideas* vol. 29, no. 2 (April–June 1968), 253–68; Ray Allen Billington, *America's Frontier Heritage* (New York, Holt, Rinehart and Winston, 1966), 15; Robert Galen Bell, "James C. Malin and the Grasslands of North America," *Agricultural History* vol. 46, no. 3 (July 1972), 423; Wilbur R. Jacobs, "The Many-Sided Frederick Jackson Turner," *Western Historical Quarterly* vol. 1, no. 4 (October 1970), 368; Ekirch, *Ideologies and Utopias*, 83; James MacGregor Burns, *Roosevelt: The Lion and the Fox* (New York, Harcourt Brace, 1956), 142–43; David M. Wrobel, *The End of American Exceptionalism: Frontier Anxiety from the Old West to the New Deal* (Lawrence, University Press of Kansas, 1993), 122–42. A pamphlet announcing the creation of the USDA's Resettlement Administration began by arguing that "America's frontiers are exhausted." Cara A. Finnegan, *Picturing Poverty: Print Culture and FSA Photographs* (Washington, D.C., Smithsonian Books, 2003), 29.

254 Ekirch, *Ideologies and Utopias*, 142–43. On the "trend toward stratification," see Howe, "This Age of Conformity," 9.

255 Gilbert, "Eastern Urban Liberals and Midwestern Agrarian Intellectuals," 162–80 (quote on page 166); Gilbert, "Agrarian Intellectuals in a Democratizing State," 213–39; Lawrence J. Nelson, "The Art of the Possible: Another Look at the 'Purge' of the AAA Liberals in 1935," *Agricultural History* vol. 57, no. 4 (October 1983), 429.

256 Gilbert, "Eastern Urban Liberals and Midwestern Agrarian Intellectuals," 177.

257 Gilbert, "Agrarian Intellectuals in a Democratizing State," 237–38. Gilbert also notes the inspiration provided by midwestern historians such as Frederick Jackson Turner and John D. Hicks. The agrarian and republican ideal, Gilbert explains, "lived on in supposedly backward regions of the country like the rural Midwest" and influenced groups such as the midwesterners in the USDA and midwestern historians. Gilbert, "Agrarian Intellectuals in a Democratizing State," 221, 224, 235, n. 36.

258 Gilbert, "Eastern Urban Liberals and Midwestern Agrarian Intellectuals," 166 (Wilson quotation); Jess Gilbert, *Planning Democracy: Agrarian Intellectuals and the Intended New Deal* (New Haven, Yale University Press, 2015); Kirkendall, *Social Scientists and Farm Politics in the Age of Roosevelt*, 12.

259 Allan M. Winkler, *Home Front USA: America during World War II* (Arlington Heights, IL, Harland Davidson, 1986), 1, 26.

260 Anthony J. Badger, *The New Deal: The Depression Years, 1933–1940* (London, 1989), 310, 10 (juggernaut); Richard Polenberg, *War and Society: The United States, 1941–45* (Philadelphia, J. B. Lippincott, 1972), 4 (radically altered); Pells, *Liberal Mind in a Conservative Age*, 3; Jon Lauck, "Garrison Keillor: An Interview," *Salmagundi* no. 184 (Fall 2014), 50; Alan Brinkley, "World War II and American Liberalism," in Lewis A. Erenberg and Susan E. Hirsch (eds), *The War in American Culture: Society and Consciousness during World War II* (Chicago, University of Chicago Press, 1996), 313–27.

261 Fisher to Ruth Suckow, January 7, 1939, Series 1, Box 3, Suckow Papers, University of Iowa.

262 Masters to August Derleth, August 24, 1942, Derleth Papers, WHS.

263 David Jordan, "Representing Regionalism," *Canadian Review of American Studies* vol. 23, no. 2 (Winter 1993), 101.

264 Neil A. Wynn, "The 'Good War': The Second World War and Postwar American Society," *Journal of Contemporary History* vol. 31, no. 3 (July 1996), 466; Hawley, "The New Deal and Business," 55–56; James T. Sparrow, *Warfare State: World War II Americans and the Age of Big Government* (New York, Oxford University Press, 2011); Bruce Catton, *The War Lords of Washington* (New York, Harcourt, Brace, 1948).

265 John Morton Blum, *V War for Victory: Politics and Culture during World War II* (New York, Harcourt Brace, 1976), 141.

266 Winkler, *Home Front USA*, 17, 43, 46.

267 Rovit, "Regions versus the Nation," 91; Jon K. Lauck, "The Death of the Midwest," *Belt Magazine*, March 24, 2014; Lauck, "Garrison Keillor," 50–51.

268 Carl Van Doren to Stuart Pratt Sherman, February 6, 1916, Box 4, Sherman Papers, University Archives, University of Illinois (peace-at-any-price); Herbert Hoover to Karl Mundt, December 2, 1941, Box 465, FF 4, Mundt Papers, Dakota State University (war-mad). Van Doren, a midwesterner, thought the "country ought to be thankful that there is one part of it which geography has made able to go through a crisis without hearing the din as it is heard on less favored coasts where the din multiplies the crisis and makes new crises daily." Van Doren to Sherman, February 6, 1916, Box 4, Sherman Papers. On the supposed backwardness of those who opposed foreign intervention during this era along with membership in the League of Nations, see Paul A. Carter, *Another Part of the Twenties* (New York, Columbia University Press, 1977), 35–37; and David A. Horowitz, *Beyond Left and Right: Insurgency and the Establishment* (Urbana, University of Illinois Press, 1997), 19–42.

269 See chapter 3.

270 W. S. Foulis to Karl Mundt, December 17, 1941, Box 465, FF 4, Mundt Papers, Dakota State University.

271 Winkler, *Home Front USA*, 77; Tremaine McDowell, *American Studies* (Minneapolis, University of Minnesota Press, 1948), 90–94.

272 Winkler, *Home Front USA*, 34.

273 Dorman, *Revolt of the Provinces*, 304 (italics in original).

274 Donald R. McCoy, "Republican Opposition during Wartime, 1941–1945," *Mid-America* vol. 44 (1967), 174–89; Jon K. Lauck, "Karl Mundt's Foreign Policy from 1938–1947: Portrait of an American Transformation," *Papers of the Twenty-Fifth Annual Dakota History Conference* (The Center for Western Studies and the South Dakota Humanities Council, 1993), 473–507. The transition could be seen at the September 1943 Mackinac Conference in Michigan attended by Senators Arthur Vandenberg and Robert Taft and other midwestern GOP political leaders.

275 Lawrence S. Kaplan, *The Conversion of Senator Arthur Vandenberg: From Isolation to International Engagement* (Lexington, University Press of Kentucky, 2015).

276 See chapter 3.

277 Peter Novick, *That Noble Dream: The "Objectivity Question" and the American Historical Profession* (New York, Cambridge University Press, 1988), 309–10.

278 The Institute for Social Research in Frankfurt, Germany, for example, moved
to Columbia University in 1934. In Manhattan, Frankfurt School scholars gave
rise to critical theory and "declared themselves to be social activists as well
as analysts." They were largely influential within the academy until the 1960s
when they were embraced more broadly. Simone Chambers, "The Politics
of Critical Theory," in Fred Rush (ed), *The Cambridge Companion to Critical
Theory* (Cambridge, Cambridge University Press, 2004), 219–29; John Patrick
Diggins, *The Proud Decades: America in War and Peace, 1941–1960* (New York,
W. W. Norton, 1989), 229 (arguing that the Frankfurt School thinkers "were
uncompromising Marxist radicals who first played down their politics to
become affiliated with Columbia University and to work for the government
during the war years"); Gorman, *Left Intellectuals*, 176–78. See also chapter 3.
Theodore Adorno of the Frankfurt School "claimed that a sense of alienation,
of not feeling at home even in your own home, was the only correct moral
attitude for an intellectual to adopt." Ian Buruma, "Cult of Exile," 23.

279 Blum, *V War for Victory*, 86. Also of note is the postwar impact of J. D. Salinger's *The Catcher in the Rye* (1951), which emerged out of the trauma of the
war and aimed to expose phony and inhibiting traditions. Michiko Kakutani,
"Hunting Again for Salinger within the Silences and Secrets," *New York Times*,
August 25, 2013. *Catcher* sold sixty-five million copies and had a "cultural
weight and penetration nearly unmatched in modern literature." David Shields
and Shane Salerno, *Salinger* (New York, Simon and Schuster, 2013), xiiv.

280 "Rosie the Riveter's World War II–era factory saved from demolition," *Reuters*,
May 1, 2014; Emily Yellen, *Our Mothers' War: American Women at Home and at
the Front during World War II* (New York, Free Press, 2004); Margaret Paton-
Walsh, *Our War Too: American Women Against the Axis* (Lawrence, University
Press of Kansas, 2002).

281 Richard M. Dalfiume, "The 'Forgotten Years' of the Negro Revolution,"
*Journal of American History* vol. 55, no. 1 (June 1968), 93–95; Rafael, "Regionalism, Area Studies, and the Accidents of History," 472 (quotation); Brinkley,
"World War II and American Liberalism," 315–17 (noting the immediate
prominence of racial issues in the wake of Gunnar Myrdal's 1944 book on race
relations); Robert L. Harris and Rosalyn Terborg-Penn, *Columbia Guide to
African American History since 1939* (New York, Columbia University Press,
2006), 18. Richard Wright also pointed to Hitler as a source of the new consciousness of the treatment of minorities. Wright, "Introduction," in Drake

and Cayton, *Black Metropolis*, 25. On the role of World War II, see Drake and Cayton, *Black Metropolis*, 90.

282 Ekirch, *Ideologies and Utopias*, 93; Winkler, *Home Front USA*, 2, 57, 59; Rafael, "Regionalism, Area Studies, and the Accidents of History," 471; Neil A. Wynn, "The Impact of the Second World War on the American Negro," *Journal of Contemporary History* vol. 6, no. 2 (1971), 45–51; Harvard Sitkoff, "Harry Truman and the Election of 1948: The Coming of the Age of Civil Rights in American Politics," *Journal of Southern History* vol. 37, no. 4 (November 1971), 597–616.

283 Mary L. Dudziak, "*Brown* as a Cold War Case," *Journal of American History* vol. 91, no. 1 (June 2004), 32–42; Thomas Borstelmann, *The Cold War and the Color Line: American Race Relations in the Global Arena* (Cambridge, Harvard University Press, 2001); Mary L. Dudziak, "Desegregation as a Cold War Imperative," *Stanford Law Review* vol. 41, no. 1 (November 1988), 61–120; Kevin Gaines, "A World to Win: The International Dimension of the Black Freedom Movement," *OAH Magazine of History* vol. 20 (October 2006), 15; Jon K. Lauck, "'I'm a Rootless Man': Richard Wright and the Limits of Midwestern Regionalism," vol. 44 *MidAmerica* (2017).

284 Andrew Delbanco, "The Decline and Fall of Literature," *New York Review of Books*, November 4, 1999 (dogma, race, exclusion); Michael O'Brien, "On Observing Quicksand," *American Historical Review* vol. 104, no. 4 (October 1999), 1203 (false); Joan Acocella, *Willa Cather and the Politics of Criticism* (Lincoln, University of Nebraska Press, 2000), 67–75; Michael Martone, review of Jason Lee Brown, Rosellen Brown, and Shanie Latham (eds), *New Stories from the Midwest* (Milwaukee, New American Press, 2014), *Middle West Review* vol. 1, no. 2 (Spring 2015), 117–20.

285 Sanders, *Staying Put: Making a Home in a Restless World* (Boston, Beacon Press, 1993), 103. Sanders attempts to counter the "orthodoxy," as personified by Salman Rushdie's writings, that "staying put is bad" and "that to be modern, enlightened, fully of our time is to be displaced." Sanders, *Staying Put*, 106 (commenting on Rushdie, *Imaginary Homelands: Essays and Criticism, 1981–1991* [New York, Viking, 1991]). See also Michael Steiner's commentary on Salman Rushdie's cosmopolitanism in Steiner, "Introduction," 10; and Buruma, "Cult of Exile," 23–27.

286 Hutner, *What America Read*, 3.

287 Nicholas Carr, *The Shallows: What the Internet Is Doing to Our Brains* (New York, W. W. Norton, 2011), 217.

CHAPTER THREE

1  R. Carlyle Buley to John T. Flanagan, June 19, 1945 (quotation) and December 4, 1944, Flanagan Papers, University of Illinois Archives. Buley was discussing his own work on a two-volume history of the Midwest and Flanagan's effort to collect materials for an anthology of midwestern literature, which would become Flanagan, *America Is West: An Anthology of Middlewestern Life and Literature* (Minneapolis, University of Minnesota Press, 1945).

2  James R. Shortridge, *The Middle West: Its Meaning in American Culture* (Lawrence, University Press of Kansas, 1989), 39. C. Vann Woodward commented in the early 1950s that "the regional historian [was] likely to be oppressed by a sense of his unimportance." Woodward, "The Burden of Southern History" (1952), in *The Burden of Southern History* (Baton Rouge, Louisiana State University Press, 1968), 187.

3  Richard Hofstadter, *The Progressive Historians: Turner, Parrington, Beard* (New York, Knopf, 1968), 68.

4  Ray Allen Billington, *Frederick Jackson Turner: Historian, Scholar, Teacher* (New York, Oxford University Press, 1973), 74.

5  David S. Brown, *Beyond the Frontier: The Midwestern Voice in American Historical Writing* (Chicago, University of Chicago Press, 2009), 25; Laurence R. Veysey, *The Emergence of the American University* (Chicago, University of Chicago Press, 1965), 110.

6  Harry N. Scheiber, "On the Concepts of 'Regionalism' and 'Frontier,'" in Harry N. Scheiber (ed), *The Old Northwest: Studies in Regional History, 1787–1910* (Lincoln, University of Nebraska Press, 1969), xvi; Earle D. Ross, "A Generation of Prairie Historiography," *Mississippi Valley Historical Review* vol. 33, no. 3 (December 1946), 392–93; Frederic L. Paxson, "A Generation of the Frontier Hypothesis: 1893–1932," *Pacific Historical Review* vol. 2, no. 1 (March 1933), 34–51; Michael C. Steiner, "The Significance of Turner's Sectional Thesis," *Western Historical Quarterly* vol. 10, no. 4 (October 1979), 440; Michael C. Steiner, "Frontier to Region: Frederick Jackson Turner and the New Western History," *Pacific Historical Review* vol. 64, no. 4 (November 1995), 486.

7  Turner to Theodore Blegen, March 16, 1923, FF Turner, 1923, Box 6, Blegen Papers, University of Minnesota Archives.

8  Curtis P. Nettels, "History Out of Wisconsin," *Wisconsin Magazine of History*

vol. 39, no. 2 (Winter 1955–1956), 116; Fulmer Mood, "The Theory of the History of an American Section in the Practice of R. Carlyle Buley," *Indiana Magazine of History* vol. 48, no. 1 (March 1952), 14.

9    Clarence Walworth Alvord, "The Relation of the State to Historical Work," *Minnesota History Bulletin* vol. 1, no. 1 (February 1915), 6; Paxson, "A Generation of the Frontier Hypothesis," 37; R. Carlyle Buley, *The Old Northwest: Pioneer Period, 1815–1840*, vol. 2 (Indianapolis, Indiana Historical Society, 1950), 551–56; Andrew R. L. Cayton and Susan E. Gray, "The Story of the Midwest: An Introduction," in *The Identity of the American Midwest: Essays on Regional History* (Bloomington, Indiana University Press, 2001), 22; Eric Hinderaker, "Liberating Contrivances: Narrative and Identity in Midwestern Histories," in *Identity of the American Midwest*, 65, 215, n. 34; Benjamin F. Shambaugh, *The Constitutions of Iowa* (Iowa City, State Historical Society, 1934), 11; Alan M. Schroder, "Benjamin F. Shambaugh," in John R. Wunder (ed), *Historians of the American Frontier* (Westport, Greenwood Press, 1988), 614. The "central west" took the lead in developing strong state historical societies. Julian P. Boyd, "State and Local Historical Societies in the United States," *American Historical Review* vol. 40, no. 1 (October 1934), 28, 33.

10   O. G. Libby, "The New Northwest," *MVHR* vol. 7, no. 4 (March 1921), 345–46.

11   Bogue to Malin, July 13, 1958, Mss. Coll. 183, Malin Papers, Kansas State Historical Society; Jon K. Lauck, "The Last Prairie Historian: An Interview with Allan Bogue," *Middle West Review* vol. 1, no. 1 (April 2014), 91–105.

12   E. Bradford Burns, *Kinship with the Land: Regionalist Thought in Iowa, 1894–1942* (Iowa City, University of Iowa Press, 1996), 53. The emerging New Critics of the era, on the other hand, were increasingly deemphasizing the role of authors' backgrounds in their work and focusing solely on the work itself. See Richard W. Etulain, "The American Literary West and Its Interpreters: The Rise of a New Historiography," *Pacific Historical Review* vol. 45 (August 1976), 324. Henry Nash Smith also saw the New Critics as the "repudiation" of literary realism, which is commonly seen as a product of the Midwest. Smith to Richard Hofstadter, July 15, 1954, FF 35, Box 2, Smith Papers, Bancroft Library.

13   Charles Grier Sellers Jr., "Andrew Jackson versus the Historians," *Mississippi Valley Historical Review* vol. 44, no. 4 (March 1958), 619. Peter Novick explains how "the professionalization of history had served as a dramatically successful ladder of personal, social, and economic mobility for dozens of small town

NOTES TO PAGE 71      197

boys in lower-middle-class backgrounds." Peter Novick, *That Noble Dream: The "Objectivity Question" and the American Historical Profession* (New York, Cambridge University Press, 1988), 169.

14    Novick, *That Noble Dream*, 182. Novick explains how, in the 1930s, universities still tended to the value of "regionalism" and how administrators looked to hire professors "spiritually attuned to the region" in which they would work. Novick, *That Noble Dream*, 180–85.

15    Benjamin F. Shambaugh, "The Sixteenth Annual Meeting of the Mississippi Valley Historical Association," *Mississippi Valley Historical Review* vol. 10, no. 2 (September 1923), 111.

16    Michael C. Steiner, "Regionalism in the Great Depression," *Geographical Review* vol. 73, no. 4 (October 1983), 434 (reverence); Suckow, "The Folk Idea in American Life," *Scribner's Magazine* vol. 88 (September 1930), 246–49.

17    Theodore Calvin Pease, *The Frontier State, 1818–1848* (Springfield, Illinois Centennial Commission, 1918), 23 (pervasive); Beverly W. Bond Jr., *The Civilization of the Old Northwest: A Study of Political, Social, and Economic Development, 1788–1812* (New York, Macmillan Company, 1934), 19, 25, 465; Buley, *Old Northwest*, 417.

18    John Hicks to Louis Pelzer, November 14, 1940, FF Correspondence September–December 1940, DB 10, John D. Hicks Papers, Bancroft Library. Pelzer served as editor of the *MVHR* from 1941–1946. William D. Aeschbacher, "The Mississippi Valley Historical Association, 1907–1965," *Journal of American History* vol. 54, no. 2 (September 1967), 348.

19    Pelzer to Paul Gates, February 3, 1941, Gates Papers, Cornell University; Malcolm J. Rohrbough, "Louis Pelzer," in Wunder (ed), *Historians of the American Frontier*, 483 (identified; absorbed); Herbert A. Kellar, "Louis Pelzer: Scholar, Teacher, Editor," *Mississippi Valley Historical Review* vol. 33, no. 2 (September 1946), 204 (concerned). The University of Minnesota historian Philip D. Jordan recalled that Pelzer "loved the width and breadth of the generous, liberal vision of the great Valley of Democracy." Jordan, "Louis Pelzer: Scholar, Teacher, Editor," *Mississippi Valley Historical Review* vol. 33, no. 2 (September 1946), 214. Pelzer gave a paper at the first MVHA meeting in 1908, presided as president in 1935–1936, served on the executive board and as an editor, and "probably attended more meetings than any other member of the Association." William C. Binkley, "Louis Pelzer: Scholar, Teacher, Editor," *Mississippi Valley Historical Review* vol. 33, no. 2 (September 1946), 201; Louis Bernard

Schmidt, "A Dedication to the Memory of Louis Pelzer, 1879–1946," *Arizona and the West* vol. 2, no. 4 (Winter 1960), 304.

20  Theodore C. Blegen, *Grassroots History* (Minneapolis, University of Minnesota Press, 1947), 12.

21  N.a., "Memorial Tribute to John D. Barnhart," *Indiana Magazine of History* vol. 64, no. 2 (June 1968), 110.

22  John D. Barnhart, *Valley of Democracy: The Frontier versus Plantation in the Ohio Valley, 1775–1818* (Bloomington, Indiana University Press, 1953); Deborah J. Hoskins, "John Barnhart," in Wunder (ed), *Historians of the American Frontier*, 86 (magnum opus).

23  Buley to Stanley Pargellis, August 15, 1944, Buley Papers, Indiana Historical Society.

24  R. Carlyle Buley, "Glimpses of Pioneer Mid-West Social and Cultural History," *Mississippi Valley Historical Review* vol. 23, no. 4 (March 1937), 510.

25  Buley, *Old Northwest*; Buley to John Flanagan, July 19, 1949, Flanagan Papers, University of Illinois Archives. Knopf revoked Buley's contract (letting Buley keep the advance) because his book was too long and not written for a general audience. Buley intended the book to be a "scholarly history." Buley to Charles D. Anderson, August 20, 1947, Buley Papers, Indiana Historical Society; Buley to Bernard DeVoto, May 11, 1943, FF 160–162, Box 8, DeVoto Papers, Stanford University. Bobbs-Merrill said the costs of publishing Buley's book "stop us cold" despite the "unquestioned merit" of the book. Rosemary B. York to Buley, May 6, 1948, Buley Papers, Indiana Historical Society. Viking was "tremendously impressed" with Buley's "brilliant scholarship" but thought sales would be too low. Arthur W. Wang to Buley, July 7, 1948, Buley Papers, Indiana Historical Society. So did McGraw-Hill. Edward C. Aswell to Buley, August 16, 1948, Buley Papers, Indiana Historical Society.

26  If he could not succeed in publishing a book on the American Midwest, Buley said, he would "break in via a book of dirty limericks." Buley to Bernard DeVoto, December 27, 1943, FF 160–162, Box 8, DeVoto Papers, Stanford University.

27  Curti interview, June 11, 1992, FF Curti, William Appleman Williams Papers, Special Collections, Oregon State University; E. David Cronon, "Merle Curti: An Appraisal and Bibliography of His Writings," *Wisconsin Magazine of History* vol. 54, no. 2 (Winter 1970–1971), 119 (retained). Curti, the Frederick Jackson Turner Professor of History at Wisconsin, examined the settlement

of Trempealeau County, Wisconsin, and found much to vindicate Turner's views on the workings of frontier democracy in his *The Making of an American Community* (Stanford, Stanford University Press, 1959). In Curti's *The Growth of American Thought* (New York, Harper & Brothers, 1943), which won the Pulitzer Prize in 1944 and was dedicated to the memory of Turner, Curti also emphasized the rise of democratic modes of thought in the West. See also Curti, "The Democratic Theme in American Historical Literature," *Mississippi Valley Historical Review* vol. 39, no. 1 (June 1952), 10, 12–13; and Paul Hass, "Reflections on 150 Years of Publishing," *Wisconsin Magazine of History* vol. 88, no. 2 (Winter 2004–2005), 5. Curti confessed, despite his "childhood in Papillion, Nebraska," that *The Making of an American Community*, which relied on new social science research methods, was a "venture into a kind of research which for me was new and very different and certainly very hard." Merle Curti to Paul Gates, February 15, 1959, Gates Papers, Cornell University. Curti is primarily remembered for his work in intellectual history, but his midwestern orientation remained strong.

28   Blegen had served as superintendent of the MHS since 1931 and prior to that had served for eight years as assistant superintendent under the midwestern historian Solon Buck, who moved to the new National Archives. Blegen had also served as a professor of history at the University of Minnesota since 1925 and at Hamline University before that. Solon Buck memo, September 13, 1935, Box 6, Buck Papers, National Archives; Buck to Blegen, August 2, 1939, Blegen to Buck, August 8, 1935, Blegen to Buck, May 13, 1940, all in Box 6, Buck Papers, National Archives. The University of Minnesota Press, the University of North Carolina Press, and the University of Oklahoma Press all were launched during the 1920s and thus became the "three oldest regional presses." Joseph A. Brandt, "A Pioneering Regional Press," *Southwest Review* vol. 26 (Autumn 1940), 27 (quotation); "An Adventure in Regional Publishing," FF 12, Box 3, Brandt Papers, Western History Collections, University of Oklahoma Libraries; "Scholarly Publishing as Viewed by the University of Nebraska Press," 1959, FF 11, Box 2, Virginia Faulkner Papers, University of Nebraska Archives; "Univ. of Minnesota Press, 1927–1937," *Publisher's Weekly* (March 27, 1937), 1402 (setting forth the University of Minnesota Press's focus on the "Upper Mississippi Valley"); "Ten Years of Publishing by the University of Minnesota Press," in FF UM Press, 1930–37, Box 42, Office of the President Papers #841, University of Minnesota Archives.

29  Solon Buck memo, September 27, 1935, Box 6, Buck Papers, National Archives; Jon K. Lauck, *The Lost Region: Toward a Revival of Midwestern History* (Iowa City, University of Iowa Press, 2013), 83–84. Blegen said, "Ford was a tower of strength to me during the period of his presidency" at Minnesota. Blegen to Buck, February 11, 1938, Box 6, Buck Papers, National Archives. Ford appointed Blegen to the University of Minnesota Press board of directors, on which he served for many years as chairman. John T. Flanagan, *Theodore C. Blegen: A Memoir* (Northfield, Minnesota, Norwegian-American Historical Association, 1977), 72–73. Buck and Blegen pushed Ford, who was forced by retirement rules to step down as president of the University of Minnesota, to take over as editor of the *American Historical Review*, which he did. Blegen to Buck, May 17, 1940, and Blegen to Buck, June 15, 1940, Box 6, Buck Papers, National Archives. During these years, University of Minnesota historian Lester B. Shippee also lent support to the MVHA and edited the *MVHR* in 1923–1924.

30  Blegen to Helen Clapesattle, December 1, 1943, and Malcolm M. Willey to David H. Stevens, December 21, 1943, both in FF Fellows, Box 5, Blegen Papers, UM Archives; Flanagan, *Theodore C. Blegen*, 73–74. Blegen praised the University of Minnesota for providing writing fellowships for regional writers and the University of Minnesota Press for making a "place, and a large place, for books interpreting the Upper Midwest." Blegen, *Grassroots History*, 11. Blegen secured the funding for the Regional Writing Fellowships from the Rockefeller Foundation, and the fellowships were designed to "secure the writing of sound but readable interpretations of regional life for as wide a popular audience as possible." The results of these fellowships included the novels *The Thresher* (1946) by Herbert Krause (a Minnesotan) and *This Is the Year* (1947) by Frederick Manfred (an Iowan). Committee on Regional Writing news release, April 15, 1944, FF Fellows, Box 5, Blegen Papers, UM Archives; Flanagan, *Theodore C. Blegen*, 73–74.

31  The organizational planning for the University of Minnesota Press, led by historians Guy Stanton Ford and Samuel Harding, began in 1924. See memos in FF UM Press 1922–31, DB 42, Office of the President Papers #841 and FF Press Committee Minutes, 1925–42, DB 1, University Press Committee Papers, both in the University of Minnesota Archives.

32  John D. Hicks to Solon Buck, October 31, 1935, Box 8, Buck Papers, National Archives; Minutes, Proposed Regular University Faculty Meeting, University

of Wisconsin, April 13, 1936, University of Wisconsin Press Papers. Livia Appel, the assistant manager of the University of Minnesota Press, had worked on Hicks's book on Populism and later moved to the University of Wisconsin Press, which began a concerted effort to publish books about Wisconsin around the time of World War II. Chronology of University of Wisconsin Press, provided by Sheila Leary, June 7, 2013; Buck to Hicks, November 7, 1935, Box 8, Buck Papers, National Archives. The University of Nebraska Press, another important regional outlet, was founded in 1940.

33  The Rockefeller Foundation sponsored the University of Wisconsin's organization and publication of the survey of regionalist thought entitled *Regionalism in America* (Madison, University of Wisconsin Press, 1951), edited by the midwesterner Merrill Jensen. See "Editor's Preface," vii. In 1944, Lawrence College in Wisconsin organized a series of lectures and community discussions about midwestern history that led to a book praised by Merle Curti. William F. Read, William F. Raney, Henry May, Dorothy Waples, and Wallace S. Baldinger, *The Culture of the Middle West* (Appleton, Lawrence College Press, 1944); Curti review in *Wisconsin Magazine of History* vol. 28, no. 2 (December 1944), 228–30.

34  Ian Tyrrell, "Public at the Creation: Place, Memory, and Historical Practice in the Mississippi Valley Historical Association," *Journal of American History* vol. 94, no. 1 (June 2007), 31–32.

35  The 1949 MVHA meeting in Madison included "conferences on Regionalism." Gates to Curti, April 22, 1949, FF 16, DB 17, Curti Papers, WHS. The 1949 MVHA included a session devoted to "The Mississippi Valley: Its Changing Relations with the Nation and the World." Billington to Gates, October 29, 1948, Gates Papers, Cornell University.

36  Pargellis to Lewis Atherton, March 7, 1947, NL 03/05/06, Box 2, FF 46, Pargellis Papers, Newberry Library (character); John T. Flanagan to Stanley Pargellis, April 9, 1947, NL 03/05/06, Box 2, FF 46, Pargellis Papers, Newberry Library; Pargellis to Flanagan, February 3, 1947, Pargellis to Flanagan, January 20, 1947, and Buley to Flanagan, December 4, 1944, all in Flanagan Papers, University of Illinois Archives; n.a., "The Newberry Fellowships in Midwestern Studies," *Newberry Library Bulletin* 1st series, no. 1 (November 1944), 13–15. In a sign of the competition for such fellowships, the regionalist August Derleth failed to receive a Newberry fellowship for his work on *Walden West*. Derleth to Pargellis, June 10, 1952, and W. T. Couch to Pargellis, January 17, 1950,

NL 03/05/02, Box 1, FF 45, Pargellis Papers, Newberry Library. Newberry fellows included midwestern historians such as Lewis Atherton, R. Carlyle Buley, Everett Dick, and Bessie Pierce. See NL 03/05/03, Box 4, Newberry Library. On the special issue for the *Chicago Sun*, see NL 03/05/06, Box 2, FF 46, Pargellis Papers, Newberry Library. Stanley Pargellis, the director of the Newberry, also tried to prod the Newberry to focus its manuscript gathering efforts on midwestern writers. Pargellis to Flanagan, October 17, 1950, Flanagan Papers, University of Illinois Archives. The Newberry fellowships were funded by the Rockefeller Foundation. See also Ray Allen Billington, "Stanley Pargellis: Newberry Librarian, 1942–1962," in Heinz Bluhm (ed), *Essays in History and Literature: Presented by Fellows of the Newberry Library to Stanley Pargellis* (Chicago, Newberry Library, 1965), 8; John Hicks to Stanley Pargellis, March 8, 1948 (promoting Everett Dick for a "Newberry Fellowship in Mid-Western Studies"), and John Hicks to Stanley Pargellis, March 3, 1948, FF January–March 1948 Correspondence, DB 14, John D. Hicks Papers, Bancroft Library. The details of the Newberry's 1947 exhibit on the Midwest are in NL 9/01/61/01, Envelope 21, Box 1, Newberry Library, and the details of its 1947 exhibit on "Prominent Midwesterners" are in Envelope 23 of same. Pargellis retired as director in 1962 when the Newberry had a staff of sixty. Billington to Gates, January 29, 1962, Gates Papers, Cornell University. For another discussion of Newberry-funded writing about the Midwest, see Michael J. Lansing, "An *American Daughter* in *Africa: Land of My Fathers*: Era Bell Thompson's Midwestern Vision of the African Diaspora," *Middle West Review* vol. 1, no. 2 (Spring 2015), 1–28.

37   Flanagan, *Theodore C. Blegen*, 74.

38   Oscar Handlin, *Truth in History* (Cambridge, Harvard University Press, 1979), 75–77; John Higham, *History: Professional Scholarship in America* (Baltimore, Johns Hopkins University Press, 1965), 212.

39   Kellar, "Louis Pelzer," 205 (hastened); Pelzer to Paul Gates, April 28, 1943, Gates Papers, Cornell University.

40   William J. Peterson, "Louis Pelzer: Scholar, Teacher, Editor," *Mississippi Valley Historical Review* vol. 33, no. 2 (September 1946), 208.

41   Jean Kern to Paul Gates, June 30, 1946, Gates Papers, Cornell University.

42   Pelzer to Malin, July 5, 1944, Mss. Coll. 183, Malin Papers, KSHS. The "insanity" of the war also took Sinclair Lewis's son Wells (named after H. G. Wells), who was killed in Italy. Paul Engle to Sinclair Lewis, December 5, 1944, Box 46,

FF 488, Lewis Papers, Beinecke Library, Yale University; Barnaby Conrad, "A Portrait of Sinclair Lewis: America's 'Angry Man' in the Autumn of His Life," *Horizon* (March 1979), 42; Richard Lingeman, *Sinclair Lewis: Rebel from Main Street* (New York, Random House, 2002), 104, 484.

43  Hicks to Curti, October 1, 1942, FF 17, Box 19, Curti Papers, WHS. Hicks also noted how the Wisconsin requirement to study in Europe "complicated matters for the Europeanists" during World War II. John D. Hicks, "My Ten Years on the Wisconsin Faculty," *Wisconsin Magazine of History* vol. 48, no. 4 (Summer 1965), 309.

44  John D. Hicks to Merle Curti, October 1, 1942, FF 17, DB 19, Curti Papers, WHS.

45  Curti to John D. Barnhart, July 24, 1945, Barnhart Papers, Lilly Library, Indiana University (GIs); Merle Curti to Paul Gates, December 17, [during 1941–1945, unclear which year], Gates Papers, Cornell University (assistant).

46  Gates to Louis Pelzer, December 24, 1943, Gates Papers, Cornell University (1,300); Gates to Merle Curti, February 1, 1943, FF 16, DB 17, Curti Papers, WHS; Paul Gates to Merle Curti, November 13, 1942, Gates Papers, Cornell University (all-out); Ian Tyrrell, *Historians in Public: The Practice of American History, 1890–1970* (Chicago, University of Chicago Press, 2005), 192.

47  Gates to James Malin, July 7, 1943, Mss. Coll. 183, Malin Papers, KSHS (swamped); Gates to James Malin, December 10, 1943, Mss. Coll. 183, Malin Papers, KSHS (writing).

48  Clarence E. Carter to John D. Barnhart, June 9, 1942, Barnhart Papers, Lilly Library.

49  Buley to Stanley Pargellis, August 15, 1944, Buley Papers, Indiana Historical Society.

50  Malin to John Hicks, January 17, 1942, FF Correspondence January–June 1942, DB 10, Hicks Papers, Bancroft Library.

51  Paul Gates to Merle Curti, February 1, 1943, FF 16, DB 17, Curti Papers, WHS.

52  Richard H. Pells, *The Liberal Mind in a Conservative Age: American Intellectuals in the 1940s and 1950s* (Wesleyan, Wesleyan University Press, 1989), 12. On the widespread belief in the Midwest as the "traditional home of isolationism," see LeRoy N. Rieselbach, *The Roots of Isolationism: Congressional Voting and Presidential Leadership in Foreign Policy* (Indianapolis, Bobbs-Merrill, 1966), 106 (quotation); and Rieselbach, "The Demography of the Congressional Vote on Foreign Aid, 1939–1958," *American Political Science Review* vol. 58, no. 3

(September 1964), 583 (noting how the Midwest was seen as the "isolationist capital of America"); Robert P. Wilkins, "Middle Western Isolationism: A Re-examination," *North Dakota Quarterly* vol. 25, no. 1 (Summer 1957), 69–76; Ralph H. Smuckler, "The Region of Isolationism," *American Political Science Review* vol. 47, no. 2 (June 1953), 391–94; Ray Allen Billington, "The Origins of Middle Western Isolationism," *Political Science Quarterly* vol. 60, no. 1 (March 1945), 44–64. Arthur Schlesinger Jr. recalled the power of the Iowa isolationists in the 1920s—"they were very much in the majority"—when his father taught at the University of Iowa. Arthur M. Schlesinger Jr., *A Life in the Twentieth Century: Innocent Beginnings, 1917–1950* (Boston, Houghton Mifflin, 2000), 27. On the major shift in outlook caused by the world wars and the Cold War, see C. Vann Woodward, "The Age of Reinterpretation," *American Historical Review* vol. 66, no. 1 (October 1960), 1–13; and Philip Gleason, "World War II and the Development of American Studies," *American Quarterly* vol. 36, no. 3 (1984), 343–58. At least half of historians aged twenty-five to forty during the era participated in some form of war-history activities. Tyrrell, *Historians in Public*, 187.

53  Paul Gates to Merle Curti, December 30, 1943, FF 16, DB 17, Curti Papers, WHS.

54  Novick, *That Noble Dream*, 247.

55  Novick, *That Noble Dream*, 283; Pells, *Liberal Mind in a Conservative Age*, 125; Tyrrell, *Historians in Public*, 195. MacLeish became head of FDR's Office of War Information. Sydney Weinberg, "What to Tell America: The Writers' Quarrel in the Office of War Information," *Journal of American History* vol. 55, no. 1 (June 1968), 75.

56  Brown, *Beyond the Frontier*, 51. For a review of the South's distinctive and un-midwestern bellicosity in the years prior to World War II and for the South's strong hostility to the midwestern-based America First Committee, see Joseph A. Fry, *Dixie Looks Abroad: The South and U.S. Foreign Relations, 1789–1973* (Baton Rouge, Louisiana State University Press, 2002), 197–205; Wayne S. Cole, "America First and the South, 1940–1941," *Journal of Southern History* vol. 22, no. 1 (February 1956), 36–47; and Carl N. Degler, "Thesis, Antithesis, Synthesis: The South, the North, and the Nation," *Journal of Southern History* vol. 53, no. 1 (February 1987), 17.

57  Novick, *That Noble Dream*, 253. Becker praised Turner's influence on his work and thanked Turner for helping him when he was just "a green boy from the

sticks." Becker to Guy Stanton Ford, April 10, 1936, FF Correspondence January–December 1936, Box 6, Ford Papers, UM Archives.

58  Novick, *That Noble Dream*, 282, 302.

59  Novick, *That Noble Dream*, 247.

60  John Hicks to Frederic Logan Paxson, August 14, 1940, FF Correspondence September–December 1940, DB 10, Hicks Papers, Bancroft Library; Novick, *That Noble Dream*, 247.

61  Tyrrell, "Public at the Creation," 43.

62  Hicks to Solon Buck, December 30, 1944, Box 8, Buck Papers, National Archives.

63  Novick, *That Noble Dream*, 292.

64  Beard to Curti, January 19, 1948, FF Curti, William Appleman Williams Papers, Special Collections, OSU.

65  Novick, *That Noble Dream*, 308–9 (quotations); Justus D. Doenecke, "Beyond Polemics: An Historiographical Re-appraisal of American Entry into World War II," *History Teacher* vol. 12, no. 2 (February 1979), 217–20; Brown, *Beyond the Frontier*, 130–31. William L. Langer and S. Everett Gleason wrote a two-volume history about American entry into World War II that sought to undermine isolationism. Novick, *That Noble Dream*, 305. See Langer and Gleason, *The Challenge to Isolation, 1937–1940* (New York, Harper & Brothers, 1952), and *The Undeclared War, 1940–1941* (New York, Harper & Brothers, 1953). This work was funded by the Rockefeller Foundation and sponsored by the Council on Foreign Relations. During its writing, Langer was head of research for the CIA, and Gleason worked for the National Security Council. Novick, *That Noble Dream*, 305. Charles Beard saw Langer as a "court historiographer." Beard to Merle Curti, January 19, 1948, FF Curti, William Appleman Williams Papers, Special Collections, OSU.

66  Geoffrey Matthews, "Robert A. Taft, the Constitution, and American Foreign Policy, 1939–53," *Journal of Contemporary History* vol. 17 (1982), 508, 522 (noting the postwar struggles of isolationist Republicans in the "Mid-West wing of the party" and isolationism's "sources of support in the Mid-West"); James T. Patterson, *Mr. Republican: A Biography of Robert A. Taft* (Boston, Houghton-Mifflin, 1972); Justus D. Doenecke, *Not to the Swift: The Old Isolationists in the Cold War* (Lewisburg, PA, Bucknell University Press, 1979); Richard Norton Smith, *The Colonel: The Life and Legend of Robert R. McCormick, 1880–1955* (Evanston, Northwestern University Press, 1997); Wayne S. Cole, *America*

*First: The Battle Against Intervention, 1940–41* (Madison, University of Wisconsin Press, 1953); Cole, *Charles A. Lindbergh and the Battle Against American Intervention in World War II* (New York, Houghton Mifflin Harcourt, 1974); Donald F. Drummond, *The Passing of American Neutrality, 1937–1941* (Ann Arbor, University of Michigan Press, 1955); Ruth Sarles, *A Story of America First: The Men and Women Who Opposed U.S. Intervention in World War II* (New York, Praeger, 2002); Manfred Jonas, *Isolationism in America, 1935–1941* (Ithaca, Cornell University Press, 1966); Lynne Olson, *Those Angry Days: Roosevelt, Lindbergh, and America's Fight Over World War II, 1939–1941* (New York, Random House, 2013); Susan Dunn, *1940: FDR, Willkie, Lindbergh, Hitler: The Election amid the Storm* (New Haven, Yale University Press, 2013); Lawrence J. Haas, *Harry and Arthur: Truman, Vandenberg, and the Partnership That Created the Free World* (Lincoln, University of Nebraska Press, 2016); Lawrence S. Kaplan, *The Conversion of Senator Arthur Vandenberg: From Isolation to International Engagement* (Lexington, University Press of Kentucky, 2015). For a defense of Lindbergh against the criticism mounted during the 1930s, see Cole, *Charles A. Lindbergh*; and James P. Duffy, *Lindbergh v. Roosevelt: The Rivalry That Divided America* (New York, MJF Books, 2010).

67 Douglas Reichert Powell, *Critical Regionalism: Connecting Politics and Culture in the American Landscape* (Chapel Hill, University of North Carolina Press, 2007), 19; John L. Thomas, "The Uses of Catastrophe: Lewis Mumford, Vernon L. Parrington, Van Wyck Brooks, and the End of American Regionalism," *American Quarterly* vol. 42, no. 2 (June 1990); Michael C. Steiner and David M. Wrobel, "Many Wests: Discovering a Dynamic Western Regionalism," in Michael C. Steiner and David M. Wrobel (eds), *Many Wests: Place, Culture, and Identity* (Lawrence, University Press of Kansas, 1997), 6; Burns, *Kinship with the Land*, 11, 163, 167, 176.

68 Novick, *That Noble Dream*, 314–15.

69 Paul Engle to Sinclair Lewis, December 21, 1946, Box 46, FF 488, Lewis Papers, Beinecke Library, Yale University; Eric Bennett, *Workshops of Empire: Stegner, Engle, and American Creative Writing during the Cold War* (Iowa City, University of Iowa Press, 2015).

70 Vernon Carstensen to Merle Curti, December 4, 1950, FF 18, DB 8, Curti Papers, WHS.

71 Pells, *Liberal Mind in a Conservative Age*, 122; Woodward, "Age of Reinterpretation," 9.

72  Lasch, "A Voice of Dissent," *Iowa Alumni Review* (October 1965), 18; Lasch, letter to editor of undesignated newspaper (probably the *Daily Iowan*), "Some disconcerting views on SUI fallout shelters," Lasch records, Staff Vertical File, University of Iowa Libraries; Patricia Eckhardt, "Schaeffer Hall," *Books at Iowa* vol. 57 (November 1992).

73  Norman A. Graebner, *The New Isolationism: A Study in Politics and Foreign Policy since 1950* (New York, The Ronald Press Company, 1956); Novick, *That Noble Dream*, 306-7.

74  Novick, *That Noble Dream*, 316-17.

75  Novick, *That Noble Dream*, 311-12.

76  Bogue to Gates, February 18, 1955, Gates Papers, Cornell University; Lauck, "The Last Prairie Historian," 93.

77  W. N. Davis Jr., "Will the West Survive as a Field in American History? A Survey Report," *MVHR* vol. 50, no. 4 (March 1964), 675; Novick, *That Noble Dream*, 310.

78  Novick, *That Noble Dream*, 310; William Palmer, *From Gentlemen's Club to Professional Body: The Evolution of the History Department in the United States, 1940-1980* (Lexington, KY, BookSurge, 2008), xv; Vicente L. Rafael, "Regionalism, Area Studies, and the Accidents of History," *American Historical Review* vol. 104, no. 4 (October 1999), 1209; Michael E. Latham, *Modernization as Ideology: American Social Science and "Nation Building" in the Kennedy Era* (Chapel Hill, University of North Carolina Press, 2000); Nils Gilman, *Mandarins of the Future: Modernization Theory in Cold War America* (Baltimore, Johns Hopkins University Press, 2007), 1-23.

79  John Barnhart to John Hicks, January 7, 1949, FF Correspondence January 1949, DB 14, Hicks Papers, Bancroft Library.

80  Palmer, *From Gentlemen's Club to Professional Body*, 177-78; Handlin, *Truth in History*, 78.

81  Merle Curti to Paul Gates, December 11, 1959, Gates Papers, Cornell University.

82  Novick, *That Noble Dream*, 372; Pells, *Liberal Mind in a Conservative Age*, 201.

83  See generally Daniel Bell (ed), *The New American Right* (New York, Criterion Books, 1955), and Daniel Aaron's review of the same in *Political Science Quarterly* vol. 71, no. 1 (March 1956), 128-30. On the postwar tendency to see the Midwest's traditions as reactionary, irrational, and anti-intellectual and for a rebuttal of the critics of the Midwest and a finding that there was "no correlation between support for agrarian radicals and support for McCarthy,"

see Michael Paul Rogin, *The Intellectuals and McCarthy: The Radical Specter* (Cambridge, Massachusetts Institute of Technology Press, 1967), 5. See also the review of Rogin by then University of Wisconsin historian Paul Glad in the *Journal of American History* vol. 54, no. 4 (March 1968), 930–32. Glad, who also wrote a history of Wisconsin and a biography of William Jennings Bryan, later moved to the University of Oklahoma. Robert Dorman, the author of perhaps the greatest history of regionalism, *The Revolt from the Provinces*, attended the University of Oklahoma where Glad's focus on local history inspired Dorman's interest in regionalism. Dorman interview, November 19, 2012. Of course, midwesterners were critics of McCarthy, too. Vernon Carstensen saw such anti-Communists, for example, as "cretins." Carstensen to Curti, July 26, 1954, FF 18, Box 8, Curti Papers, WHS.

84    Brown, *Beyond the Frontier*, 82 (quotation); Alan Brinkley, "World War II and American Liberalism," in Lewis A. Erenberg and Susan E. Hirsch (eds), *The War in American Culture: Society and Consciousness during World War II* (Chicago, University of Chicago Press, 1996), 321–22. On the McCarthy isolationism nexus, see Nathan Glazer, "McCarthyism as Isolationism," in Allen J. Matusow (ed), *Joseph R. McCarthy* (Englewood Cliffs, NJ, Prentice-Hall, 1970), 134–35.

85    Richard J. Walton, *Henry Wallace, Harry Truman, and the Cold War* (New York, Viking Press, 1976), 249–54; Pells, *Liberal Mind in a Conservative Age*, 30, 35, 102, 104, 110. In 1948, a poll found that 51 percent of Americans thought the Communist Party dominated the Wallace campaign. Karl M. Schmidt, *Henry A. Wallace: Quixotic Crusade, 1948* (Syracuse, Syracuse University Press, 1960), 259. On Communist control of the Wallace campaign, see Thomas W. Devine, *Henry Wallace's 1948 Presidential Campaign and the Future of Postwar Liberalism* (Chapel Hill, University of North Carolina Press, 2013).

86    Hesseltine, "Introduction," in Jensen, *Regionalism in America*, 143; Celia Applegate, "A Europe of Regions: Reflections on the Historiography of Subnational Places in Modern Times," *American Historical Review* vol. 104, no. 4 (October 1999), 1159–60.

87    Hesseltine, "Introduction," 143.

88    Palmer, *From Gentlemen's Club to Professional Body*, 160.

89    Palmer, *From Gentlemen's Club to Professional Body*, xvii, 175.

90    Palmer, *From Gentlemen's Club to Professional Body*, xvii.

91    Palmer, *From Gentlemen's Club to Professional Body*, 161.

92  Vernon Carstensen to Merle Curti, April 6, 1957, FF 18, Box 8, Curti Papers, WHS; Allan Bogue to James Malin, December 21, 1966, Mss. Coll. 183, Malin Papers, KSHS (source of quotes); Hicks, *My Life with History*, 83, 158, 215. Wisconsin historian William Appleman Williams thought his obligation to manage forty graduate students was "a practical and a general joke." Williams to Warren Susman, July 22, 1961, FF Susman, Williams Papers, Special Collections, Oregon State University. Vernon Carstensen thought the rise of the "gigantic university" in places like Berkeley helped cause the "[Berkeley] student revolt." Carstensen to Merle Curti, February 12, 1965, Box 8, FF 18, Curti Papers, WHS.

93  Palmer, *From Gentlemen's Club to Professional Body*, 126–27.

94  Palmer, *From Gentlemen's Club to Professional Body*, xvii, 126. During the 1930s, Berkeley hired Frederic Logan Paxson and, during the 1940s, hired John D. Hicks, both from Wisconsin. Both of them had focused on midwestern history. At Berkeley by mid-century, Henry May commented, the "[c]ampus political argument" came to be "carried on between New Dealers on one side and Marxists on the other." Linda Gordon, *Dorothea Lange: A Life Beyond Limits* (New York, W. W. Norton, 2009), 187.

95  Novick, *That Noble Dream*, 362. During the 1960s, 5,884 history PhDs were granted. From 1873 to 1960, only 7,695 history PhDs had been granted. Handlin, *Truth in History*, 24. The "frantic growth" of the "bloated postwar years" later looked like a "long wild binge" during the academic depression of the 1970s. Theodore Hamerow, *Reflections on History and Historians* (Madison, University of Wisconsin Press, 1987), 6, 8. Billington also noted the "overexpansion" of the postwar years. Ray Allen Billington, "From Association to Organization: The OAH in the Bad Old Days," *Journal of American History* vol. 65, no. 1 (June 1978), 84. During the 1970s, in a sign of the coming job crisis for historians, the number of undergraduate history majors declined by nearly 60 percent. Higham, *History*, 238.

96  Novick, *That Noble Dream*, 406.

97  Higham, *History*, 237.

98  Novick, *That Noble Dream*, 363.

99  Hamerow, *Reflections on History and Historians*, 92. If a young PhD's first job was at a "small, obscure, impecunious school," there was little chance to "get out" because the person would not have the time and support to do the necessary research to move up. Hamerow, *Reflections on History and Historians*, 119.

100 Palmer, *From Gentlemen's Club to Professional Body*, xix.

101  Novick, *That Noble Dream*, 367.

102  Novick, *That Noble Dream*, 367–68.

103  Hamerow, *Reflections on History and Historians*, 5.

104  Hamerow, *Reflections on History and Historians*, 27.

105  Novick, *That Noble Dream*, 181, 372.

106  Novick, *That Noble Dream*, 363. The rise of faculty governance meant key administrators or leading lights such as Turner could no long shape and control the direction of departments. Palmer, *From Gentlemen's Club to Professional Body*, xxiii.

107  Tyrrell, "Public at the Creation," 44; Higham, *History*, 262.

108  "Report of the MVHA Committee to Study the Relationship between the Association and the Secondary Schools," November 30, 1958, in Box 5, FF Correspondence MVHA 1931–57, James Sellers Papers, University of Nebraska Archives; Novick, *That Noble Dream*, 362. In 1912, the MVHA formed a "Teachers Section" that was active; teachers had their own program at MVHA meetings and served on the organization's executive committee; and the *MVHR* included a "Teacher's Section" until 1947, when it was terminated. By the early 1950s, the MVHA had dropped all its work on promoting history in high schools. The University of Minnesota historian Philip D. Jordan regretted that the teaching program had become a "farce." Jordan to A. D. Sageser, September 30, 1947, FF 3, Box 222, Tom Clark Papers, University of Kentucky (farce); Aeschbacher, "The Mississippi Valley Historical Association, 1907–1965," 350; Novick, *That Noble Dream*, 368; Tyrrell, "Public at the Creation," 28; Robert B. Townsend, *History's Babel: Scholarship, Professionalization, and the Historical Enterprise in the United States, 1880–1940* (Chicago, University of Chicago Press, 2013).

109  Novick, *That Noble Dream*, 373.

110  Novick, *That Noble Dream*, 372.

111  Aeschbacher, "Mississippi Valley Historical Association, 1907–1965," 344.

112  Tyrrell, *Historians in Public*, 43; Hamerow, *Reflections on History and Historians*, 56.

113  Allan Nevins, "What's the Matter with History?" *Saturday Review of Literature*, February 4, 1939 (noting that the *Mississippi Valley Historical Review* had to date "kept fairly well out of [the] clutches" of the "pedants"); Nevins, "Not Capulets, Not Montagus," *American Historical Review* vol. 65, no. 2 (January 1960), 253–58; Tyrrell, *Historians in Public*, 63; Kammen, *In the Past Lane*, 60–62, 66–68.

114 Hamerow, *Reflections on History and Historians*, 60. For Allan Nevins's survey of approaches to history, see Nevins, *The Gateway to History* (New York, D. C. Heath, 1938). Nevins supported *American Heritage* after the failure of his efforts to start a popular history journal under the auspices of the American Historical Association. Nevins, "What's the Matter with History?"; Nevins, "Not Capulets, Not Montagus," 267; Tyrrell, *Historians in Public*, 66. *American Heritage* sought to promote "roots and place," which caused it to be condemned for "nostalgia." Tyrrell, *Historians in Public*, 71, 276, n. 50. On the similar work by the Michigander and newspaperman Bruce Catton, who found a "way to appeal to the earnest sensibilities of midwestern readers," see Dave Dempsey and Jack Dempsey, *Ink Trails: Michigan's Famous and Forgotten Authors* (East Lansing, Michigan State University Press, 2012), 135. Catton was from Benzonia, Michigan, an Oberlin College (Ohio) graduate, and later took over as editor of *American Heritage*, a quarterly published by the American Association for State and Local History, and is remembered as a midwesterner: "If he loved the values of the old Midwest, he held a special fondness for his home state of Michigan. He still preferred the small towns of his boyhood." Dempsey and Dempsey, *Ink Trails*, 135, 138 (quotation); John J. Miller, "He Rewrote History," *My North*, June 3, 2009; Robert Cook, "Bruce Catton, Middlebrow Culture, and the Liberal Search for Purpose in Cold War America," *Journal of American Studies* vol. 47 (2013), 114–15. On his affection for his early life in Benzonia, see Catton, *Waiting for the Morning Train* (Garden City, NY, Doubleday, 1974).

115 John Higham, *Writing American History: Essays on Modern Scholarship* (Bloomington, Indiana University Press, 1970), 17–19; W. Stull Holt, *Historical Scholarship in the United States and Other Essays* (Seattle, University of Washington Press, 1967), 73–82; Hamerow, *Reflections on History and Historians*, 11–12; Handlin, *Truth in History*, 10–16, 78; Higham, *History*, 244–46; Woodward, "Age of Reinterpretation," 1. Nearly half of historians thought such grants were "corrupting" institutions and historians. Hamerow, *Reflections on History and Historians*, 70. At the same time, resources available for midwestern historical research, such as fellowships provided by the Newberry Library and the University of Minnesota, dried up.

116 Hamerow, *Reflections on History and Historians*, 61–66. Social science was driven by a "faddishness" and "diverted disproportionate energy into the study of the recent past and of the United States." Handlin, *Truth in History*, 18. The Rockefeller Foundation, founded in 1913, funded some midwestern

studies in the 1940s, but these had ceased by 1952. Other prominent foundations included the American Council of Learned Societies, the Social Science
Research Council, the Guggenheim Foundation, and the Ford Foundation,
founded in, respectively, 1919, 1923, 1925, and 1936. Hamerow, *Reflections on
History and Historians*, 61. Grants also spurred the professionalization that
"put an end to the reign of the amateurs." Hamerow, *Reflections on History and
Historians*, 72.

117  At Wisconsin, Merle Curti turned to social science during the 1950s for his *The
Making of an American Community* (1959), which at least focused on the Midwest and was supportive of Turner. At Iowa, Allan Bogue, who replaced Pelzer,
also became intensely interested in social science (and thought Curti used it
ineffectively in *The Making of an American Community*) and his research was
funded by the Social Science Research Council. In the end, Bogue ended up
thinking a lot of the social science theory was "fool's gold" and worried that
such forays by his fellow historians ended up making history "unintelligible to
the public." He persisted, however, and helped found the Social Science History Association in 1975. Bogue to James Malin, January 10, 1954, December
22, 1954, April 5, 1955, March 19, 1959 (fool's gold), March 6, 1967 (unintelligible), August 14, 1968, and July 15, 1975, Mss. Coll. 183, Malin Papers, KSHS.

118  Gates to Ray Allen Billington, April 14, 1953, Gates Papers, Cornell University.

119  Billington manuscript, "A Plea for Clio," appended to Billington to Paul Gates,
April 9, 1953, Gates Papers, Cornell University.

120  Hamerow, *Reflections on History and Historians*, 21.

121  Michael Kammen, "The Historian's Vocation and the State of the Discipline
in the United States," in Kammen (ed), *The Past before Us* (Ithaca, Cornell
University Press, 1980), 26.

122  Hamerow, *Reflections on History and Historians*, 31.

123  Hofstadter, *Age of Reform*, 12 (myths); Alexander Bloom, *Prodigal Sons: The
New York Intellectuals and Their World* (New York, Oxford University Press,
1986), 307–8; Don S. Kirschner, *City and Country: Rural Responses to Urbanization in the 1920s* (Westport, CT, Greenwood Publishing, 1970), xvi; Novick,
*That Noble Dream*, 340; Brown, *Beyond the Frontier*, 78; Pells, *Liberal Mind in
a Conservative Age*, 150–53. Hofstadter later admitted he purposely exaggerated the anti-Semitism of the Populists. Novick, *That Noble Dream*, 338. For
a review of the evidence disproving Hofstadter's charges of anti-Semitism,
see "Preface to the Second Edition," in Walter Nugent, *The Tolerant Populists:*

*Kansas Populism and Nativism* (Chicago, University of Chicago Press, 2013 [1963]), ix–xi. On the anti-Semitism within the isolationist movement, which one of its leading chroniclers saw as a "minor" aspect of isolationism, and isolationists' denunciations of anti-Semitism and their focus on the "treachery" of England, munitions makers, and Roosevelt, see Jonas, *Isolationism in America*, 253–57.

124  Novick, *That Noble Dream*, 337. On the prominence of Hofstadter's books, see Bogue, "The New Political History in the 1970s," in Kammen, *Past Before Us*, 231.

125  Novick, *That Noble Dream*, 337.

126  Novick, *That Noble Dream*, 337 (agrarian); Pells, *Liberal Mind in a Conservative Age*, 331 (provincial), 334–35, 336 (midwestern mind); Brown, *Beyond the Frontier*, 77. Dwight Macdonald saw McCarthy as a small-town district attorney who promoted the illusion that Americans lived in a "small, neat, understandable world" where problems could be solved through fact-finding and Congressional hearings. Pells, *Liberal Mind in a Conservative Age*, 330.

127  Peter Viereck, "The Revolt Against the Elite," in Bell, *New American Right*, 95.

128  H. Stuart Hughes, *The Sea Change: The Migration of Social Thought, 1930–1965* (New York, Harper & Row, 1975), 150–53; Martin Jay, *The Dialectical Imagination: A History of the Frankfurt School and the Institute of Social Research, 1923–1950* (Berkeley, University of California Press, 1973), 242–52; John Patrick Diggins, *The Proud Decades: America in War and Peace, 1941–1960* (New York, W. W. Norton, 1989), 227; Novick, *That Noble Dream*, 338; Brown, *Beyond the Frontier*, 82; Pells, *Liberal Mind in a Conservative Age*, 217, 332; François Cusset and Jeff Fort, *French Theory: How Foucault, Derrida, Deleuze, & Co. Transformed the Intellectual Life of the United States* (Minneapolis, University of Minnesota Press, 2008), 18. See generally Bell (ed), *The New American Right*, most of which was written by Columbia University–affiliated scholars. None of the authors was from the Midwest, the West, or the South. Brown, *Beyond the Frontier*, 82. David Riesman also criticized the gregariousness and joining common to small-town culture as a form of "other-directedness" that disrupted inner peace, caused psychological maladies, and justified personal acts of rebellion and eccentricity. Pells, *Liberal Mind in a Conservative Age*, 244.

129  Novick, *That Noble Dream*, 339; Hicks, *My Life with History*, 147.

130  Novick, *That Noble Dream*, 340. On Hofstadter's "antiregionalist bias," note

William Cronon, "Revisiting the Vanishing Frontier: The Legacy of Frederick Jackson Turner," *Western Historical Quarterly* vol. 18, no. 2 (April 1987), 173.

131 Carl Becker to Guy Stanton Ford, April 10, 1936, FF Correspondence January–December 1936, Box 6, Ford Papers, UM Archives; Gerald D. Nash, *Creating the West: Historical Interpretations, 1890–1990* (Albuquerque, University of New Mexico Press, 1991), 32, 222; Gene M. Gressley, "The Turner Thesis: A Problem of Historiography," *Agricultural History* vol. 32, no. 4 (October 1958), 233.

132 John Hicks to Merle Curti, August 7, 1942, FF Correspondence June–August 1942, DB 10, John D. Hicks Papers, Bancroft Library.

133 John Hicks to G. W. Pierson, November 25, 1941, FF Correspondence July–December 1941, DB 10, John D. Hicks Papers, Bancroft Library.

134 John Hicks to G. W. Pierson, November 25, 1941, FF Correspondence July–December 1941, DB 10, John D. Hicks Papers, Bancroft Library.

135 George Wilson Pierson, *The Frontier and Frontiersmen of Turner's Essays: A Scrutiny of the Foundations of the Middle Western Tradition* (Indianapolis, Bobbs-Merrill, 1940); Pierson, "American Historians and the Frontier Hypothesis in 1941," *Wisconsin Magazine of History* vol. 26, no. 2 (December 1942), 453–58. Pierson thought Turner was "too provincial." See Jon K. Lauck, "The Old Roots of the New History: The Intellectual Origins of Howard Lamar's *Dakota Territory*," *Western Historical Quarterly* vol. 39, no. 3 (Autumn 2008), 270.

136 Benjamin F. Wright review of Turner, *The Significance of Sections in American History* (New York, Henry Holt, 1932), in *New England Quarterly* vol. 6, no. 3 (September 1933), 630–34 (noting Turner's "preoccupation with the Middle West" on page 632); Benjamin F. Wright, "American Democracy and the Frontier," *Yale Review* vol. 22 (December 1930), 349–65; Nash, *Creating the West,* 36; Warren I. Susman, "The Useless Past: American Intellectuals and the Frontier Thesis, 1910–1930," *Bucknell Review* vol. 11 (March 1963), 17.

137 Merle Curti to Paul Gates, March 7, 1941, Gates Papers, Cornell University.

138 Allan G. Bogue, "Frederick Jackson Turner," *History Teacher* vol. 27, no. 2 (February 1994), 204.

139 Novick, *That Noble Dream,* 337.

140 In "postwar scholarship, much that had been described as southern or western either lost significance or merged into national configurations." Higham, *History,* 214.

141 Veysey, "Myth and Reality in Approaching American Regionalism," *American Quarterly* vol. 12, no. 1 (Spring 1960), 31.

142 See, generally, Hofstadter, *Progressive Historians*. See also Pells, *Liberal Mind in a Conservative Age*, 148.

143 Brown, *Beyond the Frontier*, 75.

144 Pells, *Liberal Mind in a Conservative Age*, 162, 184–87.

145 Gates to Merle Curti, February 1, 1961, FF 16, DB 17, Curti Papers, WHS. Gates was also happy to see the new agriculture department under Kennedy rely less on the more conservative Cornell College of Agriculture, which found favor with Eisenhower's Secretary of Agriculture Ezra Taft Benson.

146 Despite the overall support of the New Deal, out in the Midwest, R. Carlyle Buley observed, one could "still expectorate even against the wind without hitting more than a dozen New Dealers and beady-eyed racketeers." Buley to Bernard DeVoto, February 21, 1945, FF 160–162, Box 8, DeVoto Papers, Stanford University.

147 Novick, *That Noble Dream*, 243.

148 Hamerow, *Reflections on History and Historians*, 128.

149 Hamerow, *Reflections on History and Historians*, 155; Kammen, "Historian's Vocation and the State of the Discipline in the United States," 22; Nash, *Creating the West*, 51; David Harlan, *The Degradation of American History* (Chicago, University of Chicago Press, 1997), xv–xix.

150 Hamerow, *Reflections on History and Historians*, 156.

151 Hamerow, *Reflections on History and Historians*, 157.

152 Novick, *That Noble Dream*, 401. On Malin's marginalization, see also Thomas Burnell Colbert, "'My profession is history teaching and I am determined to make a success of it': James C. Malin as Historian and Educator," in author's possession.

153 Gates to Frederick Merk, September 17, 1971, Gates Papers, Cornell University.

154 Malin to Fred Shannon, April 4, 1947, Box 1, FF 1942–1963, RS 15/13/21, Shannon Papers, University of Illinois Archives. Shannon believed, as did others, that Malin suffered from the "nursing of a persecution complex." Shannon to Malin, April 7, 1947, Box 1, FF 1942–1963, RS 15/13/21, Shannon Papers, University of Illinois Archives.

155 Buley to Philip D. Jordan, May 24, 1951, Buley Papers, Indiana Historical Society.

156 Kirk, *The Conservative Mind: From Burke to Santayana* (Chicago, Henry

Regnery Company, 1953); Kirk to Stanley Pargellis, December 1, 1952, FF 89, Box 3, NL 03/05/02, Pargellis Papers, Newberry Library; E. V. Walter, "Conservatism Recrudescent: A Critique," *Partisan Review* vol. 21, no. 5 (September–October 1954), 512–23; Irving Howe, "This Age of Conformity," *Partisan Review* vol. 21, no. 1 (January–February 1954), 16–17; Stuart Gerry Brown, "Democracy, the New Conservatism, and the Liberal Tradition in America," *Ethics* vol. 56, no. 1 (October 1955), 1–9. *The Conservative Mind* was featured on the cover of *Time* magazine on July 4, 1953. In the spring of 1954, the MVHA held a session, chaired by Stanley Pargellis, on conservatism that included Kirk (speaking on "The American Conservative Character"), which was "exciting" and for which the "competition" to participate was "keen." Paul Gates to Fred Shannon, January 2, 1954, Box 2, FF Gates 1936–1955, RS 15/13/21, Shannon Papers, University of Illinois Archives (quotations); Kirk to Stanley Pargellis, October 21, 1954, FF 89, Box 3, NL 03/05/02, Pargellis Papers, Newberry Library. Kirk's work was supported and published by the "right-wing publisher Henry Regnery" of Chicago, to borrow Peter Novick's description. Novick, *That Noble Dream*, 309, n. 48. The third Newberry Library Conference on American Studies in November 1952 was also focused on the theme "The Tradition of Conservatism in America" and included Kirk, Merle Curti, Ray Allen Billington, Vernon Carstensen, and Henry Nash Smith as speakers. See FF 54, Box 2, NL 03/05/02, Pargellis Papers, Newberry Library.

157 Russell Kirk, *The Sword of Imagination* (Grand Rapids, Michigan, William B. Eerdmans, 1995), 178. I thank Allan Carlson for noting this citation for me. Carlson also notes the link between Kirk and Liberty Hyde Bailey, a Michigander who valued rural life and chaired Theodore Roosevelt's National Commission on Country Life. Bailey taught at Michigan State before moving to Cornell and creating the College of Agriculture at Cornell. See Allan Carlson, "Russell Kirk: Northern Agrarian," in *The Natural Family Where It Belongs: New Agrarian Essays* (New Brunswick and London, Transaction Publishers, 2014), 91–102; and Dempsey and Dempsey, *Ink Trails*, 97–110 (on Bailey's efforts to preserve "rural civilization"). On Kirk and Michigan, see Louis Filler, " 'The Wizard of Mecosta': Russell Kirk of Michigan," *Michigan History*, September/October 1979, 1218; and Scott P. Richert, "Ghosts of the Midwest: Russell Kirk's Moral Imagination," *Chronicles*, February 2002, 18–21. Carlson also notes that Kirk was a co-founder of the Philadelphia Society, an annual gathering of conservative intellectuals that always met in Chicago "for

as long as [Kirk] held sway." Carlson to author, June 20, 2013. Kirk resigned from Michigan State University in 1953 in "protest against a deliberate lowering of standards (to fill the new dormitories) and other administrative follies." Kirk to Stanley Pargellis, October 4, 1953, FF 89, Box 3, NL 03/05/02, Pargellis Papers, Newberry Library.

158  Kirk to Stanley Pargellis, December 1, 1952, FF 89, Box 3, NL 03/05/02, Pargellis Papers, Newberry Library. Ade looked fondly on the growth and development of the Midwest. Ade to H. S. Latham, September 30, 1917, Box 809, Hamlin Garland Papers, University of Southern California. On Ade, see Meredith Nicholson, *The Valley of Democracy* (New York, Charles Scribner's Sons, 1918), 87; R. F. Bauerle, "A Look at George Ade," *American Speech* vol. 33, no. 1 (February 1958), 77–79; John Ade, *Newton County, 1853–1911* (Indianapolis, Bobbs-Merrill, 1911) (written by George Ade's father); Van Wyck Brooks, *The Confident Years: 1885–1915* (New York, E. P. Dutton, 1952), 69–70. On Ade and the "Hoosier Golden Age" of literature, see James Woodress, *Booth Tarkington: Gentleman from Indiana* (New York, Greenwood Press, 1954), 13–19.

159  With the exception of *Prairie Schooner* (at Nebraska) and the *University of Kansas City Review*, Kirk thought the "great reservoir of thought and creative imagination in Illinois, Indiana, Michigan, Ohio, Minnesota, Wisconsin, Iowa, Kansas, Missouri and neighboring states has no means of expression except in the vulgarized form of the popular press." Kirk, "The Principles of a Monthly Journal," FF 89, Box 3, NL 03/05/02, Pargellis Papers, Newberry Library.

160  Kirk, "The Principles of a Monthly Journal," and Kirk to Stanley Pargellis, May 24, 1954, both in FF 89, Box 3, NL 03/05/02, Pargellis Papers, Newberry Library. These efforts ultimately led to the creation of the journal *Modern Age* in 1957. See "Apology for a New Review," *Modern Age* vol. 1 no. 1 (Summer 1957), 2–3. During the 1960s, another Michigan State professor, David Anderson, became frustrated with the Modern Language Association for rejecting his regional work and therefore launched the Society for the Study of Midwestern Literature. Lauck interview of David D. Anderson, November 11, 2011. On Anderson's career, see the special issue of *Midwestern Miscellany* vol. 44 (Spring 2016).

161  Kirk, "Principles of a Monthly Journal," FF 89, Box 3, NL 03/05/02, Pargellis Papers, Newberry Library.

162  John Higham, "The Cult of the 'American Consensus,'" *Commentary* vol. 27 (February 1959), 99; Bradley J. Birzer, "More than 'Irritable Mental Gestures':

Russell Kirk's Challenge to Liberalism, 1950–1960," *Humanitas* vol. 21, nos. 1 and 2 (2008), 64–86.

163  The search for an "American Mind" by certain American Studies scholars certainly flattened out American history and was not conducive to studying regional distinctions. John Higham, "The Cult of the 'American Consensus,'" *Commentary* vol. 27 (February 1959), 95. *American Quarterly*, the official journal of the American Studies movement, was launched at the University of Minnesota in 1949 but moved to Philadelphia by 1951. Flanagan, *Theodore C. Blegen*, 78. Soon after World War II, as many as eighty-one universities began offering American Studies programs. Edward F. Grier, "Programs in American Civilization," *Journal of Higher Education* vol. 25, no. 4 (April 1954), 180. On the prominence of the Minnesota program and its one-time emphasis on regionalism, see Tremaine McDowell, *American Studies* (Minneapolis, University of Minnesota Press, 1948), vi, 72–73. The midwesterner Theodore Blegen was critical to the launch of the Minnesota program. Tremaine McDowell, "An Evaluation of the Minnesota Program in American Studies," 1, FF AH3.1 #83, Box 3, American Studies Papers, UM Archives.

164  Smith, *Virgin Land: The American West as Symbol and Myth* (Cambridge, Harvard University Press, 1950). *Virgin Land* was based on Smith's Harvard dissertation and was considered the first dissertation written in the field of American Studies. Etulain, "American Literary West and Its Interpreters," 328; Smith interview, August 18, 1975, FF 6, Box 5, Smith Papers, Bancroft Library. Yale offered the first course in American Studies in 1931 and then created a program, which arguably preceded Harvard's. Gene Wise, "An American Studies Calendar," *American Quarterly* vol. 31, no. 3 (1979), 414–15; Lauck, "Old Roots of the New West," 270–71. The focus of Smith's dissertation on myth began as a reaction to Frederick Merk's "vigorously factual approach" to western history. Henry May, *The Divided Heart: Essays on Protestantism and the Enlightenment in America* (New York, Oxford University Press, 1991), 55. Merk, a Wisconsinite and Turnerian, was Turner's replacement at Harvard. Rodman W. Paul, "Frederick Merk, Teacher and Scholar: A Tribute," *Western Historical Quarterly* vol. 9, no. 2 (April 1978), 142; Lauck, *Lost Region*, 34–35, 38.

165  Smith, *Virgin Land*, 259–60 (interior); Richard Bridgman, "The American Studies of Henry Nash Smith," *American Scholar* vol. 56, no. 2 (Spring 1987), 265. On Smith's criticism of Turner for being "anti-intellectual" and for the "unfortunate" influence of Turner's ideas, see Smith, "The West as an Image of the American Past," *University of Kansas City Review* vol. 18 (1951), 29–40.

166 Smith to Walter Prescott Webb, April 4, 1950, FF 5, Box 2, Smith Papers, Bancroft Library. Walter Prescott Webb, a regionalist, thought Smith's treatment of farmers was too severe and suffered from an attitude of "superiority" and asked Smith to recognize that "these people were probably trying to do the best they knew." Walter Prescott Webb to Smith, April 6, 1950, FF 5, Box 2, Smith Papers, Bancroft Library.

167 Smith to Paul Brooks, April 4, 1948, FF 17, Box 1, Smith Papers, Bancroft Library. Although *Virgin Land* ultimately criticized Turner, the plan for Smith's dissertation-turned-book was to focus on the plains and mountains, not the Midwest. Smith, "Tentative Outline of the Dissertation to Be Called the Virgin Land: American Attitudes toward the Far West, 1803–1843," FF 19, Box 1, Smith Papers, Bancroft Library (with handwritten notation "probably composed in summer of 1939").

168 Higham, *History*, 215. Higham notes that Turner, with the exception of Ray Allen Billington, "received hardly any effective support in postwar research." Higham, *History*, 216. Billington later became a target of the New Western Historians. Jon K. Lauck, "How South Dakota Sparked the New Western History Wars: A Commentary on Patricia Nelson Limerick," *South Dakota History* vol. 41, no. 3 (Fall 2011), 353–81. Some critics noted that Smith focused on certain bold claims made about the West by elites, not what average people actually experienced. Barry Marks, "The Concept of Myth in *Virgin Land*," *American Quarterly* vol. 5, no. 1 (Spring 1953), 73. On this distinction between the "image" and the "facts," see Alan Trachtenberg, "Myth, History and Literature in *Virgin Land*," paper presented to the American Studies Association of Northern California, August 30, 1967, in FF 18, Box 1, Smith Papers, Bancroft Library.

169 Hofstadter, review of *Virgin Land*, in *American Studies* vol. 2 (Fall 1950), 279–82 (quotations); Hofstadter to Smith, n.d., 1950, FF 35, Box 2, Smith Papers, Bancroft Library (praising *Virgin Land*); David S. Brown, *Richard Hofstadter: An Intellectual Biography* (Chicago, University of Chicago Press, 2006), 108; Hofstadter, *Progressive Historians*, 103, 120. Hofstadter sought out Smith's advice on Populism. Hofstadter to Smith, n.d., FF 35, Box 2, Smith Papers, Bancroft Library. Smith made it clear to Hofstadter that Hofstadter was not "too hard on the Populists" and praised his linkage of Populism, isolationism, and McCarthyism. Smith to Hofstadter, July 15, 1954, FF 35, Box 2, Smith Papers, Bancroft Library.

170 Hofstadter, *Progressive Historians*, 88.

171  Steiner, "Regionalism in the Great Depression," 437 (from Steiner interview
     with Smith) (dovecotes); Steiner, "Introduction," 1 (reactionary). In keeping
     with the village revolt tradition, Smith actively supported the work of Sacvan
     Bercovitch, whose well-known work was critical of Puritanism. Smith to
     Gerald Freund, April 29, 1981, and Smith to George W. Williams, November
     6, 1985, FF 11, Box 1, Smith Papers, Bancroft Library (calling Bercovitch the
     "most impressive scholar in his age group in the field of American Studies"
     and recommending him for the MacArthur award). "Saki," in turn, called
     Smith the "single most important and influential figure in American Studies."
     Bercovitch to Frances W. Kaye, November 4, 1983, FF 11, Box 1, Smith Papers,
     Bancroft Library. Early in his career, Smith identified isolationism, region-
     alism, and criticism of New York as elements in an American form of fascism.
     "Can the American Way of Life Foster Fascism?" FF 8, Box 1, Smith Papers,
     Bancroft Library. Henry May, Smith's colleague at Berkeley, wrote a summary
     of Smith's early life in Texas that Smith read and approved. May explained
     how Smith found the religious and sports-oriented atmosphere of Dallas
     depressing and monotonous, and he explained Smith's early attraction to
     Mencken ("the Mencken influence was especially significant"), his political
     "journey toward the Left," his vote for Norman Thomas, and his criticism of
     Turner, but also notes his one-time respect for studies of the American South-
     west, which Smith took pains to distinguish from the South, and his work on
     the *Southwest Review*. May, *Divided Heart*, 33–60. John Higham argued that
     Smith's "*Virgin Land* was the valedictory of a man alienated from the Texas
     in which he grew up in the 1920s." Higham, *History*, 228, 229 n. 26. Smith
     was "sickened" by events in Texas, supported Henry Wallace in 1948, and
     embraced the "Marxist hope for peace at last after world revolution and the
     establishment of a classless society." Neil Jumonville, *Henry Steele Commager:
     Midcentury Liberalism and the History of the Present* (Chapel Hill, University of
     North Carolina Press, 1999), 210.

172  Bogue to James Malin, June 10, 1953, Mss. Coll. 183, Malin Papers, KSHS;
     Buley to Philip D. Jordan, May 24, 1951, Buley Papers, Indiana Historical
     Society; Carstensen to Merle Curti, October 29, 1950, FF 18, Box 8, Curti
     Papers, WHS.

173  Bogue to James Malin, June 10, 1953, Mss. Coll. 183, Malin Papers, KSHS.

174  *Virgin Land* was selected as one of the ten "most significant works published in
     American history during the decade of 1950" by way of a sample of American

historians. John E. Johnson to editor of Harvard University Press, July n.d., 1972, FF 18, Box 1, Smith Papers, Bancroft Library. *Virgin Land* "influenced interpretations of western literature more than any other study," and "specialists in the field place it at the top of the list of books that have shaped their thinking and writing." Etulain, "The American Literary West and Its Interpreters," 328. Michael P. Malone said *Virgin Land* was "one of those few [books] which truly changed the way we think." Malone, "Introduction," in *Historians and the American West* (Lincoln, University of Nebraska Press, 1983), 7; Ronald Weber, *The Midwestern Ascendancy in American Writing* (Bloomington, Indiana University Press, 1992), 17. As late as 1967, *Virgin Land* sold twenty-five thousand copies a year. Smith to Mark Carroll, April 16, 1968, FF 17, Box 1, Smith Papers, Bancroft Library. After being distributed by Random House, it sold seventy-seven thousand copies. Carroll to Smith, June 4, 1968, FF 17, Box 1, Smith Papers, Bancroft Library. May notes that *Virgin Land* sold "well over 100,000 copies." May, *Divided Heart*, 59.

175 William Diamond, "On the Dangers of an Urban Interpretation of History," in Eric F. Goldman (ed), *Historiography and Urbanization: Essays in American History in Honor of W. Stull Holt* (Baltimore, Johns Hopkins Press, 1941), 67–70; Eric E. Lampard, "American Historians and the Study of Urbanization," *American Historical Review* vol. 67, no. 1 (October 1961), 52 (on the rapid growth of urban history during the 1950s); Blake McKelvey, "American Urban History Today," *American Historical Review* vol. 57, no. 4 (July 1952), 919–29; James A. Henretta, "The Making of an American Community: A Thirty-Year Retrospective," *Reviews in American History* vol. 16, no. 3 (September 1988), 508–9. The Urban History Group first formed in 1953, and in ensuing years the number of universities offering urban history courses rapidly expanded. Michael H. Ebner, "Urban History: Retrospect and Prospect," *Journal of American History* vol. 68, no. 1 (June 1981), 70.

176 Hofstadter, *Progressive Historians*, 93.

177 Hofstadter, *Progressive Historians*, 150–51.

178 Barry Gross, "The Revolt That Wasn't: The Legacies of Critical Myopia," *CEA Critic* vol. 30, no. 2 (January 1977), 4.

179 Gross, "Revolt That Wasn't," 5. On the continued decline of rural influence, see Mary Clare Jalonick, "USDA Chief: Rural U.S. Getting Less Relevant," Associated Press, December 9, 2012.

180 The creation of the Southern Historical Association during the 1930s

necessarily diverted attention away from the Midwest. Tyrrell, "Public at the Creation," 29.

181 John Higham, "From Immigrants to Minorities: Some Recent Literature," *American Quarterly* vol. 10, no. 1 (Spring 1958), 83–88; Andrew Hacker, "The Rebelling Young Scholars," *Commentary* vol. 30, no. 5 (November 1960), 411; Novick, *That Noble Dream*, 348–60; Handlin, *Truth in History*, 391.

182 Darnton, "Intellectual and Cultural History," in Kammen, *Past Before Us*, 327 (queen); John Hicks to Merle Curti, April 16, 1947, FF 17, Box 19, Curti Papers, WHS. This boom included the creation of the New York–based *Journal of the History of Ideas*. Franklin L. Baumer, "Intellectual History and Its Problems," *Journal of Modern History* vol. 21, no. 3 (September 1949), 191; John Higham, "The Rise of American Intellectual History," *American Historical Review* vol. 56, no. 3 (April 1951), 464; Novick, *That Noble Dream*, 380, 382.

183 James C. Malin, "Space and History: Reflections on the Closed-Space Doctrines of Turner and Mackinder and the Challenge of Those Ideas by the Air Age," Part 2, *Agricultural History* vol. 18, no. 3 (April 1944), 125–26 (folk and little); James C. Malin, "On the Nature of Local History," *Wisconsin Magazine of History* vol. 40, no. 4 (Summer 1957), 228 (particular, abandonment, locality, and top down).

184 Earl Pomeroy, *The American Far West in the Twentieth Century* (New Haven, Yale University Press, 2008), 2 (noting that, into the last half of the nineteenth century, states such as Iowa and Wisconsin had greater populations by themselves than the entirety of the sixteen states of the American West).

185 Jo Tice Bloom, "Cumberland Gap versus South Pass: The East or West in Frontier History," *Western Historical Quarterly* vol. 3, no. 2 (April 1972), 156–58.

186 See the conference program for the 1961 meeting of the Conference on the History of Western America in Santa Fe, in FF 88, Box 34, James Olson Papers, NSHS (void). When the MVHA was first formed, the Midwest was then largely considered part of "the West." James R. Shortridge, "The Emergence of 'Middle West' as an American Regional Label," *Annals of the Association of American Geographers* vol. 74, no. 2 (1984), 212. The emergence of a clear differentiation between the Midwest and West paved the way for the Western History Association to emerge later.

187 Billington to Paul Gates, February 5, 1952, Gates Papers, Cornell University. Praising his new California house "with its view of the mountains and swimming pool," Billington said his new position at the Huntington and life in California "more nearly approaches that of heaven than I had ever hoped to

achieve, in this world or the next." Billington to MVHA Working Party, n.d., FF 16, Box 222, Tom Clark Papers, University of Kentucky. Praise of the Huntington was common. Gates to Curti, February 26, 1968, FF 16, DB 17, Curti Papers, WHS. Billington resigned from Northwestern University and moved to Pasadena in 1963 to serve as a senior researcher in western history and to generally "settle down to research and writing for the rest of my life." Billington to Paul Gates, March 19, 1962, Gates Papers, Cornell University. After moving from Minnesota to Berkeley, Henry Nash Smith also noted (during the winter) the "wonderful golden afternoons" and ocean access. Smith to Alfred Kazin, February 7, 1955, FF 6, Box 3, Smith Papers, Bancroft Library. The midwesterner Allan Nevins also retired to the "salubrious pastures of the Huntington" during the 1950s. Tyrrell, *Historians in Public*, 71. Hamlin Garland had earlier retired to southern California and praised the "serene skies of the coast." Garland to Leland Case, June 18, 1938, Box 1269, Hamlin Garland Papers, University of Southern California.

188 After the war, Berkeley had four thousand graduate students that, according to the recently arrived midwesterner John D. Hicks, made Berkeley's graduate program the "largest in the world." Hicks to Merle Curti, April 16, 1947, FF 17, Box 19, Curti Papers, WHS. Berkeley's history department also grew dramatically in the postwar years. Vernon Carstensen to Merle Curti, August 5, 1958, FF 18, Box 8, Curti Papers, WHS.

189 Gates to Merle Curti, November 13, 1943, FF 16, DB 17, Curti Papers, WHS (race); Brown, *Beyond the Frontier*, 94–95. On trying to find a young professor a job, Perry Miller noted the "problem is the old one of the Jew" (the applicant finally found a job in Kansas City). Miller to Henry Nash Smith, April 13, 1948, and April 28, 1948, FF 6, Box 5, Smith Papers, Bancroft Library. For the typical skepticism toward Jews by midwestern writers Hamlin Garland and Willa Cather, see Donald Pizer, *American Naturalism and the Jews: Garland, Norris, Dreiser, Wharton, and Cather* (Urbana, University of Illinois Press, 2008). Paul Gates recognized that the profession would change with the emergence of new students with immigrant backgrounds. When teaching at Bucknell, Paul Gates saw the diversification of the student body and noticed the rise of young students from Italian, Jewish, and Catholic families and commented that the "old American stock" of "Anglo-Saxon students" "seems to be pretty well washed out." Gates to Frederick Merk, November 10, 1930, Gates Papers, Cornell University.

190 Novick, *That Noble Dream*, 365; James Atlas, *Bellow: A Biography* (New York,

Random House, 2000), 205. Arthur Schlesinger Jr. rather outlandishly argued that the holocaust might lessen the extant criticism of the Midwest: "next to Himmler, even Babbitt began to look good." Brown, *Beyond the Frontier*, 106.

191 Palmer, *From Gentlemen's Club to Professional Body*, xiii–xiv; Hamerow, *Reflections on History and Historians*, 121–22; Brown, *Beyond the Frontier*, 83. It should be noted, however, that midwestern schools such as the University of South Dakota and the University of Iowa hired Jewish history professors before this era. South Dakota hired Bert Loewenberg during the 1930s, and Iowa hired George Mosse in the 1940s. George L. Mosse, *Confronting History: A Memoir* (Madison, University of Wisconsin Press, 2000), 135.

192 Pells, *Liberal Mind in a Conservative Age*, 74 (hinterlands); Novick, *That Noble Dream*, 339; Brown, *Beyond the Frontier*, 98. They were "suspicious of populist sentimentality," Pells notes, because they saw it "as a prelude to pogroms." Pells, *Liberal Mind in a Conservative Age*, 74.

193 Brown, *Beyond the Frontier*, 112. For a contrast between staid Minnesota-born graduate students and the "wild" New Yorkers at Wisconsin, see Brown, *Beyond the Frontier*, 115. When describing Theodore Blegen's years at Hamline in Minnesota, John T. Flanagan noted how the students of this "pre-hippy period were pleasant and well behaved." Flanagan, *Theodore C. Blegen*, 26.

194 Brown, *Beyond the Frontier*, 112.

195 Brown, *Beyond the Frontier*, 112. On the midwestern temperament, see R. Douglas Hurt, "Midwestern Distinctiveness," in Andrew R. L. Cayton and Susan E. Gray (eds), *The Identity of the American Midwest: Essays on Regional History* (Bloomington, Indiana University Press, 2001), 160–79.

196 Turner to Archer Hulbert, January 29, 1930, FF 222, Box 18, Hulbert Papers, Colorado College. John Frederick's Iowa-based journal *The Midland*, while certainly focused on realism and the difficulties of rural life, was also "prone to a quiet optimism, the stories reflecting love for the land, cheerful humor, and faith in man's ability to build a dignified life." Frederick J. Hoffman, Charles Allen, and Carolyn F. Ulrich, *The Little Magazine: A History and a Bibliography* (Princeton, Princeton University Press, 1946), 144.

197 Cather to Lewis, January 14, 1938, Box 46, FF 470, Lewis Papers, Beinecke Library, Yale University. On the lack of cynicism among midwestern historians such as Turner and Frederick Merk, see Howard Lamar, "Frederick Jackson Turner," in Marcus Cunliffe and Robin W. Winks (eds), *Pastmasters: Some Essays on American Historians* (New York, Harper & Row, 1969), 109;

and David C. Smith, "Frederick Merk and the Frontier Experience: A Review Essay," *Wisconsin Magazine of History* vol. 63, no. 2 (Winter 1979–1980), 145.

198  Cather to Lewis, January 14, 1938, Box 46, FF 470, Lewis Papers, Beinecke Library, Yale University. On the idealistic streak in midwestern history, see Carl Ubbelohde, "History and the Midwest as a Region," *Wisconsin Magazine of History* vol. 78, no. 1 (Autumn 1994), 46.

199  Pells, *Liberal Mind in a Conservative Age*, 137.

200  This story was first told to me by Ted Kooser in May 2013. Glenna Luschei to author, August 10, 2013; Luschei, "Originals," *Matriarch: Selected Poems, 1968–1992* (Brooklyn, NY, The Smith, 1992), 88.

201  James Breslin, "Allen Ginsberg: The Origins of *Howl* and *Kaddish*," in Lee Bartlett (ed), *The Beats: Essays in Criticism* (Jefferson, NC, McFarland, 1981), 68–69. Ginsberg's "talent for self-promotion" soon had him speaking from the same platforms that T. S. Eliot had occupied only recently. Diana Trilling, "The Other Night at Columbia: A Report from the Academy," *Partisan Review* vol. 26, no. 2 (Spring 1959), 216. On Ginsberg's trouble with historical accuracy, see Gregory Curtis, "The Mystery of the Allen Ginsberg-Diana Trilling Feud," *Daily Beast*, June 12, 2013.

202  Warren I. Susman, "History and the American Intellectual: Uses of a Usable Past," in Lucy Maddox (ed), *Locating American Studies: The Evolution of a Discipline* (Baltimore, Johns Hopkins University Press, 1999), 34–35; Peter Michelson, "Rearview Mirror," *New Republic* (December 22, 1973).

203  Mark Schorer to August Derleth, March 10, 1958, Derleth Papers, WHS (literature and renaissance); Schorer to Derleth, March 20, 1968, Derleth Papers, WHS (square); Brown, *Beyond the Frontier*, 113 (uptight).

204  Kammen, "Historian's Vocation and the State of the Discipline in the United States," 20 (guard); Higham, *History*, 236 (sweeping); Handlin, *Truth in History*, 81–82; Nash, *Creating the West*, 51.

205  Pells, *Liberal Mind in a Conservative Age*, 188 (prophets), 368, 374–77; John Higham, "Changing Paradigms: The Collapse of Consensus History," *Journal of American History* vol. 76, no. 2 (September 1989), 463 (hunger); Brown, *Beyond the Frontier*, 126; Lauck, *Lost Region*, 61 (straight).

206  Aileen S. Kraditor, "American Radical Historians and Their Heritage," *Past & Present* no. 56 (August 1972), 136 (noting "those on the Left who have endeavored to find in American history justifications for and forerunners of their own party or movement—and I may note here that many historians on the

Left have been interested in little else"); Howard Schonberg, "Purposes and Ends in History: Presentism and the New Left," *History Teacher* vol. 7, no. 3 (May 1974), 448–58; David Donald, "Radical Historians on the Move," *New York Times Book Review*, July 19, 1970; Novick, *That Noble Dream*, 417–57; Hamerow, *Reflections on History and Historians*, 159; James Pierson, *Camelot and the Cultural Revolution: How the Assassination of John F. Kennedy Shattered American Liberalism* (New York, Encounter Books, 2007), 89–133. On the organization of a "Left Caucus" within the American Historical Association, see "For a Left Caucus in the AHA," FF Susman, William Appleman Williams Papers, OSU.

207 Lasch to James Weinstein, November 21, 1968, FF 47, Box 16, Weinstein Papers, WHS (highlighting the usefulness of Gramsci for a new socialist party); Novick, *That Noble Dream*, 433–34 (strategy); Lasch to James Weinstein, November 18, 1968, FF 47, Box 16, Weinstein Papers, WHS (consciousness); Eugene Genovese, "On Antonio Gramsci," *Studies on the Left* vol. 7 (1967), 83 (deeming Gramsci "the greatest Western Marxist theorist of our century"); Donald, "Radical Historians on the Move."

208 Christopher Lasch and Eugene Genovese, "The Education and the University We Need Now," *New York Review of Books* vol. 13 (October 9, 1969); Novick, *That Noble Dream*, 436.

209 Palmer, *From Gentlemen's Club to Professional Body*, 161.

210 Novick, *That Noble Dream*, 423 (godfather); Brown, *Beyond the Frontier*, 106 (empire), 113; Palmer, *From Gentlemen's Club to Professional Body*, 174. Williams saw the study of history as a means of "breaking the chains of the past." Williams, *The Contours of American History* (Cleveland, World Publishing, 1961), 479. The historian Fred Harrington, who taught Williams at Wisconsin and went on to become president of Wisconsin during the 1960s, thought Williams's work "incited" students. Brown, *Beyond the Frontier*, 134.

211 Carstensen to Merle Curti, April 10, 1966, Box 8, FF 18, Curti Papers, WHS (ugly); Carstensen to Curti, October 20, 1967, Box 8, FF 18, Curti Papers, WHS. On the "emerging radicalism" of these young historians and their embrace of the "language of revolt," see Andrew Hacker, "The Rebelling Young Scholars," *Commentary* vol. 30, no. 5 (November 1960), 404–5.

212 Warren Susman to James Weinstein, June 15, 1962, FF 13, Box 8, Weinstein Papers, WHS (commonwealth); Palmer, *From Gentlemen's Club to Professional Body*, 172 (Christian) (emphasis added); Brown, *Beyond the Frontier*, 135

(blue-eyed). Susman thought Williams's "radical vision" was "essentially . . . a plea for a return to TRADITIONALISM." Warren Susman to James Weinstein, June 15, 1962, FF 13, Box 8, Weinstein Papers, WHS (capitalization in original). On Williams's opposition to the "metropolitan bias of twentieth-century radicals" and his embrace of religion and regionalism, see Williams, "Radicals and Regionalism," *democracy* vol. 4, no. 1 ( July 1981), 87–98.

213   Brown, *Beyond the Frontier*, 114 (quoting George Mosse).

214   Higham, *History*, 257. Higham also notes that Hofstadter's criticism of Progressivism was "largely from within" and premised on "empathy and detachment," not a repudiation of its basic principles. Higham, *History*, 256.

215   Curti interview, June 11, 1992, FF Curti, William Appleman Williams Papers, Special Collections, OSU.

216   Williams to Merle Curti, January 29, 1967, FF Curti, Williams Papers, Special Collections, OSU; Brown, *Beyond the Frontier*, 111, 135–37. The historian Wayne S. Cole, a Wisconsin PhD and a native of Manning, Iowa, believed Williams "may have been more of a western populist than a Marxist." Brown, *Beyond the Frontier*, 208. Cole criticized "derogatory and emotion-laden" critiques of isolationism and attempts to "portray the isolationists as more evil or obtuse than they actually were." Cole review of Selig Adler, *The Isolationist Impulse: Its Twentieth-Century Reaction* (New York, Abelard-Schuman, 1957), in *MVHR* vol. 45, no. 1 ( June 1958), 162. Williams could admire his fellow midwesterner Robert Taft, for example, because Taft did not attempt to become "an American Century James Bond." Williams to David A. Horowitz, October 1, 1983, FF Horowitz, Williams Papers, SCOSU (referring to Henry Luce's conception of an "American Century" of global dominance). Williams said, "Kennedy scares [the] hell out of me." Williams to Warren Susman, November 1, 1960, FF Susman, Williams Papers, SCOSU.

217   Brown, *Beyond the Frontier*, 137.

218   Brown, *Beyond the Frontier*, 78, 135. On Williams as part of a "left-wing anti-statist communitarian tradition," see Doug Rossinow, "Restless Natives," *Reviews in American History* vol. 25, no. 1 (March 1997), 168. For a similar account of North Dakota Senator Gerald P. Nye's agrarian isolationism, see Wayne S. Cole, "Gerald P. Nye and Agrarian Bases for the Rise and Fall of American Isolationism," in John N. Schact (ed), *Three Faces of Midwestern Isolationism* (Iowa City, Center for the Study of the Recent History of the United States, 1981), 1–10.

219  Palmer, *From Gentlemen's Club to Professional Body*, 181 (deplored); Handlin, *Truth in History*, 82 (anti-Amerikanism); Williams to Warren Susman, September n.d., 1967, FF Susman, Williams Papers, SCOSU; Higham, "Changing Paradigms," 466; Brown, *Beyond the Frontier*, 145. Williams agreed on the need for a "frontal attack" on the "younger militants." James Weinstein to Williams, October 8, 1968 (source of quotations), and Williams to Weinstein, October 8, 1968, FF 21, Box 8, Weinstein Papers, WHS. George Mosse, while rejecting the notion that Williams was anti-Semitic, describes Williams's rejection of "students' aggressiveness, which ran counter to his ideal of well-thought-out and intellectually prepared change. But the fact that he disliked the student leadership, which was largely eastern and Jewish, played its part." Brown, *Beyond the Frontier*, 114 (quoting Mosse). See Mosse, *Confronting History*, 157. For an account of the rioting on the Wisconsin campus, see unidentified to Williams, n.d., 1968, FF University of Wisconsin, Williams Papers, SCOSU. One Wisconsin teaching assistant denounced the history professor he was helping as a "pig, pig, pig" in front of his class. Morton Rothstein interview, University of Wisconsin Collection #92, 1976. Williams's student Ronald Radosh recalled that Williams left Wisconsin "because of the New Left. The last straw was the front page *NY Times* article describing how New Left students broke into his lecture dressed as monkeys carrying bananas and throwing them at the podium where he stood." Radosh to author, June 28, 2012; Paul M. Buhle and Edward Rice-Maximin, *William Appleman Williams: The Tragedy of Empire* (New York, Routledge, 1995), 160.

220  Frederick Jackson Turner had long been urging, quite directly, a recognition of the "importance of studying 'from the bottom up.'" Turner to Theodore Blegen, March 16, 1923, FF Turner, 1923, Box 6, Blegen Papers, UM Archives.

221  Schlesinger, *Life in the Twentieth Century*, 27. Although Arthur Schlesinger Jr. came to know about the "anti-small town literature of the Twenties, Winesburg, and Spoon River and Gopher Prairie," he did not "detect" the failings of the Midwest supposedly revealed by these books. Schlesinger, *Life in the Twentieth Century*, 27.

222  Arthur M. Schlesinger, *In Retrospect: The History of a Historian* (New York, Harcourt, Brace & World, 1963), 3–4, 10.

223  Schlesinger, *In Retrospect*, 59. For another product of this research, see Schlesinger, "The Khaki Journalists," *MVHR* vol. 6, no. 3 (December 1919), 350–59, which examined the soldier newspapers written in several midwestern regiments during the war.

224 Schlesinger, *In Retrospect*, 60–61. Jessup was known for hiring a number of great talents. Schlesinger, *In Retrospect*, 64. After earning his B.A. from Ohio State, Schlesinger earned his PhD from Columbia and returned to teach at Ohio State in 1912 until he was hired by Iowa. In Iowa City, he was elected to the Iowa City Lions Club. In 1923, Schlesinger was hired by Harvard, where he joined Frederick Jackson Turner and Frederick Merk as expatriate midwesterners. Schlesinger, *Life in the Twentieth Century*, 5, 18, 29, 34–35; Schlesinger, *In Retrospect*, 74–75, 79. Schlesinger recalls the august Harvard history professor Edward Channing "delighting to deride the 'crude' Middle West," but Schlesinger was buoyed by the presence of the "perfectionist" Wisconsinite Merk, a Turnerian. Schlesinger, *In Retrospect*, 85–86. In graduate school at Columbia, Schlesinger also became interested in the "new history" of Charles Beard and James Harvey Robinson. Schlesinger, *Life in the Twentieth Century*, 13; Schlesinger, *In Retrospect*, 34–35.

225 Schlesinger, *In Retrospect*, 68. Schlesinger also directed the dissertations of Bessie Pierce, who wrote about the history of education and then a three-volume history of Chicago and later taught at the University of Chicago, and Fred Shannon, who wrote a history of the Union Army and later taught at Kansas State and Illinois. Schlesinger, *In Retrospect*, 68–69; Michael Kammen, *In the Past Lane: Historical Perspectives on American Culture* (New York, Oxford University Press, 1997), 32.

226 Schlesinger, *In Retrospect*, 71.

227 Schlesinger, *Life in the Twentieth Century*, 10.

228 Schlesinger, *New Viewpoints in American History* (New York, Macmillan, 1922) (which begins with a quote from Frederick Jackson Turner); Schlesinger, *In Retrospect*, 72; Schlesinger, *Life in the Twentieth Century*, 43; Handlin, *Truth in History*, 71. The *A History of American Life* series (1927–1948) ran to thirteen volumes. Volume 6, *The Rise of the Common Man, 1830–1850* (New York, Macmillan, 1927), was written by the Wisconsin historian Carl Russell Fish. On Dixon Ryan Fox's dedication to local history, see Michael Kammen, *Mystic Chords of Memory: The Transformation of Tradition in American Culture* (New York, Knopf, 1991), 376. The midwestern historian John Hicks also taught social history at Wisconsin. Hicks, *My Life with History*, 159. Schlesinger's *American Life* volume on cities also presaged the later growth of urban history. See also Schlesinger, "The City in American History," *MVHR* vol. 27, no. 1 (June 1940), 43–66 (noting, also, Turner's recognition of the growing influence of cities).

229 Schlesinger, *Life in the Twentieth Century*, 44–45. John Barnhart worked with both Frederick Jackson Turner's successor Frederick Merk and Arthur Schlesinger Sr. on his dissertation about Nebraska Populism at Harvard, and Schlesinger took the lead. Frederick Merk to John Barnhart, February 16, 1926, and February 19, 1926, Barnhart Papers, Lilly Library. Turner admired Barnhart for keeping regionalism central to his work. Turner to Barnhart, April 1, 1931, Barnhart Papers, Lilly Library.

230 Kammen, "Historian's Vocation and the State of the Discipline in the United States," 34; Joan Hoff, "The Challenges to Traditional Histories," in Richard S. Kirkendall (ed), *The Organization of American Historians and the Writing and Teaching of American History* (New York, Oxford University Press, 2011), 111; Lauck, *Lost Region*, 87–88.

231 Darnton, "Intellectual and Cultural History," 329, 332.

232 Laurence Veysey, "The 'New' Social History in the Context of American Historical Writing," *Reviews in American History* vol. 7, no. 1 (March 1979), 10–11, n. 5; Hamerow, *Reflections on History and Historians*, 199. Diplomatic, intellectual, and economic history also "suffered heavy losses," and constitutional history "disappeared almost entirely." Hamerow, *Reflections on History and Historians*, 199.

233 Beverly W. Bond Jr., *The Civilization of the Old Northwest: A Study of Political, Social, and Economic Development, 1788–1812* (New York, Macmillan Company, 1934), vii (quotation); James A. Henretta, "Social History as Lived and Written," *American Historical Review* vol. 84, no. 5 (December 1979), 1302–5; David Hackett Fischer, *Historians' Fallacies: Toward a Logic of Historical Thought* (New York, Harper & Row, 1970), 810.

234 Fred Matthews, "'Hobbesian Populism': Interpretative Paradigms and Moral Vision in American Historiography," *Journal of American History* vol. 72, no. 1 (June 1985), 101–3; Hamerow, *Reflections on History and Historians*, 165–66; Kammen, "Historian's Vocation and the State of the Discipline in the United States," 25. The focus on "social control" and finding evidence of protest was inspired by the radical critiques of society advanced during the 1960s. Peter N. Stearns, "Toward a Wider Vision: Trends in Social History," in Kammen, *Past Before Us*, 211–16. "For a while there was indeed no end to books on social control." Higham, *History*, 258. On the broad sweep of social control studies, Lawrence Stone observed that it could "include anything from using forced labor in the Gulag Archipelago to teaching children to brush their teeth." Matthews, "Hobbesian Populism," 103 (quoting Stone).

235  Thompson, *The Making of the English Working Class* (London, Victor Gollancz, 1963); Martin Ridge, "Populism Redux: John D. Hicks and *The Populist Revolt*," *Reviews in American History* vol. 13, no. 1 (March 1985), 150.

236  Hamerow, *Reflections on History and Historians*, 166, 168.

237  Terrence J. McDonald, "Theory and Practice in the 'New' Social History: Rereading Arthur Meier Schlesinger's *The Rise of the City, 1878–1898*," *Reviews in American History* vol. 20, no. 3 (September 1992), 435.

238  R. Carlyle Buley, "Glimpses of Pioneer Mid-West Social and Cultural History," *Mississippi Valley Historical Review* vol. 23, no. 4 (March 1937), 510.

239  Schlesinger, *Life in the Twentieth Century*, 45. Peter Stearns also noted how the new social history was driven by "delight in claims of newness." Stearns, "Toward a Wider Vision," 211. William Appleman Williams was also critical of historians for their failure to understand "how history from the bottom integrates with history from the top." Williams to David A. Horowitz, July n.d., 1988, FF Horowitz, Williams Papers, SCOSU. Schlesinger's earlier social history was more "descriptive" than the later version. Higham, "Rise of American Intellectual History," 464.

240  Schlesinger, *Life in the Twentieth Century*, 46.

241  Tyrrell, "Public at the Creation," 39. Blegen helped form the Forest History Society in 1946, for example, but such efforts were focused not on "ecological" treatments but on the "efficient use of resources." Tyrrell, "Public at the Creation," 40.

242  Tyrrell, "Public at the Creation," 40. E. Bradford Burns argues that the "race to embrace the planet negates that individual search for self and the unique. Basically, it denies a sense of place." Burns, *Kinship with the Land*, 177.

243  Tyrrell, "Public at the Creation," 23; Richard W. Leopold, "The MVHA and the OAH," *OAH Newsletter* (February 1983), 3–4.

244  Tyrrell, "Public at the Creation," 24.

245  Paul Gates to Guy Stanton Ford, September 22, 1951, FF MVHA 1951, Box 15, Ford Papers, UM Archives (Gates served as "chairman of the committee to investigate" the name change). Billington and Gates, in keeping with their progressive views, both supported Henry Wallace's campaign in 1948. Novick, *That Noble Dream*, 322. Billington was also the mentor of the young PhD George McGovern and worked hard to have him hired at the University of Iowa (the other finalist for the position, Samuel P. Hays, prevailed over second-place McGovern, a decision that set in motion a long and prominent political career). Billington to W. O. Aydellotte, November 2, 1952, and

Aydellotte to Billington, March 4, 1953, Billington Papers, Huntington Library. Gates was later remembered as an "old radical." Morton Rothstein interview, University of Wisconsin Collection #92, 1976 (quotation); Gates to Frederick Merk, November 10, 1930, and March 7, 1936, Gates Papers, Cornell University; Gates to Merle Curti, November 13, 1943, and March 17, 1948, FF 16, DB 17, Curti Papers, WHS.

246 Billington, "From Association to Organization," 75.

247 Billington to Gates, October 29, 1948, Gates Papers, Cornell University (unknowns); Billington to Fred Shannon, November 4, 1948, Box 1, FF 1942–1963, RS 15/13/21, Shannon Papers, University of Illinois Archives (mediocrity).

248 Billington to Paul Gates, February 13, 1953, Gates Papers, Cornell University (sturdy); Billington to Gates, February 19, 1952, Gates Papers, Cornell University (reactionaries).

249 Billington to Fred Shannon, January 10, 1952, Box 1, FF 1942–1963, RS 15/13/21, Shannon Papers, University of Illinois Archives. The matriarch, Clara Paine, "opposed vigorously the loss of the [MVHA's] regional identity." Tyrrell, *Historians in Public*, 220.

250 Billington to Paul Gates, February 5, 1952, Gates Papers, Cornell University.

251 Gates, "A Plea for Nationalizing Our Name and Review," in Box 5, FF MVHA 1956–60, James Sellers Papers, University of Nebraska Archives (regional); Gates to Merle Curti, January 7, 1954, FF 16, DB 17, Curti Papers, WHS, "Little Imagination"; Gates, "Report: Committee on Change of Names," FF MVHA 1951, Box 15, Ford Papers, UM Archives.

252 Billington, "From Association to Organization," 78. The historian Tom Clark called them the "juvenile reformers." Clark to Clara Paine, October 8, 1951, FF 3, Box 222, Tom Clark Papers, University of Kentucky.

253 On the segregation issue, see Billington, "From Association to Organization," 79; Billington to Fred Shannon, January 10, 1952, Box 1, FF 1942–1963, RS 15/13/21, Shannon Papers, University of Illinois Archives; Paul Gates to Fred Shannon, May 21, 1953, Box 2, FF Gates 1936–1955, RS 15/13/21, Shannon Papers, University of Illinois Archives; Paul Gates to Merle Curti, April 25, 1950, FF 16, DB 17, Curti Papers, WHS; Brown, *Beyond the Frontier*, 92–94. On the efforts to end discrimination without creating tensions in the MVHA, see Tom Clark to Howard K. Beale, May 26, 1953, and Beale to Clark, May 21, 1953, FF 4, Box 222, Tom Clark Papers, University of Kentucky.

254 Buley to Philip D. Jordan, May 24, 1951, Buley Papers, Indiana Historical Society.

255 Buley to Philip D. Jordan, May 24, 1951, Buley Papers, Indiana Historical Society.

256 Buley to Philip D. Jordan, May 24, 1951, Buley Papers, Indiana Historical Society. On these earlier leaders of the MVHA, see Lauck, *Lost Region*, 29–52.

257 Buley to Merle Curti, May 17, 1951, Buley Papers, Indiana Historical Society (lost). The April 1951 meeting in Cincinnati heard a committee report about the name change issue. Elmer Ellis to Paul Gates, n.d. (probably summer 1951), in Box 5, FF Correspondence MVHA 1931–57, James Sellers Papers, University of Nebraska Archives. Curti thought the "arguments for keeping the old name are stronger." Curti to James Sellers, September 27, 1951, in Box 5, FF Correspondence MVHA 1931–57, James Sellers Papers, University of Nebraska Archives.

258 Buley to Merle Curti, May 17, 1951, Buley Papers, Indiana Historical Society.

259 N.a., "Changing the Name of the Mississippi Valley Historical Association," in Box 5, FF MVHA 1956–60, James Sellers Papers, University of Nebraska Archives. Harold W. Bradley to James Sellers, September 22, 1951, and William Binkley to Sellers, October 2, 1951, in Box 5, FF Correspondence MVHA 1931–57, James Sellers Papers, University of Nebraska Archives, indicate that University of Nebraska historian James Sellers wrote the position paper.

260 Ford to Paul Gates, October 8, 1951, FF MVHA 1951, Box 15, Ford Papers, UM Archives.

261 N.a., "Changing the Name of the Mississippi Valley Historical Association," in Box 5, FF MVHA 1956–60, James Sellers Papers, University of Nebraska Archives.

262 Harold W. Bradley statement, n.d., in Box 5, FF MVHA 1956–60, James Sellers Papers, University of Nebraska Archives (quotations); Harold W. Bradley to James Sellers, September 22, 1951, in Box 5, FF Correspondence MVHA 1931–57, James Sellers Papers, University of Nebraska Archives.

263 Billington, "From Association to Organization," 83. Theodore Hamerow noted how schools in the Midwest were always left a "little uneasy" about the "aristocratic elegance" and pretensions of the Ivies. Hamerow, *Reflections on History and Historians*, 118.

264 Buley to Merle Curti, May 17, 1951, Buley Papers, Indiana Historical Society (Negro); Buley to Philip D. Jordan, May 24, 1951, Buley Papers, Indiana

Historical Society (keeping); Tom Clark to Carl Wittke, May 15, 1951, FF 3, Box 222, Tom Clark Papers, University of Kentucky.

265 J. G. Randall to Guy Stanton Ford, November 30, 1951, FF MVHA 1951, Box 15, Ford Papers, UM Archives; MVHA meeting summary, December 28, 1950, FF 3, Box 222, Tom Clark Papers, University of Kentucky; Aeschbacher, "The Mississippi Valley Historical Association, 1907–1965," 345–46; Clara Paine to James Sellers, June 28, 1951, in Box 5, FF Correspondence MVHA 1931–57, James Sellers Papers, University of Nebraska Archives. For Indiana historian John Barnhart's opposition to the name change that he argued would undermine the MVHA's original intent, see Barnhart statement, *MVHR* vol. 38, no. 2 (September 1951), 352.

266 Paul Gates to Guy Stanton Ford, September 22, 1951, FF MVHA 1951, Box 15, Ford Papers, UM Archives.

267 Ray Allen Billington to James Olson, June 11, 1963, FF 43, Box 30, James Olson Papers, NSHS (rapid); "Areas for Investigation by the Committee Studying the Future of the MVHA," June 1963, FF 43, Box 30, James Olson Papers, NSHS (regional); Billington to Paul Gates, June 11, 1963, Gates Papers, Cornell University; Aeschbacher, "Mississippi Valley Historical Association, 1907–1965," 347. At the 1962 MVHA meeting, an expanded "Organizing Committee" of the budding western history effort also met to make its plans for a fully functioning Western History Association, another sign of the coming demise of the MVHA. John Porter Bloom report on 1961 meeting of the Conference on the History of Western America, October 12–14, 1961, FF 88, Box 34, James Olson Papers, NSHS.

268 Billington to James Olson, June 11, 1963, FF 43, Box 30, James Olson Papers, NSHS. Billington chose Tom Clark of the University of Kentucky as chairman of the Committee on the Future. Billington to Clark, May 10, 1963, Billington to Clark, May 26, 1963, and Billington to Clark, June 10, 1963, FF 16, Box 222, Tom Clark Papers, University of Kentucky. Clark, in keeping with Billington's plans, supported making the MVHA a "national organization." Tom Clark to Colleagues, December 9, 1963, FF 16, Box 222, Tom Clark Papers, University of Kentucky.

269 Billington to Paul Gates, January 14, 1964, Gates Papers, Cornell University (volcanic; obstructionists); MVHA Executive Committee Minutes, May 3, 1963, FF 43, Box 30, James Olson Papers, NSHS. Nebraska historians James Sellers and James Olson fought the changes. Billington to Paul Gates,

December 11, 1963, Gates Papers, Cornell University. Olson wanted to preserve the "old and honored" MVHA. James C. Olson to Thomas D. Clark, March 24, 1964, FF 39, Box 29, James Olson Papers, NSHS. See also Olson to Bennet H. Hall, April 24, 1964, FF 44, Box 30, James Olson Papers, NSHS. The Executive Committee explained how the "rapid increase in membership" had made the MVHA a "national organization" that had more members from New York than any other state and how the *MVHR's* focus on regional history had dramatically declined and its old mission was "outmoded." Ray Allen Billington, "Official Notice to Members of the Mississippi Valley Historical Association," *Journal of American History* vol. 51, no. 2 (September 1964), 351–52.

270 Tom Clark to Oscar Winther, January 13, 1964, FF 17, Box 222, Tom Clark Papers, University of Kentucky. The chairman was proud of his effort to "break the old Nebraska stranglehold" on the MVHA. Tom Clark to Ray Allen Billington, November 11, 1963, FF 16, Box 222, Tom Clark Papers, University of Kentucky.

271 Billington to Executive Committee, January 27 and February 26, 1964, both in FF 43, Box 30, James Olson Papers, NSHS.

272 W. D. Aeschbacher to Tom Clark, January 13, 1964, FF 17, Box 222, Tom Clark Papers, University of Kentucky (unwise; haste; discussion); W. D. Aeschbacher to Tom Clark, January 3, 1964, FF 16, Box 222, Tom Clark Papers, University of Kentucky (improper). At a meeting held during the American Historical Association convention in Philadelphia in December 1963, eight members of the eighteen-member Committee on the Future voted to support a name change for the journal and sent their recommendation to Billington, chairman of the Executive Committee. The vote of the Committee on the Future was eight to three. Seven members of the committee were not present. Only a minority of Billington's hand-picked Committee on the Future, therefore, supported the name change. In February 1964, the Billington-led Executive Committee voted twelve to six by mail-in ballot to change the name of the journal despite "vehement" objections. Billington to Tom Clark, February 25, 1964, FF 17, Box 222, Tom Clark Papers, University of Kentucky. The procedural objections raised by MVHA secretary-treasurer Bill Aeschbacher were dismissed by the chairman of the Committee on the Future based on Aeschbacher's "stand-patism." He saw Aeschbacher as "highly emotional." Tom Clark to Ray Allen Billington, January 9, 1964, FF 17, Box 222, Tom Clark Papers, University of Kentucky.

273 Billington to Tom Clark, January 14, 1964, FF 17, Box 222, Tom Clark Papers, University of Kentucky. Billington ordered the use of the new name for the journal starting with the June 1964 issue. W. D. Aeschbacher to Tom Clark, May 18, 1965, FF 17, Box 222, Tom Clark Papers, University of Kentucky. Billington blamed the opposition to his maneuver on the "remnants of our Lincoln background." Billington to Tom Clark, January 6, 1964, FF 17, Box 222, Tom Clark Papers, University of Kentucky.

274 Bennett H. Wall to James Olson, April 7, 1964, FF 44, Box 30, James Olson Papers, NSHS.

275 Billington to Tom Clark, February 25, 1964, FF 17, Box 222, Tom Clark Papers, University of Kentucky.

276 Billington to Executive Committee, February 26, 1964, FF 43, Box 30, James Olson Papers, NSHS. Tom Clark, chairman of the Committee on the Future, argued that once the journal's name was changed the MVHA had an "obligation" to change its name. Tom Clark to W. D. Aeschbacher, March 5, 1964, FF 17, Box 222, Tom Clark Papers, University of Kentucky. Others correctly wondered why there was such an "obligation." James Olson could not "agree that a change in the title of the Journal necessitates immediate concern with the question of changing the name of the Association" and defended the "old and honored" name of the MVHA. James C. Olson to Tom Clark, March 25, 1964, FF 17, Box 222, Tom Clark Papers, University of Kentucky. Despite such objections, as soon as the journal's name was changed, Clark's Committee on the Future immediately went to work to change the association's name. Tom Clark to Special Committee, March 16, 1964, FF 17, Box 222, Tom Clark Papers, University of Kentucky. Clark suggested the name Organization of American Historians in the spring of 1964. W. D. Aeschbacher to Tom Clark, May 18, 1965, FF 17, Box 222, Tom Clark Papers, University of Kentucky. Soon after successfully advocating that the association change its name, the Committee on the Future was disbanded. Tom Clark to W. D. Aeschbacher, January 21, 1965, FF 17, Box 222, Tom Clark Papers, University of Kentucky.

277 Billington to Paul Gates, January 6, 1964, Gates Papers, Cornell University. Aeschbacher served as director of the Nebraska State Historical Society from 1956 to 1963, succeeding James Olson (1946–1956), James Sellers (who filled in for Olson during 1943–1946, while Olson was a historian with the Army Air Corps), Addison Sheldon (1917–1943), and the MVHA co-founder Clarence Paine (1909–1917). Aeschbacher took the secretary-treasurer post with him

to Abilene. MVHA Executive Committee Minutes, December 28, 1963, FF 39, Box 29, James Olson Papers, NSHS. The position had been at the historical society in Lincoln since the inception of the MVHA in 1907. "Historical Note," RG014, Nebraska State Historical Society Records, NSHS; Anne Polk Diffendal, "A Centennial History of the Nebraska State Historical Society, 1878–1978," *Nebraska History* vol. 59 (1978), 385, 406–7.

278 Gates to Billington, January 8, 1964, Gates Papers, Cornell University.

279 Thomas D. Clark to Billington, June 12, 1964, Gates Papers, Cornell University.

280 William Aeschbacher to Billington, January 13, 1964, Gates Papers, Cornell University.

281 William D. Aeschbacher, "The Mississippi Valley Historical Association, 1907–1965," *Journal of American History* vol. 54, no. 2 (September 1967), 344.

282 Thomas D. Clark to Colleagues, November 25, 1964, FF 39, Box 29, James Olson Papers, NSHS (landslide); Aeschbacher, "Mississippi Valley Historical Association, 1907–1965," 339.

283 Buley to Philip D. Jordan, May 24, 1951, Buley Papers, Indiana Historical Society. The loss of leadership in midwestern history occurred rather quickly during the postwar period. Orin G. Libby died in 1952; Clarence Carter in 1961; Solon Buck in 1962; James Sellers in 1966; John Barnhart in 1967; R. Carlyle Buley in 1968; Theodore Blegen in 1969. John D. Hicks moved to Berkeley in 1942 and soon went into administration and focused on writing textbooks and headed toward retirement, although he tried to console his old friends with his vow to continue his "deep-seated interest in the Mississippi Valley Historical Association" after being "upbraided" for "leaving the Middle West." John Hicks to Louis Pelzer, April 13, 1942, FF Correspondence January–June 1942, DB 10, John D. Hicks Papers, Bancroft Library (deep-seated); John Hicks to James Malin, July 2, 1942, FF Correspondence January–June 1942, DB 10, John D. Hicks Papers, Bancroft Library (upbraided); Hicks, *My Life with History*, 194. Hicks had followed Paxson to California and would himself be followed to the West Coast by Billington and Vernon Carstensen. Wisconsin also lost its earlier midwestern focus. Brown, *Beyond the Frontier*, 114. Clara Paine retired in 1952. In 1968, soon after Nebraska lost the MVHA, James C. Olson left Lincoln to become chancellor of the University of Missouri–Kansas City. More and more historians who had once focused on the Midwest and a newer generation of historians joined the Western History Association. For the sake of midwestern history, it may have wise to either keep the MVHA

as is and promote the creation of a separate nationally oriented organization of American historians or, after the MVHA changed its mission, to create a new organization focused on the Midwest (Billington reported that a "large group of traditionalists in the upper Mississippi Valley" were "plotting to form their own society" if the MVHA was changed), but this was not done. Billington, "From Association to Organization," 80. The Midwestern History Association, formed in 2014, adopted this approach and formed an entity focused on advancing the study of the history of the Midwest.

284 Aeschbacher, "Mississippi Valley Historical Association, 1907–1965," 349–50.

285 Buley to John T. Flanagan, February 23, 1945, Flanagan Papers, University of Illinois Archives.

286 Tyrrell, "Public at the Creation," 19.

287 Tyrrell, "Public at the Creation," 46.

288 Tyrrell, "Public at the Creation," 21 ("structure" quote is Tyrrell; "indifference" quote is from David Glassberg).

289 Pells, *Liberal Mind in a Conservative Age*, 156.

290 Higham, *History*, 235.


CONCLUSION

1   Robert D. Johnston, " 'There's No "There" There': Reflections on Western Political Historiography," *Western Historical Quarterly* vol. 42, no. 4 (Autumn 2011), 334. For a similar attitude by Marxists toward regionalism during the 1930s, see Constance Rourke, "The Significance of Sections," *New Republic*, September 20, 1933, 148, and chapter 2. Henry Nash Smith believed, "Nothing is more anathema to a serious radical than regionalism." Michael Steiner, "The Politics of Place: Carey McWilliams and Radical Regionalism," in Jeff Roche (ed), *The Political Culture of the New West* (Lawrence, University Press of Kansas, 2008), 135.

2   Jon K. Lauck, "Finding the Rural West," in David D. Danbom (ed), *Bridging the Distance: Common Issues of the Rural West* (Salt Lake City, University of Utah Press, 2015), 7–34.

3   Jennifer Schuessler, "Plowing Deeper: A New Historical Association for the Midwest," *New York Times*, October 22, 2014; Margery A. Beck, "Historians Seek Revival of Studying the Midwest," Associated Press, March 8, 2014; Jon

K. Lauck, "The Origins and Progress of the Midwestern History Association, 2013–2016," *Studies in Midwestern History* vol. 2, no. 11 (October 2016), 140–49.

4   N.a., "Literary Journal 'Midwestern Gothic' Paints a Portrait of the Region," *Michigan Public Radio*, April 16, 2015; McKenzie Pendergrass, "New Magazine Launched to Spread the Good Word about the Midwest," *Columbia Missourian*, June 10, 2016.

5   Claire Kirch, "Belt Publishing Celebrates the Industrial Midwest," *Publishers Weekly*, July 23, 2015.

6   Marcia Noe, "Reconceptualizing the Midwest: A Review Essay," *MidAmerica* vol. 42 (2015), 132–38; Jon Lauck, "Regionalist Stirrings in the Midwest," *The New Territory* vol. 1, no. 1 (May 2016), 17–19.

7   Scott Russell Sanders, *Staying Put: Making a Home in a Restless World* (Boston, Beacon Press, 1993).

8   Theodore C. Blegen, *Grassroots History* (Minneapolis, University of Minnesota Press, 1947), 12. The absence of "intellectual dogmas," Thomas Hart Benton believed, made the Midwest the "least provincial area of America." Erika Doss, *Benton, Pollock, and the Politics of Modernism: From Regionalism to Abstract Expressionism* (Chicago, University of Chicago Press, 1991), 126. Of course, an urban cosmopolitanism can only persist, Moses Rischin wisely notes, if others maintain their regional and ethnic attachments. Rischin, "When the New York Savants Go Marching In," *Reviews in American History* vol. 17, no. 2 (June 1989), 292, discussing Terry A. Cooney's identification of a flaw "at the heart of cosmopolitan theory" in *The Rise of the New York Intellectuals: Partisan Review and Its Circle, 1934–1945* (Madison, University of Wisconsin Press, 1986), 268; Douglas Reichert Powell, *Critical Regionalism: Connecting Politics and Culture in the American Landscape* (Chapel Hill, University of North Carolina Press, 2007), 19–20; Tom Lutz, *Cosmopolitan Vistas: American Regionalism and Literary Value* (Ithaca, Cornell University Press, 2004), 20; Stephen C. Behrendt, "Regionalism and the Realities of Naming," in Mahoney and Katz (eds), *Regionalism and the Humanities*, 153; Rockwell Gray, "Three Midwestern Writers," *Great Lakes Review* vol. 3, no. 1 (Summer 1976), 93. Flannery O'Connor remarked, "To know oneself is to know one's region. It is also to know the world." O'Connor quoted in Michael J. Rosen, "Is There a Midwestern Literature?" *Iowa Review* vol. 20, no. 3 (Fall 1990), 101.

9   Ray Allen Billington, *The Genesis of the Frontier Thesis: A Study in Historical Creativity* (Pasadena, Huntington Library Press, 1971), 122.

10    Turner, Martin Ridge noted, "each year asked his seminar students to write two papers—the first on a narrow frontier subject and the second on why it was important in the nation's history. His theory is valid today: there is no western history without a national context." Ridge, "The American West: From Frontier to Region," *New Mexico Historical Review* vol. 64, no. 2 (April 1989), 140–41.

11    Lasch, "Preserving the Mild Life: Neighborhood Hangouts and the Social Spirit of the City," *Pittsburgh History* vol. 74 (Summer 1991), reviewing Ray Oldenberg, *The Great Good Place: Cafes, Coffee Shops, Community Centers, Beauty Parlors, General Stores, Bars, Hangouts, and How They Get You Through the Day* (New York, Paragon House, 1989), 90. The regionalist John T. Frederick said, "New York's literary despotism is bad," and "what is bad about the despotism is that it is a kind of provincialism." Frederick quoted in Tom Lutz, "The Cosmopolitan *Midland*," *American Periodicals* vol. 15, no. 1 (2005), 83. David Anderson also criticized the "alien provincialism" of Carl Van Doren, the author of the "village revolt" thesis, and noted the stereotyping of "provincial journals" such as the *New Yorker* and the *New York Review of Books.* David D. Anderson, "Notes Toward a Definition of the Mind of the Midwest," *MidAmerica* vol. 3 (1976), 11, 15–16.

12    Lasch, "Preserving the Mild Life," 88–89. Lasch also admired Lewis Mumford, who offered two principles for embracing regionalism and using it to promote a broader vision: "One is, cultivate whatever you have, no matter how poor it is; it is at least your own. The other is, seek elsewhere for what you do not possess: absorb whatever is good wherever you may find it; make it your own." Mumford quoted in Earl Rovit, "The Regions versus the Nation: Critical Battle of the Thirties," *Mississippi Quarterly* vol. 8 (1960), 96.

13    W. Stull Holt, *Historical Scholarship in the United States and Other Essays* (Seattle, University of Washington Press, 1967), 93 (England); David C. Pierce and Richard C. Wiles, "A Place for Regionalism?" *Hudson Valley Regional Review* vol. 11 (1994), 8; Karen Halttunen, "Groundwork: American Studies in Place," *American Quarterly* vol. 58, no. 1 (March 2006), 5; Lucy R. Lippard, *The Lure of the Local: Senses of Place in a Multicentered Society* (New York, The New Press, 1997), 10; Scott Russell Sanders, "Writing from the Center," *Georgia Review* vol. 48, no. 4 (Winter 1994), 734; Sanders, *Staying Put*, 106, 114; Frank Luther Mott, "Literature with Roots," *Midland* vol. 19, no. 3 (May–June 1932), 82; Tremaine McDowell, "Regionalism in American Literature,"

*Minnesota History* vol. 20, no. 2 ( June 1939), 118; McDowell, *American Studies* (Minneapolis, University of Minnesota Press, 1948), 86; H. G. Merriam, "Expression of Northwest Life," *New Mexico Quarterly* vol. 5 (1934), 128; Josiah Royce, "Provincialism," in *Race Questions, Provincialism, and Other American Problems* (Freeport, New York, Books for Libraries Press, Inc., 1967 [1908]), 105–7; Walter Havighurst, "The Midwest as Hearthstone," *Midwestern Miscellany* vol. 29 (Spring 2001), 20; Michael Kowaleski, "Writing in Place: The New American Regionalism," *American Literary History* vol. 6, no. 1 (Spring 1994), 180; Jim Wayne Miller, "Anytime the Ground Is Uneven: The Outlook for Regional Studies and What to Look For," in William E. Mallory and Paul Simpson-Housely (eds), *Geography and Literature: A Meeting of the Disciplines* (Syracuse, Syracuse University Press, 1987), 13; Larry Woiwode, *Words Made Fresh: Essays on Literature and Culture* (Wheaton, IL, Crossway, 2011), 25; Allen Tate, "The New Provincialism," *Virginia Quarterly Review* vol. 21, no. 2 (Spring 1945), 263–64. Tom Lutz concluded that "literary regionalism is necessarily cosmopolitan." Lutz, "Cosmopolitan *Midland*," 83.

14  George R. Stewart, "The Regional Approach to Literature," *College English* vol. 9 (April 1948), 374. Despite the perception of increasing mobility and lessened attachments to home, fewer Americans are now moving than in earlier decades, making regionalism more relevant. Annie Lowrey, "Inertia Nation: Americans Are Staying Put at a Greater Rate Than Ever," *New York Times Magazine*, December 15, 2013.

15  Robert L. Dorman, *Hell of a Vision: Regionalism and the Modern American West* (Tucson, University of Arizona Press, 2012), 14; and Jon K. Lauck review, *Western Historical Quarterly* vol. 44, no. 2 (Summer 2013), 195; Royce, "Provincialism," 64; Michael C. Steiner, "Regionalism," in John Mack Faragher (ed), *The American Heritage Encyclopedia of American History* (New York, Henry Holt and Company, 1998), 775; Michael C. Steiner, "Region, Regionalism, and Place," in Joan Shelley Rubin and Scott E. Casper (eds), *Oxford Encyclopedia of Cultural and Intellectual History* (New York, Oxford University Press, 2013), 275–88 (noting regionalism's "multiple loyalties" in comparison to "regionalism's evil twin, sectionalism").

16  Suckow, "The Folk Idea in American Life," *Scribner's Magazine* vol. 88 (September 1930), 252; E. Bradford Burns, *Kinship with the Land: Regionalist Thought in Iowa, 1894–1942* (Iowa City, University of Iowa Press, 1996), 132, 142.

17 Helen Clapesattle to David Stevens, June 14, 1944, FF UM Regional Writing Fellows, Box 5, Theodore Blegen Papers, University of Minnesota Archives. On the persistence of a global focus and the prominence of an "interpretive scale that often privileges the planetary," see Terrell Scott Herring, "Micro: Region, History, Literature," *American Literary History* vol. 22, no. 3 (2010), 627.

18 Michael C. Steiner, "The Significance of Turner's Sectional Thesis," *Western Historical Quarterly* vol. 10, no. 4 (October 1979), 460–61; Michael C. Steiner, "Frontier to Region: Frederick Jackson Turner and the New Western History," *Pacific Historical Review* vol. 64, no. 4 (November 1995), 492; David S. Brown, *Beyond the Frontier: The Midwestern Voice in American Historical Writing* (Chicago, University of Chicago Press, 2009), 191; Jon Lauck, "The 'Interior Tradition' in American Historical Writing," *Annals of Iowa: A Quarterly Journal of History* vol. 69, no. 1 (Winter 2010), 82–93.

19 Dorman, *Revolt of the Provinces*, 100.

20 Royce, "Provincialism," 79; Nathan Glazer, "Foreword," in Raymond D. Gastil, *Cultural Regions of the United States* (Seattle, University of Washington Press, 1976), viii–ix; Pico Iyer, *The Global Soul: Jet Lag, Shopping Malls, and the Search for Home* (New York, Alfred A. Knopf, 2000), 24; Kent C. Ryden, *Mapping the Invisible Landscape: Folklore, Writing, and the Sense of Place* (Iowa City, University of Iowa Press, 1993), 253.

21 On the growth of a "regional adversary culture" in the 1930s among those intellectuals who developed an "intensely felt sense of their place in the indigenous landscape as the root American experience," see John L. Thomas, "Lewis Mumford: Regionalist Historian," *Reviews in American History* vol. 16, no. 1 (March 1988), 163.

22 Nelson, "Ideal of Nature and the 'Good Farmer,'" 29; Paul R. Gorman, *Left Intellectuals and Popular Culture in Twentieth-Century America* (Chapel Hill, University of North Carolina Press, 1996), 4; Royce, "Provincialism," 77.

23 Dorman, *Hell of a Vision*, 21; Burns, *Kinship with the Land*, 1–26.

24 Jon K. Lauck, "The Prairie Populism of Christopher Lasch," *Great Plains Quarterly* vol. 32, no. 3 (Summer 2012), 183–205.

25 McDowell, "Regionalism in American Literature," 110, 115.

26 Russell Lynes, "The New Snobbism," *Harper's*, November 1950.

27 Dorman, *Revolt of the Provinces*, 37, 39.

28 Mary Austin, "New York: Dictator of American Criticism," *The Nation*,

July 31, 1920. After settling in New Mexico, Austin promoted a "number of prominent regionalists scattered across the awakening West." Dorman, *Revolt of the Provinces*, 39. In 1920, Austin wished she had been more successful in her effort to be a part of the "good books coming out of the middle west." Austin to Sherwood Anderson, December 12, 1920, Box 15, FF 733, Sherwood Anderson Papers, Newberry Library. See John R. Milton on the difficulty of "getting the professors and critics, (and often they are the same persons) to put aside the long-established misconceptions" of Western writing. Milton, "The Western Novel: A Symposium," *South Dakota Review* vol. 2, no. 1 (Autumn 1964), 4. Milton was a Minnesotan who founded the literary journal *South Dakota Review*. See Milton, "The West and Beyond: *South Dakota Review*," *South Dakota History* vol. 13, no. 4 (Winter 1983), 334.

29  Manfred to Bernard DeVoto, March 24, 1953, FF 325, Box 16, DeVoto Papers, Stanford University; "Milton, Manfred, and McGrath: A Conversation on Literature and Place," *Dacotah Territory* nos. 8/9 (Fall/Winter 1974–1975), 21.

30  Louis Bromfield, "A Critique of Criticism," in Horace Winston Stokes (ed), *Mirrors of the Year: A National Revue of the Outstanding Figures, Trends, and Events of 1927–8* (New York, Frederick A. Stokes Company, 1928), 60.

31  Burns, *Kinship with the Land*, 40.

32  John T. Frederick, Editorial, *The Midland* vol. 1 (January 1915), 1.

33  Dorman, *Revolt of the Provinces*, 86; John L. Thomas, "The Uses of Catastrophe: Lewis Mumford, Vernon L. Parrington, Van Wyck Brooks, and the End of American Regionalism," *American Quarterly* vol. 42, no. 2 (June 1990), 223–51.

34  Dorman, *Revolt of the Provinces*, 96.

35  Dorman, *Revolt of the Provinces*, 96 (quoting Turner). Paul Gorman notes that the interpretive models that present a stark break between an older folk culture and a new modernized mass culture miss the development of new hybrid or coexisting forms of culture, or the "possibility that 'folk' characteristics could survive alongside the new ways." Gorman, *Left Intellectuals and Popular Culture in Twentieth-Century America*, 106.

36  Dorman, *Revolt of the Provinces*, 13, 105–6; Dorman, *Hell of a Vision*, 14; Anthony Channell Hilfer, *The Revolt from the Village, 1915–1930* (Chapel Hill, University of North Carolina Press, 1969), 22. On the meeting of Iowa regionalists and the Irish writer George Russell (AE), see Burns, *Kinship with the Land*, 94. Russell also praised the Iowa poetry of Jay Sigmund. N.a., "Poetry

Is for All of Us, Iowa Business Man Holds; Jay Sigmund Presents This View in Talk at School of Business Here," *Mason City Globe-Gazette*, November 20, 1934. Hamlin Garland was also first inspired to writing by the "ballads of Ireland and Wales" and the "epics of Ireland." James C. Rosse, "Hamlin Garland: Realist," *Prairie Schooner* vol. 2, no. 1 (Winter 1928), 76. See also John Hutchinson, *The Dynamics of Cultural Nationalism: The Gaelic Revival and the Creation of the Irish Nation State* (New York, Unwin Hyman, 1987); Edward W. Said, "Yeats and Decolonization," in Barbara Kruger and Phil Mariani (eds), *Remaking History* (Seattle, Bay Press, 1989), 3–27; Robert Bernard Davis, *George William Russell ("AE")* (Boston, Twayne Publishers, 1977), 92–93; and Michael Hechter, *Internal Colonialism: The Celtic Fringe in British National Development* (Berkeley, University of California Press, 1975), 264–93.

37    David M. Emmons, *Beyond the American Pale: The Irish in the West, 1845–1910* (Norman, University of Oklahoma Press, 2010), 336.

38    Emmons, *Beyond the American Pale*, 336; Havighurst, "The Midwest as Hearthstone," 21. Kent Ryden conjectures that perhaps the Midwest "never witnessed a trauma or decline so apocalyptic and regionally focused that it made a heroic, colorful past an urgent psychological necessity for the region's elites." Kent C. Ryden, "Writing the Midwest: History, Literature, and Regional Identity," *Geographical Review* vol. 89, no. 4 (October 1999), 530. A woman describing her town in Ohio noted that it "makes no demands on its children," and, because it suffered no historical horrors or burdens, its children "are free to dream their dreams in peace." Yi-Fu Tuan, "Rootedness versus Sense of Place," *Landscape* vol. 24 (1980), 6.

39    Emmons, *Beyond the American Pale*, 337.

40    Emmons, *Beyond the American Pale*, 336–37.

41    Emmons, *Beyond the American Pale*, 336. On midwesterners being too "self-effacing, self-deprecatory" in comparison to the Irish, see Robert Sayre, "Rethinking Midwestern Regionalism," *North Dakota Quarterly* vol. 62, no. 2 (Spring 1994–1995), 125.

42    In a pattern similar to Irish resistance to English control, Lewis Mumford was inspired in part by the work of Patrick Geddes on Geddes's Scottish "valley section." Mumford, *Technics and Civilization* (New York, Harcourt, Brace and Company, 1934), 475; Van Wyck Brooks, "Lewis Mumford: American Prophet," *Harper's*, June 1952, 47; Thomas, "Lewis Mumford," 159, 163, 166; Casey Nelson Blake, *Beloved Community: The Cultural Criticism of Randolph*

*Bourne, Van Wyck Brooks, Waldo Frank, and Lewis Mumford* (Chapel Hill, University of North Carolina Press, 1990), 191–201. Geddes likewise interested Turner. Michael Steiner, "From Frontier to Region: Frederick Jackson Turner and the New Western History," *Pacific Historical Review* vol. 64, no. 4 (November 1995), 486, n. 15. Walt Whitman's evocation of the rural Midwest in "The Prairie States" was also written "for the Irish famine" of 1879, a reprise of the earlier, deadlier famine. Ed Folsom, "Walt Whitman's Prairie Paradise," in Robert F. Sayre (ed), *Recovering the Prairie* (Madison, University of Wisconsin Press, 1999), 52. On Yeats's criticism of the "leveling and erasure" of Irish culture and resistance to the Irish "becoming British," see Stephen C. Behrendt, "Regionalism and the Realities of Naming," in Mahoney and Katz (eds), *Regionalism and the Humanities*, 152–53. See also Cleanth Brooks, "Regionalism in American Literature," *Journal of Southern History* vol. 26, no. 1 (February 1960), 35–37. The regionalist Mary Austin praised the fact that "Irish regionalism" had not been stymied by British control. Mary Austin, "Regionalism in American Fiction," *English Journal* vol. 21, no. 2 (February 1932), 97.

43  On how regionalism has been "underexamined and undertheorized" and how "region has been largely omitted from the ongoing scholarly project to diversify the study of U.S. history and culture" by focusing on race, class, and gender, see Edward Watts, "The Midwest as a Colony: Transnational Regionalism," in Timothy R. Mahoney and Wendy J. Katz (eds), *Regionalism and the Humanities* (Lincoln, University of Nebraska Press, 2008), 166–67.

44  Jon K. Lauck, "Why the Midwest Matters," *Midwest Quarterly* vol. 54, no. 2 (Winter 2013), 170–80; Michael C. Steiner, "The Midwestern Mind of Jane Addams: Cultural Pluralism and the Rural Roots of an Urban Idea" (forthcoming; in author's possession).

45  John Dewey, "The American Intellectual Frontier," *New Republic*, May 10, 1922; Ruth Suckow, "Middle Western Literature," *English Journal* vol. 21, no. 3 (March 1932), 179 (italics in original); Diane Johnson, "The Heart of the Heart of the Country," *New York Review of Books*, November 19, 1981. Of the Midwest, Johnson says, "most people aren't alienated." See also Janet Wondra, "Mid: One Tentative Taxonomy of a Region," in Becky Bradway (ed), *In the Middle of the Middle West: Literary Nonfiction from the Heartland* (Bloomington, Indiana University Press, 2003), 49.

46  Dan Guillory, "Being Midwestern," in Bradway, *In the Middle of the Middle*

*West*, 193; Nancy Bunge, "Two Midwestern Teachers: William Stafford and Frederick Manfred," *Northern Review* vol. 4, no. 1 (Spring 1990), 11–16.

47  Wallace Stegner, "The Trail of the Hawkeye," *Saturday Review of Literature*, July 30, 1938, 17.

48  Robert Wuthnow, *Remaking the Heartland: Middle America since the 1950s* (Princeton and Oxford, Princeton University Press, 2011); and Jon K. Lauck review, *Omaha World Herald*, July 17, 2011. See also Marvin Bergman, "Reconsidering the Heartland: A Review Essay," *Annals of Iowa* vol. 72 (Summer 2013), 161–67.

49  Quoted in James R. Shortridge, "The Emergence of 'Middle West' as an American Regional Label," *Annals of the Association of American Geographers* vol. 74, no. 2 (1984), 215.

50  Terry Teachout, *The Skeptic: A Life of H. L. Mencken* (New York, HarperCollins, 2002), 219.

51  Cynthia Ozick, "The Buried Life," *New Yorker*, October 2, 2000.

52  Daniel Joseph Singal, "Towards a Definition of Modernism," *American Quarterly* vol. 39, no. 1 (Spring 1987), 21. Marcus Klein saw the critics as acting "along the idols that are already fallen, searching through the potsherds for something still substantial enough to smash yet once again." Klein, *After Alienation: American Novels in Mid-century* (Cleveland and New York, World Publishing Company, 1964), 29.

53  Cynthia Ozick, "Against Modernity: Annals of the Temple, 1918–1927," in *A Century of Arts & Letters* (New York, Columbia University Press, 1998), 82.

54  Ozick, "Against Modernity," 82.

# INDEX

IOWA AND THE MIDWEST EXPERIENCE

*The Archaeological Guide to Iowa*
By William E. Whittaker, Lynn M. Alex, and Mary De La Garza

*Carnival in the Countryside: The History of the Iowa State Fair*
By Chris Rasmussen

*The Drake Relays: America's Athletic Classic*
By David Peterson

*Dubuque's Forgotten Cemetery: Excavating a Nineteenth-Century Burial Ground in a Twenty-First-Century City*
By Robin M. Lillie and Jennifer E. Mack

*Duffy's Iowa Caucus Cartoons: Watch 'Em Run*
By Brian Duffy

*Equal Before the Law: How Iowa Led Americans to Marriage Equality*
By Tom Witozky and Marc Hansen

*From Warm Center to Ragged Edge: The Erosion of Midwestern Literary and Historical Regionalism, 1920–1965*
By Jon K. Lauck

*Iowa Past to Present: The People and the Prairie, Revised Third Edition*
By Dorothy Schwieder, Thomas Morain, and Lynn Nielsen

*The Iowa State Fair*
By Kurt Ullrich

*The Jefferson Highway: Blazing the Way from Winnipeg to New Orleans*
By Lyell D. Henry, Jr.